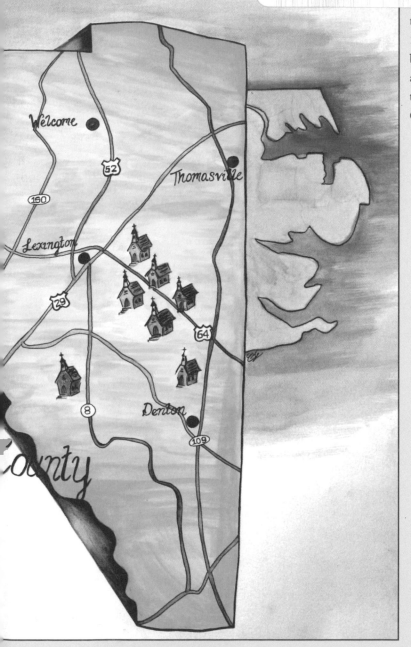

...ays shown in ...on County, ...Carolina, as they existed in the 1940s. Map produced by Candace Frieden, an art major at the University of Georgia.

WE ARE WHAT WE WERE

Memories of Rural North Carolina

To Craig,
Growing up together.
What a precious time.
We were so close to the
country (County) life yet
so far. Hope you enjoy.
Hoss

WE ARE WHAT WE WERE

Memories

of Rural North Carolina

Gene Younts

Stratford Press

ATHENS, GEORGIA

Published 2006 by Stratford Press, Athens, Georgia
© 2006 by Gene Younts

Set in 10 on 12.5 Dante
Printed and bound by Edwards Brothers, Lillington, N.C.

The paper in this book meets the guidelines
for permanence and durability of the
Committee on Production Guidelines
for Book Longevity of the Council
on Library Resources

Printed in the United States of America
10 09 08 07   C 5 4 3 2

ISBN 0-9671886-7-9

MARTHA YOUNTS SWING
1938–2006

For Martha,
a remarkable person and sister
whose encouragement provided inspiration
to complete the task.

CONTENTS

ACKNOWLEDGMENTS

Good fortune shined on my life from its beginning being born on a small dairy farm in Piedmont North Carolina at the beginning of the Great Depression as a part of a large, caring family with cousins almost too numerous to count. The surrounding community contained people attached to the land with many eking out a living by the sweat of their brow tilling the soil, cutting the forest, or working for meager hourly wages in nearby textile and furniture factories. Our world had little reach not much beyond the local town of Lexington, the county seat of Davidson County, and two or three more distant towns. This book presents an account in writing and photographs of the environment during the decades of the 1920s, 1930s, and 1940s and the effect it had on the people living there.

It would be impossible to name all of the persons and organizations that assisted me in numerous ways in gathering information and photographs. I must mention a few because without their participation the book would be much less.

Larry Younts, who obtained interviews from citizens who began their lives in the first quarter of the 20th century and experienced the Depression and World War II. I am deeply grateful to the interviewees for their candor in describing the conditions of their early years and the persons and institutions important in shaping their lives.

The University of Georgia Libraries for its assistance in procuring microfilms of the Lexington *Dispatch* for the period 1920 to 1950 and allowing me to use its equipment to read them.

Members of my graduating class at Davis-Townsend High School who shared their memories in candid sessions at class reunions. I want to particularly thank Kay McCulloch Kepley, Delores Beck Rose, Peggy Wilson, and John W. Smith for special contributions.

Ruth Parks, formerly of the Southmont community, for valuable information about her brother, Reid, who lost his life in World War II on a bombing raid over Austria. She located photographs of him and places of her youth and stayed in contact with the author while the manuscript was being written.

Velna Vawters, the sister of Efird Beck, who lost his life as an infantryman in World War II on the battlefields of Europe. She generously loaned keepsake photographs of the family some of which are included in the book. She also provided interesting details about her brother, such as his burial site in a cemetery in Holland.

Several of my cousins who shared with candor details of their own lives and comments about people who comprised the community.

Betty Leonard Younts, who provided pictures of her husband when he served in the United States Navy in the Pacific Theater in World War II.

Ann Swing Bryant who found and mailed special photographs from the family collection.

The Davidson County Historical Museum for allowing me to use a number of photographs from its collection that were made during the period covered by the book.

Melinda Hawley, a former colleague at the University of Georgia and my principal editor, who reviewed the manuscript in detail with her professional eye offering many suggestions for improvement.

Barry Jones, a former colleague at UGA, for examining carefully much of the manuscript in its beginning stages and encouraging me to stay the course.

Debbie Robinson for transcribing the tapes made during the numerous interviews.

The several persons who provided information and photographs about the churches highlighted in the book. Special consideration goes to David Smith of the Jersey community and Janice Abernathy of the Mt. Tabor community.

My brother, Richard and his wife, Gail, who took a special interest in the book from the beginning providing feedback about the manuscript and relating interesting events experienced during their early lives.

Much gratitude goes to the countless number of persons in Davidson County, North Carolina, who influenced my life in its formative years by giving me needed pats on the back for deeds well done and also for jerking me up when my efforts fell short of expectations.

To the members of my family: wife Ruth, son Greg, and daughter Leslie for their input into the substance of the book.

Much gratitude goes to Betty McDaniel of Stratford Press whose superior talents are reflected in the quality of the publication.

ONE
INTRODUCTION:
BACKWARD GLANCES

"Things are not what they used to be and who knows, perhaps they never were...."

John Howard Payne, author of "Home Sweet Home," began
the poem in this way:
> *Mid pleasures and palaces though we may roam,*
> *Be it ever so humble, there is no place like home.*

And, L. L. Cash, author of "The Old Home Place," ended his
poem with the following verse:
> *Oh the scenes and sounds of childhood*
> *From my life I cannot erase;*
> *As my mind is prone to journey*
> *Back to my old home place.*

Nothing matches the feelings generated when visiting the old home place, especially when you have lived away for more than fifty years. During this span of time, I would return every year or so, but a visit in 2004 shifted my mind into overdrive because the decision to write this book had been made a few months earlier. I was determined to recall and capture as much as I could about the place and the general area in which I grew up.

Life for me began in Davidson County, North Carolina, around the middle of the first half of the 20th century. The gallop through the Great Depression and World War II, and the innovations in the years beyond, had created a life vastly different from the one I knew back when. Standing in the yard of my home place on old U.S. Highway 64 south of Lexington, the county seat, and thinking about the past gave me unlimited pleasure. It was nostalgia at its best. Fleeting visions of yesteryear kept running through my head, and I desperately wanted to take them into custody like a county sheriff and hold them just long enough to show them to the 21st century and say, "You are not what you are cracked up to be with your high-powered technology."

We had it all in our generation, so we thought, just like the claim made by each generation. Goodness knows our possessions lacked pizzazz. We treasured what few we had, but possessions did not consume us. The pace of living allowed us time for studying and examining our surroundings, to get to know our neighbors, and to have enough space to daydream about the future and imagine what existed beyond our visible world. Radios, books and community storytellers, who stirred our imaginations, were our television sets, and in the hot summertime, a fresh breeze through an open window gave us our air conditioning.

Memory allows us to go home again, to smell roses in December, and to access the computer chips in the back of our minds, to construct any set of circumstances ever experienced. I relished strolling about the yard that day, and first glanced toward the garden fence which circled around a plot of overworked land. About an acre in size, this soil produced much of what the family had to eat in the summertime; any surplus was being canned for the coming winter. A team of mules usually pulled the turning plow and harrow that conditioned the soil for planting, and soon, at the encouragement of caring hands, rows of vegetables sprang up as if by magic, later filling buckets with their harvests. Nothing equaled the taste of vine-ripened tomatoes, fresh butter beans and corn, cooked white potatoes, grated cabbage laced with a dash of vinegar, salt and pepper, with sliced cucumbers and onions on the side.

To my back stood the old family home, now owned and lived in by a nephew and his family. Dad and Mom raised (reared) seven children—six boys and one girl. The house was constructed in the late 1920s, initially resting on pillars of either bricks or stones, with enough crawl space for a young boy to explore the mysteries of such shaded space. Two things discovered came quickly to mind, the presence of a laying hen or two that had stolen their nests under the house sitting on at least a dozen eggs waiting for young chicks to hatch and a cone-shaped home of a doodle bug or ant lion in the loose, dusty soil. The larva of the doodle bug would build a conical crater in the soil to trap ants and other insects for food. A curious boy would excavate the larva by poking a twig in the cone or by loudly raising his voice and saying, "Doodle bug, doodle bug, bring a load of corn up." Such disturbance made the doodle bug move, revealing his location. By the time I was six years old or so, the crawl space around the house was underpinned solid with bricks, putting an end to such fascinating exploration.

I remembered when the sleeping capacity of the house was increased after the sixth or seventh sibling was born to include the attic so each of us could have our own bed, quite a luxury in those days. Of course, the memory of World War II flashed back reminding me of two of the beds becoming empty as the oldest two siblings went off to war. In many ways, it was my good fortune to be the middle child of the seven, given the advantage of spending time with each sibling before leaving the security of home.

Turning my head a little to the right brought the farmyard into view. The buildings showed some wear and tear from the years of weathering, but the mental picture of the activities within and outside them remained undimmed. Immediately over the fence, to the right side of the garden, perched the family outhouse (outdoor convenience). It stayed there for a number of years before being moved to a new location. Sometime earlier, the careless use of matches set its Sears-Roebuck catalog on fire. Next to the outhouse a hog vat perched on a foundation of bricks and mortar. This apparatus served the useful purpose of scalding freshly killed hogs in order to remove the hair before hanging and butchering. For many years, a persimmon tree large enough to produce fruit in the fall stood about 25 feet from the hog vat. Mom would make persimmon pudding from the fruit just after the first killing frost. My older brother, Homer, used to joke about how he once broke his arm falling out of the persimmon tree while eating breakfast, which was his verbal illustration of how poor he was during his youth.

Not too far away came the milking parlor, and it was because of this structure that the county health department mandated removal of the outhouse to a more distant location. Unfortunately, one has to look hard to find fond memories in the "milk house," as we called it. Milking at least 10 cows by hand every day, morning and evening without a day off, not even Christmas, can take the romance out of country living. If you are not careful, you smell like a milk cow wherever you go. But being in the dairy business gave Dad pride and a regular milk check for the family. Davidson County, too, was a state leader in dairy production.

Outside the milk house in a corner of the pasture, a faucet and a galvanized tub provided water for the cows. Funny how some things stick in your mind more than others. Ingrained in my brain is a scene of three or four young turkeys (poults) lying on the ground after being drowned in the tub. A few of their feathers were missing, plucked by one of my younger siblings. Such action always led to a severe scolding and in all likelihood several stings from a stiff switch delivered by the sure hands of an angry parent.

The barn housing the milk cows stood adjacent to the milk house, and I could see the oldest and main barn on the farm up the hill. We parked the two-horse wagon in the breezeway there, and the stables on the ground level housed the mules and horses, a few cows, and the king of the barnyard, a large Guernsey bull. The children and women of the area always remained as quiet as possible when walking near the bull. One woman who lived in the neighborhood and visited Mom occasionally, would always stop and yell to the top of her lungs before entering the barnyard. She would inquire about the where-abouts of "the old man cow." If the coast was clear, she scurried rapidly into the house. Around the perimeter of the barnyard, Dad had constructed a number of sheds to house the larger farm equipment, particularly the small grain reaper. We young folks always marveled at a reaper because its many parts worked in unison (usually) as it cut the grain fields. Grain harvest time meant that wheat threshings were just around the corner, one of the great community social events of the year.

Two other buildings caught my attention. One was known as the wheat house, where freshly threshed grain (wheat, oats and barley) was stored in large open wooden bins. The other was the corncrib where corn ears found a place after the shucks (husks) had been removed. Both buildings held a special fascination for young folks. When grown-ups were out of sight, open bins of wheat especially offered an invitation for youngsters to climb in and play. Many a child received harsh verbal discipline, usually, or even spankings for committing such violations. Our parents told us that the small grain could cover us up and suffocate us, or we could get grains in our ears and go deaf, both of which were very likely. As far as I know, none of us came close to smothering, but some grains found their way into the outer ear where they became moldy and difficult to extract. Whippings ensued from such misbehavior.

A full corncrib offered at least two opportunities for special recreation. Sooner or later an insect known as the weevil would find its home among the corn ears, and if the ears were stirred vigorously, weevils would fill the air, especially at dusk. Bats circling through the evening air in the barnyard loved to catch weevils, and the airborne bats would swoop down to catch them. All of this presented an amusing creative challenge in the form of taking a long stick, preferably a reed of fishing pole length, and knocking the bats from flight as they dived for weevils.

Like all farm families, we always had a flock of chickens, and corn grain comprised the main source of feed. Of course, grain must be shelled from the corncobs which often had a very special use of their own in the outhouse. Youngsters looking for something to do on a lazy Sunday afternoon discovered the cobs made excellent missiles for a corncob fight.

Winning required an accurate throwing arm and cobs of some weight which could be obtained by soaking them in a bucket of water. The ones that made the best missiles by far were the cobs that had been left on the ground where the combination of both moisture and mud added weight and increased your chances of besting your opponent. As far as I could remember, no serious injuries resulted from such warfare other than a few knots on the head.

Looking in the distance beyond the hog pens down a pasture lane, the back of Beck's Lutheran Church came into view. During my early years, trees grew on the land that is now pasture land, which was cleared gradually year by year. We used wood from the trees as a source of fuel for the kitchen stove and for fires in the fireplaces during cold winter months. Dad made certain that all the children old enough to handle an axe participated in the land-clearing process. I was the youngest and smallest sibling at the time, so Dad purchased a junior size axe for my use. Being the unskilled rookie that I was at chopping wood, the axe slipped and cut the shin of my right leg, which to this day carries the scar of that mighty blow.

Across old U.S. Highway 64 stands a home that my grandpa Lohr, Mom's father, built more than a century ago. It is no longer in the family, but remains in good condition. Grandpa made much of his living from operating a filling station and country store next to the highway to the right of the house. In addition to gasoline and oil, he sold basic food items, candy, bottled soft drinks, cigarettes, snuff and chewing tobacco. When he passed away in the late 1930s, Grandma leased the store to a number of operators, but after a few rentals, the building was sold and moved about a mile down the highway for another use.

Old Highway 64 runs east and west, and when I was very young I thought it had no end. I knew it ran east as far as Silver Valley, some 10 miles, and west to the county seat of Lexington and perhaps a few miles farther. The world was a small place then, and no one could have convinced me that this old highway traversed the entire country, running from North Carolina's outer banks on the Atlantic Ocean to southern California where it touched the Pacific.

About 100 yards east of Grandpa's store, an unpaved county road, Smith Road, intersected the highway and led to a piece of Dad's farmland on Pounders Fork Creek. I learned to fish there baiting a hook with red worms and casting for minnows and an occasional sun perch. Dolan, a neighbor and second cousin, some five years older than I was, taught me my first swimming strokes in three-foot-deep water under a bridge, even though my form was slightly more than the basic dog paddle. My brothers and I and a few school buddies made great recreational use of the creek where it cut through Dad's farmland. We spent carefree nights walking the creek bed, frog gigging and looking for suckers. Unfortunately, all that we usually extracted from the creek were wet pants to the hips, sore feet cut on creek bed rocks, very tired bodies and an occasional frightened water snake. After a down-pouring rain, red soil from nearby plowed fields would be carried in run-off water that fed into the creek giving it a heavy red-muddy look. Catfish love to frolic in this environment providing an ideal opportunity for us to set hooks along the creek bank in hopes of catching a few.

When we came out of the driveway to our home onto Highway 64 and turned left, we soon came to an intersection to the right called the County Home Road, the route the school bus traveled as it carried us to Davis-Townsend

School about three miles away. The road was not paved for many years, and during winter months it stayed muddy most of the time. Heavy rains washed soil and silt into the road's side ditches, requiring the county road maintenance crew to bring in a road scraper from time to time to clean out the fill. The scraper left much of the loose soil material from the side ditches in the middle of the road, which added to the mud problem. Even when completely dry, the road surface went lacking for quality, having the appearance and feel of a hand washboard, challenging the driver and giving the students a bumpy ride. Buses could never be driven fast due to the governors having been installed on the engines. Even in the best of conditions, traveling faster than 28 miles an hour was out of the question.

We rode bus number 38, and the driver stopped in front of our house before proceeding to Davis-Townsend School. Bus bodies were painted the same bright yellow as they are today, a visible color especially in inclement weather. The seat arrangement in the body of a school bus has long since been changed. Rather than the seats installed today that allow all passengers to face the front of the bus, students sat on four long seats running the length of the bus's interior. Two were higher and larger on either side (for older students), and two were small ones (for younger students) down the center of the bus body. After riding the bus the first few days of school, everyone more or less claimed the same spot for the entire year.

Growing up involved experiencing a few rituals necessary to be recognized as a teenager, and an important one was to move permanently from the little seat in the middle of the bus to the big seat on the side. This required bargaining and diplomatic skills unmatched in any other human negotiation as far as I know. If the move toward the big seat was made by a brave youngster before the older students declared him or her eligible, back to the little seat the interloper went with an admonition, usually very stern, not to attempt such a move again until permission was granted. Then one day when least expected, without the older students saying a word, a teen simply knew the time had arrived to occupy the big seat unchallenged. Every school boy and girl that rode a bus remembers this rite of passage, a silent ceremony certifying becoming a bona fide teenager.

School bus operators, chosen from the student body, were males who had reached the age of 16 years and had passed a bus driver's test, and lived near the beginning of the bus route in the morning. Make no mistake about it, the driver was in complete charge of the bus and its passengers with the full support of the school principal. The driver was the "captain of his ship," so to speak, with the authority to maintain discipline and the responsibility to safely transport students to and from school in a timely fashion. Bus drivers earned about $11.00 per month for their efforts, which was more than a modest sum for a 16-year-old in the late '20s, '30s and early '40s.

Not all students rode the school bus, especially those who lived a mile or less from the school. They were required to walk whether rain or shine. No students owned cars of their own because parents could afford only one. On rare occasions, students might bring a parent's car to school if he or she had a driver's license and the principal's consent.

GOING ALONG BECK'S CHURCH ROAD

Proceeding up a hill beyond the turnoff toward Davis-Townsend School, there was an intersection that turns sharply to the left, Beck's Church Road. In my early youth, it also lacked a hard surface, but it seemed to be better maintained than the County Home Road, probably because it served a much more heavily populated community. Prior to 1931, the children living on Beck's Church Road had their own grammar school, Sandy Grove, with grades one through seven, named for the community. Another institution along the road was Beck's Lutheran Church built in 1937, and a couple miles farther was Beck's Evangelical and Reformed Church. Years later its name was changed to Beck's United Church of Christ and now Beck's Reformed. Brief histories of both churches appear in another section of this book.

Driving along Beck's Church Road beginning at the junction with U.S. 64, I can still remember the houses that existed in the late 1930s and early 40s as if it were yesterday. My eyes strained to locate the older dwellings since twice as many exist today. Looking right and left, the structures (some greatly altered over time) and names of the original families brought back unparalleled memories long since lodged in the crevices of my cranium. Where did time steal itself? How much I must have missed the past 50 years, not witnessing peers growing into adulthood and rearing their families and having the chance to say goodbye to older folks passing away. I had fleeting memories of the many community activities, the good socials, the tales told in the barber shop, the hunting and fishing outings with cousins skilled in the art of doing both, the baseball and basketball games, the breaking of land in the spring, most of the family reunions and the revivals at church. I had missed so much in my half-century absence. The list of lost opportunities seemed regrettably endless.

The first home on Beck's Church Road was that of John Briggs, built at the corner of U.S. 64 in the late '30s or early '40s when I was about eight or nine years old. Traveling for a mile or two more as far as Beck's Reformed Church, a few dozen additional homes from the past rise out to greet a visitor as their owners once did: Tom Swing, Ira Leonard, Dewey Briggs, Clyde Briggs, Thurman Crotts, the Workmans, Edgar Morris, Grady Younts, Sid Gallimore, Thurman Briggs, Dave Burkhart, Florence Burkhart, Walter Younts, Alec Swing, Jesse Kepley, Elwood Younts, Pete Fritts, Pierce Swing, Bob Swing, Tom Burkhart, Roy Burkhart, Hedrick family, Isaiah Beck, Carl Burkhart, Jake Burkhart, Crawford Swing, Emmitt Swing, Lindsay Briggs, Howard Greer, Curt Lohr, Elmo Lohr, Oscar Allred, Bob Allred, Sam Burkhart, Charlie Swing and then Beck's Evangelical and Reformed Church. Beyond the church the homes of such people as Crawford Miller, Tom Everhart, Arnold Miller, Sam Tussey, Grover Parks, Harvey Parks, Everette Swing, the Harveys, and others came to mind. Another dozen homes located on several side roads intersecting with Beck's Church Road also housed families that were well known: Walter Watkins, Bob Fritts, Lee Burkhart, Gurney Burkhart, Howard Hines, Charlie Leonard, Oscar Allred, Vee Davis (Curt Lohr's tenant), Clyde Young, Crawford Hedrick and Artese Beck.

The land held these people, on which most of them extracted their living and formed a community bonded by heritage, religion and close family ties. People of the community possessed the traits of integrity, a hard-work ethic and honesty. Each person, with his or her own individual personality, gave the place a special richness and character. Except for an occasional visit to Lexington, this was my world for many years, but once the grammar and high school years arrived, it began to expand exponentially.

On that day in 2004, I thought of other nearby communities where many schoolmates lived—Holly Grove, Mount Tabor, Hedrick's Grove, Jerusalem and Silver Valley. Families with names like Regan, McCulloch, Everhart, Beck, Conrad, Albertson, Smith, Foust, Byerly, Garner, Hedrick, Swing, Hege, Kepley, Metters, Harris, Lookabill, Hughes, Black, Bowers, Fritts, Rhodes, Young, Leonard, Curry, Crotts, Grimes, Watkins, Plummer, Greer, Williams, Bryant, Nifong, Sumner, Anderson, Carter, Grubb, Ward, Sink, Varner, and Floyd. Other communities came into mind, such as Linwood, Southmont, and other distant locations in the county: Denton, Reeds, Tyro, Churchland, Welcome, Fair Grove, Pilot, Wallburg, Midway, Arcadia and Thomasville, another town of some size. I also recalled the Junior Order Orphan's Home on Cotton Grove Road, and then began to wonder about the lives of scores of relatives living all throughout the area, a total of 67 first cousins.

Every person and place impacted our lives, at least in some small way. Our parents set the standards by which we lived, and the familial bond developed through trust, faith, and dependence among neighbors near and far had a strong impact on what we became.

TWO

OUR HERITAGE

The first Europeans to come to Davidson County and the date of their coming are unknown. Sink and Matthews, in their book, *Pathfinders Past and Present*, provide a thorough discussion of the early settlers and their origins. John Lederer, a German doctor in Virginia in 1670 traversed what is now the Piedmont in North Carolina and wrote an account of his experiences at Trading Ford, a place just south of the I-85 highway bridge on the Davidson County side of the Yadkin River. For several years other explorers, mostly English, followed Lederer's course encountering both friendly and hostile Indians. What kind of country did these early explorers find? Several visitors coming to Trading Ford around the year 1730 said this of the Yadkin Valley:

> The soil is exceedingly rich on both sides of the Yadkin, abounding in rank grass and prodigiously large trees, and for plenty of fish, fowel [sic], and venison; is inferior to no part of the Northern Continent. There the traders commonly lie still for several days to recruit their horses' flesh as well as to recover their own spirits.

The available records that Sink and Matthews studied suggest that Davidson County was never a permanent Indian home. Early explorers encountered Indians, but they are known to have fled to other regions for safety. However, the present-day Davidson County was part of a great hunting area for American Indians. They sought and killed animals for food and clothing, and fought and killed men when they met hostile groups on the same mission.(1)

One of the early settlements on the left bank of the Yadkin River was known as Jersey and was composed of people who came from the Province of New Jersey. They were principally of Scotch-Irish, English and German heritage. The date of the settlement of Jersey cannot be exactly stated, but it was probably around the middle of the 18th century. Governor Arthur Dobbs in a letter dated August 24, 1755, to Lords of the Board of Trade described the land as being of such quality to be attractive for establishing a settlement. Many of the people were of the Baptist persuasion. Geographically the Jersey settlement began at the present location of Linwood, Davidson County. One of the oldest churches in the county, the Jersey Baptist Church, was founded about the same time.(2)

The German Lutherans and German Reformeds settling along Abbotts Creek and its stream tributaries get most of the attention. They established six churches of emphasis: Beck's Lutheran, Beck's Evangelical and Reformed, Hedrick's Grove Evangelical and Reformed, Mount Tabor Evangelical and Reformed, Holly Grove Lutheran and New Jerusalem Evangelical and Reformed. (The Evangelical and Reformed congregations changed their names to United Church of Christ in the latter half of the 20th century.)

When I was in my formative years in the central part of lower Davidson County, we did not discuss our cultural heritage very often, although it was generally recognized that for most of us our ancestors had come from Germany. A common mistake was that we often said we were of Dutch origin, not German, when actually we were of Deutsch (meaning German) descent. This error persists today. Records show that the Palatinate Province on the left bank of the Rhine River in Germany supplied a vast majority of the German settlers who eventually made their way in the middle and latter parts of the 18th century to the broad area which surrounds the Yadkin River.(2) They fled their German homelands after suffering and enduring untold horrors of starvation, disease and torture. Hardly any part of Germany had suffered worse from the repeated devastations than that beautiful province on the left bank of the Rhein (Rhine). The lovely old town of Heidelberg became victim to the Catholic armies who plundered the priceless library and presented the spoils to the Pope. The industrious farmers and artisans of sunny Rhineland showed tremendous resilience in recovering from the devastation; however, the pillage and persecution continued as Palatines were driven from their homes in the late 17th century.(2)

The exodus from the Palatinate surpassed anything seen in Europe. Chief among the causes motivating this mass migration were: the destructive wars; religious persecutions and oppression by tyrannical rulers at home; the extravagant accounts of what the New World had to offer; and the hope of religious freedom that had been denied in the Old World.

Hundreds of thousands found refuge in Holland and England for a while, and later the seaports of the Netherlands and England formed a gateway to America. Historians write of stops refugees took in Pennsylvania before coming south to North Carolina. The three principal religious denominations among the Pennsylvania Germans were Lutherans, German Reformeds and Moravians. It is estimated that 12,000 Germans reached Pennsylvania from Europe in the year 1749, and that by 1775, 110,000 people of German birth or descent had relocated there. It should be noted that the number would have been much larger if not for the fact that more than a third of the Pennsylvania Germans and their descendants had begun moving toward the South in a search for more accessible and spacious lands.(3)

In addition to being a place where many Germans settled, Pennsylvania served as a jumping-off point for less densely-populated regions. The German migrants moved from the western regions of Pennsylvania such as Lebanon and Dauphin, crossed the Susquehanna River and followed the mountain slopes through Maryland into Virginia passing though the Shenandoah Valley. Their journey followed the Staunton River through the Blue Ridge and peeled southward across the Dan River proceeding as far as central North Carolina to the present areas of Davidson, Rowan, Stanly, Cabarrus, Alamance, Orange, Guilford, Iredell, Catawba, Lincoln and counties nearby. A few German ancestors came directly to North Carolina skipping western Pennsylvania after passing through the port of Philadelphia where they took the oath of allegiance to the Crown of England.

The trip from Pennsylvania to present-day area of Davidson County covered a distance of 435 miles, an arduous journey at best, following "The Great Wagon Road" briefly described earlier. Sink and Matthews in *Pathfinders Past and Present: A History of Davidson County, North Carolina* (1972), give additional details of the route often labeled as the "bad road." The authors quote the Reverend G. D. Bernheim in his *History of the German Settlements and the Lutheran Church in North Carolina* (1872) providing a vivid picture of the redundant mile journey:

> The Pennsylvania Germans journeyed in much the same manner as did later colonists to the Western states...every available article for home and farm use, capable of being towed away in their capacious wagons, was taken with them; their cavalcade moved on, every able bodied person on foot, women and children on bedding in the wagons, and cattle, sheep and hogs driven before them, they traveled by easy stages, upon the roads of the picturesque Cumberland and Shenandoah valleys...

> It is impossible to date precisely the arrival of all of those German colonists from Pennsylvania as they all depended upon themselves for leaving home and journeying southward; they arrived continuously for a number of years in succession, usually leaving home in the fall season, after all of the harvesting was over and the proceeds of the year's labor could be disposed of; they arrived at their places of settlement before the commencement of the winter season. First arrival of the pioneer train may have occurred about the year 1745, but the large body of these German colonists did not commence to settle in North Carolina until about 1750; this may be gathered partly from tradition, partly from old family records in their German Bibles, but mostly from the deeds of their lands, which were always dated some years after their actual settlement...

Just when the first Germans appeared in central North Carolina is debatable with some claiming 1745 as the year while others say 1747 is more accurate. A variance of two years' difference two and one-half centuries later seems hardly worth mentioning, but historians are challenged to be accurate. Hammer in his *Rhinelanders on the Yadkin*, page 26, puts forth a good argument contending that 1747 would seem to be the correct date, not 1745. The inflow of Germans hit full stride between 1750 and 1755 continuing even after the Revolutionary War over a period of at least 40 years. Our German ancestors settled in the most fertile sections, usually the rich creek and river bottoms. Farming was their way to make a living; they exhibited a hard-working ethic. They lived in close-knit communities and asked for little—just good land and freedom in which to live, work and worship. After choosing a location to homestead, the first challenge was to start clearing the land and constructing log houses and barns. Women and children did their part by working in the home, garden and fields. Each member of the family helped to pay for the land. Usually they brought their German Bibles, catechisms and hymnbooks as they journeyed southward. Churches and schools were soon established, often with one building serving two purposes. One person, likely the most educated in the community, had the responsibility for teaching the children and reading the sermons and prayers on Sunday.

The settlers spoke only German initially. For more than 50 years, German was the only language used in worship services, and even for 25 years thereafter the sermons were read in both German and English. Emphasis placed on education for their children cannot be overstated. They believed only in church schools, because for them religion and education went hand in hand.(3)

Not all settlers were of German origin, although in some settlements in the lower middle part of the county, people of a different background were rare. An examination of names on grave markers in the older sections of a few cemeteries reveals an occasional person of English, French, Irish or Scot origin, but the preponderance of German is overwhelming. Hammer mentions rather succinctly that "simultaneously with the Germans, many Scotch-Irish came from Pennsylvania in search of new homes. The two peoples had lived on friendly terms in that province, and the harmonious relationship continued in North Carolina. Although they often settled side by side, a great number of the Scotch-Irish occupied vacant lands to the west or south of the Germans. Both took part in the inevitable westward push, and eventually became about equally numerous in the valley of the Catawba River." And, of course, England governed the colony; hence, a number of people from that country were also among the first to arrive in Piedmont North Carolina.

"These German settlers," wrote Dr. Bernheim, "were all industrious, economical, and thrifty farmers, not ashamed of hard labor, and they were soon blessed with an abundance of everything which the fertile soil and temperate climate could furnish them. As they were...agriculturists, they generally avoid settling...in town."

The names of these Germans are themselves an interesting study since each name is distinctive and usually reveals the origin of its possessor. Many have been changed from their original spellings or translated—or anglicized —in such a way as to lose German identity. For this reason, many families today do not know their ancestral history and are not knowledgeable of the fact they are of German descent. They think they are English when they could be as Deutsch (German) as sauerkraut itself. For example, the name Carpenter could be English, but the German word Zimmerman means Carpenter as well. Little and Small often come from the German name Klein, which means small or little. Taylor looks so definitely English that people of this name may shun the idea they could possibly be German. Actually, Taylor is a translation of the German Schneider, meaning a tailor, and the name Snider comes from it as well.(3)

C. J. Leonard culled a list of names from the Pennsylvania archives in writing his book to illustrate the manner in which many names in use today were changed from the original German. Following are examples, but note that in many instances the German names have remained unaltered:

> *Frey, Fritz* (Fritts), *Meyer* (Myers), *Zimmerman, Kuntz* (Koonts), *Khun* (Coon), *Diehl* (Deal), *Hartman, Hoffman* (Huffman), *Klopp* (Clapp), *Mueller* (Miller), *Sygrist* (Sechriest), *Jung* (Young), *Arndt, Hage* (Hege), *Thar* (Darr, Derr), *Sauer* (Sowers), *Kratz* (Crotts), *Eberhardt* (Everhart), *Lohr, Bierly* (Byerly), *Frank, Boger, Suther, Hedrick, Beck* (Peck), *Lopp, Leibegut* (Livengood), *Wildfang* (Wilfong), *Schaaf* (Schoaf), *Kondradt* (Conrad), *Lingle, Berger* (Barrier, Berrier, Barger), *Wagner, Huyet* (Hyatt), *Lantz, Zinck* (Sink), *Leonhardt* (Leonard), *Wentz* (Vance), *Waltzer* (Walser), *Jantz* (Younts), *Weber* (Weaver), *Hoch* (Hoke), *Krauss* (Crouse), *Henkel* (Hinkle), *Brinkley, Schwang* (Swing), *Parks, Heinz* (Hines), *Keppele, Koeppel* (Kepley, Capley), *Fischer* (Fisher), *Schmidt* (Smith).(3)

The Germans gave this section of North Carolina distinctive characteristics which remain widespread among their descendants. Traits such as being sturdy, religious, and liberty-loving people are easily recognized. Also, certain elements of the way of life of those early Germans can be found among many descendants today, especially those still engaged in agriculture and sawmilling in some way. Work and play were frequently mixed in such activities as barn-raising, neighborhood wood chopping, or corn shucking. Especially the latter had several distinctly entertaining components. Since girls were always among the huskers, red ears of corn were placed throughout in the pile of unhusked corn. If a male perchance should find one of the red ears, he possessed an entitlement to kiss a girl, if and when the young lady was agreeable. After the corn was shucked, everyone partook of a bountiful supper prepared by the women folks. Sometimes a calf or a hog had been butchered just for that meal; sometimes a wholesale slaughter of chickens occurred. A lavish display of cakes and pies followed the eating of meat. The huskers ate and ate and ate. This custom remained strong well into the 20th century, but in the 21st, shuckings are largely a happy memory among fewer and fewer people.(2)

The Germans gave the impression they were highly superstitious, at least more than their neighbors, but evidence to support the claim is lacking. Beliefs about the influence of the supernatural in rural communities populated by the English and the Scotch-Irish were just as prevalent. Like the farmers of British descent, Germans held staunchly to the notion that the moon and zodiac signs influenced the weather, and many descendants even in late 20th century would undertake certain tasks only when the zodiac sign was right.

Outside the home, the church and its attendant school formed the center around which the lives of the German Rhinelanders revolved. They took their religion very seriously, and on occasions walked miles to services. Few rode horseback except the aged and the infirm, because they believed that their beasts of burden should likewise rest on Sunday. Since tanning of leather was a tedious process, the members of the congregation conserved their shoes by walking almost to church barefooted, pausing the last few hundred feet to wash their feet in a nearby stream. This custom continued late enough to be remembered by a few old people who lived into the 1940s.(2)

The early Germans kept to themselves, being modest, and seldom pushed themselves into public affairs as did the English and Scotch-Irish neighbors. Many reasons have been suggested for this public reticence, chief among them their use of the German language. As mentioned previously, they continued to speak their native tongue from time to time for at least 100 years after arriving in Piedmont North Carolina. They loved German, and I was surprised in conducting research for this book to discover that many of the older people living during my teenage years could still speak some of the German they learned from the lips of their mothers and fathers.(3)

German is a beautiful language, capable of expressing shades of meaning that no other language can begin to express. It is preeminently the language of science, theology and poetry. Our ancestors were reluctant to give up the tongue of the fatherland, but North Carolina became an English-speaking state with all business and government activities being conducted in English. In the churches, worship services continued to be held in German as late as 1825–1830. When congregations had a preponderance of English speaking members, interpreters were used on a regular basis. Many congregations still needed bilingual ministers from 1825–1850. When the Tennessee Synod convened at Beck's Church (Davidson) in 1849, services were conducted in German, probably for the last time at any synodical gathering in North Carolina. German preaching essentially disappeared after 1850, and following the Civil War, only one account of it is found. In the summer of 1883, a Reformed minister, near China Grove in Rowan County, apparently delivered the last sermon in German in this section. According to the records hundreds came from far and near to hear that service. While some worshippers were attracted by the opportunity of listening once again to religious discourse in their native tongue, many more attended merely out of curiosity, never having heard anything except English.(2)

With the passing of time, the knowledge of the language gradually became confined to some of the old people and an occasional bright young person. I learned in interviewing one of my oldest cousins living in the Beck's Church community that my father's mother (1869–1937) could speak German fluently. Roaming through the graveyard of my old church, founded in 1787, I found an occasional word or two of German on tombstones placed before 1825. A large stone marker stands at the foot of the grave of Peter Hedrick, the person who took the leadership in establishing our church. Engraved on it, both in German and English, is a tribute to Mr. Hedrick and the people of the Palatinate region of Germany. Mr. Hedrick was born in Germany on December 17, 1733, and died in America on January 24, 1798.(3)

In his final chapter of *Rhinelanders on the Yadkin*, Hammer has this to say of the early German settlers and their descendants:

Thus our citizens of German blood have followed consistently in the footsteps of their ancestors from the Palatinate. Those Rhinelanders were poor immigrants, mainly farmers and artisans. With strong willing hands, resolute minds and reverent hearts, they set to work and made their hopes of a promise land come true.

To posterity they bequeathed no great wealth, but rather the heritage of diligence, constancy, sincerity, and withal (archaic with) kindliness— qualities which have lived on among Carolina folk of Rheinish extraction. Among the more enlightened there is still a proud consciousness of that lineage, not withstanding occasional slurs at the hands of time-serving political chicanery and despite aspersions cast by those who are ignorant of heroic past and worthy present belonging to the German element in the Old North State. Even their forefathers helped establish a great country, so successive generations have unfalteringly built upon that foundation...Theirs have been the world sustaining arts of peace, and upon that merit they have stood and will stand. While making no spurious claims to once-great ancestry or imaginary relationships with royal or ducal families, they can look back, with well-deserved satisfaction, to "nobility of labor, the long pedigree of toil."(2)

> *And the rain descended, and the floods came, and the winds blew, and beat*
> *upon that house; and it fell not: for it was built on a rock.*
> —Matthew 7:25

Even though my section of the county was settled by a heavy concentration of German immigrants and their immediate descendants, the area was part of a larger whole, an English colony. It was heir to English traditions, government rules and structure, customs, ideas, general living practices and language. Germans eventually adopted the English language in their homes and churches, but many of their traits were passed down to generation after generation such as German temperament, the desire to be orderly, obedient and efficient—a combination that tends to ensure everything works more or less as it is supposed to do.

Today, a visitor to Germany finds timeliness to be one of the strong society virtues. It is said you can set your watch accurately by observing the arrival and departure of the trains—never late, never early. Obedience and following instructions are other virtues. Somehow I cannot remember witnessing a German crossing a street against a red light or even jaywalking when the streets were devoid of traffic.

During the last three decades of the 20th century, my good fortune resulted in the opportunity to travel to Germany at least 12 times, several of which allowed me to visit the area from which our ancestors migrated. What I learned on these trips has passed through my mind many times, and I have long since concluded that the land and terrain in central Davidson County must have been very attractive to these early settlers reminding them in many ways of their "Old Germany." They left home to find a good soil, a good climate and a well wooded and well-watered country, suitable for diversified farming and the raising of grain and livestock. This they found when they arrived here.

Stopping for lunch in the town of Lohr on the Main River one day, I requested a meal typical of the region without examining the menu. In due time, the waiter set before me a plate laden with fried pork tenderloin, green beans, potato salad, a small portion of sauerkraut, a large pickle and a few beets. My thoughts were, "I am home again."

THREE

BRIEF HISTORIES OF DAVIDSON COUNTY, LEXINGTON, THOMASVILLE, RELEVANT TOWNSHIPS, AND SEVEN CHURCHES IN THE LOWER-CENTRAL SECTION OF THE COUNTY

The geographic area of the lower-central section of Davidson County encompasses two major cities—Lexington and Thomasville; four townships—Conrad Hill, Cotton Grove, Emmons and Silver Hill; and seven churches of my early world—Beck's Lutheran Church, Beck's Reformed Church, Hedrick's Grove United Church of Christ, Mount Tabor United Church of Christ, Holly Grove Evangelical Lutheran Church, New Jerusalem United Church of Christ, and Jersey Baptist Church. The short histories presented provide background information to enrich the story.

From 1749 to 1822, the territory that became Davidson County was a part of Rowan County whose county seat was the town of Salisbury. Rowan County at one time covered much of the whole of western North Carolina, actually extending to the Mississippi River and beyond, a region which was subdivided on several occasions creating a number of new counties as well as the state of Tennessee. In 1822, Davidson County, North Carolina, (a county with the same name already existed in the state of Tennessee) was formed by carving off the portion of Rowan east of the Yadkin River. The name of the county was selected to honor Revolutionary War hero, General William Lee Davidson, born in Lancaster County, Pennsylvania, in 1746. According to Leonard, in his *Centennial History of Davidson County*, Davidson's father immigrated to North Carolina in 1750. General Davidson's early years are shrouded in obscurity, though records show he attended school at the Charlotte Academy.(1)

General Davidson distinguished himself as a hero by rising through military ranks to Brigadier General after exhibiting bravery and battle skills in a number of skirmishes against the British. He fought with General Greene in his famous march across North Carolina. At Cowan's Ford on the Catawba River, Davidson stationed himself and 300 men where Cornwallis tried to cross. When the British first attempted to get to the other side of the river, it was impassable, swollen by recent rains. Davidson's men fired on the enemy causing them to veer from the original point at which they were expected to cross. The general, observing what was occurring, started to ride from his position. British soldiers sighted him and fired a fatal shot through his heart dislodging him from his horse. Davidson County bears a worthy name, and its name honors a worthy man.(1)

By the latter part of the 18th century, Rowan County was showing considerable growth in population with settlements stretching out along both sides of the Yadkin River as well as around its county seat. Some of the population increase could be attributed to migrations from the northern sections of the country, but the bulk of the growth came from naturally high birth rates prevalent among the large German families. It was common for many families to have more than eight to ten children. An indication of the rate of population growth can be seen in census data which showed Rowan County with 15,828 people in 1790 of which 1,742 were slaves. By 1820, the total number of persons living in the county had risen to 26,009, among them 5,514 slaves.(2)

As a result of the growing population and the fact that Rowan citizens residing east of the Yadkin River were essentially disenfranchised from the county seat of Salisbury, especially in bad weather, the notion of dividing the county took on special significance. During seasons of rain and snow, the crossing of the Yadkin became almost impossible, resulting in citizens postponing trips to Salisbury as long as possible. A number of streams east of the Yadkin also had to be forded. Another factor also came into play. The western part of the state needed a larger representation in the General Assembly to match the dominant majority from the East. An additional county would help equalize legislative power. On November 22, 1822, a bill was introduced in the North Carolina Senate calling for the division of Rowan County. After considerable debate and a number of votes, the bill known as "The Act of Creating Davidson County by dividing the territory of the county of Rowan" was passed and ratified by the General Assembly on December 9, 1822.(1)

With its creation came taxation and government spending on public buildings for lawmakers and law breakers. Private Laws 1822, Chapter 48, Article IV—"That the acting Magistrates for the county of Davidson shall, on the fourth Monday of January next (1823) convene in Lexington; and they shall proceed, a majority being present, to lay a tax of not less than seventy-five cents on the white and black polls, and of not less than ten cents on every hundred dollars valuation of lands and lots within said county, for the purpose of erecting a courthouse and jail in said county and for other public uses." Article VII of the same law—"And be it further enacted, that until the jail of Davidson County is completed, all offenders may be recognized or committed to the jail of Rowan County in the same manner as if the offenses had been committed in Rowan...."

General Davidson, the county's namesake, was one of the most celebrated men in the country. *The Dispatch*, in the issue of September 14, 1922, the centennial year of creating Davidson County, contained the following statement of general historical interest: "Davidson County, which begins the celebration of its centennial of September 26 (1922), is the second North Carolina county of the same name...one of the early sessions of the legislature (when Rowan County extended to the Mississippi River) created the county of Davidson with Nashville as its capital. Shortly after the creation of Davidson County, the territory of the west seceded and formed the state of Tennessee. In 1784, the state of North Carolina ceded the territory of the Union as an independent state. The name was then changed to Tennessee, after the river that winds itself across the state several times and which got its name from the Indians that still roamed the county toward the Mississippi.

"Davidson County, Tennessee, still remains, and Nashville, its county seat, is the capital of the State. It was named after General William Lee Davidson, who fell at Cowan's Ford on May 1, 1780."(1)

Soon, the settlement of Lexington, North Carolina, was named as the shire town (a British term meaning county town). In fact, the name of the town of Lexington antedates the name of Davidson County. On April 19, 1775, the skirmish of Lexington, Massachusetts, was fought, one of the first battles of the Revolutionary War. News traveled very slowly in those days, and word about the battle in Lexington, Massachusetts, did not reach this community for several weeks. When it did come, the patriots at once gave the name of Lexington to the settlement in honor of the New England Lexington.(1)

The territory out of which the new county was formed contained few inhabitants, with thick forests covering most of the land. Probably not more than 1,500 people lived in the entire county. Two villages at the time were Lexington and Clemmonsville neither of which contained more than 100 people. Stagecoach routes ran through the county to Raleigh, to Danville and to Fayetteville. One of the initial challenges for the citizens was to construct a public building(s) to be used as a courthouse and a jail. For a brief period of time, the location of the county seat remained undecided. Land was purchased in the exact center of the county with the intention of building the county seat there, and the name Marion was actually given to the undeveloped site. In the final analysis, Lexington won the bidding, and the General Assembly chose Lexington in early 1823.

Once the decision was made, a committee of three persons was appointed by the courts to contract for and superintend the courthouse and jail construction. It was further directed that the cost of the courthouse was not to exceed

$5,000. The site selected for the courthouse was the center of the public square, known as Washington Square, located where Center Street intersects Main Street. According to available records, the building was two-story of brick construction completed in the late spring of 1823 with courtrooms above and offices below. Early in 1824, a wooden jail, whipping posts and stocks were built near the courthouse site.

In the February 1856 session, the Court ordered that "building of a new courthouse in the town of Lexington is necessary for the safekeeping of records of several courts on this county." Five county commissioners were appointed to locate the courthouse, and they selected a lot adjoining the public square. The structure was to be 80 feet long and 60 feet wide, two stories high, and when completed would be the finest in the state. Cost was estimated to be $20,000, and it was christened in October 1858. This magnificent building served as the county courthouse for over 100 years, and today it houses the Davidson County Historical Museum.(2)

Thomasville, a second town of some size in Davidson County, was planned and placed by its founder, John W. Thomas, on the North Carolina Railroad after its route was established.(2) Incorporated in the 1850s, Thomasville remained a village for half a century until the possibilities of it becoming an industrial center emerged. Its population in 1900 was but 751 people, but by 1910 it had grown to 3,877 and by 1920 to 5,676.(1)

Mr. John Thomas, in 1852, built a large store on the present corner of West Main and Salem, facing the railroad. The structure was two-story frame with a porch across the entire front, considered a marvel of skill and architecture. This was the place where men sat and talked over their business, as well as affairs as wide as their knowledge would reach. People came from a large area to sell their farm surpluses and purchase needed goods.(2) The General Assembly of North Carolina ratified a bill on January 8, 1857, incorporating the town of Thomasville, named after its founder Thomas and his friend, Dr. Henry Rounsaville. *The Greensborough Patriot and Flag* on March 6, 1859, wrote of the town: "Its citizens are said to be enlightened, sober, moral, and industrious, and the rapid growth of the place shows they are characterized by a great deal of enterprise and a laudable ambition to excel in all that is good and commendable."(2)

Thomasville has enjoyed a proud history of growth and economic development, and even though it was founded later than Lexington, it showed a higher census population in 1920 than the county seat. A claim to fame for Thomasville resided in its having the largest chair factory in the nation, and for much of its history, it has been known as The Chair Town. In 1922, when it could honestly claim to be the largest producer of chairs in the South, a "Big Chair" was erected on the town commons near the main square. It was constructed with enough wood to make one hundred regular-size chairs—The Big Chair was

13 ft. 6 in. in height with its seat 6 ft. by 5 ft. 6 in. The entire hide of a Brown Swiss steer covered the seat, the largest such hide obtainable. The Big Chair remained in place for more than 40 years, but the years of weather caused the wooden chair to deteriorate, and hence, it was removed. In 1949, the Chamber of Commerce of Thomasville sponsored the building of another big chair, this time constructed of steel and concrete.(2) A great thrill for me and my siblings was to ride in the family car through Thomasville and see the Big Chair.

Early in the history of the county, the white population was sharply divided in support of slavery. As a result between 1840 and 1860, many of the best citizens went west seeking new homes on government land rather than live where men were "half slave and half free." Even though the slavery question enraged many people, some slave owners were described by the press as noble people dealing with a just and gentle hand. Most farmers did not own slaves, guided by personal beliefs, but the owners of some of the larger plantations, such as Plummer, Finch, Carson, Moore, and Cox, had many slaves, numbers of which could not be determined.

Following the Civil War, Davidson progressed slowly. The war had broken its economic back, but enough resilience remained in the hearts and souls of the hard-working families to begin to reshape the county, making it an improved place to live. The gap between black and white narrowed ever so slightly, but genuine concern was shown eventually by the county leaders to provide for the education of all children. Leonard wrote in 1922, "Davidson is a great county. It embosoms valuable ores and precious metals. Its soil is fertile and richly rewards the labors of its numerous happy farmers. Its streams of water turn many factory wheels and also convert latent power into electrical energy. Its forests after ruthless denudation still cover thousands of acres. Davidson County is the home of numerous cotton mills, furniture factories, flour mills, chair factories and numerous enterprises. It has strong banks and large mercantile establishments. There are fine public and private schools and academies together with finely equipped orphans' homes."(1)

Historian Leonard describes the advancements achieved during the first 100 years of the county giving a graphic comparison between what existed 100 years earlier and what had come about by 1922.

The men and women who lived in Davidson County one hundred years ago never saw a railroad, an automobile, a harvesting machine, a photograph in its present perfection, a telegraph line, a wireless instrument, a daily paper, a printing machine, a sewing machine, a phonograph, a typewriter, a telephone, an electric light, a railroad train, a trolley car, a kerosene lamp, an ocean steamer, a twine binder, a hospital, an anesthetic, a temperance society, a peace society, a Red Cross society, a

Young Men's Christian Association, a Young Women's Christian Association, a Christian Endeavor Society, a church organ or piano, a brick schoolhouse, a furniture factory, a department store, a roller rink, a paved street, a concrete sidewalk, an ice factory, a brick machine, a flying machine, a gasoline engine, an electric motor, a washing machine, a public laundry, a high school, a graded school, a planing machine, a tractor, a concrete bridge, a radio outfit, a cotton mill, a steam shovel, a mowing machine, a steam thrasher, a sky-scraper, an electric fan and a fruit jar.(1)

The first permanent settlements of Davidson County were made by honest, hard-working, frugal and industrious people from Pennsylvania, New Jersey and Old World countries. They carried all their belongings in wagons drawn by horses, mules and oxen. Their cows and sheep were driven for days, weeks and sometimes months over unknown lands; the travelers forded turbulent streams and made their way over rough trails and bad roads and camped in the open, bravely facing and enduring all kinds of weather and adverse conditions. These courageous people settled in Davidson County. When they reached here, they went no farther.

When Davidson County was created in 1822, it contained military districts with an appointed captain over each. In a few short years, the military districts were dropped in favor of townships, which exist today. Four of them—Conrad Hill, Silver Hill, Emmons and Cotton Grove—receive special attention since they contain the rural areas and churches so important in our child and teen years.(1,2)

Conrad Hill(3) has the distinction that can be claimed by no other township—it contains within its borders the center of the county. When being settled, much gold and silver were found beneath its surface. Prospectors and miners spent considerable quantities of capital and time attempting to recover the two metals. The township owes its name to the Conrad Hill Gold Mine located near Hedrick's Grove. One of the larger plantations in the county existed near the county line next to Randolph County. Philemon Plummer owned the plantation and a number of slaves who helped work the land. Agriculture contributed much to the economy for years consisting mainly of livestock, small grain, corn and pasture production with a few farmers growing cotton and tobacco. Sawmilling and lumber provided substantial income as well. Four of the churches mentioned are located in Conrad Hill Township—Mount Tabor, Holly grove, Hedrick's Grove and Beck's Lutheran.

Silver Hill Township(4) takes its name from the Silver Hill Mine opened by settlers in 1840 and offering the first public employment in the county with the number of employees ranging from 50 to 100. A small settlement grew up around the mine as well as the Cedar Grove grammar school. Another community, Sandy Grove in the northern part of the township, also had a grammar school. Beck's Lutheran Church had its origin in the Silver Hill Township but relocated in Conrad Hill. Beck's Reformed and Beck's Lutheran shared an original structure constructed in 1787 on Four Mile Branch. Many of the inhabitants in the township derived their living from sawmilling as well as from general farming—row crops, cattle, sheep, and other livestock. In the southwestern section, the backwaters of High Rock Lake have presented opportunities for development of lakefront real estate and water recreational activities.

Emmons Township(5) lies in the southeast section of the county bordering four other townships, two of which are Conrad Hill and Silver Hill. In colonial times, Emmons was sparsely populated. Roads qualified for nothing more than trails, but many travelers found the township favorable for camping. By 1770 by actual count, 127 families, or a total of 823 whites and 55 slaves lived within its borders. Emmons was also a mining district with mines having such names as Emmons, Cid and Silver Valley. The mines yielded gold, silver and lead and provided employment for many workers. Communities were established at Cid and Silver Valley, the latter being a stagecoach stop where drivers changed horses before proceeding to Asheboro. Before the Civil War, a plantation owner, Richardson Finch, owned many slaves with a substantial farming activity.

Special emphasis needs to be given to the town of Denton, the largest incorporated area in the southern part of the county.(5) Young Denton got off to a good start with a couple of stores and a private school building erected along with a Baptist Church. By the beginning of the 20th century, Denton had a balanced community, and a railroad led to the rise of a sizeable lumber industry and the establishment of a livery stable. As in other townships in the area, diversified farming was a way of life for many families that built many mutual connections through commerce.

Some of the first European settlers formed the community of Jersey in Cotton Grove Township(4) in 1740. Since farming was the principal economic enterprise of that time, the settlers found the rich soils of the area much to their liking. Years ago the village of Cotton Grove served as a rendezvous point for farmers with wagons laden with cotton before traveling in caravan to a cotton market to the east. The popularity of the gathering point grew with each harvest making Cotton Grove the possible source of the name of the township.

One of the oldest Baptist churches, Jersey Baptist, in North Carolina was founded in the Cotton Grove Township. Two railroads cut across the township with the villages of Linwood and Holtsburg situated along one and the village of Southmont area on the other in the southern part of the township.

The backwaters of High Rock Lake rise near the Southmont region making it attractive for second homes and a wonderful place for swimming and boating. When the county bested the competition for the Junior Order Orphans Home, the committee selected the Cotton Grove Township for its location.

HISTORIES OF SEVEN CHURCHES

Rural churches played a significant role in the growth and development of the area. They served several functions—as a place of worship, the site where a formal education could be obtained, as the center of social activities and as a gathering location for community discussions. Protestant churches soon dropped the responsibility for providing a basic education when it became a public responsibility but retained their religious, cultural and social roles. Without question, the rural church had a tremendous impact on the community at large as well as individual citizens. Not only was it a provider of religious education, but many of its programs built individual leadership skills and confidence. The ability of persons to function in society can often be traced to the many church experiences such as participating in worship services, attending and teaching Sunday school, vacation Bible school, youth fellowship, backyard parties, playing on church athletic teams, singing in the choir and the list goes on and on. For many rural residents, the church provided the primary opportunity for social development and interactions.

Of the many churches that made contributions to the quality of life in the area, three United Church of Christ, two Lutheran, and one Reformed have special significance because their congregations shared a similar heritage, honored mutual values and other close cultural and historical linkages. A seventh church, Jersey Baptist, has been a pillar of strength for more than 200 years. The Lutheran and Reformed churches were strong from their beginnings, and throughout the history of the region these churches have maintained their organizations. I knew many of the people who attended the churches during my formative years, moving among them almost daily in community settings of work and recreation and interacting with them in grammar and high school as well.

Beck's Lutheran Church(7)

As most of the early German settlers were of both Lutheran and Reformed faiths, a close association between the two groups existed at some locations. Beck's Lutheran and Beck's Reformed are an example of this union, and just exactly how they functioned initially remains unclear. Nevertheless, it is safe to say the two denominations were "joined at the hip" so to speak for a number of years. Beck's Lutheran Church is one of the older Lutheran congregations in Davidson County, first located some six miles east of Lexington. The deed for the land on which Beck's was located was made on November 7, 1787, conveying some 53 acres from Dr. John Billings, L. Smith and others. The conveyance went to both the Lutherans and the German Reformeds known as "the Church of the Dutch Settlement." Dutch is a misnomer when it really refers to the word Deutsch which translates into English as German.

The first building was a log house located on the property when the land was purchased. It is possible that a second log structure was built soon after the congregation organized. At Beck's, in the early 1800s, there was disagreement over the form of worship which led to two groups of Lutherans. One group belonged to the North Carolina Synod and the other to the Tennessee Synod. Those belonging to the Tennessee Synod held their worship on alternate Sundays from the North Carolina Synod Lutherans and the German Reformeds. This arrangement lasted until about 1878 when the Tennessee faction decided to build a church for themselves. Accepting a gift of land from Mr. George Hedrick, the Tennessee group constructed a frame building on the property. But through the years, their numbers decreased and gatherings were essentially discontinued. The two Synods merged in 1918, and at the time of the merger, Beck's Lutheran was a part of a parish consisting of five other churches. Soon the Rev. R. Bruce Sigmon came from seminary to serve the parish where he labored faithfully until 1928.

During the struggle for survival, two men were influential in keeping the old church alive. One was George Washington Beck who often came to church when no one else did. He found himself alone in the sanctuary and served as Sunday school superintendent, teacher and as church organist. Mr. Washington has been credited for holding the church together when its future appeared to be in doubt. The other man of significant influence was J. Ed Young, who supported the church liberally and gave it wise counsel as it struggled along.

In 1928, Rev. Roy L. Fisher began his service as pastor of the parish that included another church. During his ministry, Beck's Lutheran Church changed greatly, and the most significant change was its relocation. The congregation purchased six and one-fourth acres of land from Mr. R. L. Bowers located some two miles north on Beck's Church Road toward Lexington. A new modern brick building was constructed on the property, and the congregation moved into it in 1937. Rev. Roy Fisher served until 1942, and Rev. Charles F. Kyles succeeded him. During Pastor Kyles' ministry, Beck's Lutheran Church became independent. Kyles served as pastor until 1947.

Beck's Lutheran has shown continued growth over the years, not only in the size of the congregation, but in the extent to which the physical facilities were expanded and renovated. Capable and dedicated ministers have served the church, and today, Beck's Lutheran Church is very much alive and well.

Beck's Reformed Church
(formerly Beck's United Church of Christ)(8)

Officially, Beck's Reformed Church began November 5, 1787, but records of worship activities prior to that date put the beginning several years earlier. The origin of the name Beck's Church remains speculative largely because none of the early prominent members carried the name Beck. Other churches seemed to have been named in this fashion. Records show the first settler by this name as Devault Beck whose property bordered the 53 acres deeded to the church, and a logical conclusion could be that the church was known for its location as the church next to Mr. Beck's and simply shortened to Beck's Church.

The oldest tombstone at Beck's (as well as in all of Davidson County) is that of Jacob Byerly dated 1771. Frederick Goss, Peter Hedrick, Jr., and John Billings made a land entry in 1779 "so as to induce a church belonging to Lutherans and Calvinists (the Reformeds) in company." This same parcel of land was later made as a state grant to John Billings and David Smith, Sr., in 1784. Then on November 5, 1787, the transfer of the 53 acres "including a meeting house and burial ground" was made to the church. Trustees of the union church at that time were Martin Frank and Frederick Billings of the Lutheran Church and David Smith, Sr., and Henry Lookabill of the Reformed Church.

The pastor of the Reformed congregation in 1787 was Rev. Mr. Schneider. He organized the congregation for services in a log house that had been constructed under the leadership of Rev. Suther. Much suffering occurred among the members of the congregation during the Revolutionary War, and the tribulations of Peter Hedrick, Jr., and his family serve as a notable example. Mr. Hedrick was born December 17, 1733, in the Palatinate area of Germany. His father and family, including his two sons, Peter, Jr., and Johann Adam, migrated to America in 1738 settling in Pennsylvania where they remained until after the Revolutionary War began. In fact, the father and the two sons became soldiers in the Continental Army. As they approached adulthood, the two boys moved to the North Carolina Piedmont with Peter Hedrick, Jr., settling along Four Mile Branch. On one of Peter's trips away from home, a band of Tories (English loyalists) pillaged his property, then abused his wife and left her and the children helpless. When Peter Hedrick returned a few weeks later and discovered the situation, he took his wife and children to Virginia, returning after the war. Peter, one of the founders of Beck's Church, was buried in its graveyard when he died in January 1789.

Beck's Church lost a portion of its congregation when the Lutherans split off in 1878; and in 1891, Beck's lost additional members, chiefly Hedricks, when

Hedrick's Grove Reformed Church was founded. The Hedrick families and a few others wanted a place of worship closer to their homes.

Prominent names listed in the Beck's congregation at that time included Robert Allred, Frank Burkhart, Zeno Tussey, Andrew Younts, Henry Hedrick, Robert Swing, Vance Miller, Bud Parks, Ed Crotts and the Greers.

Shortly after the Reformed/Lutheran split in 1878, the remaining Beck's Reformed congregation erected a new frame church to which a sizeable addition was made in 1924. Many members living today remember the old frame church which served for worship until 1950 when the congregation moved to a newly constructed brick building containing a sanctuary and Sunday school rooms on a high hill overlooking the cemetery.

From its inception in 1787 until 1934, when a merger occurred with Evangelical Church, Beck's was a member of the German Reformed denomination. The denomination continued as Evangelical and Reformed until 1961 when another merger occurred with the Evangelical and Reformeds joining the Congregational and Christian Churches to form the United Church of Christ. Similar denominational changes were experienced by most of the areas "reformed" churches.

Hedrick's Grove United Church of Christ
(formerly Hedrick's Grove Evangelical and Reformed Church)(9)

Traveling to their church at Beck's Reformed Church with horses, wagons and buggies was a great inconvenience for many folks in the Hedrick's Grove community. For many, the trip was so difficult to make that they chose to forgo attending church altogether.

Planning for a solution began in the spring of 1889. A group of people met in the old storehouse in a grove of trees near the site of the present parsonage and organized a Sunday school, selecting Daniel Hedrick as superintendent. The group prospered, and they looked ahead to building a sanctuary and facilities for religious and public education. Land was given by George W. Hedrick, Sr., Philip E. Hedrick and John Long. Members cut needed timber from their own land and gave of their time and money. On Thanksgiving Day, 1889, the cornerstone was laid for the new building. Using volunteer labor, the building was enclosed, and the floors were laid during the winter. The ground floor consisted of three rooms to be used for religious and public educational needs, and the second floor was to serve as the sanctuary, seating some 200 persons. Completion came during the fall of 1891 and the winter of 1892. Dedication occurred July 31, 1892.

At a joint consistory meeting of the Lower Davidson Charge held March,

1891, the church was accepted as a part of that body under the name of "Hedrick's Grove." This name apparently came into usage because of the many Hedricks in the area and the beautiful grove of trees which framed its location. The congregation was officially organized May 8, 1891. Allen Hedrick, John L. Black and R. Eli Hedrick were elected elders, and H. Frank Hedrick, Henry Hedrick and Robert L. Beck were elected as deacons. Charter membership of the church numbered 41 persons. Transferring from Beck's were: Emily Regan, Jacob Younts, Mrs. Alexander Smith, Alexander Smith, Mrs. Washington Smith, Laura Young, Issac Rhodes, Chrissie Leonard, Lamuel Allred, Allen Hedrick, Mrs. Neaty C. Hedrick. Elizabeth Hedrick, Phillip E. Hedrick, Wiley C. Hedrick, A. Eli Hedrick, Henry E. Hedrick, Jacob Hedrick, George W. Hedrick, Mrs. Jane Hedrick, Thornton Hedrick, Adeline Hedrick, Joseph Hedrick, Minnie E. Swing, R. Eli Hedrick, Mary E. Hedrick, G. Mathias Hedrick, Rachael Hedrick and Betty Hedrick. Additional persons transferred from the Emmanuel Church: David Grubb, Susanna Grubb, John L. Black, and Frances Black. Received by confirmation were: Ida Regan, Laura Regan, Robert L. Beck, Samuel W. Beck, Jones Tilden Hedrick, Sara J. Hedrick, H. Frank Hedrick, Henry H. Hedrick and S. Adnet Hedrick.

A weekday school for children in the community was held in the new building in 1892 and 1893 under the supervision of the church. This function was assumed by the county and continued until 1924.

Hedrick's Grove Church became a member of the Lower Davidson Charge consisting of Beck's, Mt. Tabor, Jerusalem and Hedrick's Grove. A parsonage to serve the Charge was constructed at Hedrick's Grove in 1923, and for many years the minister allocated his time among the churches.

The church property was enlarged by a grant of land from Grover Hedrick for parking purposes, and at the same time, a hut was constructed providing indoor facilities for social gatherings. Hedrick's grove voted to become an independent church in 1954. In 1953 some 60 members withdrew from the church to form Memorial Evangelical and Reformed Church. Even so, Hedrick's Grove continues to experience modest growth with more land being acquired and additional physical facilities constructed.

Mount Tabor United Church of Christ
(formerly Mt. Tabor Evangelical and Reformed Church)(10)

Mount Tabor's origin and heritage are similar to those of the other churches rooted in the Reformed faith being founded by people who came to North Carolina from Germany by way of Pennsylvania following "The Great Wagon Trail" from Philadelphia through Virginia to the Yadkin River. The church is located approximately three miles east of Lexington on the Holly Grove Road in the Crotts community and was established there to accommodate citizens who experienced difficulty traveling to Pilgrim Reformed Church to worship some six miles away. At the time of establishment in 1883, long distance transportation had its problems, and the Classis (District) of North Carolina granted the authority to organize a Reformed congregation. Several men and boys pitched in to build a tent-like brush arbor structure where worship services were held for a few months.

Charter members numbered 22 persons, having the names of Crotts, Burkhart, Lohr, Beck, Tysinger, Musgrave, Fritts and Smith. Most of them had traveled to Pilgrim, but some had connections to the Beck's Reformed Church. Elected consistory men included David H. Tysinger, David Crotts, Jr., Alexander Burkhart and John H. Crotts. For several years after incorporation, Mount Tabor was associated with the Upper Davidson Charge of the Reformed Church, but in 1896, a detachment process moved it to the Lower Davidson Charge where it remained as one of four member churches until 1947 when it withdrew from the Charge and employed its first full-time minister.

The first permanent church structure was constructed in 1884 on land purchased for $1.00 from Robert and Rachael Crotts, and Mary Ann and Catherine Crotts.

Twenty-five years later, the original building was torn down and a new one put in its place. Nearly three decades later, the congregation once more constructed a new building to which an addition has been made.

The Mount Tabor Church has rendered invaluable service to the community as a special place for religious and social activities since it was established nearly 125 years ago. The men and women who are products of the church have been and continue to be leaders in the community. As with many rural churches, many young people have left the Mount Tabor community seeking opportunities elsewhere; and it is likely wherever they have gone, the solid religious and family foundations developed in the Mount Tabor Church have stood them well.

Holly Grove Evangelical Lutheran Church(11)

Holly Grove Evangelical Lutheran Church held its centennial celebration in 1985 and has an extensive and rich history. Historians typically link the stories of the Church with Holly Grove Academy, which was established in the fall of 1884 on the old Raleigh Road about five miles east of Lexington. The Rev. Professor W. P. Cline saw the great need for education after he arrived in Davidson County to assume pastoral responsibilities at Pilgrim, Emmanuel, Beck's and New Jerusalem Lutheran congregations. He opened the Academy in the abandoned Quinn schoolhouse near his home at Holly Grove and taught the first year. In the summer of 1885, Rev. Cline started the movement to construct a new academy building; after a discouraging beginning, it was completed by December. Professor Cline gained the confidence of many people in the area, and a right-hand man, Eli Younts, gave land for the construction of the academy building and a parsonage for the professor and his family.

The project was truly an effort of dedicated persons from the Holly Grove community, and when completed in December 1885, the Academy building was two-story with a large auditorium above and one small and two large recitation rooms below. As someone quipped, "The Academy building is a great example of what a community can do that does not know itself." The cost of the building and furnishings was estimated to be $500, but its actual value to the growth and development of Holly Grove itself can never be measured in dollars and cents. In what was truly a community-wide effort, each participant had some part in making the building a reality. When the young school moved into the building, there was great rejoicing and hopefulness beyond Holly Grove because this was at a time when education was at low ebb in the county. The public schools averaged no more than three months a year, being taught by teachers having only meager training, teaching in dilapidated schoolhouses with practically no equipment. Some of the parishioners, aware of the poor schooling opportunities, desired a minister like the Rev. Cline who also could teach school. Holly Grove Academy held great promise for delivering a high quality education, and it served as a beacon for the establishment of academies in other church communities.

Holly Grove Lutheran Church dates its beginning in 1885, the same date the Academy was established. Rev. Cline's calling was to be the new church's minister, and the first worship service was conducted on Christmas Day that year in the Academy auditorium. On May 30, 1886, the first communion service was conducted with 20 participants. Like other Lutheran churches and the German Reformed churches in this section of Davidson County, many of the ancestral pioneers at Holly Grove came south from York and Lancaster Counties in Pennsylvania bringing a heavy German influence. In fact, the initial membership was largely made up of members from the Pilgrim, Beck's and New Jerusalem Lutheran congregations.

The impact of the Holly Grove Lutheran Church and the Holly Grove Academy on the area is legendary. Many of the students attending the Academy were from local homes, but other students would come from more distant places, some of whom were boarders in a two-story house constructed for this purpose, others in the parsonage and private homes. The Rev. Professor W. P. Cline served the Holly Grove community in the dual role of being the minister of the Holly Grove Lutheran Church and conducting the Holly Grove Academy, which he did with remarkable success. The Academy enjoyed a solid reputation as an institution of learning. Both the Church and the Academy were pioneering accomplishments, and he remained as their leader until 1891 when he answered the call to a greater work joining three other educators in founding Lenoir College in Hickory, North Carolina.

The Holly Grove Academy continued to be an educational leader after the departure of Professor Cline. During later years, the old building serving both the Academy and the church was moved and dismantled, and another school building was constructed. At the same time, members of the congregation decided to build their own sanctuary nearby. As fate would have it, the Academy building burned in the 1920s, and folks near the school opened their homes to the students and teachers to finish out the school term. Until Davis-Townsend School was opened in 1931, the students went to other schools in the county. Some attended Thomasville, Fairgrove, Lexington, and as far away as Linwood. Unquestionably, the Holly Grove Academy became a moving force for education in Davidson County as well as in the state.

Holly Grove Lutheran Church enjoys a long and proud history of providing religious, social and cultural opportunities for the residents of the community. For more than 70 years it was a part of a parish with Beck's, Lebanon, Emanuel, Pilgrim and New Jerusalem Lutheran churches as members; but later Emanuel went its own way. In 1956, the Holly Grove congregation voted to become self-supporting leaving the parish and purchasing the other churches' portion of ownership in the parsonage. Holly Grove Church has served the community for more than 120 years, and during that time nearly 30 ministers have provided spiritual leadership.

New Jerusalem United Church of Christ(12)

New Jerusalem United Church of Christ, located in the region has had a long-time historical association within both the Reformed and Lutheran denominations. In fact, during its early years of existence, Baptist and Methodist congregations worshipped in the church...New Jerusalem was the classical example of a Union Church for 106 years until 1962 when it dissolved from the Lutherans, leaving the United Church of Christ as the sole proprietor. Like other churches of this faith, New Jerusalem United Church of Christ had its roots with the German Reformeds, followed by the Evangelical and Reformeds. Nestled in the rolling hills near Three Hat Mountain in the lower part of the county, just off of old Highway 64, close to Willomore Springs, the church enjoys a most serene and beautiful site.

New Jerusalem stood as a symbol of Protestant cooperation, something that was a throw-back to the horse and buggy days when for practical reasons congregations of more than one faith shared the same physical facilities. One must wonder how such an arrangement functioned harmoniously at New Jerusalem for more than a century, but it did. For example, when owned by the Lutherans and the Reformeds, the church had two pastors with Reformed services conducted every first, third, and fifth Sundays and Lutheran services every second and fourth Sundays. The same people attended church almost every Sunday, and except for the pastor and the type of service, it was impossible to determine whether the church was Lutheran or Reformed on any particular Sunday. Each congregation paid its pastor and made benevolent donations. When the Reformed pastor held service, the offering went to the Reformed fund; when the Lutheran pastor preached, the offering went into the Lutheran fund. Members of both congregations made up the choir.

There was only one Sunday school for both the Lutherans and Reformeds, held every Sunday, which functioned in a cooperatively and congenial fashion. During one year, Lutheran materials were used, and the following year Reformed materials were studied. All operational expenses such as heating, electricity, repairs and general upkeep were paid out of the Sunday school treasury. In 1962, the Reformed members (United Church of Christ) purchased the interests of the Lutheran congregation, which saw the passing of an era of union congregations between the two denominations in lower Davidson County.

Jersey Baptist Church(13)

The church takes its name from a colony from New Jersey which settled in the Yadkin valley in the middle of the 18th century. Garland A. Hendricks in his book, *Saints and Sinners at Jersey Settlement: The Story of Jersey Baptist Church*, chronicles in explicit detail the origin and development of one of the oldest Baptist churches in America.

Hendricks said the settlers came from New Jersey "to the Yadkin Valley in order to claim more adequate land holdings for themselves...these honest, hard-working, frugal people drove their sheep and carried their families and belongings on carts and wagons drawn by oxen and horses along a road which led from Lancaster, Pennsylvania, to Trading Ford."

They valued religion, practicing two ordinances only—baptism by immersion and the Lord's Supper. According to Hendricks, two ministers, Benjamin Miller of Pennsylvania and John Gano of New Jersey, were appointed to minister to the spiritual needs of the people. These two men "were instrumental in gathering a group of Baptists for worship and service with some degree of regularity and momentum...they were invited back every year...they visited the settlement and preached as they could."

John Gano attracted large numbers of people to his services, and no building structure existed in the settlement large enough to accommodate the crowds. In looking for a place to construct a meeting place where Baptists and others could gather to worship, Elder Gano and his followers selected a building site on a hill overlooking the River Valley.

The history of the Jersey Baptist Church is a storied one throughout its formative years. Trying times befell its supporters from external sources such as raids by the Cherokees and controversy about taxes with the Governor of the Province. Many families dispersed into the wilderness in search of relief. Very little, if any, movement occurred until the early 1780s when the scattered members came together and formed under new leadership with fourteen members. From that day forward, the church became heavily engaged in Christian work, and amid trials and tribulations, the church moved forward through the next century and three-quarters.

A bicentennial celebration in 1955 was a very special event. First and foremost, reaching 200 years of age was a lofty milestone few churches had achieved. Members readied the church for a week of special services. Even the governor of the state, The Honorable Luther Hodges, addressed the congregation.

Jersey Baptist Church has anchored the development and expansion of the denomination in western Davidson County. A minimum of 16 churches owe their start to the support rendered by the Jersey Baptist congregation. Included among the number is the Holloway Baptist Church which stands with Jersey among the leading churches of the region.

Given the contemporary division among religious denominations, the apparent harmony between Lutherans and Reformeds appears remarkable today. Early Settlements in lower Davidson County and surrounding areas contained a preponderance of both denominations often worshipping in the same church even though variances in doctrine kept them apart. The Lutherans followed the catechetical precepts of Luther while the Reformeds adhered to the Heidelberg Catechism. Apparent disagreement existed between the two sects in the attitude toward the sacrament; the Lutherans believed that the participants at the communion table ate the body of Christ as transmuted into bread, but the Reformed Church professed that the wafer is merely a symbol. In the early days, when German was continuing to be spoken, the issue of the differences was raised between two gentlemen. One man asked another: "What is the difference between the two denominations anyway?" "Why," said the other, "it is all in the way they begin the Lord's Prayer. The one says 'Unser Vater' (Our Father) and the other 'Vater Unser' (Father Our)."(14)

The brief accounting of the history of the seven churches most closely associated with the German settlers illustrates the citizens were a religious people. In 1920, church membership in the county numbered a total of more than 17,000 persons. Sink and Matthews(2) place the population of the entire county in the same year at 35,201, showing that 50 percent of the population were church members. The impact of the church on daily lives is obvious. Leonard surmises that the large number of church-going citizens "make it (the county) a fit place in which to live." He concluded that "the more church members we have, the stronger and more reliable will be the moral worth and integrity of our people."

Beck's Lutheran Church, one of the oldest Lutheran congregations in the region. Its members worship in this structure completed in 1937. (Photo by author)

Beck's Reformed Church (formerly United Church of Christ) members worshipped in this frame structure for more than 72 years. (Family collection)

Hedrick's Grove United Church of Christ (formerly Evangelical and Reformed) was organized in 1891. Sanctuary shown above has served the congregation since 1922. (Photo by author)

Holly Grove Evangelical Lutheran Church was founded in 1885. The building shown above has served as the sanctuary and educational quarters since 1913. (Photo by author)

Jersey Baptist Church is one of the oldest Baptist churches in North Carolina, established in 1755. The building shown here was constructed in 1842 and still remains as a part of the total church plant. (David Smith)

The members of Mt. Tabor church used this sanctuary from 1910 to 1966. (Janice Abernathy)

The congregation of New Jerusalem Church of Christ worships in a beautiful frame structure just off Highway 64 in the Three Hat Mountain area. (Photo by author)

FOUR
OUT OF WORLD WAR I
AND THROUGH THE 1920s

Children of the 1920s, '30s and '40s came through some tough times during the depression years and the frightful events of World War II. These events gave them a character and set of values different from most generations. They learned to do for themselves or to do without, and they developed an awareness of their surroundings and a deep understanding of human behavior. If they faced a difficult situation, the challenge became to solve it through logic and the use of a good dose of common sense.

If at first they did not succeed, they tried and tried again until they made it. My peers and I were shaped by a tough environment, the tough mindedness of our elders, and a caring community of adults who taught us right from wrong. It was a time of measured goal-driven living; life moved at a slower pace than it did after World War II. I am what I was, and all of us are what we were; our children and grandchildren ought to know the forces that molded us. The memories of those days are treasured, and we believe they will never appear again—or will they?

The year 1920 arrived without much fanfare for the residents of lower Davidson County, especially since World War I had been in full swing less than two years ago, and nothing could top it in significance. The "Great War to End All Wars" came to an end on November 11, 1918, when an armistice was signed at midnight with the German government accepting the Allied terms. All hostilities ceased promptly at six a.m. on a Monday morning, Paris time. Before leaving for his office at the capitol that day, President Wilson addressed his fellow countrymen issuing the following proclamation:

> The Armistice was signed this morning. Everything for which America fought has been accomplished. It will now be our fortunate duty to assist by example, by sober, friendly counsel and by material aid in the establishment of just democracy throughout the world.(1)

Like all wars, the cost was heavy, not only in material goods, but in human life as well. Germany simply ran out of manpower with its final recruits being boys of 14 years of age and men in their sixties. It had no more food or supplies because of a solid blockade laid down by the Allies, but in a way, the country was fortunate since no battles destroyed its fertile soil. Yet, its economy was in shreds. More than ten million people perished, of which six million were civilians. The United States War Department reported 53,169 American war deaths.(2) Closer to home, a total of 932 men from Davidson County went into service, about 782 were white and 150 colored, as people of color were known at the time.

Many of these men were from the area of my birth, lower Davidson County, and two of them were uncles, Walter G. Younts and Ivey W. Lohr, and another a cousin of my father and neighbor, Henry R. Smith. By the time the war ended, 39 men from Davidson County had lost their lives, 37 white and two colored.(3) *The Dispatch* carried a story of the loss of Robert Lee Fritts from the Conrad Hill Township in its November 13, 1918, edition. As a young boy, I can still remember the World War I veterans recounting their war experiences. One thing that really stuck with me was the fact that so many U.S. soldiers faced the horrors of poison gas deliberately leaked by the Germans into the trenches and on the battlefields. The physical effects such as nerve damage from being exposed to the gas were permanent.

As if war was not enough, an epidemic of influenza raged across the globe with estimates of the number of deaths reaching 20 million persons. The U.S. Bureau of Public Health said that the deaths among civilians far exceeded those among troops abroad and that more servicemen died from the influenza than on the battlefield. More than 80,000 civilian deaths were counted among the large cities of the country, and during the last two weeks of October 1918 when the disease peaked, 40,000 deaths were recorded nationwide. Attempts to develop a vaccine had failed.(2) An uncle of mine, my mother's brother, died in 1920 at 24 years of age during the epidemic.

Celebrations following the victory lasted for several days as Americans cheered and marched through the streets all over the country. Other than sending troops to Cuba for the Spanish-American War, 20 years earlier, World War I marked the first time in the history of our republic that young Americans fought on foreign soil in large numbers. They could not have been more jubilant climbing out of the trenches of France that November 1918 day to make their way back across the Atlantic.

Victory had been achieved, but the story did not end there. For most of the servicemen, going off to war represented the first time traveling more than fifty miles away from home. They trained with persons with unusual accents and were teased for their Southern drawl. When overseas, dramatic changes in the scenery and language confronted them at every turn. Most of them just wanted to get home, but others had liked the experience of change of getting off the farm and did not want it to end. Naiveté and simplicity had been tempered considerably. New York's Broadway playwrights caught the metamorphosis and responded with an appropriate stage musical show titled, "How Ya' Gonna Keep 'em Down on the Farm after They've Seen Paree?"

Since World War I ended with the signing of an armistice, further negotiations were necessary because neither side was defeated. The Allies considered themselves the victors and wanted Germany to suffer and pay for what they had done. What turned out to be a serious mistake by the Allies was not inviting Germany to the Paris Peace Conference, and in the long run, this high handedness resulted in the planting of a germ for war for the next generation. In the year 1919, the Allies did sign a peace treaty with the German Empire, as well as the countries of Austria and Bulgaria. A year later, peace treaties were signed with Hungary and Turkey. The general conclusion was, since no one really won the war outright, no one could establish a lasting peace.(2)

The impact of the Great War found its way into the thoughts and hearts of the people of my area for many years, even into the period of World War II, which raged from 1939–1945. Many songs that were written to characterize World War I stayed on the lips of people. The publishing house of Leo Feist churned out songs at an impressive rate, and folks began almost immediately to sing them. Most of them were catchy marching tunes said to raise the spirit of the soldiers more than letters from home.

School teachers on the home front and many years later taught the songs to students on a regular basis, and we sang them in our homes... *The Saturday Evening Post* published tributes to the songs:

> A nation that sings never can be beaten; each song is a milestone on the road to victory," and "Songs are to a Nation's spirit what ammunition is to a Nation's army." Their sometimes whimsical titles captured a soldier's experience of war and homesickness: "It's a Long Way to Tipperary," "Pack Up Your Troubles in Your Old Kit Bag," "Oh! How I hate to Get Up in the Morning," "Keep the Home Fires Burning," and "Till We Meet Again." Others portrayed the American's consternation when in another's country such as: "Hinky Dinky Parlay Voo," and "Tramp, Tramp, Tramp."

Literature written in World War I made its way into the hearts of Americans in the form of hundreds of books and articles as well as in poetry. We were required to read some of these works during grammar and high school. One such work that has stuck with me even until now is the memorable war poem written by John McCrae, a medical officer in World War I, titled, "In Flanders Fields."(4) The poem portrayed the bloody deaths of thousands of young soldiers. I recall having to memorize the poem in school, and during the recitation sessions, you could have heard a pin drop as we struggled to say the words and to catch the full meaning of the author's lines. We learned much from memorizing the words, but even more, we gained a deeper understanding of life and what is expected from us.

Another important occurrence of historical significance to the South was the advent of the cotton boll weevil. This insect came out of Mexico and migrated all across the Southern Cotton Belt reaching to the eastern coast of Virginia in the early twenties. As it made its way through the South, the damage inflicted devastated cotton farming. Yields were cut by as much as 85 percent, and this debacle, coupled with falling cotton prices at the mills, put the cotton farmers into a serious economic and psychological depression.

Fortunately, the percentage of farmland devoted to cotton production in lower Davidson County was minimal on most farms, but farmers with cotton suffered severe income losses. Depression arrived early for them, nearly ten years before the national crisis that was to occur later.

Getting into the 1920s

At the beginning of the decade of the twenties, the population of the United States stood at 106,521,537 people with life expectancies of 54.6 years for females and 53.6 years for males. Davidson County counted 35,201 persons with 9,878 living in Lexington and 8,730 in Thomasville. Populations of townships in central and lower Davidson County were the following: Conrad Hill—1,431; Cotton Grove—1,721; Emmons—2,142; and Silver Hill—979.(3,6) Woodrow Wilson was president of the country, and Thomas W. Bickett was governor of North Carolina.(5)

In manufacturing, our state was earning the distinction of being first in tobacco, textiles and furniture. The labor force of the state averaged only five years of schooling, slightly less than for the country as a whole. North Carolina had the largest number of farms (estimated to be 275,000) of any state in the U.S., but the average number of acres per farm was one of the lowest in the nation. We were definitely an agrarian state in every sense of the word with 80.8 percent of the people living in rural areas as compared to 48.8 percent for the entire nation.

Like the rest of the southern states, per capita income lagged behind the North by any measurement. The carryover of the ravages of the Civil War plus a stumbling agriculture for nearly a half century gave the North Carolina resident an annual income no more than two-thirds of that of the average U.S. citizen's. For example, per capita income in N.C. in 1920 was just below $1,000 per year, while persons in the states of Michigan, Ohio and Illinois had average incomes of $1,500 per year.(5)

On the other hand, we were not in the dire straights of other southern states such as Georgia and South Carolina, where yearly incomes averaged less than $700. All of this meant fewer dollars for education, the building of roads and other infrastructure important to support economic development.

The Dispatch established in 1882 in Lexington had for its motto, "The Paper of the People, for the People and with the People," and was printed weekly at a yearly subscription rate of $1.50. People living in central and lower Davidson County looked to the publication as a dependable source of information about events of the time. In the eastern part of the county in and around Thomasville, the News and Times of Thomasville was a valuable source of local and state news.

An inordinate amount of time was spent scanning The Dispatch(1) from 1920 to 1950, as well as national and international sources of information, for example, 20th Century Day by Day by Dorling Kindersley, to obtain an understanding of what people in Davidson County were learning at local, state, national and international levels. What follows are selected news items characterizing the decade of the twenties as the people of lower Davidson County faced it. Quotation marks indicate headlines and stories lifted directly from the publications.

From *The Dispatch*, 1920(1)

A general store, Gilmer Brothers' Company, in Lexington sold everything from food to millinery items to men's overcoats, and the following items were listed for a sale:

Food
  Kellogg's Corn Flakes 2 boxes for 23 cents
  Uneeda Biscuits 3 boxes for 33 cents
Millinery Department
  $5 hats reduced to $3.49
  $12 hats reduced to $7.99
Men's clothing
  $18.50 overcoats reduced to $12.98

The Lyric Theatre ran an advertisement about the current silent film attraction titled, "A Virtuous Vamp," starring Constance Tallmadge. The price of admission was 15 cents for children and 25 cents for adults.

Ads for Fletcher's Castoria explained it had been in use for 30 years, and Bull Durham Tobacco, in its drawstring sack, touted roll your own cigarettes or mix it pipe tobacco.

Horses and mules provided the power for heavy farm work, and the advent of the Fordson Tractor promised to make farm work easier and more efficient.

The Dispatch carried a story written by Wilbur F. Cannon, Colorado's Pure Food and Drug Commissioner, reflecting to some extent the low level of scientific understanding of the nature of things in the early twenties. The Commissioner associated the prevalence of pellagra in humans to women using self-rising flour in their baking and cooking. He began his article this way—"They have about concluded that it (pellagra) is caused by the lack of an element called vitamines [sic]. Nobody knows what exactly vitamines [sic] is. No one has been able to catch one. None are on exhibit in the national museums. But still, it is known to exist."

"Commissioners of Rowan and Davidson County are meeting to consider building a 'free bridge' across the Yadkin River, something needed for many years." One of the main reasons Davidson County was formed in 1822 was to eliminate the problem of crossing the Yadkin River in the rainy season to reach Rowan County's seat of Salisbury.

"Davidson County Road Board ordered the Beck's Church road in Silver Hill Township built."

"Noise of hack saw arouses jailor, who prevents escape of prisoners, and they confess."

In Washington, D.C., the valor of Indians in World War I was told. The Commissioner of Indian Affairs recalled the deeds of 10,000 Redskins who fought Kaiserism in France. At that time, there were 333,702 Indians in the United States with 8,216 living in North Carolina.

On December 20, 1920, *The Dispatch* announced that Lexington will be the second city in N.C. to have the automatic telephone system.

The 1920s Sense of Humor

1. *Just a man*
The bride: But why do you look so blue deary? You know papa has promised he will still buy my dresses.
The groom: Yes, but I am wondering what the dickens we shall have to eat.
2. *Good church man*
Visitor: And you sit here day after day painting nothing but animal pictures?
Artist: Well, on Fridays I paint fish.

Around the Nation and the World, 1920(2)

"Pitcher Babe Ruth sold to the Yankees,"

"It's the Law: Prohibition takes effect." Beer, wine and liquor were officially banned by the 18th Amendment.

February 24, 1920: Hitler advocated anti-Semite policy.

Short became the watchword for feminine apparel, and American women won the right to vote.

By February, the Germans balked at paying the war reparations demanded by the European Allies, which was followed by the Allies occupying Germany to collect the debt. Germany offered to pay less than a quarter of the amount and finance the remainder, but Allies said no to the offer.

Warren G. Harding of Ohio was installed as the 29th president. He ordered the doors of the White House thrown open to the public, the first time in four years. One month later, he turned down the League of Nations, an organization that Woodrow Wilson had labored so hard to fashion.

The Roaring Twenties, a term coined to describe the tenor of the times, came on like gang busters. Dance marathons were the rage in U.S. cities. On May 15, 1921, the New York State Legislature passed a law giving the state commissioner the right to censor dances. In Utah, a statute was pending providing for the imprisonment of women wearing skirts more than three inches above the ankle. American youth were kicking up their heels and indulging themselves in what seems to be a frenzy rebellion against standards of their parents and grandparents. New styles and dances were singled out as the chief culprits.

From *The Dispatch* in 1921 and 1922(1)

United Furniture Company gets a charter and has $200,000 to capitalize the company.

Law enforcement officers demolished whiskey stills all over the county.

School consolidation vote passes for Tyro school districts with five more consolidation votes scheduled in March 1921.

Cameron Morrison became Governor of North Carolina.

Cotton prices hit rock bottom.

A glorious July 4th celebrated at the fairgrounds under the auspices of the American Legion with a parade followed by free exhibition in the grounds by acrobats, a baseball game between Lexington and Thomasville.

Around the Nation and the World—1922, 1923, and 1924(2)

Mahatma Gandhi imprisoned in India—put behind bars for six years by the British for sedition—advocating civil disobedience to oppose British colonial presence.

Alexander Graham Bell, inventor of the telephone, died at his home in Nova Scotia.

Mussolini's fascists march on Rome.

Nazi Party holds first congress in Munich, January 1923. The decline of the mark in Germany called desperate—at no time in the month of June 1923 would 20,000 marks fetch even one U.S. dollar. Hitler was arrested in Munich on November 12, 1923, after his effort to take over the national government fails. One dollar now worth four trillion marks.

President Warren Harding died from apoplexy in a San Francisco hotel at the age of 57.

Tokyo and Yokohama destroyed by the greatest earthquake in Japanese history—300,000 persons killed.

Wall Street boom sets record—2,226,220 shares traded.

Lenin, Soviet founder, died at age of 54.

Woodrow Wilson died—a shattered man with a shattered dream of a League of Nations—on February 3, 1924. To some he seemed as much a casualty of war as the men who died on the battlefields of Europe.

Calvin Coolidge won re-election in November 1924.

Adolph Hitler freed after eight months in prison.

From *The Dispatch*, 1923 and 1924(1)

Rotary Club endorses move to secure a library for the county to be located in Lexington.

Ford sedan for $595 f.o.b. Detroit.

Yadkin River bridge under construction connecting Davidson and Rowan counties.

School terms for county schools increased to a full six months.

The struggle to get children to attend school at all has been a problem for many counties.

Plans were being made to secure the Junior Order Orphanage for Davidson County.

Brick plant will be located in Conrad Hill Township and owned by Cunningham Brick Company of Greensboro.

In December 1923, thirty-three cases of smallpox in the county, four cases of measles, two cases of scarlet fever, seven of chicken pox, and one of typhoid fever.

Junior Order picks Davidson County site for orphanage.

Buick four-passenger car sold for $1,545 and Studebaker for $1,150. The new Ford touring car priced at $295; Studebaker, 1924 model, light six-cylinder touring car $995, Big six $1750, Big six sedan $2643.

Another one of those more or less relics, a genuine copper still came rolling up to the courthouse in Deputy Green's fliver. He had found the still, complete with cap and worm, reposing peacefully in a large pile in Atlantic Township Monday afternoon. The still was almost 35 gallons capacity.

"Colored Farmer finds Gold vein on Place"...J. H. Koontz, a colored farmer who lives on Cotton Grove Road two miles north of Southmont, informed *The Dispatch* yesterday that there was a vein of gold running through his 36-acre farm that he believed was highly valuable.

A tribute to Memorial Day, 1924 by Fredrick B. U. Fritts(1)

Tomorrow is Memorial Day. Between cloudy sunrise and red sunset the hymns of a nation's triumphs cease. Music of mournful remembrances fills the streets and churches.

It is the day of the dead. They have been asleep in their shaded beds through snowy winter and rainy spring...On this day we call the spirits back to us that they may see with their clear eyes and judge with their wiser wisdom...

They have had their day with us. They have seen that our sorrow and troubles still are as quiet as when they themselves lived upon the earth. Between sunrise and sunset they have shared the day with us.

On July 17, 1924, the Lexington Country Club was thrown open to the public for the first time; golf course was added later.

The Davidson County-Rowan County bridge across the Yadkin River opened to the public on August 15, 1924...

The dedication of the Junior Home in the Cotton Grove area held on August 15 also. Following is a portion of the main editorial that appeared in *The Dispatch* that day.

"...Saturday at 1:30 p.m., the Junior Orphanage Home site will be formally dedicated to the service of God and childhood. Lexington and Davidson County should be proud of this entity which will mean much to the community."

At the end of last year, North Carolina stood first among Southern states east of the Mississippi in total wealth, growing from $1,647,791,000 to $4,943,110,000 during the past 10 years.

From *The Dispatch*, 1925(1)

The Silver Hill News column: Schools of Arey and Cedar Grove suspended a few days on account of epidemics of whooping cough and chicken pox among the scholars. Clyde Peeler, teacher at Cedar Grove, was right indisposed several days suffering from rheumatism.

Denton voters beat increased tax for school. Lexington Township voted to apply over one-half of its tax for the entire county.

"Liquor Car Wins Race but Accused Man Surrenders":—Luther Shaw won one race but lost another to the Deputy Sheriff; he outraced the deputy in his Ford roadster; as officers approached Shaw's car, whiskey jars began to go through the air. He stopped near a bridge and turned around. After a mile or so, the Ford took to the ditch, and its occupant took to the woods. Shaw turned himself in the next day.

Doctors raised the obstetrics fee at their monthly meeting; increase went from $20.00 to $25.00 per month.

Letters to Santa Claus: (1)

"Dear Santa Claus,
This is what I want you to bring me a cap buster, some caps, fire crackers, spit devils, a pocket knife with two blades, also some candy, nuts, apples, and oranges. I go to school at Hedrick's Grove. I have been a good little boy.
Harlan Hedrick
Lexington, Route 2, Box 158

"Dear Santa Claus,
I want you to bring me for Christmas a dolly that sleeps, cries, and walks with long curly hair and some candy, nuts, apples, oranges and also a train. I guess I won't ask you for anything else.
Your little friend,
Marie Hedrick
Lexington, Route 2

"Dear Santa Claus,
I love you so much and I want you to bring me a silk bathrobe and a pair of slippers to match. I want some oranges, and candy apples. I would like a baby doll that cries "mama."
Remember the little orphans and be sure and not forget me. I am a little girl in the N.C. Sanitorium with T. B.
Elizabeth Faust
Sanitorium, N.C."

Around the Nation and the World, 1925 and 1926(2)

"Tennessee bans teaching of evolution..."

Mein Kampf disclosed Hitler's policies. In the book, Hitler called for a national revival and a battle against communism and Jews...

Charleston is newest dance craze—"Up on your heels, down on your toes."

Duke has become the richest university. James Buchanan Duke, tobacco king and philanthropist, died. Mr. Duke rose from extreme poverty. Duke established the university earlier by a trust fund of $40 million to give North Carolina preachers, teachers, lawyers, engineers and doctors.

Grand Ole Opry began Saturday night "Barn Dance" broadcast on WSM, Nashville, Tennessee...

American Association of University Professors assailed college football as a moral menace saying college football promotes drinking, dishonesty and neglect of academic work.

Marilyn Monroe was born in June 1926.

Bobby Jones won British Open title.

Babe Ruth caught baseball dropped from a plane.

From *The Dispatch*, 1926 and 1927(1)

False alarm was responsible for a tragic accident by fire truck when crossing Main Street at 3rd Avenue. It sideswiped a Buick Coach and overturned killing three and badly injuring two.

Jeffrey Lanning died of injury from pitchfork; sliding down a straw stack, the handle of fork penetrated his body about eight inches.

Market Prices
Eggs 30 cents per dozen
Butter25–40 cents per pound
Hens (gross)18–20 cents per pound

Less boll weevil feared in N.C. now. Weevil first came in 1919 and covered the cotton area of the state by 1922. N.C. not hit as hard as states to the South. Best method of boll weevil control was dusting with calcium arsenate.

Carload of better dairy cattle sires arrived in Davidson County. Twenty-nine purebred bulls purchased by Davidson County farmers. 22 of the 29 bulls are Guernsey, four are Jerseys and three are Holsteins. J. C. Crouse and John Beck, Lexington, route 2 purchased several.

North Carolina has 63 millionaires out of 11,000 in the U.S.

By the year 1927, the largest construction project ever imagined for Davidson County and counties bordering on the west and northwest was in progress. In fact, the venture rivaled anything else in the entire state. January 10, 1927, edition of *The Dispatch* devoted much of its space in describing the details of what was transpiring in the building of a dam to form High Rock Lake. When completed, the rising dam will hitch the end of the hills banking the mighty Yadkin River on either side and turn the great basin from the town of High Rock to Davie County into the South's most expansive artificial lake.

Interesting new figures about the Great High Rock Lake: will be the second largest artificial lake in the U.S.; will cover 20,600 acres and extend 26.3 miles up the Yadkin River; will come up Abbott's Creek 20 miles. Around the lake shore within one mile, 35-40,000 people will live eventually.

Local News: Out in Holly Grove section, they raised some mighty good hogs and have slaughtered a few. Charlie Everhart recently killed several nice ones, including one weighing 475 pounds and another about 440 pounds. A. H. Kepley butchered one weighing 415 pounds.

Great snowfall broke record in March 1927. Twenty inches was the average depth, and there were deeper drifts in many places.

Around the Nation and the World, 1927(2)

America was the land of the automobile. According to a January report, there were nine million cars registered in the United States, a whopping 39 percent of the world's total: one car for every six citizens. In England, there was one car for every 57 people, and in Germany it was one for every 289.

Television broadcasts had successful tests in New York.

Mae West found guilty of sexy acting. Courts ruled the show had lewd improvisations and ordered it closed.

Charles Lindbergh flew the Atlantic alone. Nearly 100,000 Parisians rushed onto the tarmac of Le Bourget Airport on the evening of May 21 to cheer a new international hero. Charles Lindbergh completed the first solo non-stop flight from New York to Paris. He took off from Roosevelt field on Long Island, overloaded with gasoline. His plane, the *Spirit of St. Louis*, sailed like a drunken seagull, barely clearing trees at the end of the runway. He flew by dead reckoning, sometimes dipping to within ten feet of the sea, sometimes climbing as high as 10,000 feet.

Lou Gehrig of the New York Yankees hit three home runs in one day in a defeat over the Boston Red Sox.

"The Babe hits his Number 60." George Herman "Babe" Ruth added to his already-existing legends by smashing his 60th home run of the season.

Iraqis discovered oil in Kirkuk.

From *The Dispatch*, 1928(1)

Triplets were born to Holly Grove couple on Saturday, two girls and one boy.

Parents have named them Mary, Martha, and John. They made the 9th, 10th and 11th children of Mr. and Mrs. John Younts. Dr. Bryce Hunt of Lexington was the attending physician. A 2nd set of triplets for this section of the county. Two boys and one girl were born to Mr. and Mrs. Deaton Young of Silver Hill Township. Dr. J. A. Smith was the attending physician.

"Brothers Held for Causing Trouble at Christmas Tree, December 1928." At the Christmas exercise at Holloways Baptist Church in December 1928, two brothers of Silver Hill Township were arrested for disturbing the program. Charges grew out of a disturbance caused by one of them being drunk and the other assisting him in assaulting a Mr. Cook who was attending the religious service. The drunk brother held Cook from the back while the other struck him with his fist; at the same time, the drunk man was alleged to have ripped Cook's clothing from the rear with a knife. All men were released from jail on bond,

and the two brothers were fined at a hearing before the judge. Members of the church said they had not seen anything like this for at least 20 years.

Sandy Grove Corn Club Takes First Honors in County Contest

Sandy Grove boys' 4-H Club in its first year of operation took first honors for being the only club in the county to complete the club work for the year. A boy grew one acre of corn with Gilbert Burkhart having the top yield of 69 bushels per acre. Arvil Burkhart presented the best exhibit and won 1st prize...

Industrial Bank of Lexington paid five percent interest last year from the day of deposit to the day of withdrawal.

On the lighter side:

1. Willie's idea of a new Christmas is to begin to have father get tired of playing with the electric train before school starts again.

2. A tax on bachelors would prove to be unpopular because every single man would object.

3. People who never brag should not brag about it.

Around the Nation and the World, 1928(2)

Millions heard Will Rogers's radio broadcast. Will Rogers and stars across the nation entertain an audience of millions tonight (January 4, 1928). NBC hooked up all 48 states to a giant studio where entertainers miles apart sang, laughed, and bantered. Prices swing madly in record trading on Wall Street. Fortunes were made and lost on March 27 due to the erratic stock behavior. Even within the space of just ten minutes, price swings made the difference in millions of dollars in the open market value of leading securities.

Amelia Earhart became the first woman to fly over the Atlantic. Trip took 22 hours from Boston to Cartmenshire, South Wales.

Hoover said the U.S. is near the end of poverty as he accepted the Republican Party's nomination for president (August 11). Said he was running on the platform slogan, "A chicken in every pot, a car in every garage."

Hirohito was crowned Emperor of Japan. In a confident voice, the 27-year-old emperor declared that the spiritual union between the sovereign and the people was the essence of Japanese nationality. He vowed to work for world peace.

Herbert Clark Hoover won a landslide victory for president in the November elections. He defeated the Democratic candidate, Governor Alfred E. Smith of New York, by carrying most of the states.

During same election, Franklin D. Roosevelt won the governorship of New York.

The National Association for the Advancement of Colored People claimed nine Negro lynchings in 1928, the lowest in 40 years.

From *The Dispatch*, 1929(1)

O. Max Gardner of Shelby, became the new Governor of North Carolina.

Sandy Grove news: school has 68 pupils.

Mr. Dermont Lohr returned to the University at Chapel Hill after spending the holidays with his parents, Mr. and Mrs. A. C. Lohr.

City extended electric lines by Beck's Church—a distance of some four miles—a section the most thickly settled in the county. The line followed along the road known as Beck's Church Road which connects with highway 90 and Silver Hill Road.

Big still found running in broad daylight in the Hampton Township. It was a 75-gallon copper still holding 20 gallons of liquor and 2,000 gallons of mash.

Debate continued about highway 90. Some proposed it come into Lexington by way of Holly Grove, but the route was fixed because going by Holly Grove would have added the cost of one more bridge over Abbott's Creek.

Ruey Downy of Denton was arrested for allegedly boiling a black cat alive... Downy said this resulted from seeking the advice of a black man, a "conjure doctor," in an effort to make sure of the love of a woman.

Chicken "bites" woman in county. Mrs. Henry Shaw in a call to Raleigh found that chickens are not subject to rabies.

County had 1,500 phones.

Thousands attended ceremony for laying the cornerstone of the North Carolina Building at Junior Orphan's Home.

Confederate veterans—43 veterans and 90 widows—continued to receive pension checks—43 vets received $182.50 each—each widow received $50.00.

Road sentence was given to a man for using a pitchfork on a mule. Earl Benge of Winston-Salem went into a barn near Thomasville and took a pitchfork and severely stabbed the mule in several places. Benge said he was so drunk he did not know what he was doing.

Population of N.C. stood at 2,938,000 on July 1, 1928—growth of 41,000 over the previous year.

The new Davidson County Court House is completed; cost $295,000.

Lexington football went to Atlanta, Georgia, for the big contest between the University of North Carolina and Georgia Tech.

Bowers family met at Holly Grove to welcome a native son home. "Before and after the picnic dinner, the crowd was most active in greetings, hand shakings, talking, laughing, and rejoicing. On all sides one could hear, 'Don't you know me?' 'I am so glad to see you.' 'Well, well, if that isn't old so and so.' The meeting came to an end with the singing of 'God Be with You Till We Meet Again.' "

The Davidson County Fair opened on Tuesday on grounds located to the rear of Smith Lumber Company on West Center Street. Manager Dave Leonard said that he had spared no expense in securing exceptional free acts. The fair included clowns, acts of air-devilry, Higgins Uniform Band, high diving and fireworks each night.

County schools are near complete consolidation with Board of Education planning two new schools to bring this about in an area from Lexington to the Randolph County line. Area embraced the school districts of Holly Grove, Hedrick's Grove, Sandy Grove, Cedar Grove, Burkhart, Ember, Clarksburg, Plummer, Jerusalem, and Kindley...One of the new schools was a combined elementary and high school and the other a standard elementary school...

There was little mention in *The Dispatch* of "Black Friday" on the New York Stock Exchange. Davidson County industries showed little slippage. The situation was not as serious as in many large Northern cities. Many workers at the Davidson County factories especially the textile mills were put on furlough because of the economic slide.

On the Lighter Side:
1. Bald headed men can not believe that parting would be sad.
2. Jim Reed now says he did not say all members of congress are jackasses. He ought to be more specific.

Around the Nation and the World, 1929(2)

Germany reported 3.2 million unemployed.

Martin Luther King, Jr., civil rights leader, was born January 15, 1929.

Billy Sunday packed them in for religious meetings. Former baseball pitcher became a flamboyant Presbyterian minister and started touring the country.

Arkansas girl 17 years old married a man 92 years of age recently. She said he is a good talker.

STOCK MARKET CRASHES, October 24, 1929(2) From one end of the country to the other, financial uncertainty and fear fed on rumor and cascaded into panic; frightened investors ordered their brokers to sell at whatever price, and the stock market crashed. This was a day that will be known as "Black Thursday." It was hard to count the losses, but estimates put them into billions of dollars. Thousands of accounts were wiped out with many accounts literally given away. What happened was something that had been building for weeks, and it crippled the country as no single event had ever done. The end of 1929 found President Hoover searching for ways to bolster the economy and keep it from crashing as the stock market did a month earlier. On the positive side, Hoover forecast a big surplus of farm products in a message to congress.

A Recap of the 1920s

The United States, the "land of opportunity," ran in overdrive during the 1920s. Prosperity was said to be on the doorstep, and all of the energy and vitality of the people seemed to be unleashed at once. Whatever North Americans did they did it with gusto and to excess usually. There was no tomorrow, or so it seemed. Appropriately named the "Roaring Twenties" or as some called them, the "Soaring Twenties," people very seldom showed restraint, and the outcome for many was prosperity shrouded in an aura of optimism. It was as if someone were on the sidelines encouraging everyone to "let it all hang out" and let the good times roll. Innovation showed up in inventions, the way games were played, in music, in dance, in fashions, in social reform, in literature and in politics. Things happened fast, and no one seemed to get enough of whatever was the "in" thing. Television had been invented and tested for reliability.

There were downsides as well with the Ku Klux Klan having its most active decade in its history, displaying their hate by killing hundreds and destroying the lives of many others. Prohibition ushered in by the passage of the 18th amendment in January 1920 and staying in effect for the next 13 years aided and abetted an illegal alcohol business and a rise in crime.

Many people gave caution to the wind, investing their personal money and/or what they were able to borrow on whims as the value of the stock market and tangible holdings continued to skyrocket. What goes up must come down, or so says the song writer, and it occurred in painful measure for the economy on October 24, 1929. The crash of the U.S. stock market made itself heard around the world with a resounding thud.

However, the entire nation did not have a chicken in every pot or a car in every garage as Herbert Hoover had used as his campaign slogan for president. Most of the former Confederate states were on hard times at the beginning of the 1920s and were stuck there when the stock market tumbled.

The boll weevil blanketed the South from Texas to eastern Virginia by 1920, reducing incomes from cotton to a subsistence level. Sharecroppers had no viable cotton fields, and many of them left for possible work opportunities in the large northern cities of New York, Philadelphia, Chicago, and Detroit.

Those areas where cotton was not king did not feel the boll weevil devastation. Yet incomes in such regions were still far below the national average. Most Southerners had no idea what it meant to invest in the stock market because they had no wealth to invest. In Lexington, N.C., the local newspaper did not run a column about the Wall Street catastrophe on Black Thursday. Farmers and small landholders were surviving on the food produced on their land while the urban people were employed largely in textile and furniture manufacturing, industries not immediately affected, even though they were low-wage.

In my section of Davidson County, N.C., the roaring twenties had an impact but perhaps less dramatic than in states like New York and California. Dress styles changed, more automobiles made the scene, movies shown in theaters were the same as those being seen in other parts of the country, educational opportunities improved, electric power became available to some rural residents, new roads were built, radios came to many living rooms, and music saw changes. Baseball was the sport most played and followed nationally. Even though only a handful of people had been close to New York, everybody knew about Babe Ruth and his mighty bat. The same thing can be said for Detroit and a player named Ty Cobb from Georgia who played for love of the game and stole home plate 50 times during his career. The name of the national and international hero, Charles Lindbergh, was on everybody's lips. They marveled at his feat of flying his single-engine plane, the *Spirit of St. Louis*, from New York to Paris nonstop.

Throughout the decade silent films predominated, but talking movies did come on the scene near its end. Names of the silent screen stars were handed down to the next generation (mine): Gloria Swanson, Tom Mix and his horse Tony, Norma Talmadge, Rudolph Valentino, John Barrymore, Greta Garbo and Janet Gaynor.

Music titles and words often reflected the tenor of the times. "Keep Your Skirt Down Maryann" cautioned against raising hemlines above the knee. "I Wish I Could Shimmy Like My Sister Kate" held out the desire to be able do the Lindy Hop or the Charleston in two-time rhythm. "I Married the Bootlegger's Daughter" probably spoke to the large amount of moonshine being made during prohibition on isolated streams. Of course, other songs emerged from the 20s that stood on their own. For example, "I'll Be with You In Apple Blossom Time," "Yes, We Have No Bananas," "Ain't She Sweet," "Carolina Morning," "Alabama Bound," and "Tip Toe through the Tulips" made the charts for many years.

One of the great advents in the music world was the birth of the Grand Ole Opry in 1925, a Saturday night show of country and hillbilly music broadcast by radio from Nashville, Tennessee.(1) Not everyone had a radio in rural Davidson County, but those who did often invited their neighbors to listen to shows such as Amos 'n Andy, the nation's most popular radio show at the time. Boxing matches often brought neighbors together, and to a great degree, radio drew the nation together. People in every section of the nation could technically listen to the same programs at the same time. Radio programs did not select their audiences, the audience selected them.

Many very important events and actions occurred in lower Davidson

County, and those that stood head and shoulders above all others should be highlighted. The construction of the High Rock dam across the Yadkin River to form High Rock Lake, the second largest artificial lake in the country, was to impact our lives in many ways yet unseen.

Perhaps the most important thing that happened was the final act of school consolidation that closed the one-room schools in favor of a new physical plant. The opening of the Junior Order Orphan's Home was also a major accomplishment.(1) Furniture factories and textile mills were continuing to be constructed in both Lexington and Thomasville. Davidson County's income from agriculture rivaled other counties in the state. Opening the Davidson Creamery was to boost a growing dairy industry among county farmers. Bootlegging remained the biggest matter for law enforcement.

The Peter Kepley house, built in the early 19th century, exemplifies the architecture of the period for rural homes. (Kay Kepley)

Copy of a painting of the Bob Swing home on Beck's Church Road built in the 19th century. (Artist, Jane Younts Hayes)

Riding in horse and buggy was common in the early 20th century both for pleasure and point-to-point transportation. (Davidson County Historical Museum)

Grady sits behind a T-Model Ford, an automobile manufactured in the decade of the twenties. His dress reflects the dapper look of the times. (Family collection)

Thomasville, once claimed the title of "The Chair Town," constructed the largest chair in the world in 1922. The chair measured 13 feet 6 inches in height and had a seat 6 feet by 5 feet 6 inches. (Davidson County Historical Museum)

The first telephones were mounted on the wall, and the small crank on the right side was turned to dial other parties. No privacy was possible since as many as 16 families shared the same party line. (Family collection)

Ty Cobb, a native of Georgia and a star baseball player for the Detroit Tigers, paid a visit to Lexington in the fall of 1919. Mr. Cobb holds a child on his knee. (Davidson County Historical Museum)

High Rock dam, under construction here, on the Yadkin River created a large lake that has provided recreational opportunities since the late 1920s. (Davidson County Historical Museum)

Davidson County Court House in the late 1920s. Note the variety of automobiles and an absence of parking meters. (Davidson County Historical Museum)

Two small farm boys pose with a rooster and a straw hat nearby. Note their dress in overalls. (Family collection)

Pork shoulders being barbecued over a bed of hickory coals has been a trademark of Lexington for many decades. (Davidson County Historical Museum)

FIVE

THE 1930s:
THE DEPRESSION ERA

The population of the United States for the 48 states totaled 123,188,000 people in 1930, for North Carolina 3,170,276 people, and for Davidson County 45,219. Life expectancy for the U.S. as a whole stood at 58.1 years for males and 61.6 years for females.

Black Thursday, or the stock market crash of October 24, 1929, triggered a series of economic disasters that were to impact every section of the United States and most countries round the world for years to come. Interestingly enough, the states in the southern region of the country did not appear to suffer as much as many states to the North. One might say the South did not have as much wealth to lose because it was already in a depression, especially in the cotton belts, from the damage inflicted by the onslaught of the boll weevil in the early 1920s. Low wages meant that citizens had known much about belt tightening in tough times.

In North Carolina, the furniture and textile industries took it on the chin, but agriculture other than cotton seemed to weather the storm more easily despite the fact that farm prices skidded to all-time lows. Farms were not large plantations in lower Davidson County, being essentially self-contained. First and foremost, food was produced to feed the farm family, with surplus productions taken to local markets and sold to neighbors or relatives in town or anywhere it could be redeemed for something, no matter how small.

From *The Dispatch*, 1930(1)

Moving beyond the beginning of a sagging economy, one of the first orders of business in 1930 for Davidson County was to pick sites for two new schools and begin construction so they might be completed by the opening of the next school session. Closure was not reached until mid-May. The high or union school was built near the Holly Grove community and the elementary school near the intersection of highways 109 and 90 at Silver Valley. Names of the two schools: Davis-Townsend High School and Silver Valley Elementary School.

The Davidson County School System has made no arrangements yet for handling Negro buses. The Supreme Court of North Carolina stated that bus companies must provide for the handling of Negroes on buses.

The Dispatch adopted the slogan "Make Davidson County the Dairying Center of North Carolina."

September 15, 1930: Davis-Townsend School Building completed , and Principal was Austin Bivens.

The big mills that cut production partially because of the economic situation in the country have begun operating a full schedule again.

News of Colored People: The following program presented by Dunbar High School:

Tues: How the School Helps to Promote Patriotism and World Understanding

Wed: The Schools of Yesterday—by Paul Evans, County Superintendent

Sunday: The School of Tomorrow and the Future of America—by President of Livingston College, Salisbury

The Negro branch of Davidson County Library was located in the Dunbar High School.

Around the Nation and the World, 1930(2)

Babe Ruth earned more money than President Hoover—$80,000 per year to play baseball for the New York Yankees. "The Babe explained that he had a better year than the president did."

The Nazis Party was the second largest in Germany. Hitler's young followers were mesmerized by his fiery oratory, and the older ones were attracted to his hate for the Jews, his stand on war reparations, and the German parliamentary form of government.

President Hoover sought solutions to fight economic depression. He called on state governors and private industry to cooperate in creating jobs.

From *The Dispatch*, 1931(1)

By 1931, the economic woes in the large cities to the North began to trickle in serious fashion to the towns and farms of central North Carolina. Budget cuts became necessary for the city fathers of Lexington and Thomasville, and optimism slipped among the business community as well.

At the A & P Food Market
  Bread—(wrapped loaf)7 cents
  Flour—24 lb.72 cents
  Meal or grits—lb.3 cents
  Bananas—3 lb.20 cents

Everything closed on Easter Monday.

Wheat threshing began on time.

Quoting a national story: "Businesses glad to bid farewell to the departing year (December 28, 1931). Values tumbled like rows of dominoes, disrupting the world's businesses and belying prophets of an early upturn in the economic cycle in 1931. Banks were in trouble all over the world."

Around the Nation and the World, 1931(2)

Jobless rate exceeded more than four million workers in the U.S. President Hoover said that we are much better off than the rest of the world.

European unemployment figures set historic levels. Germany and England suffered especially hard; 2.5 million workers were without jobs in England and 5.0 million with no work in Germany.

Nazis asked Germany to leave the League of Nations.

President Hoover signed a bill making Francis Scott Key's "Star Spangled Banner," sung to old English drinking song, the National Anthem of the United States.

Empire State Building in New York City opened on May 1, 1931; the tallest building in the world standing at 1,245 feet.

From *The Dispatch*, 1932(1)

The sale prices of consumer goods and real estate reflected the impact of the depression in Davidson County. For example—800 acres covered with small timber having seven miles of good road frontage sold for $15 per acre.

Davis-Townsend School had an English club in the 6th grade; participating on the program for the first meeting were: Eldora Crotts, Lena Mae Cooper, Curry Regan, Helen Whitlock, Ruth Burkhart, Paige Beck, Roby Fritts, Otis Leonard, Clifton Allred, Raymond Burkhart, Cletus Swing, David Leonard, Dermont Beck, Beulah Clodfelter, Zeola Burkhart, Lillian Hedrick, and Frances Swing; president is Edith Crotts, vice president is Victor Foust, secretary is Leva Briggs, flower girls are Eldora Crotts, Lena Mae Cooper, and Frances Swing.

Possum hunting season opened but closed on doves.

Bank robbed in Denton.

Davidson led all counties in the number of Grade A farms.

Ray Bowers elected police chief.

County officers lost liquor car after chase.

Negro schools to be improved by the use of $4,000. 453 students in classes; land needed for rural colored school.

Cash and Negro missing from lunch stand—Red Pig Lunch—$46.00 found and Negro fled to South Carolina.

Around the Nation and the World, 1932(2)

In Albany, New York: F. D. Roosevelt enters presidential race. FDR is nominated—promises a "new deal."

Germany—Adolph Hitler was Nazi candidate for presidential elections. Hitler loses bid for the president of Germany. He was refused his request to be given a Cabinet seat, and Hitler refused limited chancellorship offered by Chancellor Hindenberg.

Lindbergh's baby kidnapped and later its body was found in woods near family home.

August 22: eleven million Americans jobless. Hoover was optimistic that the major financial crisis has been overcome. Hoover called on the leaders of the nation to attack what remains of the depression.

Roosevelt wins 472–59; carried all but six states. Roosevelt spoke of what he called a "new deal". He vowed to revive prosperity, to regulate banks, and that no person in this country would starve.

From *The Dispatch*, 1933(1)

McLellan Stores Co. went into bankruptcy in New York City but the local is not affected.

The Dispatch sold for five cents a copy, and its slogan continues—The Paper of the People, for the People and with the People.

The following films played at the movies: "Farewell to Arms"—by Ernest Hemingway—and "Bird of Paradise."

Federal relief reached largest number of folks in weeks. A total was $2,945 shared by 734 people.

Many cigarette ads popped up in the newspaper. Camel cigarettes were the most popular.

Grain threshing got underway in all sections of the county.

Wage increases announced at the Lexington cotton mills—up by 11 percent for over 1,000 employees.

Liquor cases flood the county court agenda.

Farmer attacked by vicious bull rescued by wife. Attacked by a bull in his barn, and fortunately, his wife was nearby, who drove the bull away with a large spike.

Davis-Townsend Blue Terrors defeated Welcome High School by a score of 17–14.

Around the Nation and the World, 1933(2)

U.S. jobless figure reached 15 million. Henry Ford said times are good in one way, insisting we are in ox cart stage of machine age.

HITLER IS NAMED GERMAN CHANCELLOR. The flamboyant, power hungry Hitler takes over the chancellor's job at a very difficult time in German history.

A would-be assassin attempted to kill President-elect Roosevelt as he finished a speech in Miami. The person responsible was arrested and quoted as saying, "I'd kill every president." Roosevelt was unhurt. FDR sworn in on March 4 and in his address he said, "The only thing we have to fear is fear itself"...FDR ordered four-day bank holiday to halt massive withdrawals.

Nazis ordered ban against Jews in business, professions, and schools. American Jewish Committee demanded that Washington act on Hitler. Nazis open first concentration camp near the town of Dachau ten miles outside Munich. Nazis enforced ban on Jewish merchants; signs were erected saying, "German people, defend yourselves! Do not buy from Jews!" A large pile of books was burned in front of Berlin University, books that Nazis have declared "un-German." Nazis now the only political party in Germany as Hitler's government outlawed the last major opposition party. Nazis began evicting Jews from civil service. Official confirmation from Germany was that Nazis arrested large number of Jews and sent them to concentration camps.

FDR asked for pay raise for U.S. workers under the theory that demand must be maintained for the economy to recover.

FDR ordered millions of dollars to aid the most needy. About $700 million made available for food and clothing during the coming winter.

Germany withdrew from the League of Nations claiming the world treats it as a second-class citizen.

Prohibition in America came to an end on December 5 with the repeal of the 18th Amendment.

Was a great year for films—everything from "The Three Little Pigs" to "The Private Life of Henry VIII." Other big titles included: "Little Women"; "The Invisible Man"; and "King Kong."

From *The Dispatch*, 1934(1)

Liquor provided 74 cases for the court in one month.

Two cows bitten by a suspected dog develop rabies.

"Little Women" starring Kathryn Hepburn played at the movies.

Measles raged over the county. One school, Davis-Townsend, closed for two weeks—200 pupils out.

Only eight Confederate Veterans received checks during the past six months.

The Christmas holidays in 1934 were sober with the police in the county making no arrests.

Around the Nation and the World, 1934(2)

Hitler planned vast highway system—will be network of four-lane highways that will link all parts of the Reich. Hitler stopped paying all foreign debts—he simply said he did not have the money. Hitler now the President of the country and predicted that the Reich will stand for 1,000 years. In N.Y., Nazi rally at Madison Square Garden attracted 20,000 persons.

Henry Ford restored $5.00 per day wage.

Max Baer took world heavyweight title.

Desperado, John Dillinger, killed leaving a Chicago theater. Al Capone locked up in Alcatraz.

Mussolini amasses 10,000 troops on the Austrian border. Navy triumphs over Army in football.

From *The Dispatch*, 1935(1)

Unemployment listed in the county was not very large; eighty-seven names sent to Raleigh may be placed on local relief.

Postal receipts largest the past year for the past five years.

Some signs that the economy might be improving. Clothing costs remained relatively low—school shoes, $1.35—silk hose, 59 cents per pair—dress socks, 72 cents.

At the local markets: (prices paid for) eggs—30 cents, butter—16-20 cents, dressed hens—17 cents, Irish potatoes—75 cents per bu., pork—9 cents per pound.

Twenty-three CCC camps are being constructed in 22 Piedmont counties, the enrollees of which are to be employed directly in soil conservation work.

A Rabies Brigade has been formed to help quell of rabies outbreaks in the county; there are 17 township rabies inspectors.

Threat of poliomyelitis delayed Farm and Home Week activities at N.C. State College for one year; 375 cases statewide reported so far in 1935.

Around the Nation and the World, 1935(2)

Plane flights barred over White House for disturbing President Roosevelt's sleep.

Tennessee voted to retain anti-evolution law.

Storm clouds gathered over Europe. German Reich arrested 700 pastors and military inscription re-instated.

Mussolini followed suit by expanding Italy's conscription laws. Italy had nearly 1,000,000 men armed and ready to fight.

Russia and Britain agreed to maintain peace if possible at all.

U.S. hit by dust storm in the arid states of the lower Midwest—Oklahoma, eastern Colorado, most of Texas, and parts of New Mexico. Livestock suffered miserably and crop damage was staggering in the nation's breadbasket; little relief in sight.

FDR created the Rural Electrification Administration to provide energy loans. Work Progress Administration (WPA) created by executive order.

100,000 welfare recipients in New York to get jobs under PWA.

U.S. Protestants asked for Olympic boycott by not sending any teams to participate in 1936 Berlin games.

Motion pictures offered some escape from hard times. Adventure, romance, classics, and comedy awaited attendees.

Following movies were shown all across the U.S.—"Mutiny on the Bounty," "Captain Blood," "Lives of a Bengal Dancer," "Anna Karenina," "The Devil Is a Woman," "David Copperfield," "A Midsummer Night's Dream," "A Night at the Opera."

From *The Dispatch*, 1936(1)

What did the bootleggers think of next? Officers report a find of liquor concealed in a casket.

Rotary Club in Lexington backed Knot Hole Gang at the ballpark for boys from families of limited income.

Dean of Agriculture from N.C. State College to speak at annual farmers' picnic; there will be a judging contest in the afternoon and a ball game.

The annual meeting of the Valentine Lohr Historical Association was held on August 6 at the Beck's Reformed Church. There was to be dinner on the grounds at noon.

Fall enrollment in county schools showed a decrease. 17 of 18 white schools showed a loss of 252 students, total enrollment of 5,771 students.

County reported that dairy cows increased but total milk production decreased during period of 1929 to 1934. The depression left less money to purchase feed for the cows.

At the dry cleaners: men's suits—20 cents, ladies' dresses—20 to 30 cents; everything cash and carry terms.

In the classified ad section:

For sale—$20.00 will buy my 1923 Model Ford; good tires; 1937 license. See Doc McCulloch at *The Dispatch* office.

Silver Hill Newsletter: Madison Allred fell off the porch and cut his head on a plow point fracturing his skull...He spent time at the Davidson Hospital.

Robert Bruce Greer, son of Mr. and Mrs. Howard Greer was seriously injured when the horses ran away with the wagon he was driving. It ran against the barbed wire fence and cut his legs so severely that several stitches had to be taken.

Used Cars: 1934 Studebaker, $745; T-Model Ford sedan, $15.

Record liquor haul made by county officers Saturday. 6,288 pints of bonded booze found in Abbotts Creek by Sheriff Bodenheimer.

The Dispatch wagons: all you had to do was turn in a *Dispatch* subscription stub of $6.00 and you got a little red wagon.

Around the Nation and the World, 1936(2)

Rudyard Kipling, one of Britain's great authors, died at the age of 70 in London.German Volkswagen makes its debut. Hitler sends troops into Rhineland violating earlier pact. German press warned Jews who vote will be arrested. Hitler told crowd in Munich that Germany's only judge was God and itself. Germany paraded military power on Hitler's birthday. France planned a big arms race in reply to Hitler...

Russia claimed the world's greatest air force with 7,000 planes. Mussolini announced pact with Reich. Fascist countries form Axis—Germany, Italy, Japan.

Italy conquered Ethiopia, and Mussolini annexed the country and proclaimed himself emperor. Berlin recognized the move.

Washington reported U.S. industrial output at five-year peak.

Joe Louis KO's Retzlaff in first round.

Tornadoes swept the South killing 421 while floods swept Midwest states.

Herbert Hoover called the "New Deal" fascism.

Max Schmeling KO'ed Joe Louis in 12th round.

From *The Dispatch*, 1937(1)

Agricultural extension specialists from North Carolina State College frequently in Davidson County—hogs, beef, dairy, and poultry most wanted topics.

Dr. Dermont Lohr, a native of this county, has located here and will be in the office of Dr. J. C. Leonard who is going to Philadelphia for a one-year study... Dr. Lohr is the son of Mr. and Mrs. Curtis Lohr of Route 6 and graduated from Jefferson Medical College at the T.C.I. Hospital in Fairfield, Alabama.

Local economies improved slightly on a broad front but unemployment remains high. Concern expressed by some citizens about the buildup of military forces in other parts of the world. Many still talked about World War I and certainly cannot think of another war so soon.

Around the Nation and World, 1937(2)

FDR says one-third of the nation is underprivileged. He also heralded the nation for its steady climb out of the depression.

DuPont patented a new thread, called nylon.

Golden Gate Bridge opened in San Francisco.

From *The Dispatch*, 1938(1)

Hundreds in Davidson County to file for unemployment insurance. Many areas of the economy have shown improvement.

Much to be done before full employment returns and prices received by farmers are sufficient enough to improve economic standing.

Week of September 26 set as the date for the county fair. Tuesday was children's day. Farm exhibits included poultry, cattle and hogs. The normal carnival rides came as well as evening shows of fireworks.

Around the Nation and the World, 1938(2)

Adolph Hitler resolved the tension between governing factions by giving himself unprecedented power. He named himself the Supreme Commander of the armed force. He took direct control of foreign policy. Austria falls under Nazi control. U.S. recognizes the German conquest as does Great Britain. Hitler destroyed stores owned by Jews.

U.S. census revealed some unfortunate news concerning the number of workers unemployed, reporting at least 7.8 million which could be as many as 10 million. Total employment in the country is estimated to be 44 million.

FDR calls the South the most depressed region of the nation.

Around the Nation and the World, 1939(2)

FDR asked extension of Social Security Act to cover women and children. 22,000 Nazis hold rally in New York. FDR moves Thanksgiving Day from November 30 to November 23.

"Gone with the Wind" opens in Atlanta, Georgia, receiving resounding accolades.

How long can the U.S. stay neutral in the war?

Hitler demanded return of colonies for Japan and Italy and warned U.S. not to meddle. Czechs collapse totally in wake of Hitler's triumphant arrival. All youth in Germany 10–18 conscripted. Diplomacy could not stop Hitler. September 30, Nazis swarmed all over Poland, take it and divide it with Russia.

EUROPE IS AT WAR AGAIN: condemnations came from almost every sovereign state. Britain and France declared war on Germany following the Nazis lightning invasion of Poland. German U-boats were effective in sinking British and French vessels. Britain and France rejected Hitler's hand of peace. He said, "They threw down the gauntlet and Germany has picked it up." Most of Europe agreed that lasting peace will not be possible until Hitler is defeated.

A Recap of the1930s

Events of the 1930s came with such fury that they were difficult to assimilate, much less comprehend. The decade showed few signs of optimism for restoring a viable economy or quelling unrest either in the U.S. or abroad. Each day brought unimaginable surprises as U.S. leaders struggled to find solutions to high unemployment, hunger, disease outbreaks, unlawfulness and insurrection in the larger cities. The depression, Hitler's rise to power and the beginning of what would be WORLD WAR II wrote the headlines around the world and at home.

In Davidson County, total rural school consolidation came at last with the completion of Davis-Townsend High School near Holly Grove and Silver Valley Elementary School at the intersection of highways 90 and 109. Belts tightened as the mills and factories in Lexington and Thomasville reduced labor forces and wages in attempts to beat the depression.

Farm prices skidded to unbelievable low levels for most commodities, while at the same time a growing dairy industry held on, giving the county the claim of being number one in the state of North Carolina. The sight of people wearing clothes that were tattered and torn and patched over and over again symbolized a ditched economy. A few new county roads were built and others extended, especially highway 90 to Asheboro and eventually to Raleigh. For the most part communities and people in lower Davidson County maintained their wits and adopted creative measures to "tough out" the depression.

Churches remained central to the lives of the rural people who had the advantage of owning at least some acreage of land to produce food for their families, as well as harvesting surpluses for sale in the town markets. Character, integrity and the ability to work with their hands carried them through the chaotic 30s even though many emerged on the other side with little to show for huge efforts.

Across the nation, the depression hit the economy with a vengeance unlike anything experienced for decades, if ever, in the history of the republic. No section or faction of the economy was spared by depression's knife, which put 25 percent of the nation's workforce in the soup lines. People living in the large industrial cities in the North seemed hit the hardest. Wall Street brokers, once attired in Madison Avenue pinstripes, found themselves in bare threads in living quarters without heat and water. Food became scarce forcing the unemployed into bread lines that stretched around city blocks and back, endlessly. Despair ruled the day with high suicide rates, especially among those who lost large fortunes.

Franklin Delano Roosevelt was elected president and reelected promising a "New Deal" for the citizens of the United States. Adding to all of this, a serious problem descended on several mid-western states as a prolonged drought laid dry soils barren only to be picked up by high winds that formed a dust bowl stretching from Oklahoma to Colorado and south to West Texas. Farms yielded nothing and livestock suffocated from the dust clouds placing the residents in harm's way unlike any previous natural event in the nation's history.

Mass movements of people from the states of Oklahoma, Arkansas and parts of surrounding areas took people to California, which was already having difficulty coping with its set of problems.

One of the good things coming during the '30s was the end of prohibition, which had been imposed by a constitutional amendment some 13 years earlier. Prohibition led to a colossal illegal liquor industry, a nationwide wave of crime and the emergence of gangsters, who ruled with guns and who were supported by mobs. In Davidson County, the destruction of liquor stills became the number one activity of law enforcement officers.

In the world at large, nothing rivaled the importance of Adolph Hitler's rise to power in Germany. He fomented the Nazi political party conscripting able-bodied men into a formidable war machine. Proclaiming that Nazi Germany would survive a thousand years, he formed an axis with Japan and Italy and coerced many other nations into his camp by threats and intimidation.

Czechoslovakia collapsed under the weight of Hitler's war machine. By the end of the decade, he had literally made himself the Supreme Commander of Germany—the President, the Chancellor, and the chief of all armed forces—culminating in the invasion and conquest of Poland. Hitler made the Jews his scapegoat persecuting them in ways previously thought unimaginable.

To his east in Russia, communist dictator Joseph Stalin also clattered weapons of war, building an air force of 7,000 planes and an army of well over one million men. Stalin started a war of his own by invading Finland.

Europe seethed with anxiety as both Britain and France declared war on Germany stating that no country could rest until Hitler was vanquished. President Roosevelt declared that the U.S. would maintain a neutral stance toward the "new war" and sit on the sidelines.

Stepping back from war, songs written during the 30s generally spoke to economic conditions and hopes for a better day. Titles of some of the most popular songs follow.

Brother Can You Spare a Dime?
I'm an Unemployed Sweetheart
W. P. A.
Ten Cents a Dance
We're in the Money
Happy Days Are Here Again
Wrap Up Your Troubles in Dreams
Them Good Old Times Are Coming Back Again
There's No Depression in Love

Radio was of incalculable value during the depression years. By 1939, nearly 80 percent of the American people owned a radio. However, this figure is much too high for the poorer regions of the South, and this likely applies to the people in lower Davidson County as well. Radio programs conducted by such comedians as Jack Benny, Fred Allen, George Burns and Gracie Allen, Amos and Andy, and Fibber McGee and Molly kept us laughing, providing an occasional mental escape from the tough times. The serial shows featuring the heroics of the Lone Ranger and Tonto, the Green Hornet, the Shadow and Jack Armstrong provided excellent respites as well. It was the radio that allowed us to hear the voices of news commentators H. V. Kaltenborn and Edward R. Murrow, and the radio provided FDR a medium to bring the American people closer to him with his "Fireside Chats."

Movie producers seemed to be relentless in the number of motion pictures released to theaters across the country. Names of actors and actresses became household words, and we talked about them as if they were known personally: Clark Gable, Fred Astaire, Charles Chaplin, Errol Flynn, Laurel and Hardy, The Marx Brothers, William Powell, Ginger Rogers, Shirley Temple, May West and Myrna Loy. All of us scratched around each weekend to find the required nickels, dimes or quarters to purchase a ticket.

Meanwhile, Roosevelt stayed focused on the country's unemployment problem.

He initiated a variety of government employment opportunities for the jobless. In fact, the government became about the only place to find work. The Worker's Progress Administration is thought to have put more than eight million workers in jobs all involved in improving the country's infrastructure, such as building or repairing bridges, highways and parks.

Dress during the Depression years reflected levels of income as much as any other factor. (Library of Congress, FSA-OWI photo collection, LC-USF34-020124)

(*Left*) Worn-out automobile tires had great utility for kids. This young man could roll it, tie it on a rope and make a swing, or just plain sit in it and daydream about the world about him. (Library of Congress, FSA-OWI photo collection, LC-USF33-T01-001169)

(*Below*) This young man through industriousness and by saving his meager earnings was able to purchase a used bicycle of his own during the Depression (Library of Congress, FSA-OWI photo collection, LC-USF34-020862)

County roads became almost impassable during rain; the driver of this vehicle struggles to stay in the road. (Davidson County Historical Museum)

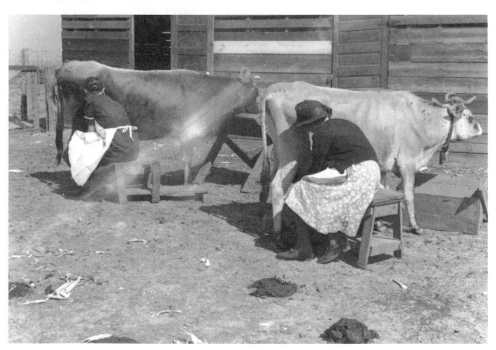

Practically every farm family owned a cow or two to supply milk and butter. The barnyard was the usual place for the morning and evening milkings. (Library of Congress, FSA-OWI photo collection, LSF-USF33-030314)

A farmer who owned mare horses would often breed them to a male donkey which produced a mule offspring. (Library of Congress, FSA-OWI photo collection, LC-USF34-054047)

Before the advent of tractors, farmers depended on horses and mules for farm power. Trading horses and mules among farmers was a big and serious business. (Library of Congress, FSA-OWI photo collection, LC-USF351-184)

During the Depression, tenant farmers had few resources to support the families. The physical appearance of these three men reflects poor living conditions. (Library of Congress, FSA-OWI photo collection, LC-USF34-T01-016336)

A local feed mill was an essential business for a farming community. Farm families came to the mill to get their grain and corn ground for animal feed and wheat ground for family flour. (Eva Rae Swing Clark)

Class of students shows school dress during the Depression. The boys are wearing overalls and most of the girls are wearing dresses made from feed sack cloth. (Wessels Living History Farm, York, Nebraska)

During the days of racial segregation, public buildings had separate toilet facilities and water fountains for colored and white persons. (Library of Congress, FSA-OWI photo collection, LC-USF33-T01-001112)

SIX

THE 1940s:
WORLD CONFLICT
AND ECONOMIC RECOVERY

World War II dominated all other events of the decade of the '40s. The entire population of a nation, 131,669,046 citizens, put everything aside to join the war effort. President Roosevelt could not keep the country in isolation after the Japanese attacked Pearl Harbor on December 7, 1941. War was declared on Japan immediately and soon thereafter on Nazi Germany.

We became engaged in a long and bitter struggle to help defeat enemies on both sides of the globe without any notion of how long the battles would last or how costly they would become. The 59,320 people living in Davidson County quickly stood up to do their part, as well as the rest of the 3,571,623 citizens of North Carolina. Nothing in the recent history of our republic, up to this time, did as much to change how we went about living our daily lives as did World War II. Men went off to war and women left the security of their homes replacing them in the factories. The economy began to emerge from its years of being in the doldrums due to increased war production.

When the war ended, a very changed nation lay before us. Farms were more mechanized, and the amount of human labor released with military discharges simply outstripped the need on the family farms. Adjustment for both men and women weighed heavily on us all, but it was the welcomed chal lenge. Getting on with our lives, making a living and raising a family became the main objectives. Everybody pitched in with so much catching up to do. Fall-out from the war included the GI Bill, a federal program to support veter- ans in furthering their education, one of the best public policies ever adopted in the United States. Enrollments at colleges and universities, as well as trade schools, swelled, bursting the campus seams with most institutions recycling army barracks to make classrooms and living quarters. Surprisingly, unlimited peace-time uses were found among the vast amount of technology developed in making weapons of war.

From *The Dispatch*, 1940(1)

New REA electric lines for the Linwood and Southmont sections installed completing the original layout for the Davidson Mutual Electric Corporation.

"Big Booze Cargo Is Taken at Thomasville Early Today"...Salisbury man caught with 168 cases of "bottled in bond liquor."

Lexington Children's Home was the new name selected for the orphanage.

"Coble's Dairy Production Capacity Expanded."

"The record of sales of electric refrigerators, electric radios, washing machines, irons, equipment for home water systems and other items which contribute much to the livability of rural homes."

In Hedrick Grove's News column: Work has begun on Grover Hunt's service station.

"The draft of young men for induction into the armed services to begin soon"... Two draft boards were formed in the county, one for Lexington and one for Thomasville. All males between the ages of 21 and 35 years of age fell under national conscription.

The Dispatch reported on October 17 that 7,051 men registered for the draft across the county with 3,503 from Lexington.

The first Selective Service Men of the county received calls for induction on November 25, 1940, 11 white and three colored young men.

Around the Nation and the World, 1940(2)

U.S. census reports population at 131 million. The decade gain of the thirties was the lowest in the nation's history.

Winston Churchill replaces Neville Chamberlain as prime minister as Reich troops storm Western Europe.

Nazis trap Allies at Dunkirk on the English Channel. Holland gives in after heavy bombing of Rotterdam. Nazis entered Scandinavia. By June 14, German troops parade through Paris as they placed signs everywhere reading... "Germany conquers all." Royal Air Force hits Berlin, astonishing German war leaders. Hitler declared all-out war on British cities in reprisal for RAF bombings. Japan joined Axis pact and entered Indochina...

The British royal navy led a successful exodus of 340,000 Allied troops from Dunkirk and imminent annihilation. Churchill warned that wars are not won by evacuations proclaiming, "We shall fight on the seas and oceans, we shall fight with growing confidence and growing strength in the air...We shall defend our island whatever the cost may be; we shall fight on the beaches...We will never surrender."

President Roosevelt nominated for a third term and wins.

The first draft numbers drawn in the U.S. (Oct 29)...U.S. Navy called up

27,591 reserves to man new ships...18,700 entered U.S. Army in peace-time draft.

Nazis continued to pound British cities. Germans began herding Warsaw's Jewish population insisting this will give Jews a new life.

From *The Dispatch*, 1941(1)

Defense demand for workers reported heavy; needed at Ft. Bragg and other military installations...

Twelfth grade to start next school year in North Carolina, the fall of 1941.

Thousands viewed the Silver Streak train across Davidson County—"The Southerner" traveling at speeds up to 90 miles per hour...

Local theatre aided in national aluminum drive. Pots and pans and golf clubs were given as admission ticket. Enough aluminum was collected over America to build several giant bombers for Uncle Sam's growing Air Corps.

Fifty-five men stood physical exam this week for military service. Others made ready as the largest contingent left for camp from Lexington for Fort Bragg.

"Buy Defense Bonds—Help Your County Help Yourself."

Issue Price	Maturity Value*
$18.75	$25.00
$37.50	$50.00
$75.00	$100.00

*Ten years to maturity

City officials approved plan for daylight saving time. President Roosevelt said it would aid in the conservation of electricity for national defense.

Great dairying industry has rapidly developed here. Coble's has bought milk at the rate of over one million dollars per year.

Congress Declares War on Japan after Surprise Attack at Pearl Harbor... Vicious attack Sunday united the nation with an estimated 1,500 dead at Honolulu. President Roosevelt in a very brief address to the joint session of congress declared that an hour before the Japanese envoy to this country delivered a note to Secretary Hull, Japanese forces had actually attacked at Honolulu causing naval and military damage. The President's speech was interrupted by tremendous bursts of applause—WAR WAS DECLARED BY BOTH HOUSES OF CONGRESS.

County farmers pledge more in food than asked...Milk, meat, eggs, and gardens promised in "Food for Freedom"...Farmers to practically double their quotas the coming year.

On December 11, Germany and Italy joined Japan in war upon the United

States. Congress made a quick response to the challenge by declaring war against Germany and Italy.

Dec 22: Special guards put on the bridges across the Yadkin River...

Dec 29: Tire Rationing Boards for the counties named by the Governor. Blame it on the Japs. Strict rationing system deprived all the average motorists, including traveling salesmen, taxi drivers and residents in isolated areas lacking other transportation, from purchasing new tires.

The Dispatch Editorial, Dec. 11, 1941
"Unity at Last"

"The Japs are good imitators, but they are not smart at least in the direction of wisdom...The attack unified the American people as nothing has done in this generation...

"For every ounce of damage done to our ships or planes, there will be pounds of new strength added every month by the spirit of America; for every man killed last Sunday, a thousand have stepped forward...Japan settled the question on that fateful Sunday."

Around the Nation and the World, 1941(2)

Massive Nazi attack made on Russia. State of siege in Moscow.

Court said that Negroes are entitled to all first-class service on railroad trains.

FDR ordered U.S. Navy to shoot first if Axis raiders enter our defense zone.

Jews in Germany must wear the Star of David.

In the Pacific, Japanese planes raided Pearl Harbor in a surprise attack. Within two hours, the Japanese had sunk or seriously damaged several U.S. battleships, destroyed 200 aircraft and killed over 2,000 seamen and almost 400 other people and wounded another 1,300.

A thunderous applause came from congress as President Roosevelt assailed the Japanese onslaught.

From *The Dispatch*, 1942(1)

Many men previously deferred from military service for various reasons called by the local Draft Boards.

Schools to sell Defense Stamps, a "Sharing America Effort."

William Cicero Miller of Thomasville died at Pearl Harbor—the second youth from Davidson County killed. The first was Harold Tussey from the Welcome community.

Daylight Savings Time will be with us for the duration of the War...

Seventy white men called for induction into the army, largest single group yet from the local district.

No aspect of living has missed the impact of the war. Farmers asked to grow more soybeans, a good defense crop. School children bought victory stamps at an accelerated rate. War began taking men teachers of county schools. Plenty of jobs for good carpenters available. Wages paid were 90 cents per hour and time and a half for overtime over the 40-hour week. County schools train men for defense tasks. Davidson County citizens rallied and purchased defense bonds.

The need to ration food became a reality starting with sugar. Citizens required to register in order to receive a certificate to purchase a sugar allotment...

May 11, 1942: Car operators registered in one of five classes in order to get gasoline.

Class A for all non-essential drivers and allowed seven units of gasoline between May 15 and June 30, inclusive.

Class B1, B2, B3 for limited essential drivers.

Class X for unlimited users such as doctors, police, taxi cabs, all trucks and a majority of their vehicles favored under the tire rationing plan.

May 21: Trial blackout called Tuesday. Fire and factory whistles sounded the alarm.

Selective Service Board planned for the registration of youngest group, 18- to 20-year-old group soon to be enrolled.

Grain threshing started. License forms required in order to issue wheat cards so grain can be released into channels of trade.

The Dispatch started carrying photos of men in service. Private David L. Leonard, son of Mr. and Mrs. R. B. L. Leonard of Route 2, Lexington, a member of U.S. Army stationed in Hawaiian Islands. Rural areas prepared to join Blackout Night. Telephones and church bells sounded the signal.

Chutists jumped as celebration feature here on the 4th of July. About 40 parachutists from Ft. Bragg jumped...Lt. Col. Robert Sink jumped at 11:00 o'clock and bailed out over the fairways of the Lexington municipal golf course. Thousands attended this unusual ceremony.

"Parachute Jumping Proven Feature of July 4th Here"—estimated 10,000 persons came—largest gathering ever assembled in Lexington.

Eighty white men called for army examinations on July 24. Many teachers, college graduates and students were in the group. Colored quota for July set at 27 men. Bikes rationed and Lexington quota was 22 for the month of July.

Rural schools throughout the county abandoned sports for the year.

County has twice as many in armed services as it did in WORLD WAR I. Davidson County and all of North Carolina to be blacked.

Farm Board asked freezing order on boys on farms due to a labor shortage.

Colored News Section in every edition of the newspaper now...News about weddings, social events, men in service, etc.

Draft age lowered to 18 to19. Total in service may reach 4,000 if war continues throughout the coming year.

Photos of men in service appeared in most issues of *The Dispatch*...Example: brothers in service, Efird D. Beck and Elmer C. Beck. Several families have as many as four sons in the armed services, some more.

Around the Nation and the World, 1942(2)

FDR asked for a budget of $59 billion of which $53 billion would be earmarked for the war effort. FDR asks governors to set speed limits at 40 mph to conserve tires. Philippines fell to the Japanese. 36,000 United States prisoners taken on Bataan.

FDR created U.S. Women's Auxiliary Army Corps (WACS). U.S. Congress created the WAVES.

Scarcity and sacrifice on the home front in the U.S.— meat, sugar, coffee, butter and shoes are scarce...U.S. gas rationing went into effect nationwide, no joy in auto land.

Nazis fix final solution. Hundreds of thousands of Jews are believed to have been murdered by Nazis. Germans broke Stalingrad line, attack the city. Russians launched a counter attack. Russians encircle Germans at Stalingrad. German losses now total 1.5 million. Nazis began sending Jews to Auschwitz. Germans executed 207, 373 Jews; figures included formal executions following trials.

Churchill went to Russia for talks with Stalin.

Eisenhower took charge in Europe.

U.S. fliers joined RAF for the first time in a bombing raid of Nazi bases.

Japanese losses at sea and in the air have mounted.

From *The Dispatch*, 1943(1)

High school graduates and parents only may use cars.

Permits must be had for slaughter of all meat animals. All meat must be stamped with number given...

Thirty colored men called for examination at Ft. Bragg.

Beck's Lutheran Church dedicated. Beck's Lutheran Church completed only a few years ago was dedicated Sunday, May 2, 1942.

Coble Dairy planned a large expansion program at the plant in Lexington. Milk now bottled in cardboard containers; a new innovation.

One hundred and fifty white men went to Camp Croft, and a call for 39 colored men to go to Ft. Bragg issued.

Sgt. Garland Crotts died in the Pacific Fighting Zone. His mother, Mary Jane Crotts, received the word of his death from the War Department—Crotts was rear gunner on a bomber assigned to the Pacific area stationed in Australia. He attended Davis-Townsend High School and was a member of Mt. Tabor Evangelical and Reformed Church.

A War Widow's Christmas: (A talk with her young son after her husband had been killed.) Ending paragraph—"Soon, dear God, let war be no more, families be united everywhere with smiles and laughter and children's voices filled with glee. Then we too shall proclaim as the angels long ago, Glory to God in the highest and on earth peace and good will toward men."

The holidays were not celebrated with the same enthusiasm as in years past with so many of the young men in service. Scarcely a family left unaffected by the war. Yet, those left at home did their best to maintain good morale among the children. Everything was dedicated to the war effort which resulted in many yuletide trees empty of the normal number of gifts. Congregations gathered for their Christmas Tree programs which brought some respite to war anxiety.

Around the Nation and the World, 1943(2)

New York Yankee star, Joe DiMaggio, joined the army as volunteer inductee.

FDR seized all coal mines on strike.

FDR asked Italian people to overthrow Mussolini and threatened devastating bombings if Germans resort to poison gas.

Race riots in Detroit worst since the days of the Great War.

Jane Russell in "The Outlaw" was a big hit...

War books were popular—such titles as "Guadalcanal Diary," "Here is your War," "Watch the Rhine," "The Fear of Freedom" received praise.

German army gave in at Stalingrad.

RAF and USAF dropped bombs on Berlin. Nazis mobilized women for military service. Jewish resistance fighters were fighting Nazis in Warsaw, Poland, knowing success was impossible—the fate of Jews at the hands of the Nazis was certain death—over 56,000 killed in the end there. 150,000 German troops surrender in North Africa.

Patton's army takes Messina in Italy.

U.S., Great Britain, and Russia agreed on plan to subdue Reich.

Over 2,000 Allied planes, including 1,300 from the U.S., hit Germany with awesome firepower.

From *The Dispatch*, 1944(1)

Davidson County women were very active in the war effort. Salvage of tin, fats, and scrap iron; preservation and canning demonstrations; dehydration and freezing project; sale of war bonds and stamps; assistance to the Red Cross and nutrition programs.

Because of so many men and women in the armed forces, marriages were very low in number.

Minister's son was killed in action in Italy—Lindsey Paul Leonard, the eldest son of Rev. and Mrs. A. Odell Leonard.

Many stories of heroism and bravery beginning to make their way home. Supervising officers pay numerous tributes for acts of courage by soldiers and sailors alike.

The effort during World War II had the complete support of the nation's citizens, and people in the South exhibited uninhibited patriotism.

News of Colored people

The Dunbar P.T.A. presented Tranai Long in a recital. All music lovers invited to attend—No admission charge.

Interracial Day was Sunday, February 13, held to create goodwill among races and was held at the Dunbar School. Theme of the meeting was "How to Win the War." Mrs. H. W. Sullivan discussed the part of the home in winning the war.

Pvt. Troy Littlejohn, in the British Isles, sent the following letter to his mother:

I will come back to you. It was a happy world we shared, you and I. There were joys and tears; long hours of idleness and the zest of being young and free. I was no hero that day I became a soldier, still less was I a hero to myself. It was a war not of my making but in it I have found a cause too precious to betray. That is why one day I will come back to you. Oh, yes, it might have been easy to have turned aside. I heard no call to battle, only a deep down conviction that was greater than myself If I had lived to love you, could I not ride death to fight for you? It was no challenge; it was a simple echo in my heart that whispers now. I will come back to you....

Throughout that battlefield may lie many of those who staked a claim to life, their souls triumphant will go marching on—cleansed by the fire of tribulation in the cause of rights. Shoulder to shoulder we will stand—even in death, and if my living comrades of the line should close their ranks for me, I too will be there fully content. God's wish will be fulfilled—a night and a little day—I will come back to you....

Signed Pvt. Troy Littlejohn

Some servicemen who have been overseas for 18 to 24 months were beginning to be rotated back to the states. Those honorably discharged were eligible for mustering out pay of $300.

Both Lexington and Thomasville Draft Boards reviewed 1,200 farm deferments.

David Metters of Holly Grove was awarded the purple heart. More and more telegrams were coming to parents of men losing their lives or missing in action. Occasionally very good news was received about men who had supposedly lost their lives but later reported as prisoners of war.

The Dispatch carried scores of stories about military activities of young men from the area. For example:

> Corporal Robert S. Swing, son of Mr. and Mrs. R. L. Swing of route 6, has arrived safely in North Africa according to word received by his wife, the former Miss Beulah Smith...
>
> Pre-induction exams for some 230 younger men—men engaged in essential work including farming—to go April 26.

The war was on almost everyone's mind, but some comfort came from the battle victories seemingly being reported more and more frequently.

Government started planning processes for absorbing the returning veterans on the farms and in factories, especially the farms.

Based on occasional items in the newspaper, not all lifestyles changed during the war. Bootleggers went about their business as usual. The sheriff and his deputies captured a liquor still and a large quantity of spirits in the Conrad Hill township.

Silver Hill News: Mr. and Mrs. Harvey Parks were very pleased to have all their sons in service home at one time.

The July 13 issue of *The Dispatch* carried story about an epidemic of polio becoming nationwide. Swimming pool in Lexington closed to keep polio from the city. Children under 15 were barred from the theaters.

Older men received calls for the draft during August. Almost every issue of paper contained a story of at least one serviceman killed or missing in action.

Hundreds of buses stood idle due to lack of tires.

Davidson County couple lost second son in war service. Sixty-seven Davidson men known dead in present war—more confirmed dead than in all of World War I.

Around the Nation and the World, 1944(2)

Washington announced that 5,200 American prisoners tortured by Japanese...Senator Maybank of South Carolina told U.S. Senate that the South will not open its polls to Negroes.

"Roosevelt signed G. I. Bill of Rights."

Supreme Court rules that Negroes can not be barred from voting in Texas Democratic Primaries.

"Democratic ticket is Roosevelt and Truman," with FDR saying, "I have as little right as a soldier to leave his position on the line"...Churchill and FDR have met to discuss strategy against the enemy and plans for postwar world.

FDR won 4th term.

"British bombs saturated Berlin."

MacArthur begins drive through Pacific Islands.

"Hungary's Jews sent to Auschwitz as Red Army Approaches."

In March, U.S. planes bombed Berlin for the first time.

U.S. bombed main Japanese island. Japanese lost 400 planes and three carriers in the battle of the Philippine Sea.

JUNE 6—"ALLIED FORCES LAND IN GREAT NUMBERS IN NORMANDY D-DAY HAS ARRIVED"...General Eisenhower addressing the people of Western Europe said, "This landing is but the opening phase of the campaign in Western Europe. Great battles lie ahead. I call upon all who love freedom to stand with us."

Nazis withdrew entire west wing as Americans gained in Normandy.

U.S. troops completed conquest of Saipan. Guam proclaimed under U.S. rule.

Russians pushed on the Eastern Front—the tide has turned there.

General Patton launched drive on Paris.

American launched air raid over Nagasaki, Japan.

Allies landed in Southern France and moved quickly inland.

Jews and Christians killed by the millions by Nazis in concentration camp in Poland.

Belgian cities liberated. Americans break onto Reich soil.

Soviet push scared off Eastern Europe allies of Germany.

MacArthur returned to the Philippines.

From *The Dispatch*, 1945 (1)

Lt. Paul R. Regan, one of the five sons of Mr. and Mrs. Remer Regan in the armed services, was promoted to 1st Lt.

Lt. Reid Parks reported killed in action in Italy on February 17. A detailed account of his death provided later.

Pfc. Efird Beck reported missing in action (April 9, 1945), one of seven sons of Mr. and Mrs. W. D. Beck accepted for military service. Pfc. Beck later confirmed killed in action (account of his death given in detail later)...

At the Carolina Theatre—"Since You Went Away," starring Claudette Colbert, Jennifer Jones, Joseph Cotton, Shirley Temple, Monty Woolsey, Lionel Barrymore and Robert Walker.

When the draft initiated the practice of inducting married men, many of them left a wife at home who was expecting a child. In many instances the father has not had an opportunity to see his child for a year or more. Pfc. Thomas

Byrd of Route 2, Lexington, left for Europe before his son was born, and the following poem was written by Pfc. Byrd to his little boy upon receiving a photo of him from the Mrs. Byrd:

I see you standing in your little pen
With eyes upturned, laughing to meet each day.
It seems to me, son, that dad can hear you 'shout'
Though you are many miles away.
Over the seas from afar your picture came today.
It shows a sweet face, son,
Unscarred by the war and not afraid of life
By Heaven's sweet grace.
Thank God, son, that you shall never know the fear
That boys in this country have known
Day after day, year after year,
Until every word uttered is a groan.
Your birthday just passed and you are one;
Dad hopes before long
He can meet you son.

Davis-Townsend news: V-E Day came on Tuesday, May 8, 1945, a day we had hoped and prayed for so many years; it was Hitler's war. There was no hellacious celebration through the communities though the stores were all closed in Lexington and Thomasville. Schools remained open and carried a full schedule. Patriotic songs were sung throughout the grammar grades and a minute of silent prayer was observed throughout the school.

Japan surrendered at 7 o'clock on August 14, 1945. Informal parading as happy citizens turned out in numbers. Factories and stores observed this as if a national holiday. Lexington literally went wild Tuesday night as its people released their pent-up emotions. Factory whistles sounded loud and long throughout the city area, and in a matter of minutes cars and trucks joined the clamor by sounding their horns. Guns sounded and firecrackers exploded. People retired to churches to worship. It had been a long and difficult struggle since Pearl Harbor and even longer for our Allies in Europe. Unconditional surrender had been obtained from the Germans and the Japanese. Everybody began looking to the future as never before.

Men and women came home victorious, but it was a costly war in terms of American lives. More than 400,000 lost their lives and a much larger number were wounded. In addition, 6,000 U.S. civilians lost their lives. All total 12,300,000 Allied soldiers were killed, and 45,500,000 civilians for a total of 57,800,000. Total Axis deaths exceeded 11,000,000. In addition, the Nazis executed more than six million Jews as well as thousands of people in the European countries. WORLD WAR II was the most costly war in terms of human life in the history of the world.

Around the Nation and the World, 1945(2)

U.S. B-29s carried out new raids on Tokyo. U.S. troops land on Luzon, 107 miles from Manila. MacArthur's troops moved on Corregidor in the Philippines.

U.S. marines stormed onto the shores of Iwo Jima. Allied planes remained relentless in bombing raid over Reich territory. Stars and stripes raised over Iwo Jima. MacArthur raised the U.S. flag on Corregidor in the Philippines. Japan closed its schools; orders all over six to war service.

Auschwitz liberated by Soviet troops finding thousands of victims of Nazis' sadism.

Big Three: Roosevelt, Churchill, and Stalin met at Yalta to plan future moves.

Roosevelt died with victory so near—at Warm Springs, Georgia, on April 12, 1945, of a cerebral hemorrhage and Harry Truman assumed the presidency. Roosevelt's body was transported by a slow train from Warm Springs to Washington with people lining the railroad banks to get a view of the funeral car. The train passed through Lexington, North Carolina, in early morning just after midnight. The author stood in silence with the hundreds.

After a quick and expedient trial, Mussolini was shot on April 28. Adolph Hitler, smelling Germany's demise, committed suicide in Berlin on April 30. Yanks and Reds join up in the heartland of Germany on the Elbe River. Germans surrendered unconditionally to Allied demands at 2:41 a.m. on May 8 after five years, eight months and six days. The end of the war was greeted with joy and celebration in the United States, but yet, no one could forget the war was still raging in the Pacific.

Okinawa battle—bloodiest land battle in the Pacific war—has finally ended…Italy declared war on Japan. U.S. fliers raised havoc on Japanese installations wherever situated in the Pacific.

Atomic bomb dropped on August 6 ravages Hiroshima.

Three days later a second atomic bomb was dropped on Nagasaki—60,000 dead at Hiroshima and 10,000 dead at Nagasaki; 60 percent of Hiroshima destroyed and 30 percent of Nagasaki.

Japan surrendered on August 15, 1945 bringing war to an end all over the world…Long-awaited V-J Day, victory over Japan, had finally come. Japanese officials signed act of unconditional surrender on board the U.S. Battleship Missouri. General Douglas MacArthur signed for the Allies. MacArthur in accepting the Japanese surrender said, "It is my earnest hope and, indeed, the hope of all mankind, that from this solemn occasion a better world shall emerge out of the blood and the carnage of the past; a world founded on faith and understanding, a world dedicated to the dignity of man and the fulfillment of his most cherished wish for freedom, tolerance and justice."

The pent-up emotions of U.S. citizens seemed to be released in unison as the streets of cities, towns and villages across the country were filled with uninhibited celebration. Minds churned with memories of sacrifices and duty during the war, but thoughts soon began swiftly turning to the long-awaited experiences of welcoming the soldiers, sailors, and marines home. Most of them had been in battle witnessing first hand the terrors of war in lands previously unknown.

Had the life of being a serviceman changed them into different persons? How much had we changed? Would we be able to understand our differences and show the tolerance required to make adjustments? The dawn of a new era had arrived, and it was up to us to make it worth the sacrifices of the war.

At home, Jackie Robinson, born into a Negro family of sharecroppers in Cairo, Georgia, became the first person of color to sign a contract in organized baseball—the Brooklyn Dodgers organization.

Pan American Airlines opened service between New York and London flying a sleek new DC-4 airliner. Arabs threaten oil embargo if the U.S. aids Zionism.

Nationwide strike shuts General Motors plants—180,000 workers idle... Nuremberg war crimes trials began.

General Patton, master of tank warfare, killed in car accident near Heidelberg, Germany.

From *The Dispatch*, 1946(1)

Peace time at last, and the returning veterans being discharged at an increasing rate wasted no time in getting on with their lives. The number of marriages soared and building permits for new homes and expanding business set records.

Bootlegging continued as stills were found and destroyed by sheriff's deputies. Veterans sought farm equipment beyond supply.

Lexington got its first licensed radio station which has 250 watts power operating on 1190 kilocycles only during the day.

Max Lanier of Denton won his fourth straight victory on the mound—best in the group of National League pitchers.

Veterans secured loans to assist them to return to the farm accounting for 24 percent of loans made by banks.

One year ago on December 5, 1945, Lexington was stunned by the greatest fire disaster in history of the town when the Carolina Theatre building, largest in town, caught fire. Estimates of the loss around $300,000.

County public speaking contest announced for high school students on the subject of soil conservation.

Around the Nation and the World, 1946(2)

WORLD WAR II ended with an unconditional surrender of Japan in August 1945 and earlier by Germany in May 1945.

Truman was now the President, and he and the Congress faced unexpected domestic issues headed by labor crises in the steel, meat packing, coal mining, automobile and many other industries. Truman in a national broadcast called on people to push Congress to act. Spectacle of 800,000 steel workers on strike along with hundreds of thousands in other industries just did not make sense to veterans who had laid their lives on the line for America's freedom. Meanwhile inflation was reaching astronomic proportions in Europe, and food shortages found people close to a starving condition.

U.S. Supreme Court rules segregation in public transportation unconstitutional.

United Nations opened its first session in January in London.

Churchill delivered a speech in which he coined the phrase "iron curtain."

Communist Mao Tse-tung ordered a showdown with Chiang Kai-shek.

In Nuremberg, Germany, nine Nazi war criminals are hanged.

From *The Dispatch*, 1947(1)

White friends in funeral for aged Negress. Mrs. Mandy Rosina Earnhardt, age 98 had four white pallbearers.

Edwin Cathell received bronze star for outstanding service in the Pacific War Theater. 27 from Davidson County died in the navy (10 were marines).

Silver Hill: Rev. C. E. Hiatt filled his regular appointment at Beck's Reformed Church. Rev. Alfred G. Sandrock of New Bloomfield, Pennsylvania, accepted call to be the pastor at Mt. Tabor Evangelical and Reformed Church.

Around the Nation and the World, 1947(2)

U.S. Congress proposed limitation of presidency to two terms.

Henry Ford is dead at the age of 83.

Secretary of State George Marshall offers plan to rebuild Europe, which is necessary to prevent western European countries from slipping into communism.

Two and one-half million students go to college in the U.S., half of which are ex-GIs.

From *The Dispatch*, 1948(1)

Edith Greer marries Joe Lee Beck. Edith was a graduate of Southmont High School and Joe a graduate of Davis-Townsend.

Grover Parks and Harvey Parks, brothers and sawmillers, filled their fish ponds.

Connie Mack himself will be with the Philadelphia Athletics when they come to Lexington April 14 for an exhibition game with the Lexington Athletics farm of the North State league.

Wade Younts made a fine basketball record at Davis-Townsend as a sophomore being named to the all Northwest Tournament Team.

Harold Harrison named Man of the Year for Thomasville.

Holly Grove Lutheran Church celebrated its 50th anniversary.

Garland Crotts remains being returned from Australia where he served as a rear gunner on a bomber and killed in an accident on June 27, 1943.

High school commencement at Linwood scheduled for May 28. The sermon to be given by the Rev. Harden A. King of the 2nd Presbyterian Church of Lexington.

Davis-Townsend commencement address to be given by the Rev. A. Odell Leonard.

Miss Maxine Swing and Carl Leonard were married in Linwood on June 4.

New Fords showed radical body changes.

Ten county men get degrees at N.C. State College; among them are John Wayne Fouts and Robert Bryce Younts.

Miss Betty Sue Leonard daughter of W. T. Leonard and Robert Bruce Younts son of Mr. and Mrs. Walter G. Younts married at Methodist Church in Winston-Salem.

Three cases of polio reported the last weekend in June. County Health Board bans children from gatherings with 35 cases of polio reported by August 5.

Some *Dispatch* humor:

Mrs. Asker: "Is Mrs. Smith an active member of the Women's Club?"

Mrs. Gabby: "Heavens no! She never has a word to say. She just sits there and sews."

A farmer met the overseer of the poor driving a cart with a man lying flat in the back. "Where are you going with the man?"

"Well, he has a farm but won't work, so I am taking him to the poor house."

Farmer: "I will give him a load of corn if that will help out."

Raising himself up, the poor man asked: "Is it shelled?"

"No," said the farmer.

"Drive on!" said the poor man as he lay back down.

Around the Nation and the World, 1948(2)

The U.S. Supreme Court ordered the state of Oklahoma to admit a Negro into the University of Oklahoma Law School.

President Truman assailed "Jim Crowism" and asked Congress to outlaw lynching and to establish a federal commission on civil rights.

U.S. Supreme Court bans pacts barring Negroes from owning real estate.

Chrysler auto maker raised wages to $1.63 per hour.

Draft act was signed requiring men from 19 to 25 to serve in the military.

Army segregation ended by President Truman.

Babe Ruth died of cancer at the age of 53.

Truman won presidential election against Dewey confounding the prophets.

State of Israel comes into existence.

Russian command blocked Berlin, but western powers are determined to fly in enough supplies to keep the population from starving.

North Korea was made a nation, and will be controlled by the Communists.

Tojo and seven others sentenced to hang for WORLD WAR II atrocities and 16 others given life in prison.

England's Princess Elizabeth and the Duke of Edinburgh named their two-day-old son His Royal Highness Prince Charles Philip Arthur George of Edinburgh.

From *The Dispatch*, 1949(1)

Denton Lumber Company leveled by fire—damage estimated to be between $50,000 and $75,000.

Chicken Pie Supper...There was a chicken pie supper on Saturday evening at Beck's Reformed Church hut with serving beginning at 5:30. Chicken pie, chicken stew, custards and cold drinks highlighted the menu.

Southmont has grown very rapidly and remodeling has been keeping pace with building.

Another cab company was mentioned for Lexington—Veterans' Cab Company.

An all-out cry for better schools was heard in the legislature in Raleigh.

Wade Younts of Davis-Townsend voted county's outstanding basketball performer in boys division. Willis Hedrick was also on the 1st all-county team. Betty Jean Burkhart of Davis-Townsend also named to the 1st all-county girl's team.

Colored News: Miss Betty Jean Hargrave celebrated her birthday with a party at Raymond Holt's café at Southmont. About 40 guests were present.

Around the Nation and the World, 1949(2)

U.S. Congress raised presidential salary to $100,000 with $50,000 expense allowance. Movie stars made more than the President in 1948—Humphrey Bogart ($467,361), Fred McMurray ($325,000), and Ronald Reagan ($169,000).

Jet bomber crossed U.S. in four hours.

Levi jeans introduced with great reception by U.S. buyers.

On the world scene, China Communists occupied Peking with Chiang government moving the capital to Canton.

Berlin airlift delivered one million tons of cargo since it began eight months ago—plane a minute lands every day. Allies organized NATO to preserve peace and security. Berlin Blockade was ended a year after the Soviets imposed it; 277,264 flights made. Three million ex-Nazis now eligible to vote in Germany.

U.S.S.R. detonated its first A-bomb in secret.

China establishes People's Republic. Communists in East Germany established a government. Nationalist China moves to Formosa.

Recap of 1940s

The 1940s was a time when the people of the United States were focused, as never before in the history of the republic, on one single issue: defeating the Axis powers of Germany, Japan and Italy. Everything else found its way to the back burner of priorities, and all future plans would have to wait. A common purpose and a common enemy united citizens in lock-step to rid the world of Axis dogma.

The "war effort" became the term of the day as we geared-up for the draft of our finest young men for military service, and more than 7,000 of them registered in Davidson County. The most able-bodied were inducted into the several branches of the armed services.

At the height of the war, more than 16 million young men and women donned military uniforms. We knew of no other way to get the job done. All bets were off for a shortcut to victory, and when the young men left the farms, villages and towns for war, persons left on the home front put their shoulders to the wheel to produce what the war effort required. Farmers raised production levels because an army cannot fight on an empty stomach, and many women shed their aprons or laid down their mops and brooms to keep factories at full production.

National policy mandated the conservation of resources vital to the war effort, which meant the rationing of gasoline, all things made of rubber, leather goods, sugar and many other food stuffs. Domestic automobile production came to a halt, but a few trucks were manufactured for civilian use in vital transportation activities.

The taste of manufactured candy became a memory, and we forgot about chewing gum because none was produced. People were challenged to be a part of scrap metal, paper and rubber drives and responded by rounding up everything they could locate. Patriotism was ingrained into every corner of our lives. We went to bed one hour earlier to conserve electric energy following the newly introduced idea of "daylight saving time."

Enemy attacks failed to reach our shores during the war, but we practiced air raid drills just in case, and occasionally the nights fell to total darkness as we learned the real meaning of a blackout. To help finance the war effort, citizens were called on to use their hard-earned savings to purchase government war bonds that yielded interest rates not previously known. School children saved their nickels and dimes purchasing war stamps at 25 cents and carefully pasting them one at a time in a prescribed book until it was completely filled for a total value of $18.75. Such could be traded for a war bond of equal value, and if it was held for ten years, its value would reach $25.00, a great lesson to young and old alike about the power of compound interest.

Practically every family had at least one close relative in military uniform with many families having a multiple number of sons in the war itself. Families Regan and Beck and several others had more than five sons each in service at the same time. Anxiety for their safety could be overwhelming, and we read and listened to every bit of war news we could find. Letters written by servicemen in harm's way were censored before reaching home so information that might be useful to the enemy never left the battle zones. The phrase, "Loose Lips Sink Ships" was drilled into the heads of citizen-soldiers to prevent inadvertent disclosure of useful facts.

Again, music played a big part in war keeping the spirits on the home front lifted with such songs as: "Remember Pearl Harbor," "Praise the Lord and Pass the Ammunition," "Bell Bottom Trousers," "My Guy's Coming Back," "It's Been a Long, Long Time," "I Don't Want to Walk without You," and "My Dreams Are Getting Better All the Time." Radio comedy shows helped us keep a few smiles on our faces. "Our Miss Brooks," "Amos and Andy," "Lum and Abner" and "Burns and Allen," to mention a few.

Accounts of the progress of the war in the newspapers helped us understand what was happening, but the radio seemed to be the better source. Each evening around 6:30 folks would gather in front of their radios to hear the comments from such newsmen as Edward R. Murrow, H. V. Kaltenborn, or Gabriel Heater. The latter broadcaster would often begin his version of the news by saying, "Ah, there is good news tonight," something all wanted to hear, and the tone of his voice oftentimes calmed some of our fears and reassured us of the importance of our commitments. The cadence in H. V. Kaltenborn's voice grabbed our attention, but none of the broadcasters communicated with us like Edward R. Murrow and the band of reporters he assembled who blanketed the war zones like dew covering the South. Murrow, a native of North Carolina born in Greensboro, was a distinguished and prominent figure. Heroes in World War II cannot be limited just to those fighting on the battlefields, because Edward R. Murrow and his colleagues emerged heroes as they brought the details of the war into our living rooms. These reporters were not trained to fight, but the lack of training did not prevent them from being on the battle stage. They traveled with the ground forces as they made their way up the Italian peninsula and across Europe from Normandy to the heart of Germany. Some went on bombing raids over Berlin and other enemy targets, and the radio reports to us back home not only carried their voices but the realistic sounds of war. Because of broadcast journalism, we somehow knew that the country was engaged in an enormous undertaking and we would win the war.

Anyone wishing to relive the broadcasts or learn about them for the first time can find an excellent summary in a book by Mark Bernstein and Alex Libertozzi, *World War II on the Air—Edward R. Murrow and the Broadcasts that Riveted a Nation*.(3) An audio CD containing 47 actual broadcasts collected from archives has been affixed to the inside cover.

Following is an excerpt from a broadcast from Leipzig, Germany, on April 22, 1945, as Murrow described an assault on the city hall by units of the American 69th Division:

> When they began to roll, they were hit with bazookas and machine guns. When they turned a corner, the wounded slipped off. The medium tanks were traveling about thirty miles an hour, and no man turned back. Lieutenant Ken Wilder started with a total of thirty-nine men, and when they reached City Hall he had eight. They had a company of 185 men. Sixty-eight reached the city hall...
>
> An hour after reaching the city hall, those boys were driving German cars and motorcycles about the streets. In a place where we were sitting, a sniper's bullet broke a pane of glass in a window. A doughboy said, "My! My! Somebody done broke a window. Things are getting rough around here. Folks are destroying things." The Germans had given up. A few had shot themselves. One said he couldn't be taken a prisoner by the Americans. He must commit suicide. A young lieutenant said, "Here's a gun." The German took it and shot himself just under the right ear...

The Impact of World War II on Human Life

Nothing impacted our lives like World War II whether you were a citizen soldier or a person on the home front. Finally, the Allies achieved victory in both the European and Pacific theaters. The lights had come on again all over the world as a song writer had promised, and we breathed a deep sigh of relief for the victories. Servicemen and women, who were scattered to the four corners of the globe, started returning home to their communities and families. Reunions took on a very special meaning, and homecoming celebrations never felt so good even when heroes carried the battle scars of war.

Wait a minute. A happy homecoming was not to be for all families. War had extracted a terrible toll on human life with 121 members of the Army and Army Air Force from Davidson County having paid the ultimate sacrifice, not to mention the 27 losses in the Navy and Marines. Yes, most of them came home, too, but in coffins draped with U.S. flags while a few remain until this day in cemeteries in foreign lands. We knew some of these fallen heroes, and we shared the best we could the sorrow and grief experienced by their loved ones. Unless you were a member of a family losing a son in battle, however, you could not fathom completely what it meant to have the life of a young member snuffed out in military action. Among all the ways that World War II affected us, nothing compared with a serviceman's next-of-kin receiving a telegram of his demise in action from the War Department. In Davidson County, the telegrams were delivered by the Red Bird Taxi Company.

Red Bird Taxis delivered at least two such telegrams to families in our community, one to the family of First Lieutenant Reid G. Parks and the other to the family of Private First Class Efird D. Beck. Both of these young men were among the area's best and held great promise for what they would become as older adults. Lt. Parks was a member of the Beck's Evangelical and Reformed Church (now Beck's Reformed Church), and Pfc. Beck was a member of Beck's Lutheran Church. Today, Lt. Parks' body lies in the cemetery at Beck's Reformed Church, and Pfc. Beck's body remains in a military cemetery in Europe at Margraton, Holland.

Reid Grover Parks was born on July 31, 1924, to Henry Grover and Minnie Young Parks of Silver Hill Township. He received his early education at Southmont High School graduating when 17 years old in the class of 1940. The class motto was, "Give to the world the best you have, and the best will come back to you." Following his education at Southmont High, he attended and graduated from Brevard Junior College in 1942. He was attending North Carolina State College (now North Carolina State University) in Raleigh when he enlisted in the U.S. Air Force on February 23, 1943. He began his air cadet training at Malden Field, Missouri, after which he had additional training at army air fields in Alabama, California, Illinois, Arkansas, Massachusetts and New York. He received his officer's commission and Pilot's Wings at Stuttgart Army Air Force Field, Stuttgart, Arkansas, in 1944.

In October of that year, he was assigned to the Air force 325th B-24 Liberator Bomber Squadron at Foggia, Italy. On February 17, 1945, returning from a bombing run over Graz, Austria, engine problems developed which could not be remedied. However, he managed to return the crippled B-24 within 40 miles of the Air Force Base at Foggia. He realized at that point he could not reach the base and ordered his crew of eight to bail out while electing to remain with the aircraft and attempt a crash landing. In this attempt, Reid was fatally injured, but the plane did not burn. His recovered body was buried in Naples, Italy, until 1948, when the U.S. government returned the body to Davidson County. Reid was 21 years old upon his death and was one of the Air Force's youngest pilots of his rank.

Reid Grover Parks, a wonderful human being of great character and courage, gave his life for his country. He responded to the call to duty willingly without complaining, carrying with him the support of a caring family consisting of a father and mother, a brother and two sisters. To him, home was as close as a pen and a piece of stationery. He wrote often and on a regular basis beginning the first day he went away from home to college. He shared his experiences, and he looked forward to letters from home. Letter writing was the principal means of communicating in the 1940s. From Malden Field, Missouri, he wrote about his first flights and the cold weather. From Maxwell Field, Alabama, he inquired about the progress of his young sister's piano lessons, and what's Hoyle (his brother) doing, indicating he was right at the top of his class in flying and how much fun he was having. The letter contained some money he wished for the family to give to the preacher. He ended by saying, "California, here I come." Later from Illinois, the thrill of flying upside down was described as being just as easy as flying upright.

The letters came every two or three days to his parents' mailbox providing a continuum of a young man's experiences becoming an army air force pilot. He was always describing the various parts of the country as he saw them from the air. When transferred to Westover Field in Massachusetts, he commented how impressed he was by Navy Waves from Smith College, and after a visit to New York City, he wrote he wouldn't live there if they gave him the place. His stop at Mitchell Field, New York, came shortly before shipping out for overseas duty. On October 14, 1944, he told his family he knew where he would be going but could not tell them. "I'm o. k. and I know what I am going to do for certain, I think. I'll let you know about things when I can. Don't worry about me. P. S.—I will be o. k. until I write again."

About mid-November 1944, Lt. Parks arrived in Italy assigned to a bomber group in the Fifteenth Air Force. A longer time was required for his letters to the U.S., but he continued to write, and he relished each communication from home. In a letter dated November 27, 1944, to his sister, Mabel, he lamented the fact he would not be able to get Christmas presents for anyone in the family, asking the folks at home to put some under the tree from him. On November 30, in a letter to the family, he described the climate in Italy about the same as it is at home. He mentioned that there were no trees in Italy, and his daddy could saw all the timber over here in half a day (his father, Grover, was a saw-mill operator). Some disappointment was expressed about receiving only one letter from home since his arrival.

During the next few months, he piloted his B-24 Liberator Bomber with his crew of eight on numerous missions against the enemy in Italy, Austria and southern Germany, paying attention to railway installations in the vicinity of the Brenner Pass. On February 11, 1945, he wrote to his brother, Hoyle, mentioning four letters he had just received from various relatives. He requested that no more candy be mailed since he was eating too much as it was. Reid promised a squadron insignia for Hoyle to place on the left side of the breast of a jacket asking him to give it care since another would not be available. Again, he asked about sister Ruth's piano lessons, and what is sister, Mabel, doing?

In his goodbye, he admonished Hoyle to plant a good watermelon patch this year. "I'm coming home in time to eat them," he said.

The next letter was written on Friday evening, February 16, 1945, addressed to his father with the salutations of "Dear Folks." He began by saying:

> Well time flies by and I see it has been a couple of days since I wrote...I'm still o. k. and just messing around. The weather is rather nice, not much rain, and it's warm. I'll be glad when the old Adriatic gets warm enough to go swimming...Well it looks as if the Russians really mean business along now—that the big three have met—things look better...well—I hope you are all well, and I'll stop now and say goodbye...Love Reid...
>
> P. S.: I'm in the Army Reserve now instead of the U.S. Army which means that even if I get out of the Army, I'll keep my commission and still have to fly a certain number of hours each year for the Army, and we get good pay too...I can't tell you all back home where I am in Italy—I'm wondering where you think I am.

This would be the last letter that Lt. Parks would write. The next day he and his crew made the bombing raid over Graz, Austria, the ill-fated flight, and the fatal crash. The family received at least two more letters of note, one from a Lt. Colonel George addressed to Reid's father, portions of which follow:

> It is with great sorrow that I write this letter to inform you of the many details as I can pertaining to the death of your son, 1st Lt. Reid Parks, 0-827034, who was killed when the plane he was piloting crashed in Southern Italy...In attempting to land his crippled plane after a very successful raid over Austria, Reid saw he would not be able to make it to his home, and he ordered the crew to bail out, which they did, but he elected to remain with the ship and attempt a crash landing...In this attempt, Reid was instantly killed, but the plane did not burn and his

body was removed from the wreckage immediately by American military personnel who had witnessed the crash...He was buried the following day in a nearby military cemetery with full honors by members of his squadron, his own chaplain conducting the ceremony, and his crew, who probably owed their lives to his coolness in time of danger, among the mourners...Reid died as he had lived; courageous, attentive to duty, and thoughtful of others. We know your grief because to some degree we share it with you. Through his efforts, eight members of his crew carry on with his shining example ever in their minds, and the love and respect of the entire squadron will always be his.

A second letter came to Mr. and Mrs. Grover Parks from a member of Reid's crew that survived the parachute jump from the ailing plane on February 17, 1945. It was written by Lt. A. T. Stolen from New York, New York. From the beginning of the letter, the writer apologizes for having to say what he was about to say in such matter-of-fact terms, but he wanted the Parks family to know exactly the circumstances surrounding Reid's death. Lt. Stolen reviewed the successful bombing mission over Graz, Austria, during which they came under heavy enemy fire disabling three out of the plane's four engines. Due to Reid's flying skills, assisted by navigator Lt. Robert D. Drennan of Rockwell, Iowa, the crippled plane made it back to their own territory with the one engine. While cruising at about 2,000 feet and 40 miles from their base, the remaining engine under the enormous strain of propelling such a heavy load caught on fire, and the plane began losing altitude rapidly. Giving all the safety to the crew, orders were given by Reid to bail out, which the crew did, and for some reason Reid did not.

"My parachute landing," he wrote, "was just a short distance from the site of the plane crash. I approached it and saw that Reid's body had been thrown clear of the plane. He had died instantly, and the next day, the body was buried in an allied military cemetery."

Because of Reid's constant letter writing and the attentiveness to them shown by his sister, Ruth, the letters have been preserved in a scrapbook in chronological order. The scrapbook holds many, many more letters than the ones quoted here. All combined, they make a historical record of a young man's achievements and personal concerns for his family as he made the journey that led to his ultimate sacrifice. The book of letters with other personnel effects of Lt. Parks can be found in the Special Collections Section of the North Carolina State University Library in Raleigh, North Carolina.(4)

Nearly four years after Lt. Parks died in action, his body was exhumed from the U.S. Military Cemetery in Bari, Italy, and brought to Davidson County for his last rites. On a cool autumn afternoon at two o'clock, November 28, 1948, at the Beck's Evangelical and Reformed Church, the Rev. Charles E. Hiatt conducted an appropriate sermon with the Lexington V.F.W. in charge of the military rites at graveside. The service was attended by a large number of relatives and friends. I was among the attendees and remember clearly these many decades later the squad of military men firing several volleys of rifle shots over a flag-draped casket before it was lowered into the ground. The sounds of exploding shells from the rifle muzzles and their echoes from a wooded hollow below the cemetery are one of my life's most vivid memories. The soldiers carefully folded the flag in military fashion and presented it to Reid's mother. I have wondered for so many years now what were the thoughts of his parents that day to this type of homecoming, so different from that of the families of servicemen who survived the War and came home to live another day.

Efird David Beck, born on September 13, 1920, was the ninth child (eighth son) of Mr. and Mrs. W. D. Beck of the Hedrick's Grove community. He attended and graduated from Davis-Townsend High School in the class of 1937. Private First Class Efird Beck entered the U.S. Army on October 6, 1942, undergoing basic training for the Military Police. Two years later, he volunteered to transfer to an infantry regiment as a rifleman. After six weeks of basic training at Camp Maxey, Texas, he was transferred to Fort Meade, Maryland, and assigned to overseas duty. After being in the field overseas for three and one-half months, he was suddenly struck by enemy machine gun fire, causing his death.(1)

Pfc. Efird Beck enjoyed tremendous popularity in his community. His immediate family was very large consisting of his mother and father, one sister, Mrs. Willie Vawter, and seven brothers: Gurney, Carlton, Clifford, Elmer, Arlie, James, and Ernest. Efird loved his family dearly, and he was close to his brothers. His service as a Military Police in the Army Air Force in Iowa would probably have kept him out of harm's way for the duration of the conflict, but two of his brothers were on the front lines in Germany, and not satisfied, he wanted to join them. One brother, Pfc. James Beck, was serving in Patton's famous Third Army, and the other, Pfc. Elmer Beck, in the noted 9th Army. Efird got his wish, and he was placed in the 120th Infantry Regiment of the famous 30th Division, an outfit that was spearheading the advance of the 9th Army across Germany. Efird fought in two major battles of the war, the Battle of the Bulge and the Battle of Northern Germany. It was toward the close of this latter battle, while Efird and his Company were attacking an enemy fortification near the town of Dorsten, Germany, he received heavy machine gun fire. The initial notification delivered to his parents indicated he was missing in action; however, three days later a telegram confirmed his death as being instant on March 26, 1945. For his valor and courage in service to his country, he received the Good Conduct Medal and a year later a Cluster and the infantry Combat Badge for his participation in the Battle of the Bulge and the Battle of Northern Europe.

Appropriate religious services were conducted in Private First Class Efird Beck's memory by the United States Army. His body was laid to rest in the United States Military Cemetery, Plot Y, Row 8, Grave 188, in Margraton, Holland, 10 miles west of Aachen, Germany. A white cross above his grave contains his name, rank and army serial number 34432271. Efird Beck died in the line of duty, and he earned the highest traditions of the Army and his country which he served so nobly well. No man could have done more in the great struggle for human freedom.

His church and Pastor, the Rev. C. F. Kyles, assisted by Chaplain R. L. Fisher, conducted a memorial service for Efird on July 28, 1946, at the Beck's Evangelical Lutheran Church. Friends made two tangible presentations in Efird's honor early in the ceremony: a religious art memorial and a pulpit Bible. Scripture and the Memorial Address were handled by Chaplain R. L. Fisher, and Pastor Rev. C. F. Kyles gave the Memorial Sermon, titled, "Jesus' Resurrection and Life." A solo, "The Lord's Prayer," was sung by Mrs. J. L. Gathings, wife of the principal of Davis-Townsend High School, to conclude the service.

Efird's father and mother like many American families made the decision to leave his remains in the cemetery in Holland, but a foot marker bearing his name was eventually placed near the graves of his parents in the cemetery of Beck's Evangelical Lutheran Church.

An interesting comment about Pfc. Efird Beck seems in order. He was the only unmarried child among the eight sons and daughter of Mr. and Mrs. W. D. Beck. While stationed in Iowa, he met and won the affections of Miss Bettie Hurd of Cherokee, Iowa, and they had planned to wed before he went overseas, but he was unable to secure a furlough for this purpose.

Returning to Normal

The latter part of the decade of the '40s saw a resumption of manufacturing for a civilian society. Old automobiles, a majority of which were produced before the decade, started being replaced by newly designed models, equipped with many operating parts based on technology developed for the war effort. Prices rose for practically every commodity consumed in society, and minimum wages started climbing to match inflation. The world and home front had changed forever, and nobody wanted to turn back.

Sixteen million men and women poured back into civilian life with an energy never witnessed before. It was as if they had calculated their post-war plans anxiously while negotiating hedge rows in Western Europe or island-hopping in the South Pacific. They had eagerly awaited the enemy's defeat to implement their plans. Marriages put on hold took place in record numbers, and birth rates occurred in equally astronomical numbers.

Congress had passed the GI Bill while they were away, and the veterans took advantage of it. Many enrolled in over-crowded colleges and universities across the country, becoming not only more useful to themselves but to the whole of society.

Returning farm boys discovered huge changes had taken place in the way food was produced. Powerful machines had replaced animal and human power. Not as many hands were required to feed a growing and grateful nation. Some who envisioned themselves being tillers of the soil began to migrate to urban and suburban areas to seek other professions. They discovered that to make a living the family farm could not accommodate them all. All this change combined to create the most advanced and highest standard of living the world had ever seen.

Society, it seemed, rushed from the 1940s into the '50s with unbounded enthusiasm. Consumerism vaulted to an unprecedented level. Housewives' kitchens took on the appearance of a totally electric or natural gas arcade with dishwashers, stoves, food mixers and toasters. In the laundry rooms, the old wringer washing machines gave way to machines with automatic washing cycles, and the outdoor clothes line disappeared from behind houses in favor of electric or gas dryers waiting to receive a machine load of freshly washed clothes.

Manpower on the farm became much more efficient with tractors, tillage machines and harvesters. One farm worker was producing more meat, milk, crops and vegetables than 10 men could before the War. Leisure blocks of time began appearing in our daily lives as technology replaced drudgery. With time on our hands, television sets made their way into living rooms as if by magic. The decade of the fifties became known as "The Golden Age of Television" as networks produced shows to entertain everyone in the family. Television screens were black and white, requiring an inordinate amount of time adjusting rabbit-ear and outside antennas in efforts to rid them of snowy patterns and get better signal reception.

Performers in the '50s did their shows live, and we were introduced to some of the greatest names ever in television entertainment. Who could ever forget Milton Berle and his antics, the Perry Como show and his mellow voice, the Hit Parade of the most popular tunes of the week, the Jack Benny show—a carry-over from radio, lonesome George Gobel, Arthur Godfrey, the Ed Sullivan Hour, the singing of Diana Shore, the fast-stepping music of Lawrence Welk and his band, the classic comedy shows of Red Skelton, the menagerie of talent on the Colgate Comedy Hour, Sid Ceasar and Imogene Coca with their situation comedy, and finally, the comedy team of Dean Martin and Jerry Lewis?

Tom Brokaw in his book, *The Greatest Generation*, describes succinctly and vividly how this generation of Americans who had lived through the Great Depression and won the war went on to build a modern America.

This generation was united not only by a common purpose but also by common values—duty, honor, economy, service, love of family and country and, above all, responsibility for oneself.(5)

The torrid pace the veterans set in becoming civilians again produced an after-draft, pulling others along with them. They were competitors in every facet of life, and for many it was produce or move aside. No longer were mediocre performances good enough in a world where the desire to excel became the norm rather than the exception. America's greatest generation once again at home in America did not know how to lose. The word was not in their vocabulary.

Peace had come by the end of the decade of the '40s, but the winds of power and politics continued to blow in the world with uncertainty in Southeast Asia. Korea was divided into the South and the North. In Europe, the Soviet Union annexed the eastern half of Poland and northeast Prussia. What was once mighty Germany became divided into an East and West. Moscow was setting up communist regimes taking the place of previous governments in Eastern Europe while Allies allowed the Western nations to restore their democracies. The globe at that time belonged to the Soviet Union or to the United States. Nations not belonging to one feared being cajoled or forced to side with the other.(2)

World War II Marriages

A twist of fate had prevented the marriage of Pfc. Efird Beck and Miss Bettie Hurd of Iowa from happening, It would have been one of many marriages that occurred around World War II when a soldier far from home met a girl, and they fell in love and married.

A marriage involving a young man from Nebraska, John Edwin King, and a young lady, Elizabeth Maxine Parks, who had graduated from Linwood High School, represents what did happen over and over again during and after the war. In wartime the mobility of people reaches unprecedented proportions, and World War II was no exception with 16 million U.S. citizens in uniform at military bases in all sections of the country and around the world.

John Edwin King, or Johnny as he was called by his friends, was such a military vagabond. Born in Falls City, Nebraska, on December 28, 1925, he was inducted into the army at Leavenworth, Kansas, at the age of 18 years on April 28, 1944. He stayed there only until May 6 and boarded a troop train for an unknown destination. After taking a circuitous route, he arrived at Fort

Jackson, South Carolina, for his Infantry Basic Training. After completing this requirement, he was assigned to the "motor pool" where he had to learn to drive trucks weighing between two and five tons. Again, the troop train came into the picture, boarding one to go to Camp Kilmer, New Jersey. A few weeks later, it was back on the troop train for New York to board the British ship, *Queen Elizabeth*, for an Atlantic crossing to Glasgow, Scotland, arriving on December 21. Again it was the troop train, an English train this time, for a trip to England. About mid-January 1945, he joined a convoy of trucks for a night trip to a seaport to get to France. In France, he became a part of the 3rd Army hauling supplies to Army units going to the front lines. After staying at the front lines for a few days, the convoy would return hauling German prisoners to camps in Belgium and France.

Being a truck driver did by no means take a soldier out of harm's way. One assignment called for loading his vehicle at night with five-gallon cans of gasoline at a fuel depot in Dusseldorf, Germany, while being shelled by German artillery during a raging thunderstorm. Sleep came hard, and he moved away later in darkness with a convoy in blackout conditions. The gasoline was left with the 3rd Army getting soldier King involved in the Battle of the Rhineland.

An unusual experience came when his unit helped liberate a German concentration camp near Mauthausen, Austria. As they entered the camp, they found corpses piled like cordwood, and their job became rounding up the escaped prisoners in the countryside bringing them back to camp to give them water, food and medical attention. If ever there was a life-changing experience, the Mauthausen Camp assignment became one for Johnny. Austrian civilians were assigned to bury the dead in mass graves dug by bulldozers driven by Army engineers. Each body in the cemetery was marked with a white cross or some other religious symbol.

From Mauthausen, the first part of July 1945, Johnny drove his truck in convoy to Le Harve, France, where by chance he saw his uncle. In about two weeks, he and 1,500 other troops boarded the U.S.S. General Bliss for the USA arriving in Boston on August 3, 1945, to a great celebration of bands playing and ships sailing out to greet them. Here, he enters another troop train headed for Fort Sam Houston, Texas. A long-earned furlough came next to visit parents and siblings. After a brief assignment at Camp Polk, Louisiana, Johnny went to Fort Bragg, North Carolina, where he continued his duty as a driver which sometimes required him to drive a bus.

On Saturday morning, November 10, 1945, he left Fort Bragg with an Army band headed for Lexington, North Carolina, for a band concert and an Armistice Day parade the next day. On Saturday evening, the band and drivers were invited to a dance at the Lexington Country Club. Johnny and two Army bud-

dies visited People's Drug Store on Main Street. While sitting on a soda foun-
tain counter stool, Johnny just happened to notice four young ladies in a booth
with one of them seeming very pleasant to him.

After finishing their Coca-Colas, the soldiers started to leave, but Johnny
was not going until he had spoken to the pleasant young lady. After asking
her, Maxine Parks, two questions in rapid fire succession, "Are you married?"
and "Would you go out with me?," he invited all four ladies to the dance.
Their reply was no because they planned to go to the movies to see "Anchors
Aweigh." Not to let the pleasant one get away, the soldiers joined the ladies at
the movie, which turned out to be "Where Do We Go from Here," a rather
ominous title.

Maxine's story of their first encounter carried a slightly different twist to it.
The four ladies actually viewed the three servicemen when they entered the
drug store with considerable scrutiny. Maxine was the first to spot Johnny, and
she remarked to her friends, "Here is my man," as he walked through the door.
Apparently, she never told Johnny of this remark because he courted Maxine with a fervor requiring countless trips to Lexington over the next several
months made by hitchhiking to Lexington and returning to camp by bus.

To conclude the story of the romance, the couple married on June 8, 1946,
at the Beck's Evangelical and Reformed Church. Johnny and Maxine have resided in the same church community ever since the wedding, and the union
has been very fruitful—three children and six grandchildren.(6)

Successful and interesting courtships also occurred in the opposite direction involving U.S. servicemen stationed overseas, mainly during years following the war. They met young ladies, fell in love, wooed them, and brought
them back to the states. No doubt, a number of men from Davidson County
married wives born in a foreign country, and one such union that comes to my
mind was between John William Smith of the Hedrick's Grove Community
and Rose Mary Schneider of Karlsruhe, Germany.

Following his graduation from Davis-Townsend High School, John William or Bill attended North Carolina State College, now University, where he
earned a degree in civil engineering in June 1952 along with a commission in
the army engineers. He was inducted into service very shortly after graduation; by December 1952, Second Lieutenant Smith was dispatched to Karlsruhe,
Germany, assigned to the 406th Engineer Combat Battalion of the 39th Engineer Combat Group. Before he had time to get much German soil on his boots,
he attended a New Year's Eve Ball at the Officers' Club where he met Rose
Mary. She caught his eye, but there would be no second dance for the couple
then because the U.S. Army shipped him to Munich to an Officers' School for a
couple of months after which Bill returned to Karlsruhe in March 1953.

Bill and Rose Mary started dating, which Bill described as being much different from dating in the U.S. For starters, an American soldier courting a German girl did not resonate well with the German people, particularly the mothers and the girls' friends in general. The year 1953 was only a few short years following a devastating war, and many people still regarded the U.S. soldiers as enemies, even though the Marshall Plan was helping rebuild the country. Bill persisted, and as he said, "Being a nice guy, I won over Rose Mary's mother and grandmother who were very protective of her."

The U.S. Army sent Bill back to the states in early 1954 to receive a discharge, and because Bill did not accept a regular Army Commission, they could not marry in Germany. Rose Mary still in Germany, had to immigrate to the U.S. Since she was born in Namibia, Africa, further difficulties arose due to a low quota for immigration from her native country. They addressed the problems for nine months, and with assistance from Bill's local State Representative, Eugene Snyder of Lexington, N.C., success was finally theirs in November 1954. When she arrived in the U.S., she went to Raleigh and stayed with a Mrs. Rhodes, Bill's landlady while he was a student at N.C. State College. Marriage occurred in a few weeks on December 18 in the Sacred Heart Cathedral in Raleigh.

The couple resides in Columbia, South Carolina, their home for many, many years. They reared two children, a daughter, Colette, who like her father is a civil engineer, married and living in Colorado. Their second child is a son, Alan, also a civil engineer, single and residing in Greenville, S.C.

Those of us who lived through World War II heard interesting and fascinating stories from returning GI's about their impressions and experiences in foreign countries, but what about the reactions of a war bride moving to the United States and leaving her comfort zone of home permanently? Rose Mary came from a large metropolitan area in Germany which was devastated by the war, and in 1954, she was amazed and delighted to see a small city like Raleigh so intact and surrounded by a large rural countryside. Compared to the closeness in Europe, distances between cities and towns surprised her and still do to this day.

On her first visit to the Hedrick's Grove community from Raleigh, she was struck by the inordinate amount of time required to make the trip and the absence of a fast train to make the journey easier. The small villages along the highway on the road to Hedrick's Grove and Lexington lacked the picturesque character of those found in rural Germany. Rose Mary says, "I still miss them," as she does Europe.

There is no place like home, and jetliner travel makes it easy to get to Germany allowing her to attend school reunions each year. She expresses it this way, "The last time I went to Germany was in September for eight days by myself. It was wonderful, the weather was perfect, the new wine was delicious, and I enjoyed sitting in the sidewalk cafes viewing the scenery and enjoying the fabulous pastries. It still amazes me that you can get around in Europe without a car. I shudder to think when the time comes that I cannot get into my car here to go where I need to go." She speaks of being fully acclimated in the U.S. and how she became a student at the University of South Carolina majoring in German and minoring in French.(7)

A Colored and White Society

During the decades of the '20s, '30s and '40s, segregation of individuals based on skin color was a way of life in Davidson County, the entire South and other sections of the country as well. Segregationist Jim Crow laws had been enacted in North Carolina as early as the 1870s, evidenced in separate water fountains, eating places, transportation vehicles, public venues and the pervasive signs stating "Colored" and "White." Laws passed in North Carolina in the early 1900s were very specific about separating students of color and white in public schools. The number of laws passed by 1957 numbered 23, speaking to the many kinds of situations where whites and colored interacted physically. A decision by the United States Supreme Court in 1896 set forth the doctrine of "separate but equal," meaning segregation had become an institution, a way of life. Louis Lomax, in his writing of *The Negro Revolt*, challenged the validity of the doctrine and said, "But if 'separate but equal' was the law, 'separate and unequal' was the practice."

Practically every experience was partitioned by color of one's skin. In Davidson County, we went about our daily lives without serious conflicts over the policy. Persons of color gained entrance wherever the public activity could provide for separation. For example, colored people usually sat in the balcony area in theaters and whites in seats on the lower level. If members of both races sat in the balcony, whites took the front seats and the colored sat behind them. On public buses, colored sat in the back of the vehicle. At professional baseball games, each race had its separate section in the bleachers. Signs designating use for Colored or White were prevalent in all public places. Signs greeted you at bus stations, at water fountains, and in government buildings.

The local newspaper, *The Dispatch*, carried society news about colored and white people under separate headings; however, in other situations, references to white and colored appeared in the same articles. For example, a report of the number of persons from Davidson County serving in the armed services in World War I indicated a total of 932 men of which 150 were colored and 782 white. The same report concluded by saying 39 men from Davidson County lost their lives, 37 white and two colored. During World War II, the number of men from the two County Draft Boards, Lexington and Thomasville, being drafted into the armed services was listed monthly, and the quantity was given by race. The first Selected Service Men of the county received their induction calls on November 25, 1940—11 white men and three colored. In July 1943, 39 colored men from Lexington went to Fort Bragg and 150 white men to camp Croft. A story in *The Dispatch* after World War II mentioned that 148 men from the County lost their lives in military operations, but no stratification of numbers by race appeared in the article. Military units continued to be segregated throughout the war, but General Dwight D. Eisenhower called for integration of all military services soon after the war ended.(1)

The most interaction of colored and white occurred in the workplace and on farms. Some white factory owners had incentive policies for the children of all workers, including colored workers. For example, the Finch family owners of the Thomasville Chair Company provided college scholarships for children of colored and white workers, and many children took advantage of the opportunity. Some colored women were employed by well-to-do white families to care for the children and perform domestic work. This gave the colored woman an income but took her away from her own home and children. In many instances, colored women stayed with white mothers during the daytime after they gave birth to their children until the mother had recovered from the stress of childbirth.

Education facilities operated on a totally segregated basis. Schools and practically all universities and colleges were designated for either white or colored students, never both. Lexington had one of the two colored high schools in the county, Dunbar High School, named after the great Negro poet, Paul Lawrence Dunbar. His name graced the buildings of many colored schools all over the South. In 1930, Dunbar High School conducted a week-long program and invited white educators. Each day focused on a single subject featuring such topics as "The Schools and the Enrichment of Life," "The Schools of Yesterday," and "The School of Tomorrow and the Future of America." Dunbar High School housed the Negro branch of the Davidson County Library.(1)

Dunbar High School held an interracial day on February 13, 1944, to create goodwill among the races. Its theme was "How to Win the War." Discussions were conducted on such subjects as the role of the home, church, and community in winning the war. One of Dunbar's teachers presented a Bible study followed by glee club singing.

In 1948, the United States Supreme Court ordered the state of Oklahoma to admit a Negro into the University of Oklahoma Law School. In that same year, the U.S. Supreme Court banned a pact barring Negroes from owning real estate.

Although the integration of many public schools would have to wait nearly two decades in much of the South, a benchmark decision by the U.S. Supreme Court on May 17, 1954(2), in the case of *Brown versus Board of Education*, stated that "separate educational facilities are inherently unequal." The court thus overturned the doctrine of "separate but equal," which had been the law since 1896. Over the next several decades, the Jim Crow laws and customs, not without considerable resistance by the defenders of the status quo, would one by one fall by the wayside.

Uncle Sam appeared on posters all over the nation admonishing all of us to join in the effort to bring the enemy to their knees. (Wikipedia, J. W. Flagg creation)

Thousands of young people from Davidson County served their country in World War II. Young men (draftees) reported for induction into the armed services. (Davidson County Historical Museum)

During the war, practically all servicemen home on leave used bus transportation to get to and from their bases. Here we see a crowded ticket counter at the bus station. (Library of Congress, FSA-OWI photo collection, LC-USF34-044102)

The War department worked diligently encouraging Americans to buy war bonds. Billboards were placed strategically in every city and town. (Library of Congress, FSA-OWI photo collection, LC-USW3-031014)

Scrap metal drives were held to collect scrap metal of all types to support the war effort. The Carolina Theater provided free admissions to persons bringing in scrap metal. (Davidson County Historical Museum)

General Eisenhower giving final instructions to paratroops in England before the Normandy invasion—June 1944. (U.S. National Archives)

G.I. taking a break to sit on one of the tanks in General Patton's army. (Family collection)

U.S. infantrymen with a captured swastika. (U.S. National Archives)

Medics attend to an injured soldier on Normandy Beach during the invasion. (U.S. National Archives)

(*Above*) Celebrating Germany's surrender at Piccadilly Circus in London. (U.S. National Archives)

(*Left*) Factory-produced tires were not available during the war, and recapping old tires became a very common practice. (Library of Congress, FSA-OWI photo collection, LC-USE6-0-008029)

Black steam engines pulled the trains until diesel engines replaced them. (Library of Congress, FSA-OWI photo collection, LC-USE6-D-006810)

Bus stations throughout the southern United States provided separate waiting rooms for colored and white passengers. (Library of Congress, FSA-OWI photo collection, LC-USF-33-20522)

The invasion of Tarakan Borneo occurred at high tide. Before the landing ships could move offshore, the tide receded leaving the ships such as the LST 1027 stranded for several days. (Family collection)

Navy buddies on the deck of LST in the Pacific ocean. Seaman Bruce Younts of Sandy Grove on the left. (Family collection)

Seaman Younts at cannon on LST 1027 in the South Pacific. (Family collection)

United States marines raise the flag on top of Mt. Suribachi during the battle of Iwo Jima on February 23, 1945. (Joe Rosenthal/The Associated Press)

The second atomic bomb dropped in Japan hit the center of the city of Nagasaki. The entire city was literally vaporized. Photo taken shortly after the bombing. (U.S. National Archives)

A formal photograph of Lt. Reid G. Parks killed in action on
February 17, 1945. (Family collection)

Reid

(*Above*) Lt. Parks took his early flight training at Malden Field, Iowa. He became a pilot of a B-24, four-engine bomber. (Family collection)

(*Facing page*) The body of Lt. Reid Parks was returned to the United States. His funeral at Beck's Evangelical and Reformed Church on November 28, 1948. (Family collection)

Efird Beck at 15 years of age standing beside his family home. (Family collection)

Pvt. Efird Beck is shown with army buddies before he shipped overseas to Europe to enter the war. (Family collection)

Pvt. Efird Beck was killed in action in Germany, and his body was laid to rest in the United States Military Cemetery in Margraton, Holland. The body remains there today. (Family collection)

Mr. and Mrs. W. D. Beck had eight sons and one daughter. Seven of the sons served in the military during World War II. Efird in the middle front row. (Family collection)

Cpl. John King from Nebraska married Maxine Parks at Beck's Evangelical and Reformed Church in 1946. (Family collection)

Lt. John W. Smith of the Hedrick's Grove community married Rose Mary Schneider of Karlsruhe, Germany. (Family collection)

Addressed V-mail envelope. Servicemen and servicewomen stationed overseas during World War II could use a V-mail service postage free to send mail home. (Martha Younts Swing)

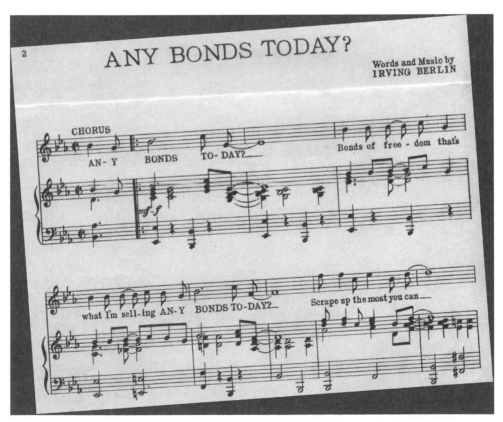

America's theme song: To aid in the war effort, Irving Berlin wrote "Any Bonds Today" which was called the Theme Song of the National Defense Program. The music and words for the first few lines of the song are shown here. (Ruth Younts)

CLOTHES RATIONING DURING WORLD WAR TWO - YEAR 5

During the Second World War, every man, woman and child was allowed 48 coupons per year for clothes.

ITEM	COUPONS
Overcoat or raincoat	5
Jacket or blazer	6
Boy's trousers	6
Girl's gym tunic/skirt	4
Girl's dress	5
Pyjamas/nightie/dressing gown	6
Cardigan/jumper	5
Underpants/knickers/vest	2
Boy's shirt/girl's blouse	4
Child's shoes/sandals/boots	2
Gloves/hat/scarf/cap	2
Socks/stockings	1
Ties/handkerchiefs	1

The number of rationing coupons needed to purchase various items of clothing. Each person limited to a total of 48 coupons per year. (Martha Younts Swing)

Rationing coupons. (Martha Younts Swing)

Nº 838148 BS

WAR RATION BOOK No. 3

Void if altered

Identification of person to whom issued: PRINT IN FULL

Martha A. Younts

(First name)   (Middle name)   (Last name)

Street number or rural route *Route 3*

City or post office *Lexington* State *N. C.*

AGE	SEX	WEIGHT	HEIGHT	OCCUPATION
5	F	50 Lbs.	3 Ft. 5 In.	

SIGNATURE ....
(Person to whom book is issued. If such person is unable to sign because of age or incapacity, another may sign in his behalf)

NOT VALID WITHOUT STAMP

WARNING

This book is the property of the United States Government. It is unlawful to sell it to any other person, or to use it or permit anyone else to use it, except to obtain rationed goods in accordance with regulations of the Office of Price Administration. Any person who finds a lost War Ration Book must return it to the War Price and Rationing Board which issued it. Persons who violate rationing regulations are subject to $10,000 fine or imprisonment, or both.

OPA Form No. R-130

LOCAL BOARD ACTION

Issued by ....

(Local board number)   (Date)

Street address ....

City .... State ....

....
(Signature of issuing officer)

Ration book. (Martha Younts Swing)

INSTRUCTIONS

1 This book is valuable. Do not lose it.

2 Each stamp authorizes you to purchase rationed goods in the quantities and at the times designated by the Office of Price Administration. Without the stamps you will be unable to purchase those goods.

3 Detailed instructions concerning the use of the book and the stamps will be issued. Watch for those instructions so that you will know how to use your book and stamps. Your Local War Price and Rationing Board can give you full information.

4 Do not throw this book away when all of the stamps have been used, or when the time for their use has expired. You may be required to present this book when you apply for subsequent books.

Rationing is a vital part of your country's war effort. Any attempt to violate the rules is an effort to deny someone his share and will create hardship and help the enemy.

This book is your Government's assurance of your right to buy your fair share of certain goods made scarce by war. Price ceilings have also been established for your protection. Dealers must post these prices conspicuously. Don't pay more.

Give your whole support to rationing and thereby conserve our vital goods. Be guided by the rule:

"If you don't need it, DON'T BUY IT."

16—32299-1 ☆ U. S. GOVERNMENT PRINTING OFFICE : 1943

Instructions for using the World War II ration book. (Martha Younts Swing)

Sunday nite
Feb. 11, 1945

Dear Hoyle —

I got your letter, from mama, and Ritta + Sissy Lloyd today — they were mailed between Jan 29 and Feb. 2.

So you have mailed another box of candy — well you had better keep it for I eat too much already. you all eat it at home.

So you are going along in basketball at Southmont. well — don't beat everyone — Are you doing any hunting along now? we get to shoot about all we wa[nt]

Page 1 of 3-page letter Lt. Reid Parks wrote to his brother Hoyle.

to at the gunnery range.

I'm sending our Squadron insignia — hoyle you can wear it if you have a coat or jacket — put it on the left side breast — take care of it — I paid $2.50 for it and doubt if I can get another — sew it on if you use it — otherwise keep it at home for me.

you never did let me know if you are going to speak or not — that $.25 is waiting for you.

How is Ruth doing with her piano lessons. and what

Page 2 of letter from Reid Parks to his brother Hoyle.

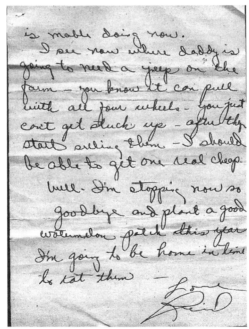

is mable doing now.

I see now where daddy is going to need a jeep on the farm — you know it can pull with all four wheels — you just can't get stuck up — after they start selling them — I should be able to get one real cheap.

well. I'm stopping now so goodbye and plant a good watermelon patch this year I'm going to be home in time to eat them —

Love
Reid

Page 3 of letter from Reid Parks to his brother Hoyle. (Ruth Parks)

Friday evening
Feb. 16, 1945

Dear Folks,

Well - time really flies by & I see it has been a couple days since I last wrote.

Today I got a letter from Margie but I haven't been getting much mail lately.

I'm still ok and just messing around over here. The weather is rather nice, not much rain and it is warm. I'll be glad when the old Adriatic gets warm enough to go in swimming.

I'm sending home a money order - I got kind of carrying the money around, was going to send it several days ago but was too lazy to walk to the Post office -

Well, it looks as if the Russians really mean business along now - that the big three have met - things look better. Well. I hope you are all well & so I'll stop now & goodbye -

Love
Reid -

P.S. I'm in the Army Reserve now instead of the U.S. Army - which means that even if I get out of the Army I'll keep my commission and I'll have to fly a certain number of hrs each year for the Army - & we will get good pay for it - (over)

Page 1 of letter Lt. Reid Parks wrote to his folks the day before he was fatally injured.

Page 2 of letter Lt. Reid Parks wrote to his folks the day before he was fatally injured.

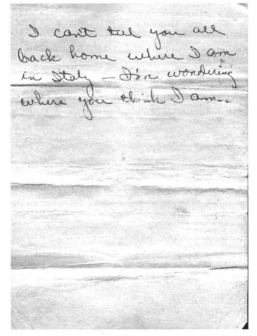

I can't tell you all back home where I am in Italy - I'm wondering where you think I am...

Page 3 of letter Lt. Reid Parks wrote to his folks the day before he was fatally injured. (Ruth Parks)

IN GRATEFUL MEMORY OF

First Lieutenant Reid G. Parks, A.S.No. 0-827934,

WHO DIED IN THE SERVICE OF HIS COUNTRY AT

in the Mediterranean Area, February 17, 1945.

HE STANDS IN THE UNBROKEN LINE OF PATRIOTS WHO HAVE DARED TO DIE

THAT FREEDOM MIGHT LIVE, AND GROW, AND INCREASE ITS BLESSINGS.

FREEDOM LIVES, AND THROUGH IT, HE LIVES—

IN A WAY THAT HUMBLES THE UNDERTAKINGS OF MOST MEN

Franklin D Roosevelt

PRESIDENT OF THE UNITED STATES OF AMERICA

President Franklin Roosevelt's letter to Reid Parks' family. (Ruth Parks)

Lt. Reid Parks' Purple Heart citation. (Ruth Parks)

SEVEN
CHURCH ACTIVITIES:
PREACHING, PRAYING, SINGING
AND EATING

The church held a central position in our lives, being the place where we worshipped and experienced much of our social life. Baptism rites involved head sprinkling for some congregations and total immersion for others, and the type of communion drink varied from church to church. For the most part, however, Sundays meant not working and going to church. Not much took place around the church during the week, because farm families worked from daylight to dusk and the trip to church and back would have consumed too much time. Also, several churches shared the same minister, making it impossible for him to meet with each congregation two or more times a week. Parishioners who failed to appear were referred to as "backsliders."

Getting to and from church could be a chore. In the decade of the '20s, and to some extent in the '30s, families often relied on the horse and buggy and mules and wagons for transportation. In the early '20s, churchgoers would marvel at the large number of horses and mules tied to wagons and buggies standing quietly in the church yard as if they were participating in the service.

During the World War II, the scarcity of gasoline forced either restricted driving or even giving up the automobile entirely. Many neighbors and friends shared rides in order to get to church. I remember very well we routinely stopped on our way to give an uncle, aunt and/or cousin a lift. It was a common practice in those days, something people were very willing to do, a virtuous deed.

One uncle loved to talk almost incessantly. On the way home when we stopped in his driveway to let him out of the car, he would continue talking with one foot on the running board and his head practically in the car window. The challenge for the driver was to ease the car forward slowly and gently in order to dislodge him from the running board without causing him to fall or crush his foot beneath the tires. As we drove away slowly, he would always invite us in, saying the "madam," our aunt, has prepared something for Sunday "dinner." It was an invitation we would politely decline. Rural folks called the midday meal "dinner" and the evening meal "supper." The term lunch was reserved for what was eaten at noon at school from a brown paper bag or in the cafeteria.

A Sunday at church consisted of two major events, Sunday school followed by worship service. On occasion, the two occurred in reverse order. Together, both activities usually lasted slightly less than two and one-half hours. "Sunday school" meant precisely what it said, a school for the study of the Biblical scriptures as they related to the events of everyday life. Classes were divided and named according to age and / or gender—Old Men's Class, Young Men's Class, Senior Class, Junior Class, Old Women's Class, Young Couples' Class, Young Ladies' Class, Primary Children's Class, Cradle Roll, etc. Such arbitrary distinctions of age created reluctance on the part of many to move from the "young" to the "old" classes.

Teachers were selected by the Sunday school superintendent from the church roll, and they assumed their tasks without special training. The treasurer received and counted the class offerings, and a secretary kept records of class attendance. Teachers leaned on what they had learned from years of attending Sunday school themselves, supplemented by what they could glean from the Bible and quarterly study materials. Many oil lamps or electric light bulbs burned late on Saturday night in the rural homes of central Davidson County as teachers prepared lessons for Sunday morning.

Each class member was expected to contribute a monetary offering no matter how small, even the children just old enough to hold a coin in their tiny hands. Parents would make sure each child had at least a penny, or brownie as our grandparents called them. This taught us the importance of giving, and it is more blessed to give than to receive. For years, even well into adulthood, a feeling of guilt would creep into my being if an offering plate were passed in front of me and I had nothing to contribute. Following the class period, all Sunday school attendees as a group would reassemble in the church sanctuary for a few minutes to hear a reading by the secretary of the attendance count and money collected in each class.

Sunday school teachers, both male and female, were special people; they worked hard in teaching us the contents of the Bible, often requiring the younger students to memorize scripture verses. Class periods often began by the teacher asking each student to quote a verse learned during the previous week, which often provoked anxiety and nervousness. Lucky was the student who was asked first to say a verse, because each student knew at least the shortest in the Bible, "Jesus wept." What followed could have been anything. One Sunday during the inquiry, the first student answered, "Jesus wept," passing the test, while the second, totally lost and paying only half attention, responded "Moses crept," a reply that left the class in stitches and the teacher speechless.

Teachers of the teenage and pre-teen classes usually organized one or two socials per year consisting of ice cream parties, weenie (wiener) roasts, and ball games or going swimming, the latter usually reserved for the all-male groups. Swimming in a creek evoked a finicky feeling for most girls, squeamish at the prospects of stepping on a tadpole or a crawfish. Having access to a backyard pool was out of the question; country folks would never consider such a luxury even if they could afford one. A local creek became the only alternative. The teacher, a male adult, would lead the boys to a site in the creek where the water was deep enough to swim but not deep enough to be considered dangerous.

Each boy brought along his bathing suit that consisted of absolutely no threads at all. Going skinny dipping meant the hastily removed clothes were scattered all along the bank of the creek, some lying on the ground and others hanging on tree limbs and bushes. On one such outing, while splashing and laughing in the creek, we boys thought we heard someone approaching. Not waiting to verify our suspicions, we immediately scampered up the muddy creek bank, putting on clothes with abandon and not taking time to notice if the clothes selected belonged to the right person. Mismatches of all descriptions resulted, with smaller boys putting on the larger-sized clothes and larger boys tugging feverishly to get into the smaller fits. Luckily, no intruder appeared, but the teacher consumed much of the remainder of the afternoon sorting out the wardrobes. Very few experiences ever matched that of a Sunday school class skinny dipping.

Ice cream socials and wiener roasts were the norm for mixed classes of boys and girls. The teacher usually made most of the plans; all the members of the class had to do was show up. Ice cream was prepared in a hand-cranked freezer on the spot, with the teacher recruiting help from the stronger boys when the crank turning became difficult. Enlisting volunteers for this duty presented no problem, since most young boys wanted to demonstrate their machismo, particularly when they hoped to catch the eye of a particular girl.

Roasting a wiener or hot dog properly required a certain amount of skill. Basic necessities included a stick about four to five feet in length to be used as a roasting instrument and a good bed of hot wood coals. Branches from a dogwood tree made excellent roasting sticks because they were strong usually forked, allowing two hot dogs to be roasted at once. As can be imagined, boys and girls approached the bed of hot coals with caution, especially when barefoot.

The wieners would be held over the coals and turned from time to time to make certain they were roasted on all sides. Catastrophe occurred during the process when hotdogs not properly affixed on the stick came loose and fell into the hot coals. All was not lost if they could be retrieved, but a coating of ashes on burned meat altered the taste considerably. Teenagers showed no concern about such mishaps because a heaping dollop of mustard helped the hotdogs go down, and food was too scarce to waste. Young people always possessed the appetite of a growing horse, and on a picnic every food morsel found its way into the stomach.

An "intermission" usually separated Sunday school and worship service, which afforded several options for the congregation: going outside for a smoke or to discuss any range of topics; visiting the toilet facilities; getting a drink of water from the church spring down the hill; or crawling into the car and sneaking away before the worship service, an act frowned upon by most adults.

Two outdoor toilet facilities were provided, one for women and one for men. At Beck's Evangelical and Reformed church, an additional option existed for the men and boys in the form of a giant oak tree located some distance from the church building across the road, down by the spring and up a hill. The path to the tree remained worn by the footsteps of men and boys of all ages as they made their way back and forth to relieve their bladders on the obscured side of the sturdy old oak tree.

A few minutes before eleven, the minister or some adult would pull the rope of the church bell signaling it was time to reassemble for "worship service." Children especially were fascinated by the bell rope, and occasionally the adult would let a child pull it, which required both of his or her small hands. In a format that remained unchanged for years, the service consisted of hymn singing by the choir and congregation and preaching by the minister, often concluded with attempts at soul-saving. This traditional template was advantageous because church bulletins showing the order of a service had yet to be invented. Church leaders felt services should be guided by the Holy Spirit, and most congregations liked to follow the same routine Sunday after Sunday. Woe be it unto the minister who attempted to invoke change. By eleven, most members of the congregation had usually settled in their pews, women sitting on one side of the church and men on the other. The youngest children sat with their mothers who also held their babies in their arms. Boys at a certain age, around nine or ten, would leave their mother's side to sit proudly with their fathers, another rite of passage to becoming an adult. Teenagers had their special pews and more or less sat together provided they behaved.

Service usually opened with a hymn led by the choir and accompanied on the piano by one of the women from the congregation. Favorite hymns included "The Church in the Wildwood," perhaps a description of the church itself being located in a grove of trees near a heavily wooded area, "Love Lifted Me," "Blessed Assurance," "Jesus Is Calling," "This Is My Father's World," "Rock of Ages," "Where You Never Grow Old," and others. During warm spring mornings especially, our spirits would be lifted by singing "In the Garden." Whatever the hymn, most carried a message of promise, beauty, rest and plenty in the hereafter. Hard-working folks of modest means yearned for better days, free from the drudgery and heartaches that often existed on North Carolina Piedmont farms.

The minister would make a few announcements and lead the congregation in reading in unison a passage of scripture found in the back of the hymnal. Sometimes the reading would be responsive, with the minister reading what was printed in black and the congregation reading the lines printed in red or vice versa. Another hymn was usually sung followed by the congregation reciting the Apostles' Creed.

Next came the taking of the collection or offering as adult men moved through the congregation with large wooden plates in which the crumpled bills and change were placed. From time to time, two young male teenagers would participate in the receiving of the collection as each of them passed a smaller container made of a stiff fabric among a portion of the congregation. I suppose this was a type of apprenticeship preparing the youngsters for the time when they would become adults and be elected to serve the church in a much broader role. As the offering takers walked down the aisles to the front of the church and placed the collection plates on the altar, the congregation would sing, "Praise God from Whom All Blessings Flow," and the minister would offer a short prayer of thanks for the gifts.

The minister would again read scripture and deliver a rather lengthy, passionate prayer to prepare the listeners for the sermon, which usually dealt with the trials and tribulations of the day and formed the heart of the service. His topics usually focused on current issues, matched as best he could with appropriate scriptures. Lamentations about the Depression, the war, tragedies, good things happening to upright people and sin came up frequently for a thorough airing. He would also pray for his church family: the safety of those away from home, the sick, the ones less blessed than the members of the congregation, for those straying from God, and those facing uphill personal and family battles. Since almost everybody farmed or was affected by farming, he would petition the Lord for good weather so crops might yield an abundant harvest. Regardless of what he said in his prayers, he never, not ever, missed the opportunity to make those who had fallen from grace squirm in their seats.

The minister usually started his sermon around 11:40 with the objective of finishing by noon, and the congregation supported him on this point. However, it seemed he seldom reached his finishing lines by noon. The preacher had a habit of placing his gold pocket watch face-up on the podium in easy view and as a signal to the congregation that he would not go overtime. In fact, the members of his flock saw the placing of his watch on the podium as a completely useless gesture. When he preached beyond twelve noon, some of the adult men would begin to sneak a peek at their pocket watches if they had one, and a few young people would sometimes scoot down in their pews as if in protest. If the preacher ever noticed the stirring, he never responded. For those ministers who had the habit of preaching too long, members of the congregation could be heard saying afterward, "No souls are saved after twelve o'clock," or "That fellow stopped preaching and went to meddling."

Closing the service with a final prayer, the minister would issue an invitation to join the church, wait a few minutes and walk toward the church exit as the choir and members would sing the last verse of the closing hymn. My memory on this point may be fuzzy, but it seemed as if the congregational singing showed more exuberance on the final stanzas than it did earlier in the service. My older cousins always said this was an expression of relief in getting through another service. By this time the minister had positioned himself at the main exit door to greet the members of the congregation, shaking hands and exchanging comments. All in all it had been a good morning, and everyone felt virtuous about being present for another sermon. For some reason, it seemed more important to be present for the sermon than to be moved by it.

During cold winter months, the congregation may have been even more virtuous. In the '20s, '30s and '40s, often the temperature of most churches was regulated by burning firewood. The main part of the sanctuary had a large wood circulator in the middle, and smaller wood heaters were placed strategically in other sections of the building. It became someone's duty to get to church early, build fires, and have it cozily warm and comfortable by the time the congregation arrived. When, for some reason, the person assigned to build fires shirked his duty, a cold building greeted disgruntled parishioners, which in extreme cold weather called for a rare cancellation of service that day.

After church, the families returned home for Sunday dinner, a welcome ritual since this was one day of the week when meat, usually pork, beef or chicken, might be found on the table. We may or may not have had meat on other days of the week, but on Sundays, meat was always there.

In summer months, the option of chicken offered the best possibility for something tasty and fresh because chickens were caught on the spot, then readied for cooking or frying. Beef and pork were best served in the winter during colder weather when the two meats could be kept fresh for longer periods of time.

Most families let their chickens run free in the yard where they scavenged for food among the grass and debris to add to the nightly handful of grain they usually received. Such a diet produced a meat with a distinctive flavor appreciated only by us who have tasted chicken from the rough. A rural housewife possessed a talent for frying freshly killed chicken to perfection using a heavy iron skillet greased with pork lard. Before the chicken meat was placed in the heated frying pan, it would be rolled in flour, and what was placed before you on the table soothed the palate unimaginably. Combine pan-fried chicken with fresh summer vegetables and a few buttermilk biscuits, and a little piece of heaven was ours for the taking, especially if the meal ended with a piece of chocolate or coconut cake. The Sunday dinner was a tradition at its best, and in a sense it was really an extension of the church service, particularly when the minister joined the family.

Most churches conducted an array of special activities such as a Christmas exercise, vacation Bible school, youth fellowship, homecoming and revivals. Each of them held a special importance, but none as much as the revival, usually held at night near the end of the summer when temperatures rose to uncomfortable levels. Small-grain threshing was over and row crops had reached maturity and were "laid-by" waiting for their harvest a few weeks later. A laid-by crop no longer required cultivation or hoeing, and farm implements were set aside for the next growing season.

As summer days shortened, churches that were not yet served by electricity lines from town required other forms of lighting. Candles and oil lamps played a big role in the very early days, but by the '30s, generators turned by gasoline engines offered a significant improvement. The generator in our church was manufactured by the Delco Company—we referred to it simply as "the Delco"—and produced sufficient wattage to burn several light bulbs hanging on cords from the ceiling, enough light for the congregation to read and the minister to see his notes. The Delco lacked reliability especially during summer thunderstorms when light bulbs would flicker and fade often into total darkness.

A few candles would come to the rescue, and a "jack-of-all-trades" member of the church would usually save the service by getting the Delco going again. Of course, church windows were held wide open by props to allow the cool evening air to blow across the members of the congregation. If this natural air conditioning did not remove the sweat beads from foreheads, parishioners would use a hand-held funeral home fan to take up the slack. Often, the light bulbs would attract a number of "candle flippers" through the open windows; these moths became serious distractions.

A revival usually lasted one week. An invited preacher from another church, perhaps some distance away, would lead the main part of the service amid stepped-up preaching, praying and singing. Rafters in the country churches would reverberate from loud, fervent messages delivered from the pulpit and exuberant, high-volume singing. Rural folks who worked daily in the fields had strong lungs. Having another crop in its final stages was reason enough to sing without inhibition. By the end of the week, the visiting minister would rejoice if new members were added to the church rolls. He had accomplished one of his missions, to save the souls of backsliders while adding a few members to the church roll. Another goal was to rejuvenate the spiritual soul of the members, ridding them of committed sins, and the hot August nights naturally helped them sweat them it out.

Teenagers watched very carefully to see if any of their peers walked down front to let the preacher know they were ready to join the church. I never knew how others felt about this very personal experience, but was relieved when finding the courage to do it. If the Holy Spirit yanked me to the front, I never felt it. I went under my own power, wobbly legs and all.

An anticipated part of revival meetings was dinner on the grounds, held after the conclusion of the Sunday morning sermon. Before it was served, the congregation walked to the cemetery a few hundred feet away for prayer and a few brief comments. We stood solemnly looking across the tombstones as we sang two hymns, "Shall We Gather at the River" and "When the Roll Is Called up Yonder."

Dinner on the grounds was a sumptuous meal prepared by the ladies of the congregation and brought to the church in cloth-covered baskets. Food was held there until the morning service was over then carried to tables set up outdoors under the thickest shade available in the churchyard. Everyone in the church knew a feast awaited them, and at times churchgoers especially the young folks—were certain that the preacher spoke too long on purpose that day in a futile attempt to rid us of the sin of temptation.

Dishes were set out on long tables temporarily fashioned from boards and sawhorses or "bucks" as we called them. An enticing aroma met the diner who approached the table with an empty plate. What a sight to behold: dishes of fried chicken, cured ham, and barbecue; plates of deviled eggs and sliced to-matoes; bowls of potato salad, cabbage slaw, sourdough biscuits, corn bread, chicken pies, sauerkraut, pickles, and vegetables of all kinds; and desserts, in-cluding banana pudding, and cakes and pies of all descriptions. If there was ever a mouth-watering experience, this had to be it.

The tables literally creaked under the weight of the food. On one table sat large tubs with sweet lemonade and water cooled by blocks of ice, if available, readied by the men. Aluminum dippers hung next to the tubs for filling paper cups and drinking glasses. If a local supply of watermelons was available, they were heaped and ready for slicing.

At last, after what seemed as a much longer blessing than usual by the resi-dent preacher, it was time to eat. Adults went to the tables, first men, then women. Children went last. Plates were heaped with a selection of the delecta-ble choices available, which usually meant a quick search of the tables so noth-ing appetizing was missed. The big eaters went for second helpings, followed by one or two helpings of dessert. If the stomach still had space, a slice of wa-termelon sometimes brought this eating ritual to a close. Flies could be a con-stant nuisance, hovering too close and lighting on the food. Men would often break branches from nearby bushes to shoo them away momentarily, but it was an exercise in futility. All edible left-over food was returned to food baskets and carried home for supper.

One additional church event, homecoming, also called for dinner on the grounds. As the name implies, homecoming was a special day when former members of the church who had left the community were encouraged to return in order to renew old bonds and rekindle old memories. This tradition would often be given a second meaning by the minister when he spoke of that day when we would all meet in heaven for the final homecoming. The earthly homecoming was filled with excitement for everybody, especially when attendees had to travel a long distance or had been away for several years. Some members of the community had moved up North or out West to find better work opportunities, and the delight in seeing them became nearly overwhelming.

It was a day that focused on the family more than any other day of the year. Music was special with quartet singing and an extraordinary performance by the choir. An invited speaker lifted worshipers' spirits by reminiscing about the past and praising members of the congregation for their efforts in helping to raise good families.

A traditional dinner on the grounds filled a long dinner hour, and in the '20s, '30s, and early '40s, the congregation reassembled in the church for an afternoon service, which consisted of a short sermon by the regular minister and plenty of singing by invited quartets. The North State Quartet from town was a favorite of many congregations, and its members sang the fast-moving hymns such as "On My Way to Glory," "I've Got a Home in Glory," "I'll Fly Away," "Just a Closer Walk with Thee," and "Do Lord, Do Lord, Do Remember Me." The accompanying pianist touched the keys with gusto, and if the church congregation ever came close to "rocking," it happened when the quartets sang.

Vacation Bible schools always came with mixed emotions. We youngsters, especially the rough and tumble boys, never appreciated fully the value of taking a week of a precious summer vacation from regular school to be at church. Whoever invented Bible school must have loathed the sweaty toil of farm work. Bible school offered the fool-proof excuse to come out of the fields or get out of the home where the orders of the day included sweeping and scrubbing floors, washing and ironing and helping cook. Like public school, it required us to study and memorize selected sections of the scriptures and use arts and crafts to express what we were learning. We would go on a picnic at the end of each week. Even though some of us never took this special schoolwork too seriously, the "togetherness" of boys and girls, a kind of country social club for kids and pre-teenagers, outweighed the ordeal of going through rituals.

Youth Fellowship occurred on Sunday evenings when the minister led services aimed at older teenagers. To a great degree, the activity represented a transition into adulthood and the mainstream of the church body. At this point, young people discovered that church could be more than fun and excitement, but these two elements were major drawing cards.

Following a Bible reading and a short message from the minister or one of the teenagers, the group enjoyed singing and social activities and refreshments. A few of the older teenagers had already secured drivers' licenses, and they often served as a "busing service" if a parent's car was available, bringing members of the fellowship to the meeting. Bolder drivers might stretch parental rules by taking a more circuitous route on the way home. This was excitement at its best, since no teenager had the luxury of having his or her own car. A chance to take a joy ride with a load of peers defied description. Loud singing and chatter among the occupants were part of the routine, and luckily the daring drivers made it home safely. Members of Youth Fellowship contributed much to the life of the church serving as role models for the younger boys and girls and as leaders in church plays.

A Christmas Exercise or Christmas Pageant, usually held at least one evening before Christmas Eve, provided one of the most memorable moments of going to church. A family affair, the sanctuary was filled to capacity for this annual event, with anxious parents and grandparents and excited children beholding a re-enactment of the birth of Christ and singing Christmas carols. The re-enactment of the birth of Jesus had top billing; eyes opened wide and voices hushed as young thespians, children of the congregation, marched on stage.

One of the more mature girls played the role of Mary, and an appropriate male counterpart portrayed Joseph. Their entrance came first, and as far as I can remember, Mary never rode in on a donkey, as the scripture says. After Joseph said his part, the shepherds made their entrance dressed in home-made robes with a large piece of colored cloth wrapped around their heads and carrying shepherds' crooks appearing like the real thing. The choir often sang "While Shepherds Watched Their Flocks" at this point. The angels, dressed in white from head to toe, made their way down the aisle next, singing "It Came upon a Midnight Clear."

Finally, the three wise men from the East dressed like kings came on stage, and the choir would sing "We Three Kings." Each boy playing a king's part would say his part. "My name is Balthasar, and we followed the star to find our way to this lowly stable. I have gold as a gift for the Magi." The second king would announce himself as Gaspar offering frankincense to the Magi, and the third king introduced himself as Melchior bearing myrrh as his gift. Mary would receive the gifts, express thanks, and the audience would offer a sigh of relief that all children had performed with distinction, especially their own. The audience would sing "Joy to the World" with gusto, and the service came to a close. Sacks of treats containing tangerines and oranges, English walnuts,

Brazil nuts, and a smaller bag of chocolate drops were distributed to each person, whether infant or 80 years old, a tradition as old as the church itself.

Mothers Day had its own special traditions. Rosebuds were worn by the men and boys to honor their mothers. A red rose signified that the mother was still living, and a person with a white rose let you know the mother had passed away and gone to her reward.

On Easter, women and girls in the congregation broke out their finest—spring hats and dresses, shoes and handbags. The minister that day did his best to develop a sermon describing the meaning of the Crucifixion and Ascension. Without exception, I expect, each rural congregation on Easter Sunday sang "The Old Rugged Cross." At the end of the service, members of the congregation would get up from their pews and walk over to the cemetery for prayer and the singing of "Up from the Grave He Arose."

Rural churches looked for ways to raise additional funds to support church activities or to build new structures. During the Depression and World War II, people seldom dined outside the home because of the cost, but a chicken-pie supper at a church hut was usually affordable. Menus could vary, but usually chicken pie, chicken stew, cole slaw, custards and sweet ice tea comprised the list.

The event would be held on Saturday evenings at about 5:30, announced earlier in the local *Dispatch* as a public service. The women of the church prepared the food, and younger folks waited on the customers. At a dollar or two at a time, the church congregations gradually met special financial needs.

Money was also raised by sponsoring an occasional pig barbecue. The Young Men's Sunday school class at Beck's Reformed Church decided just after the war that this event would be an excellent way to increase the size of the church building fund. Various committees were formed to do the work necessary for a successful event. Early Saturday mornings, appointed members of the class plus Emmett Swing, a local man with barbecue skills, assembled behind Elwood Younts' store to cook the barbecue. Pit cooking, a technique common to Piedmont North Carolina, was the method of choice for doing the barbecuing. The men lit kindling, and soon the pile of hickory wood was ablaze, forming red-hot coals placed with a shovel in the pit under fresh pork shoulders. In short order, cooks and bystanders could hear the pork slowly cooking as hot grease from the meat dripped on the burning coals, a sound like music to the ears. Blue smoke, stirred by puffs of wind, circled in the air, another signal that success was near. A large piece of thick cardboard from Elwood's store covered the several shoulders, and from time to time, Emmett would lift up the cover to apply a prepared sauce to the meat, giving it a special taste. Mouths began watering as thoughts turned to how the barbecue would taste when served at the church hut that evening.

During one lifting of the cardboard cover, the pork shoulders, now extremely hot, caught fire and the smoke turned from blue to black. Prospects of doom looked certain. Emmett yelled for water to extinguish the fire; members of the class, in panic, searched for a bucket. One member of the class spied such at a nearby faucet, grabbed it and without looking at the contents closely, dashed everything on the burning pork. As the fire subsided and the steam and smoke cleared away, observers saw pieces of tomato and potato peels, lemon slices, and a few soggy biscuits scattered across the meat.

No question about it, the bucket contained water but also Thelma Younts' table scraps to be fed to the hogs the next morning. Emmett, without saying a word, found clear water and carefully cleaned each shoulder, cooked them another hour, and sent them to the church hut. The young men, in contemplative silence, cut the meat into servings for the customers with many of them remarking it had to be the best barbecue ever eaten.

Money was added to the building fund, and this occasion may have been the origin of the saying, "What you don't know won't hurt you."

Dinner on the Grounds at the Junior Order Orphanage. (Davidson County Historical Museum)

A rural Colored church. (Library of Congress, FSA-OWI photo collection–LC-USF 34-056039)

(*Above*) A combined summer Bible school between Beck's Lutheran and Beck's Evangelical and Reformed churches. (Family collection)

(*Facing page*) Children portraying the shepherds described in the biblical story of the birth of Christ at a Christmas exercise. (Davidson County Historical Museum)

The North State Quartet presenting a program aired over WBUY, a local radio station. The Quartet often sang at revivals at churches all over the county. (Davidson County Historical Museum)

Young adults in the early twenties leaving for a ride. (Family collection)

EIGHT
DOWN ON THE FARM
AND SAWMILLING

Men living in rural areas labored hard to provide for families, and for most it meant doing farm and/or sawmill work. Other men worked in the furniture and textile factories, driving to and from Lexington or Thomasville each day. A few hundred dollars for a car and 10 cents per gallon for gasoline were tidy sums for a factory worker earning as little as 15 to 25 cents an hour, and the answer to transportation needs was shared rides with each other. Another saving grace economically for families on limited budgets was having access to land for a vegetable garden and the space to keep a milk cow and a few hogs. More people lived in the rural countryside than lived within city limits because low farming efficiency, especially in the '20s, '30s and through World War II, required large farm populations for the nation to feed itself, and not enough jobs could be found in town.

Working Farm Animals

Animal power was used on practically all farms in the South, which meant young men and boys learned to work with livestock at an early age. By trial and error, they mastered the art of holding the handles of a cultivator and guiding the horse or mule between rows of crops in the fields or vegetables in the garden.

My plowing career with a walking cultivator began when I was about 10 years old, like other farm boys in the region. Dad had fashioned a cultivator with a wooden beam rather than the heavy steel of factory-made cultivators, making it lighter in weight. One morning as I walked to the barn, I noticed Dad had harnessed and hitched a mule to the wooden-beam cultivator, signaling that a rite of passage had come. We went to a field beside the house where corn no taller than 12 inches grew in rows about 40 inches wide filled with plenty of young weeds and grass. Even though I had observed Dad and my older brothers handle a cultivator, suddenly a pit formed in my stomach as I was told to take hold of the two handles. The rear end of the mule seemed as tall and wide as the Farmer's Hardware building up town, but Dad showed no hesitation as he gave the mule the signal to start walking. Off we went, Dad holding the lines to the mule in his hands and I with the cultivator handles. Rather than staying between the rows of corn, the cultivator veered first to the right, plowing out about a dozen stalks of corn, and then to the left, up-rooting another dozen from the row on the left. The old adage of "things are never as easy as they seem," was learned in a hurry. Finally, with Dad's help, the cultivator was steadied, and we made it to the end of the corn row, which seemed like a mile, when in reality the distance was probably no more than 300 feet. Dad instructed me to lift the cultivator around as he pulled on the lines guiding the mule between the next two rows. Giving the mule "get-up" instructions, back to the other end of the field we went, plowing out no more than six or eight stalks of corn this passage, but covering many of the shorter stalks with soil. "Not good enough," Dad said. He reversed the mule, heading it again between two more rows, and I knew I had to lift the cultivator quickly as the mule turned without Dad's prodding. Away we went again, repeating the same plowing pattern four of five more times until the cultivator was at my command, plowing out the weeds and staying six to eight inches from the rows of corn.

Without saying a word, Dad placed the lines to the mule around my shoul-ders and told me to finish cultivating the field. Slowly and cautiously, the re-mainder of the field, about one-half of an acre, was cultivated, and luckily, less than a dozen additional stalks of corn met their fate in the process. Even though I was no more than a rookie at handling a cultivator, the first lesson had been passed. For the next two or three years, the wooden-beam cultivator belonged to me, and I got first choice of the gentlest mule on the farm.

After learning the art of handling a cultivator, boys soon graduated to a team of mules or horses and a walking turning plow. If the moisture in the soil was right and the team well-disciplined—two big ifs—the plowing went well. The plow would glide through the soil eight to ten inches deep, and the soil would spill over the moldboard, turning itself bottom-side up. Surface debris disappeared under the turned soil and eventually rotted away. Among all the kinds of work that farming required, I never found any task that provided com-plete contentment, but if there was one, breaking land had to be it. The unique aroma of freshly turned soil could be pleasant, unlike any other smell; and the smooth, steady sound generated by the steel plow point and moldboard, as they made their way through the soil, reassured its operator that something important was being accomplished. He could look back with pride at the fur-rows and ridges of turned soil that often took on a shiny glimmering look es-pecially in the late evening sun.

Breaking land could also be one of the worst jobs on the farm when plow-ing a new ground, one that had been cleared of trees for only a few years. Sud-denly, without warning, the plow would hit a stump just below the soil surface and stop the team and its operator dead in their tracks. The operator's teeth rattled, his stomach hit the plow handles, and the team was jerked almost to unconsciousness. Using all strength available, he struggled and struggled to extract the plow point from the underground stump and resumed plowing.

Another dreaded experience occurred when the plow turned up a bumble bee or yellow jackets' nest below the soil surface. These insects possessed a sting strong enough to inflict painful discomfort to both the operator and the team. With luck, if the insects' wrath were avoided, the operator halted the plowing and destroyed the nest by torching it with a covering of flaming dead plant residue.

Sometimes working a team of mules or horses took a lad away from the farmhouse from sunup to sundown, which meant carrying an ample supply of water to quench his thirst and a sack of food for lunch. For most farm boys, such a day was a treasured experience. The team felt the independence and so did the boys, knowing the day belonged to them and the team. Throughout the day, it was the team and a boy plowing, stopping to rest or take a drink of water. By midmorning, the water had lost much of its desired coolness, even though the boy placed the jug in the shade of the wagon pulled to the field. If a clear stream ran nearby, the boy would use a bucket to get a drink for his tired animals. Lunch break never came too soon, and when it did, the boy eagerly ate the lunch his mother had prepared and washed it down with the slightly tepid water. Although the day passed according to an understood work plan, it was always an unusual day. When the hour came to return to the house, accomplishments for the day were all theirs.

The boy had plenty of time for thinking about his world and what it might hold for his future. Background music was free; not stereophonic, but an off-key chorus of insects swarming around the animals, June bugs buzzing overhead and grasshoppers fluttering underfoot. The hotter the day, the louder the music insects produced. There was little else to distract the boy. He wanted to complete his job and please his father.

Farm families were large with as many as 10 children or more, and they became a part of a labor team mastering chores that needed to be done. Fathers took their sons to the fields and woods as soon as they were big enough to help with the planting, hoeing, cultivating and harvesting of crops or the cutting and sawing of timber. Mothers would teach their daughters the many facets of housework and child-rearing and the intricacies of cooking and preserving foods. Children observed parents struggling almost relentlessly from dawn to dark to make a better living for their family, and developed lasting impressions.

Nothing compares to waking up in a rural home when the sun has yet to break the darkness. Families arose early, and the largest part of the morning chores were finished without full daylight, allowing a head start on the rest of the day. The main tools of a person were his or her hands, so it was important to make every daylight hour count. During summer months especially, welcome and cool morning breezes came out to greet you, and the mournful call of a dove heard from the edge of the woods nearby told of the wonders of nature. Other noises pervading the air possessed special meanings. The buzzing of bumble and honey bees going from flower to flower collecting their nectar let us know that all creatures take seriously the dawning of a new day. The stirring of animals in their stalls signaled their readiness to receive morning portions of grain and hay. On the farm when the roosters crowed, the night had ended.

Buying and Breaking Mules

Horses and mules provided the power needed for heavy work on most farms in the communities at least until World War II. Rural North Carolina and the South lagged behind much of the rest of the nation in the purchase of tractors. At the beginning of the Depression years, other sections of the country owned more than four times as many tractors as did the South. Dad purchased a used tractor, a Farmall H, from a family near Denton close to the end of the war, but prior to that time, we looked totally to horses and mules to get jobs done.

Even after the tractor was bought, we kept mules and horses. Neither animal came into this world prepared to work, and their aversions to pulling a plow or a piece of machinery had to be cleared from their minds. Horses could be taught working habits with patience and proper training by letting them work beside an experienced horse, but for mules the situation was entirely different whether raised on the farm or bought from a mule trading company.

We raised a mule or two by breeding our mare horses to a jackass, but ordinarily we went to Richfield in Stanley County to make purchases from a mule trader. Due to the importance that mules played in farming at this time, the biggest man in the area was the mule trader, and his barn and auction arena was the center of trading activity. There were two people in the business, Charlie Misenheimer and Dave Casper. As far as I can remember, we traded only with Misenheimer, who had a big barn for the mules between the highway and the railroad in the middle of Richfield. He shipped in a lot of mules from the Midwest, probably from Missouri, by rail and unloaded them down inclined chutes into barns and lots where they were held until a sale day. Notices of the sales were carried in our local newspaper.

On sale day, Mr. Misenheimer displayed the animals for full view in the lots, and each mule was sold at auction. Dad had a good eye for mules, and he knew a bargain when he saw one. He always made a purchase unless none of the mules looked healthy. When the mule arrived at home, he or she would be placed in a stable where the training began. For about two weeks, the mule was given oats, corn and hay and gently rubbed and patted to develop a kinship between owner and animal. The next step in the training process was to put on a bridle and bit a couple of times a day which was accomplished easy enough. In a few days, Dad dared lead the mule from the stable for short walks around the barnyard, stopping from time to time to rub his neck and sides if allowed. Next came putting on a set of harness beginning with collar followed by the hames and attached trace chains. This task was not accomplished without resistance from the mule. In a few days, the animal felt comfortable with the changing scene. It was definitely a case of mule versus man, and neither would give up much.

Dad announced one morning that the time had arrived to put the mule to the test of pulling a cultivator. Dad knew it was a risky step, but it had to be done if the investment in the mule was to be worth anything. After harnessing the mule, he brought her to the corn patch beside the house for the cultivator test. Attaching the trace chains to the single tree took some effort, but Dad did it.

When Dad took the lines in his hands and gave the signal to start, the mule started jumping and pulled Dad and the cultivator in a complete circle at least three times, devastating the corn patch. The mule wanted no part of pulling a cultivator and was determined to free herself from it. Dad, seeing that the breaking process was far from over, went to the woods nearby and cut himself a piece of sapling about two inches in diameter and four feet long. He unhitched the mule and with the sapling in hand, he walked in front of the mule, grabbed the reins, and proceeded to hit her across the nose repeatedly. Dad would swing the piece of sapling, and the mule would rebel, stepping backwards. Dad held onto the rein never missing an opportunity to lay the sapling across her nose with authority.

Little by little, the mule succumbed to the hard lick, and finally stood still. Dad knew the breaking process was complete, and the phrase, "stubborn as a Missouri mule," had been verified. He wiped the sweat from his face and brow, laid down what was left of the piece of sapling, re-hitched the mule to the cultivator, and cultivated what was left of the field of corn with a willing mule. From that day forward, the mule never rebelled again, and Dad kept her as one of his most trusted animals for several years.

Runaway Horses and Mules

Horses and I had difficulty communicating with understanding. We worked well together when breaking land or driving a hay wagon, but in times of crisis, my command of horses left much to be desired. One day Dad and I were forking manure from a stable into the bed of a wagon to which two horses were hitched. They remained calm while listening to Dad's voice, and everything was proceeding without promise of incident. However, a man from the other side of the county who purchased young pigs from us regularly drove up in his brand new Plymouth. He had come to buy a couple of six-week-old pigs to fatten. Dad asked me to mount the wagon, sit on the seat board, and hold the horses' lines so they would not run away. He left to negotiate the sale, and when the deal was about closed, the horses became excited by horseflies and began to stomp their feet and shake their heads. In the calmest voice I could conjure, I tried to assure the horses that everything was fine and admonish them to hold still. Without warning, they lurched forward and started to run. My pulling on the lines made no difference. Around the upper side of the barn they ran, with the wagon trailing behind. I abandoned the wagon about the time it hit the front of the visitor's Plymouth smashing the right fender knocking out the headlight.

Their run was not over. They were headed downhill toward the milk barn at full speed, too fast to miss the corner of the barn, removing a good chunk of the brick foundation. A brother of mine emptying feed sacks in the milk barn thought the end of time had come. On the horses sped, splintering the pasture gate at the bottom of the hill and making a circle or two in the pasture before the coupling pin and pole dislodged from the wagon, which lost its rear wheels. The rear end of the wagon started dragging the ground, bringing the escapade to a quick halt.

By this time Mom had heard the commotion, had come out of the house, and begged Dad not to kill me. He saw no humor in it at all. He paid the owner of the Plymouth a few dollars to get it repaired and threw in a couple of pigs as well. This was not my finest day. I would have just as soon forgotten about farming altogether.

The saying of what goes around comes around has been verified time and again. About a month after the horses ran away with me, Mom and I were sitting under a large oak tree in the backyard shucking fresh corn for canning when we heard Dad coming home earlier than usual from the field. He was singing. He had left right after dinner with his team of mules hitched to the mowing machine saying he would be mowing a large field of lespedeza for hay.

Mom thought it odd, him coming in early and especially since he was singing. "I'll bet you he has done something wrong," she said. "He always sings when he's in the wrong,"—his way of begging for understanding, I supposed. He came into view, and based on the visible features of the mowing machine, wrong was an inadequate word to describe what had happened. Parts of the gear box of the mowing machine were obviously missing and the remainder was held together with bailing wire. When he saw us, he gave a loud WHOA and stopped the mules and began laughing. His story was interesting and refreshing to me since I had been victimized by a team of horses.

Apparently, while mowing in tall lespedeza, a rabbit bolted from its nest, and Dad could not resist a chase. He laid down the mule's lines, jumped off the mowing machine, and went after the rabbit. Sensing the machine was not being watched, the mules seized the opportunity to head for the barn and started running as fast as they could. Unfortunately, the mowing machine was still in gear and put to the test. Never had it been required to turn as fast, and it flew apart, cogs and all; he must have failed to catch the rabbit because we saw none. He continued laughing as he drove on toward the machine shed. Strange, I thought. Why did he not laugh when the horses ran away with me and the wagon load of manure?

Milk and Meat

Most rural families, even those who did not farm extensively, kept a milk cow or two and a few hogs to provide milk and meat for family consumption. The relatively simple chores of milking the cows and feeding the hogs commonly fell to the children; in this way they could contribute to the food needs of the family. Both were most likely done before breakfast, because the daily necessities of cows and hogs were best met on an early schedule.

Hardly a rural boy or girl made it to adulthood without having the responsibility for milking a cow on a regular basis. With pail in hand, he or she would walk through the morning darkness to the barn, pour a large tin cup or two of ground corn or wheat into a trough and watch the cows nose their way to the food. The "milker," sitting on a box or his or her haunches, would place the pail under a cow's udder from the right side and begin a gentle squeeze that yielded fresh, warm milk. The cow was not fooled by the attempt to distract her, but she was satisfied to allow the milker to fill the pail.

The task of milking came twice a day, and the evening milking offered more of a challenge whether it be summer or winter. Flies would pester cows on hot days, and they would switch their tails to shoo them away. In the winter months, the barnyard had deep, soggy mud, and a wet and dirty cow's tail could be a terrible weapon against the milker. To avoid being harmed by the tail, it could be held behind the milker's knee by clamping down on it in a sitting position. The smell of warm milk, mixed with barnyard odors, is one a farm boy or girl never forgets.

In the late 1930s, Grade A milking barns came on the scene when a large milk processor, Coble Dairy, opened a plant in Lexington. Coble needed large quantities of raw farm milk every day. My family joined others in Davidson County in operating a Grade A dairy farm. Labor intensive, Grade A farms required milkers to handle as many as 10 cows each morning and night. The chore of milking moved from the stable in the barn to a concrete-floor milk barn constructed to hold five or more cows at a time. This larger quantity of milk was placed immediately in refrigerated boxes to obtain a quick cooling. Later it would be transported to Coble Dairy and sold. Dad ran a milk route picking up five-, eight- and ten-gallon cans of milk from farms all over the northern part of Davidson County. As we boys became old enough to drive the truck and handle the larger cans, we also ran the route, and Dad stayed home to farm. Despite strict cleanliness standards, we had no idea how the milk was being handled on the farm and how much "cow" dirt was being hauled to Coble's each day.

My family owned one of the smaller Grade A farms, with some 20 milk cows. Anyone who has ever milked a cow by hand knows that on rare occasions, the cow will lift her back foot and place it squarely on the milk pail. City buddies often wondered how we disposed of the milk after this had happened. "Did you feed it to the hogs?" they might ask. My tongue-in-cheek reply was usually, "We did not dispose of it at all. We strained the milk to remove the barn lot debris, and if we did not get it clean the first time, we would strain it again."

The task of feeding the hogs had fewer challenges, but many farmers saw to it that feed of some type was provided twice a day. Housewives contributed to meeting hog feed needs by disposing of table wastes in a slop bucket usually kept on the pantry floor next to the kitchen. The person responsible for feeding the hogs would take the slop bucket from the pantry each morning, go by a feed bin in the barn, and add a few scoops of wheat bran. After stirring the mixture with a slop paddle, it would be poured into a trough as a gastronomical delight for the hogs. In the evening, the feed usually consisted of whole ears of corn, sometimes shelled, or whole stalks of green corn cut from a nearby field with ears intact.

A story made the rounds about a dirty farmer in South Davidson County who tripped over a tree root while feeding the hogs and fell into the pen among the hogs. Quickly rising to his feet, he shouted, "Move over, I am as good as airy one of you."

Harvesting What We Grew

No word other than drudgery adequately describes plowing, planting, cultivating, hoeing and weeding; but harvesting, even though often equally laborious, lifted the spirit and brought on excitement. Harvesting meant time had arrived to evaluate how well crops had performed during the growing season. Would the farm family have enough to tide them and their animals over during the winter time? With help from a good growing season, there would be extra harvest to sell at local markets providing enough money to purchase a few basic family needs.

Rural families planted a vegetable garden and gathered vegetables as they matured throughout the summer months. They placed much of the tasty produce directly on the dining table; they cooked excess harvests and canned them in glass jars to be eaten during the coming winter. Housewives tended to the canning with help from family members who were not working in the fields, and the quantity and quality of canned food became a point of pride for the housewife. Sharing canning techniques and recipes among housewives was common practice. Occasionally, a special recipe gave a housewife an advantage, and she showed much reluctance in giving it even to her closest friends. A considerable number of recipes had been in families for years, brought to this country by ancestors. By the fall season, pantry shelves near the kitchen became laden with vegetables of all types, canned in quart and half-gallon Mason jars.

Every farmer planted a patch of watermelons, cantaloupes and muskmelons, or "mush" melons as we referred to them, mostly for family consumption. However, when the harvest was bountiful, neighbors, relatives and distant friends would be invited over for a melon feast. Melons were gathered and cooled overnight before being cut and eaten the next day. A hot, boiling sun in July or August would ruin a melon party if they were eaten directly from the patch. There seemed to be an art to cutting a watermelon into slices properly sized for holding in the hand and eating clean to the rind. Of course, the presence of numerous seeds among the flesh of the melon slowed the speed of eating, but a seasoned eater of watermelon had the ability to spit seeds in one direction and swallow in another. Seeds of cantaloupes and muskmelons formed in the center of the melon which was hollow and could be easily removed.

Rinds of watermelons and peels of cantaloupes and muskmelons made acceptable hog feed, but, since the rinds were mostly water, they were often tossed to the chickens. Peels always went to the hogs. Boys found another use for watermelon rinds. About the time the party ended, one of the older boys would on the sly catch a younger boy or girl and use the rind to wash his or her face. Being the fourth boy in the family, my face experienced such frivolity on several occasions, much to the delight of the adults present. Except for being the center of attention, it was something I would have just as soon missed. Another sport created with watermelon rinds, the making of mock false teeth, brought chuckles from onlookers. The rind nearest the outside skin became very firm and could be shaped by a skillful youngster. A piece of rind about three inches long, two inches wide, and one-eighth inch thick would be carefully cut down the middle lengthwise, then notched to take on the appearance of teeth. When carefully placed in the mouth, a prankster took on the look of a country "bumpkin," buck teeth and all.

Pumpkins, another vine crop, had a special place on the farm. After corn seeds had germinated, pumpkin seeds would be planted between the young plants. The corn-pumpkin relationship was very compatible, with the corn maturing slightly earlier than the pumpkins, and corn leaves allowing enough sunlight to get to the pumpkin vines. Pumpkins had two primary uses, making pies and jack-o-lanterns at Halloween.

Of all the foods on a dining table, pumpkin pie heads my preferred list without any question. My taste for pumpkin pie must have been developed when in diapers because I have no memory of the first time I ate it. However, my memory is very clear about walking as a toddler into the pumpkin patch impatiently waiting for them to ripen. Mom was in agreement with me on this issue because she savored the taste of pumpkin as well. We would watch the young fruit grow larger and larger and wonder if it would ever begin ripening. The path that had been beaten into the patch became more heavily traveled and easily identified. Finally, in late July or early August, a few yellowish stripes would start forming near the blossom end. Responding to the persuasion of a wistful child, Mom was convinced to bring the not-yet-completely ripened pumpkin into the kitchen. She peeled it, cut it into cubes, cooked it, and mixed it with eggs and milk and a few spices, pouring the mixture into a pie crust. I had no intentions of leaving the kitchen while the pie baked, and, after what seemed an eternity, the pie emerged from the oven—a bit yellow but nevertheless a pumpkin pie by definition. When it cooled, I ravenously consumed the first piece of pumpkin pie of the season followed by as much pie as Mom would allow. To this day, I would choose a green pumpkin pie over one made with ripe pumpkin. To me, using a pumpkin carved for a jack-o-lantern was a total waste of a precious food commodity.

Small grains such as wheat, oats, and barley reached maturity earlier in the season than other field crops. Harvesting occurred in two stages: cutting the plants with a reaper, a machine which tied them in bundles and left them on the ground to be placed in shocks for drying, and bringing the shocked bundles to a threshing machine to separate the grain from the straw and chaff. All of us youngsters on the farm looked forward to these two operations each year.

A mechanical grain reaper in operation would hold my attention as long as any other machine on the farm, probably because it had so many working parts. This was one of the great labor-saving devices. We learned in grammar school that the reaper was invented by Cyrus McCormick, and the ones that farmers owned in our communities bore the distinctive name, McCormick, visibly displayed. The external features were the cutting bar and guards, and reels to push the stalks of grain toward the cutting bar and onto a moving platform canvas which carried the stalks between two upward moving canvases forming a bundle some 15 to 20 inches in girth. The bundle was encircled by an arching needle threaded with a coarse hemp twine. Before the bundle was released by machine, the twine was grabbed by a revolving "knotter" that tied the twine in a knot, and a cutting blade severed the twine and released the tied bundle. Over and over this process took place until a field of grain lay in bundles ready for farm hands to put in shocks—a vertical grouping of bundles that stood like individual temples. The reaper was pulled by a team of mules or horses, usually three in number, because putting a reaper in forward motion demanded extra horsepower for efficient operation. A main wheel, the bow wheel in contact with the ground, drove all the moving parts. Maintaining a reaper in fine working condition for the entire harvest required patience and know-how.

The task of cutting a field of small grain usually contained a sporting element for the fleet-of-foot workers in the form of a rabbit chase or two. Rabbits found the density of plants in a small grain field to their liking for raising their young, and by harvest time, the young had grown to size desirable for human consumption. As the reaper continued to circle the outside borders of a field, the area of uncut plants became smaller and smaller, seriously disturbing the rabbits. Eventually, a rabbit would bolt from the small grain seeking cover elsewhere, creating a recreational opportunity for men and boys alike. The chase was on, up and down the rows of plant stubble, as the rabbit darted right and left trying to escape the onslaught of shouts and tossed stones that usually missed their mark. In due time, either the rabbit or the pursuers tired, and the chase ended. The effort was scarcely worth the outcome. Fewer bundles of grain were shocked, and the bare feet of the young boys stung, pierced by horse nettles and ached, bruised from stepping on the hard ground and rocks. Like most pursuits, the excitement of the chase outweighed the catch.

During the peak of small grain harvesting, extra hands would be needed for shocking the bundles. A man named Jakie liked shocking small grain, and he was hired by some of the farmers. Jakie often worked in a white dress shirt and suspenders. He loved to talk and joke with the teenagers. He once asked a teenage boy if he knew what a "yca-who" was. Not hearing an answer, Jakie said. "It's a gum boil on a goose's posterior."

Threshing of small grain took top billing in the yearly cycle of farm work. It was called "wheat threshing" even though other grains were threshed, but wheat was the "king of small grains" and earned the threshing title. Farm families banded together at wheat threshing time like no other occasion, a true example of a community effort. They looked forward to and enjoyed it despite the hard work and rigorous schedule. Of course, people visited with each other at church events, but the togetherness at wheat threshing time was unsurpassed.

Wheat threshing involved as many as a dozen families or more residing in close proximity in "threshing districts." The task lasted a period of at least three weeks moving from farm to farm until it was completed. In lower Davidson, there may have been as many as 10 or more "threshing districts." Formulas were not used to determine the extent of each district, but total acres of grain had to be the principal controlling factor. No maps existed showing the districts, but put on a large scale, the countryside would have looked like a jigsaw puzzle. An enterprising person owned a threshing machine in each district. He provided a service as well as helping to make a living for his family.

Each family in a district helped other families in proportion to the size of farms; farmers with large acreages sent more workers than did families with smaller farms. In our district, the farms lay along Beck's Church Road for about two miles with a few farms on the side roads. Threshing would start at one end of the village one year and the other end the next, and the process continued day after day except on Sunday. Rain could be a culprit interrupting the cycle, because grain had to be totally dry to be threshed and cleaned properly. Extended periods of rain put farm families in melancholy moods for fear the grains would germinate in the shocks. No one became happy until all grain had been threshed and put in sacks and bins.

Of all of the machines employed in farming, the threshing machine championed the rest because of its enormous size and the noise it made while operating. Threshing machines required a powerful tractor—a steam engine in earlier times—for them to operate properly. Emmitt Swing owned the machine in our community, and he powered it with a 15-30 McCormick-Deering tractor, which also pulled it from farm to farm. We counted on him to do the threshing, which he did for years. Farmers paid for his services by giving him a percentage, or toll, of the grain collected.

"Here comes Emmitt Swing and his threshing machine," the youngsters would shout as he, the tractor, and the trailing machine neared the farm. After being directed to the location for threshing selected by the farmer, Emmitt would uncouple the hitch between the tractor and the threshing machine and get ready to receive horse- or mule-drawn wagons loaded with bundles of small grain lifted from shocks in the field. The tractor was turned around strategically to face the threshing machine, and Emmitt rolled out a long, wide belt placing one end on a pulley on the tractor and the other on a pulley on the machine. Emmitt would put the tractor in reverse and tighten the belt. A crew of knowledgeable men assumed stations on and around the machine, and the scene was set to begin threshing.

Two wagons loaded with bundles of grain drew along either side of the machine. Workers on each wagon would begin to place bundles, one at a time, on platforms in front of teenage boys who used hooked knives to cut hemp string bands used to hold the bundles intact. The boys would shove the loosened grain to the left or right in front of the feeder, a man who fed it heads first into the machine's gaping mouth. Here the heads of grain met with a rapidly revolving drum in which steel spikes knocked the grains of wheat, oats or barley from the straw and the chaff.

Through the interior of the threshing machine the straw, chaff and grain moved on shakers to assure the grain had been totally separated. About midway alongside the bottom of the threshing machine, two men collected the clean kernels of grain, fed into a half-bushel measure by an auger. After each bucket was filled, it was slid from beneath the pouring stream of grain and replaced by another. A counter automatically tallied each half-bushel bucket filled. The buckets of grain were poured into sacks, each usually holding three measures, or one-and-a-half bushels. Filled sacks were grouped to avoid spillage and later placed on a wagon or truck to be hauled to the farmer's wheat house. Men handling the half-bushel buckets remained totally focused on the task to ensure that each kernel was saved and placed in a sack. In our community, Charlie Fritts handled buckets, and his son, Wade, held the sacks. I always marveled at the professionalism displayed by farmers in conducting what looked to be a rather menial chore. We learned that any task worth doing is worth doing well.

At the rear of the machine, through the blow pipe—a long telescoping pipe nearly two feet in diameter—straw was propelled by a large fan to form a huge stack. Air surrounding the straw stack would be filled with dust, depending on the direction of the wind, and could be a nuisance to the threshing crew. Emmitt had no crew of his own, like most threshing machine owners, and he depended on the assistance of eight or ten experienced workers from the farms involved. When I became old enough to follow the machine from farm to farm, I often stood on the platform receiving grain bundles as they came off the wagons, cutting the bands of twine and pushing them in front of the feeder. Farmers would often ask me to save the bands to be used for sack ties, meaning the cut had to be made next to the knot on the twine. From time to time the blow pipe at the rear of the machine needed a change in direction or elevation, and Emmitt would elevate my stature by asking me to handle the blow pipe. Both of these assignments were also rites of passage for a farm boy.

While workers were occupied with the threshing task, farm wives and daughters and women from the neighborhood busied themselves in the kitchen, preparing both dinner and supper fare each day for the entire group. The challenge was huge, as vast quantities of food were consumed by workers who ate in shifts—first the men of the threshing crew, next the older men handling the wagons and teams, and, finally, the younger boys. When men sat down to dine, they were greeted by an array of choices that included a meat dish, usually chicken pie or ham, and many types of vegetables, including cooked Irish potatoes, baked sweet potatoes, slaw, green beans, fresh tomatoes, corn cut from the cob, sliced cucumbers, beets and pickles. Biscuits, preserves, cakes and pies topped off the servings, and the workers quenched their thirst with iced tea, milk, lemonade, ice water or coffee.

The women waited on the table and passed the food to the diners who seldom put more than one item on their plates at a time. Occasionally, a guest would join the workers for the supper meal. I remember one guest, an uncle of mine who ran a dry cleaning establishment in town, who always put several food items on his plate at once. This departure from our norm attracted considerable attention in the kitchen among the women and became a topic of conversation among the field workers. Traditions lived for a long time among rural farm people and caught attention when broken.

Camaraderie developed among workers who banded together to thresh small grain. No one performed tasks alone, which created something special between neighbors, an interdependence of confidence and trust-building relationships that lasted for years. Respect developed between two persons handling a team and wagon fetching bundles of wheat, oats or barley from shocks in the fields and transporting them to the threshing machine. The task repeated itself many times each day, and the two workers developed mutual appreciation for their respective talents, learning which tasks each could perform. Such close-working associations, while lasting only two or three weeks each year, often formed strong bonds of friendships for life.

After wheat threshing was complete for all farmers, a decision had to be made about handling the straw stack. Some farmers restacked the straw around tall poles for safer keeping, and left it in the field to be used as needed for a feed supplement or stable litter. Other farmers preferred to have their straw baled, tied with wire, and stored in the barn loft. This removed the straw from the hazards of weather and ensured it would be easily accessible when needed.

Below Beck's Reformed Church in the community where the Millers, Parks, Sheets, Harveys, and others lived, Allison Miller threshed the wheat for the farmers. Initially, he powered the threshing machine with a large steam engine. The belt running from the steam engine to the threshing machine had to be extra long to maintain a safe distance between the heat and the dry bundles; yet, one day a fire broke out. In the 1920s, while Miller was threshing in a field near the Junior Orphanage Home, sparks from the steam engine set two wagon loads of wheat bundles on fire, destroying not only the wagons and the wheat but the threshing machine as well.

After the fire incident, a 15-30 McCormick-Deering powered his next threshing machine. When Allison Miller gave up the responsibility, a man from around Denton, and later Arthur Kepley and Edgar Rhodes threshed small grain for this group of farmers. Similar situations existed for farmers in the Holly Grove and Hedrick's Grove communities. Carl Smith threshed wheat for farmers in the Mount Tabor community.

Cutting and making hay for livestock ranked high on the list of farm drudg-eries, especially the loading, hauling and forking of cured hay onto a stack or into the storage barn. Farmers favored lespedeza for hay, and they would spread seed with a cyclone seeder on the soil surface in the small grain fields in early spring. The tiny seed nestled down into the rough soil surface and ger-minated with some growth by small grain cutting time. A few weeks after the grain was threshed, usually mid-August, the lespedeza plants were ready to be cut for hay, which the farmer accomplished with a mowing machine drawn by a team of mules or horses. The machine had a mechanically driven cutting bar of some 6–8 feet in length which glided along just above the soil surface as the team pulled the mower and operator around the field. When the machine performed well, it made a soothing sound as the cutting bar with blades moved back and forth across guards, mowing off the lespedeza plants.

Cut lespedeza plants lay in the field for a day or two for sun drying and cur-ing after which they were raked into piles or rows by using an animal-drawn hay rake. Workers with pitchforks shoved the rows into small shocks later to be loaded with the same pitchforks onto wagons and transported to hay barns or placed in large stacks near the field. Forking hay by hand into a barn loft is something a farm boy never forgets. The temperature under a tin roof in Au-gust could reach nearly unbearable scorching levels, and hay dust often caused serious breathing difficulties. A worker in the loft would suck it up, so to speak, to get the job done. Eyes would water and noses run, conveying a true under-standing of the meaning of hay fever.

As farm operations became mechanized in World War II, the job of forking loose hay into a loft disappeared with the advent of the tractor-powered hay baler, which compressed the hay into rectangular-shaped bales weighing 50–60 pounds. Bales were lifted with hand-held hooks into the loft and neatly stacked. Getting cured hay out of the fields was hastened considerably if first baled, and a compressed bale consumed much less loft space in storage.

Fields of corn were planted, cultivated, and harvested for livestock feed on practically every farm. Prior to the mid-1940s, all corn harvesting was done by hand. Some farmers harvested two parts of the corn plant, the ear and the por-tion of the cornstalk above the ear. The latter was done first as the corn plant reached maturity. The farmer would cut the cornstalk above the ear, strip the leaves and save them in shocks for livestock feed. After the remaining portion of the corn plants had matured and dried, he would hand-pull ears from the stalks, pitch them in piles between the rows, to be picked up and hauled in wagons to the barnyard and dumped in long piles for shucking.

Next to wheat threshing, a corn shucking involved the largest number of neighbors and friends. By word of mouth, an announcement went out that a corn shucking would be held in a certain farmer's barnyard and anyone interested in participating should come on the designated date and hour. The farmer and his wife guaranteed good fellowship and a hearty meal following the shucking.

Adults and children alike came with their stools and shucking pegs, if used. Workers established themselves at a spot along the side of the long pile of corn and started removing the husks from corn in front of them. Throughout the evening, social chatter filled the air as did shucked or husked ears of corn as they were tossed over the remaining unhusked pile. Removed husks or shucks were tossed or pushed behind the shuckers. The farmer and members of his family kept a plentiful supply of water available for quenching thirsts. As the crowd focused on it, the pile of corn diminished, one ear at a time. Eventually, the original pile of corn disappeared as if by magic, replaced by a trough of bare ground between a heaping of shucks and a neatly cleaned mound of corn ears.

The shuckers had done their job, and all the while the farmer's wife and a few helpers busied themselves in the farmhouse kitchen preparing a late-evening feast equal to or more than those prepared for threshing crews. Everyone proceeded to the house to be greeted by the housewife with aluminum basins filled with warm water for the shuckers to remove a heavy covering of corn dust from faces and hands. Husking corn develops hearty appetites, and the shuckers made the most of the food-laden table. No monetary compensation passed hands as all involved shared the reward—fellowship, food plus the warm feeling of helping a neighbor.

Farmers usually reserved space in a cornfield for planting several rows of cane sorghum, which matured in early fall. They cut stalks just above the ground, stripped them bare of leaves and removed the seed heads. Bare stalks were then loaded on a wagon and carried to a molasses mill. The mill my dad used was owned by Tice Swing who lived in the Holly Grove community some five or six miles from home. Traveling with mules and wagon to and from the mill, plus the making of molasses, required a sun up to sundown day. We had the mules hitched to the wagon by dawn, and by the time we arrived at the mill, Tice had built a fire under the molasses cooker or boiler and was ready for us to begin the chore of squeezing sap from the stalks of cane.

One of our mules was hitched between two long poles extending from two vertical pressure rollers that squeezed the stalks of cane as the mule walked in a continuous circle around the rotating rollers. Dad or I fed the stalks between the rollers, and soon sap began to flow into the cooker. In no time at all, steam began to rise, and as the sap made its way through a labyrinth of dividers, it formed a thick, dark green liquid. Tice would test it, and declare, "Molasses is being made." As long as Dad or I kept feeding the cane between the rollers, the cooking process continued, and finally some 10 to 15 gallon jugs were filled with molasses. Tice received a portion of the finished product for his services, and for many breakfasts in the coming winter, molasses could be found on the table. The taste was bitter-sweet, a delicacy to many but shunned by others. Some people referred to molasses as a poor family's corn syrup. Sorghum syrup or molasses occupied its place in jugs on every pantry shelf.

Sweet potatoes could be found on practically every family table in the region, especially in fall and winter. Climate and the sandier soils in central Davidson County were well-suited for sweet potato production, and if properly cured and stored, the potatoes remained edible for several months. Sweet potato plants pulled from propagation beds were set out in rows after the soil had warmed from the early summer sun. The young plants needed watering for two or three days to stimulate their growth, and after several weeks, a full crop of potato roots formed beneath the soil surface. With the skill of a surgeon, the farmer would use a furrow or turning plow to loosen the potatoes from their soil sockets, and youngsters and adults would pick them up in buckets and transfer them to sacks. The housewife saved a few of the "green" potatoes for immediate use, and the remainder was put in well-ventilated bins in a curing house. Uncle Roy Burkhart had a heated curing house, and he kept a few empty bins so others could dry their sweet potatoes. When drying was completed, we would bring the potatoes home and store them in a cool dry place. Oven-baked sweet potatoes were prepared whole for dinner on most winter days, and when we came home from school, we stopped first at the kitchen table to enjoy this culinary delicacy.

No family attempted to feed its members without having a small orchard of peach, apple, plum and/or pear trees to provide fresh fruit during summer and fall. Usually a trellised grapevine or two could also be found. During peak ripening season, more fruit would be available than could be eaten immediately. Surpluses did not go to waste; women canned them in glass Mason jars or smaller jelly and preserve containers to help tide the family over the winter. Peach trees of two varieties dominated the orchards—a white-meat one called Georgia Bell and a yellow-meat one called Elberta. In addition, an occasional clingstone and/or plum peach would have been planted.

Once picked from the trees, peaches over-ripened in four to six days, which usually meant surpluses had to be processed quickly for canning. The peels of peaches were cut away either by hand with a knife or a small mechanical peeler. Skilled hands repeated the peeling process, one fruit at a time, until the day's harvest had been prepared for cooking and canning. Except for cling peaches, the seed or stone in the center of the fruit was removed before canning. Peach halves were placed in half-gallon or quart-size Mason jars which had to be sterilized and sealed airtight to prevent spoilage. Some of the halves were often cut into smaller pieces and made into preserves or jelly and put into smaller containers. White and plum peaches ripened first and yellow peaches ripened last in the season. The plum peaches were smaller in size than the whites or yellows, and rather than removing the peel, they were often halved and sliced for drying in the sun. The dried pieces were called snits after the German word "schnitten" for slices and used in making fried pies.

In many peach seasons, our trees would not bear much fruit, especially if a late killing frost occurred during blossoming time. We did not want to go into the winter without having plenty of canned peaches on the pantry shelf, which of course meant another source of the fruit had to be located. The answer to the dilemma passed by our home every summer: an old man hauling ripe peaches from the sandhill peach orchards. He drove a four-door T-model Ford with a canvas top and would travel to the orchards below Asheboro and over-load every available spot, in and on the T-Model, with bushel baskets full of ripe peaches and return to his home near Winston-Salem. Mom knew to be on the lookout for the T-model as it made its way up the hill in front of our house. The noise of the chugging vehicle could be heard well before he reached us, and one of us would run to the highway to flag him down, which was not easy since he focused firmly on his driving. Stopping a T-model with a load of peaches could not be done on a dime, but he always managed to do it. Mom bartered for a few baskets, if the peaches looked good, usually paying a dollar or less a bushel.

Apples ripened later in late summer or the fall of the year, and the fruit stayed on the trees for a longer period of time before spoiling. Trees planted included varieties such as Red and Golden Delicious, Queen, Granny Smith, Winesap, Buckingham, Crab, Stamen, and Magnum Bonus. On the family farm, apples were consumed fresh, peeled and canned, processed into jelly and preserves, and sun-dried as snits for fried pies or apple jacks. Plums ripened in early summer and pears in late fall. Both were eaten fresh or made into preserves and/or jelly. The grapes were eaten fresh or turned into jelly.

In the fall of the year, around Thanksgiving after the first hard frost formed, rural folks began saying the time had arrived to fill the meat house, which meant "hog killin'" time. Every family that owned more than an acre or two of land built a hog lot and raised at least one hog to a weight up to 250–350 pounds to provide fresh or cured pork for several months of the year. In the spring, families would purchase six- to eight-week-old piglets from a local farmer, carry them home in a hemp sack, and feed them until frost. By that time, the pigs had become hogs and reached the requisite weight for slaughtering.

Slaughtering a hog and processing the meat for human consumption required a skill learned only through experience, passed on from generation to generation like most other skills used on the farm. When the weather "got right," the hog killing itch spread throughout the community, and a person knowing how to butcher a hog was in great demand, especially if he owned a scalding vat. A hog was killed by shooting it between the eyes with a rifle at close range and sticking a long knife into its throat to cause bleeding. When totally limp, the carcass was carried to a large vat filled with water at scalding temperature. One or two stout men would plunge the hog into the water and turn it about until the hair showed signs of coming off the hog's body. Using chains that had been placed under the hog when put in the vat, the carcass would be taken from the water and rolled onto a wooden platform next to the vat. The hair would be removed by scraping the entire carcass with the blade of a hoe followed by a razor-sharp knife to assure the hog was completely clean.

Next, the hog would be hung by its hind legs, head down, to be washed and scraped down, weighed using a steelyard, and carefully gutted to remove the entrails. After cooling, it was cut into pieces—making hams, shoulders, and middlins'. Lean meat that had been taken from all parts in the process was saved for fresh frying or ground into sausage. The cut-away fat meat was diced and cooked in a large black wash pot outdoors rendering it into lard. Remaining solids called cracklings, had little use except being mixed into cornbread dough.

Hams, shoulders, and middlins' would be salted down and placed in the meat house for curing. Except for the entrails, all parts of the hog—the head, liver, kidneys, feet, melt, stomach, backbones, and ribs were used for food. Even the small intestines would be carefully cleaned and used as a sausage stuffer. Folks had a saying, "Every part of the hog was eaten except the squeal." For a rural family, hog-killing time had a very special meaning and was filled with enjoyment and excitement.

Not a better companion than eggs could be found for salt-cured country ham as a breakfast dish. Chicken meat and eggs made up part of the diets of farm families. Chicken meat found its way on the table in the form of pies and dumplings, or it was often fried or baked. No one really cared which came first, the chicken or the egg, but everybody knew baby chicks mattered immensely whether hatched on the farm or ordered from a commercial hatchery. A settin' hen became an incubator, often secretly sitting on a nest of a dozen eggs, more or less, until they hatched 21 days later. The chicks wandered about the barnyard in close proximity to the mother hen until they were several weeks old or at least fully feathered.

Commercial day-old chicks, usually in cardboard boxes with several compartments, were delivered by the rural mail carrier who placed them on the backseat of his car until he reached the point of delivery. I often wondered how the mailman survived the chirping noise that a hundred or more chicks must have made, and marveled that they arrived healthy. A farmer once told me that groups of chicks can maintain body heat by huddling together, which is why

day-old chicks can be shipped by mail. Once they arrived at the farm, transferring them to a brooder house was a simple task. When a young chicken
reached a weight of two to four pounds, whether being fed in the brooder
house or eating while roaming in the barnyard, it became fair game for frying
or broiling. Frying seemed to be the preferred method of most housewives; I
can't remember many broiled chickens.

Killing the young chicken was a duty often left to the housewife or the
teenage children. With the chicken grasped firmly in one hand and a sharp
axe in the other, the "killer" would look for a chopping block near the wood-
shed. Holding the chicken by its legs and coaxing it to place its head across the
block, an accurate blow with the axe severed the head. For a few minutes, the
headless creature kicked and moved in an aimless direction threshing around
in the wood dust until life was gone. Anyone having observed this action has
a total understanding of the saying, "He is acting like a chicken with its head
cut off." The entire carcass was then immersed in a pot of boiling water until
its feathers could be easily picked or plucked by hand. Before the picked or
plucked chicken was taken to the kitchen for gutting and sectioning, the carcass was singed with the flame of a burning piece of paper to remove coarse
hair camouflaged earlier by feathers.

Those of us reared in a rural area the first half of the 20th century have a
pragmatic perspective about slaughtering animals. Shooting a hog or removing a chicken's head was a common occurrence done to provide food for the
family. Our feelings for the food animals seldom, if ever, gravitated to becoming emotional attachments, as they often did for the work animals such as
horses and mules and those animals kept as pets. The only way to understand
the ability to keep one animal distant while giving another a name and respecting it emotionally is to have been reared in a self-sufficient environment.
We did what was required of us.

Going Hunting

Learning how to hunt wild game for food or recreation became an expected
training unit of a young boy's upbringing on the farm, which lasted for years
and covered every aspect of the art of hunting imaginable. The list of game
animals hunted on a regular basis included possums, rabbits, squirrels, crows,
and to a lesser degree deer, raccoons, ducks, geese and quail. For most of us,
hunting rabbits was at the top of our list, mainly because they were plentiful
and they had excellent value as a source of meat. Squirrels ranked second and
possums third. Because crows destroyed our growing crops, we killed them
when possible just to get rid of the menace.

It was incumbent upon the older boys to introduce the younger ones to
the folly of hunting under the pretense we were about to experience our first

glance at Heaven. Most boys were no more than five or six years old when the thrill of "possum hunting" was revealed.

Possums, being nocturnal, were hunted at night, the time they came out of hiding to rummage on the ground and in the trees. For some reason, an experienced possum hunter loved to go hunting following a rain. I was told after a rain the leaves and other debris on the forest floor masked the noise of a hunter's foot making it easier for the dogs and hunter to creep up on the possum. Also, the scent of the possum was stronger, which favored the dogs. Memory of my introduction to possum hunting is fuzzy, but it probably went something like this. By dusk as the sun slid behind the horizon, and the hunters—it would have been five of us—two cousins, a local hunter, an older brother, and I and four hound dogs—were ready to go. Even at such a tender young age, I could sense the night would be different from anything I had ever done. How lucky could you get?

Down through the pasture we went in wet grass up to my waist. The dogs and I trudged along the best we could, and by the time we reached the barbwire fence next to the woods, my shoes, socks and pants were cold and wet. I glanced back at the house, now nothing more than a flicker of the light from the back porch.

I surely did not want to climb through the strands of wire to get into the woods, but the older boys would hear nothing of it, separating two of the strands for me to safely slip through to the other side. Except for snagging the seat of my overalls on a barb temporarily, the fence was negotiated. Walking became easier, and sure enough, the leaves rattled less when wet.

We walked about ten minutes when Old Blue, one of the possum hounds, let out a prolonged yelp, and a cousin yelled, "Whoopee, I believe he has struck a hot trail." Almost in unison the other three dogs joined in the chorus with their noses to the leaf floor moving in small circles and barking at what I had no idea. The dogs picked up their gait, and so did all five of us in a mad rush, tugging at bushes and tree limbs in an effort to stay abreast with the dogs.

From my vantage point, the world was nothing more than dips and gullies on the ground that needed crossing, neither of which fit my short legs. "Come on," an older cousin yelled, carrying a kerosene lantern as he moved ahead, pushing limbs aside and releasing them to hit me in the face and spray water from their leaves, which soaked every thread on my small body.

The barking of the dogs sounded more distant but filled with excitement, and in a few minutes, one of the boys said he believed the dogs had treed a possum. Well, with those comments, our pace quickened, or at least it did for the others. Hard as I tried, my legs would move no faster. Not only was I cold and wet, but a tiredness hung over me like none I had ever known.

I looked around at the trees, and nothing was familiar. Yet, the older boys encouraged me on. Like a wind-up toy with a spring too tight, my desire to go farther broke. My tears began to flow with a few sobs, but luck was on my side, because we neared a tree surrounded by four barking dogs acting as if they wanted to scale it. One cousin said, "I believe he is up there," meaning the possum.

The barking continued as the four older boys caucused in a small circle near the base of the tree. As they broke from their meeting, one said, "You climb up and get him, Buster." Off came his shoes and up the wet trunk of the tree he scampered as those on the ground shined flashlights into the limbs overhead searching for the possum. "I see him," one cousin said full of excitement, and when I gathered my emotions and looked up, all I could see were two beady eyes, which sparkled like red reflectors on the rear fender of a bicycle. They belonged to the possum.

Buster reached the limb holding the possum and shook it vigorously until the catch let go. He hit the ground with a loud thud only to be suddenly grabbed by the jaws of the snarling pack. The possum made himself into a round ball for protection while the three older boys on the ground wrestled the dogs to free him. Almost as if by magic, the tallest cousin proudly lifted the possum by the tail high in the air for all of us to get a good look. "Man, he is a nice one," they all agreed as I wondered, how could such a frightened animal be worth a celebration?

After admiring the catch of the evening for several minutes, they placed the possum in burlap sack and gave the panting dogs a rest. By that time, Buster had slid down the trunk of the tree in good shape even though a bit tired and dirty from hugging the wet bark.

The oldest cousin decided it was time to return home, and he looked at me, remarking that I had had my lesson for one night. Indeed, I had, and the cousin, observing that I was tired to the core, led me by the hand for the trek home. One of the other boys carried the sack. Possum hunting and I were strangers no more.

Possums caught on a hunt had some utility especially if they were fat. Some people found their meat to be a delicacy when oven baked with sweet potatoes. If the possum was skinny, it would be placed in a secure cage for fattening by feeding it raw vegetables and persimmons, when available. When the possum was removed from the cage, much care had to be taken. The object was to grab it by the tail and swiftly drag it through the cage door to avoid being bitten. Possums have sharp teeth and strong jaws, and extracting a caught finger from a possum's mouth becomes critical for the person on the other end.

"Rabbit hunting" differed from possum hunting in several respects. First, it was done during the daytime, and second, the hunters normally carried guns. Trained dogs were used to scent the rabbits and follow their trail when they decided to change locations. Most hunters used four or five dogs in a pack to chase rabbits, and each dog possessed a bark with its own pitch, tone, volume and cadence readily recognized by the hunter.

Hunter and dogs entered a field where rabbits might be hiding in tall grass and weeds or in a nest along the edge of the woods. Together the hunter and dogs combed the area, and usually when least expected, up jumped a rabbit, which initiated a chase. Furious barking erupted when the dogs sighted the rabbit and continued as long as it stayed in their view. To the hunter, the barking in pursuit was music to his ears, and the thrill of the chase could be intoxicating. When the rabbit got out of sight, the pace of the dogs slowed to a trot as they followed the scent of the rabbit's trail with their damp noses close to the ground. The reduced cadence of the barking let the hunter know conditions had changed, and patience became a virtue. Sooner or later, if the dogs trailed the rabbit successfully, he would run full circle returning near to the place originally found, and the hunter got his take with an accurate gun shot.

Fathers and older brothers or relatives passed the art of rabbit hunting to the younger boys in the family. Knowing how to hunt and shoot a gun was a birthright not taken lightly, an activity sought early in life by most rural boys. Serious hunting had to wait until mastering the firing of a gun was safely demonstrated. No one desired to go hunting rabbits with a rookie who had never learned the art of handling a loaded gun. For some it came easy, but for others hitting the broad side of a barn bordered on being impossible.

Firing a .22 caliber rifle and successfully hitting a still target was no big deal, but holding of a loaded 12-gauge shotgun to the shoulder and pulling the trigger took manly courage, because the discharge of the shell would kick most young boys to the ground and leave a blue shoulder to boot. Most of us left the shotgun hanging on the back porch wall and used the rifle until we reached the age of 14 at least. Sooner or later we succumbed to using the shotgun because hitting a rabbit running at full speed with a rifle was akin to throwing a rock through a knot hole at 100 paces. With a shotgun and its scattering pellets, chances of making the kill increased significantly.

Whether hunting rabbits or possums, a dog possessing the correct bark was a prized possession, one you would brag about long and loud at the local store on a rainy day or Saturday night. Such a dog belonged to an old fellow who lived about two miles south of the church, and word of the dog's superior traits reached far and wide.

As it so happened, news of the dog's qualities became known by a man in Winston-Salem, who had never hunted and wanted to take up the sport. He wrote the owner inquiring if he would sell the dog. An affirmative answer came back in a hurry, the owner sensing the city slicker could be an easy take.

In a few days, the potential buyer showed up at the old man's place and asked to see the dog. "Sure," the old man replied, "not only will I show the dog to you, we will take him to the pasture and let you hear him bark." Off the two men and the now high-priced dog went. In no time at all, a rabbit sprang from his hiding, and the dog gave chase barking in tones he had never made before. With pride and smugness, the owner said, "Now, isn't that the most beautiful sound you have ever heard?" The man from Winston-Salem replied, "I can't hear a 'durn' thing for the racket the dog's making."

During the Depression of the '30s and early '40s, rabbit meat was much in demand by both rural and city folks, and the butcher in the meat market in town would pay us 25 cents for each rabbit we could deliver, a rather tidy sum in those days. City folks had an aversion to rabbits that had been shot because of the appearance of bullet holes and the probability of a lead shot or two buried in the flesh. We allayed their concerns by trapping rabbits in "rabbit gums" placed strategically in areas where they were most likely to be found.

Old boards and hollow logs made good materials for constructing a rabbit gum, which when completed, was closed on one end with the other containing a trap door which would shut if tripped by an entering rabbit. The entrapment occurred during cold winter nights, and we would visit as many as 20 to 30 gums early each morning to see if trap doors had been released, a signal an intruder had invaded the gum. Cautiously, the gum would be placed on the enclosed end and the trap door opened. If the intruder was a rabbit, he would be crouched in the rear of the gum. Without much hesitation, an open bare hand reached into the gum retrieving the rabbit by it hind legs, and the other hand was used to give the rabbit a killing blow behind its head. After all gums had been checked, we carried our catch home and skinned and gutted the rabbits before delivering them to the meat market.

Once in a while, the tripped gum snared an animal other than a rabbit —a squirrel, a raccoon or a possum—which created the problem of emptying the gum without being clawed or bitten by the unwelcome trespasser. An older brother making the rounds one morning discovered a squirrel in a gum. Hastily attempting to empty the gum, he placed his new leather cap over his hand and reached into the gum only to have the trapped squirrel tear his cap into shreds, a deed never to be repeated again.

Squirrels from early fall through the winter months started feeding about the time hickory nuts had become full grown and slightly hardened. The challenge was between the hunter and the squirrel as it moved among the hickory trees in search of an edible nut. The hunter would step quietly across the forest floor, stopping occasionally to listen for a squirrel feeding on a nut. Two sounds might be heard, the scraping sound of the squirrel gnawing on the nut and the soft thump of pieces of the nut falling to the ground. A squirrel hunter loved hearing either of those sounds, and he would creep slowly to the tree to avoid being detected by the squirrel. Carefully, the hunter would search the canopy of the tree, sight the squirrel, aim and fire his gun. During winter months, a dog would accompany the hunter to scent squirrel trails and trees holding squirrels.

Gigging for Frogs

"Frog gigging" was touted as being fun and something every boy had to experience. A great myth pervaded the rural countryside that frog legs when prepared properly tasted delicious, much like chicken meat, which was compelling enough for a boy to try a frog-gigging outing at least once. Four of us set out one evening about dark to tackle the frogs. The party, in addition to me, included my older brother, Homer, and two of his classmates, Gene Smith and Boyd Lee Hedrick. The four of us agreed to meet at Pounders Fork Creek about three-fourths of a mile from home.

Gene and Boyd Lee lived in the opposite direction from the creek. Homer and I arrived to the meeting place carrying necessary essentials for a frog gigging—a flashlight, a .22 caliber rifle, a gig in the shape of a pitchfork but much smaller, some leftovers from supper to be eaten as a snack later, and an empty sack to carry the frogs home. Gene and Boyd Lee brought other essentials, and Boyd Lee with a sneaky grin showed us something extra, four large El Reso, two-for-a-nickel, cigars. He passed one to each of us, saying we would have a grown man's smoke later.

The section of Pounders Fork Creek in which we planned to search for frogs ran through land belonging to our dad. At no place in the creek did the water exceed two feet in depth nor was the width more than 15 feet. Our challenge became to wade quietly and look for frogs on either bank. Rather than soaking my shoes, I decided to wade barefoot, which turned out to be a bad decision.

Off we went slipping into the stream with pant legs rolled to the knees or higher, walking in the middle and looking from side to side, aiming our flashlights and hoping to spot frogs. My steps were taken carefully because rocks of all sizes and shapes covered the bottom of the stream. Small ones cut my feet and the large ones were slippery with creek slime, making walking upright next to impossible. Being the youngest of the group and wanting to be one of the boys, I never complained, trudging ahead and praying for relief.

Where were the frogs? They made loud croaking sounds minutes earlier as we readied our gear, but now none were in sight. Even though the time of year was late summer, the temperature of the creek water chilled us adding to our discomfort. One fellow stopped suddenly and became very quiet. Had he located a frog? No, a water snake swam immediately in front of us crossing from one bank to the other, a serious distraction. My comfort quotient had sunk to near zero by now, and only a large bullfrog could restore it to anything close to normal.

Quicker than Davy Crocket, one of the other boys raised his .22, pointed toward the left bank, and pulled the trigger. The noise of the exploding cartridge shell got our attention, and the shot had hit its mark, a small toad probably out for an evening of catching mosquitoes.

Thirty or 45 minutes more passed as we continued to stalk our invisible prey. Coming up empty handed, and without saying a word, Boyd Lee struck a match and lit an El Reso. At least, if the frogs did not wish to cooperate, puffing on a good cigar might keep the evening from being a total waste. Three more matches broke the darkness as each of us joined in a smoking orgy. This was the life, boys doing a man's thing and communing with nature at the same time. My first puff on the cigar fell short of expectations, so I took a few more puffs inhaling a little deeper each time. I glanced at brother Homer the best I could out of the corner of watery eyes and noticed he was having difficulty negotiating the slippery creek bed, but he kept a good grasp on the rifle he had borrowed off Dad's gun rack. The bottom of a creek bed did not seem like a good spot to drop it.

Appearing to be slightly green in color, Homer advocated strongly that we abandon the hunt, get out of the creek, and let the frogs have it. He had enjoyed about as much of the El Reso as he could tolerate and was ready to pack up his gear and head for home. Hastily, I seconded his motion and joined him now standing on the creek bank.

Gene and Boyd Lee followed suit, we said our goodbyes, and after I had put on my dry shoes, Homer looked to the east and said, "Let's go." "Go where?" I responded, arguing as persuasively as possible that home was to the west and not the east. He refused to let me have my way as older brothers tended to do, but I would not relent.

If a judge and jury had witnessed him in his condition, they would have sentenced him to a month "on the roads." Finally, the cool night air began to clear his smoke-laden cranium, and he recognized his mistake. In silence, we headed west, and as we neared home, Homer suggested the details of our ill-fated evening remain a secret, which they have been for more than 60 years. Even Mom cooperated by never mentioning the smell of cigar smoke she detected in our clothes, and the subject of frog gigging was tabled for a while.

Goin' Fishing

Only a creditable person would utter "goin' fishing" in earnest unless he meant it. Next to "playing ball" or "let the dogs loose," you never wanted to suggest heading for a creek or lake to fish with cane poles and worms without realizing a crowd might climb on your wagon or the back of the pickup truck.

Rural folks liked to fish, and after each outing, they loved to brag about their catch and even more about the big one that got away.

Retelling details about the whopper of a fish that never landed in the boat or on the creek bank was a kind of sport in itself. No matter the eloquence and tenacity used by the person in describing his "almost accomplished" feat, the lack of supporting evidence, a fish, left him as empty-handed as the trip home from the lake.

John Steinbeck once wrote, "It has always been my private conviction that any man who pits his intelligence against a fish and loses has it coming." We learned early in life that contriving whoppers about fishing exploits was an exercise in futility, not without peril. The ribbing engendered throughout the community subsided only when another manufactured whopper let us off the hook.

Nevertheless, fishing we would go. As a small boy, I often cast a hook baited with a red worm into a "fishing hole" deep enough to grow large minnows or sun perch. Even before we could hoe corn or plow, Dad used to take us to streams that wended their way through fields, and the day might be whiled away sitting on the bank testing our fishing skills. The fishing gear usually consisted of just a cane pole, an attached line, a floating cork, a hook, a small piece of lead as a sinker, and some worms. Baiting the hook with a worm was a boy thing, not to be tackled by most girls. Boys had a hard time tolerating their yelling and squealing, which scared the fish.

With a pole in hand, I would be content to sit and watch a floating cork for hours, hoping for one fish bite and daydreaming about catching a big one. Finally, after what seemed an eternity, the cork would begin to move up and down ever so slightly. If a fish found the worm to his liking, the cork bobbing accelerated meaning the feast had commenced in earnest. With no further warning, the cork went under the water and the line tightened. I was on my own, which demanded the skill to land the fish. Giving the pole a smooth, steady jerk, I yanked the line out of the water and with it came the cork, the lead sinker, and a fish, alive and flapping its tail. A minnow no more than six inches long had taken the bait, and the fish hook would not let him go. What a catch! No one was present to witness the dexterity and technique exhibited in landing him. In my mind, the minnow was three times its actual size and totally under my control. What a story of bravery I told Dad as he hitched the team to the wagon at the end of the day.

If we wanted to catch larger fish such as crappie, bass or fresh-water catfish, we went to Abbotts Creek or to High Rock Lake, but such an excursion rarely occurred. These types of fishing trips typically were planned by older boys, usually brothers and cousins, and most of them seemed to happen when the fish were not biting. We would say, "Today was a perfect example of fisherman's luck—a wet butt and a hungry gut." Yet, never let it be forgotten, a bad day fishing was better than a good day of work. The fishing was always good; it was the catching that could be bad. If by chance we caught a string of fish large enough to clean, you could bet we did not return home in silence.

Another form of fishing, setting hooks, would follow heavy summer rains when surface runoff from the fields was sufficient enough to muddy the streams. At the end of the day about sundown, we would walk along the stream banks and "set" a large number of baited fish hooks on the end of short strings barely touching the surface of the water. Catfish loved to swim in this environment, and if they encountered the baited hooks, they were usually swallowed completely. Up and down the stream bank we walked, shining our flashlights in the direction of the hooks to see if catches had been made. With any luck at all, we caught enough fish to set in motion bragging rights at the barber shop or country store.

Young boys could slip away on a Sunday afternoon to test their luck at landing a big one without the grown-ups making much fuss about it. Van Hoy, "Squeaky," Hines and I made big plans to try such one Sunday in the spring, and our chances for success had been enhanced by attending both Sunday school and worship service that morning. We made no secret about our destination, the banks of Abbotts Creek some distance from home where it ran through the Gray Place, and we would get there and back riding a couple of sway-back mules. Riding a mule requires different skills and techniques than riding a saddle horse. Normally, no saddle is used at all on a mule, which really made no difference in this case since neither of us owned a saddle, and a mule really does not care one way or the other. We would ride bareback, just throwing a hemp sack across the mule and climbing on. Since Squeaky lived between my home and the Gray Place, it made sense for me to meet him before proceeding to the fishing site. Kate, my mule, and I arrived at Squeaky's at the designated time, and he and his mule joined us making a compatible foursome.

This was the life, a beautiful spring day warmed perfectly by the bright mid-afternoon sun under a clear sky. Off the mules trotted carrying Squeaky and me, a few cane poles with fishing lines and hooks affixed, a couple of bottles of drinking water and our overall pockets laden with peanut butter crackers, our pocket knives, and oh yes, some fishing bait. Before Kate and I had left home, I did some digging with a grubbing hoe in the moist loamy soil by the cow barn and uncovered two or three dozen fat, juicy earthworms, the kind fish find hard to resist. But, worms must stay fresh if a person is to have any luck fishing. The solution was a discarded tin can about four inches in diameter and a layer of the moist soil placed in the bottom. The worms would rest on the soil with another layer on top for good measure. Nothing lacked, and we were prepared for any challenge that Abbotts Creek and the fish could present. What a picture this must have made, two teenage boys wearing straw hats headed for the creek on mule back.

Down the dirt road we went, passing Charlie Leonard's house. His son, Otis, had taught us in Sunday school that morning. Next the mules, without being directed by the reins, turned left by the Hedrick house. In about a quarter of a mile, we crossed a small bridge over a stream before going up a hill toward the Goins' house. At the top of the hill, we made another left turn, aiming us directly toward the Gray Place and Abbotts Creek. First, a field of spring wheat, about 10 acres in size, had to be negotiated.

Our mules quickened their trot, and Squeaky let out the reins on his mule putting it into a gallop. Kate and I had done more than a little riding together, and enjoyed a very comfortable relationship as long as the gait was reasonable. She had galloped once or twice with me while in full harness, and I felt safe and secure holding to the knobs of the hames. Security was non-existent on this occasion. Kate broke into a gallop, wanting to keep up with Squeaky and his mule. In the process, she gave at least three mighty kicks and jumps with her hind legs as we reached the middle of the wheat field. In desperation, I tried to hang on by locking my legs around Kate, but failed; her mid-section must have been five feet wide so my heels would not dig in. Her mane was as short as a G.I. haircut, which offered no hope in the crisis. Into the air the hemp sack and I flew; how high, I will never know, but probably slightly lower than suborbital. In this moment of terror, I let go of the reins. The pain of the rear-end landing in the wheat field was exacerbated by the bait can located in the back pocket of my overalls. Squeaky had witnessed the entire episode and came back to see if everything was intact. Except for an aching backside, the feeling of being a little woozy, a lost fishing expedition, and the loss of my mode of transportation, having left the scene headed back the way we came—things could have been worse. After retrieving my straw hat from some tall grass, we left the wheat field, both of us now on Squeaky's mule, and headed for my home.

Mules possess a well-developed sense of home-finding, and Kate had exhibited her homing abilities on other occasions when left unattended for an inordinate amount of time. If she made it to the comfort of her stable this time, she would be record setting for distance. I had learned a long time ago not to underestimate the intelligence of most farm animals.

The load on the back of Squeaky's mule seemed unfair, but he trudged forward with determination, appearing to understand completely the gravity of the situation. He conveyed a sense of personal pride for not being unruly like Kate. We passed by a few of our friends who thought it odd that both of us were riding the same animal. The Sunday afternoon loafers sitting in front of Uncle El's store let out a few cat calls, teasing me in particular about riding ineptness. "Did someone steal your mule?" one smart aleck shouted barely smothering a loud guffaw. I stared straight ahead, not wanting to see who had asked the question. One mile away, my barnyard and Kate's stable awaited us. Why was it taking so long, I wondered. About 15 minutes later, we emerged from the woods in front of the barn, and there she stood, sheepishly looking out of the open door. For a moment, I thought I detected a grin on her face as if she were eating briars. Her homing "mechanism" had worked flawlessly, but my feelings were mixed. She left me standing disconcerted in the wheat field an hour ago, but I could get the stable door secure before Dad and Mom returned from a visit to Bob Smith's.

A postscript is in order at this juncture. For one year, the fall caused by Kate's antics in the wheat field made running difficult, but since it did not interfere greatly with farm work, no one suggested I see a doctor. Sixty-three years later during a visit to Dr. Mulherin to determine the cause of lower back pain, an x-ray showed a deviation in the spine. Recalling the Sunday afternoon experience with Kate to the doctor, he concluded the spinal divergence may not be congenital but perhaps the result of landing on a bait can in the middle of a wheat field bordering on Abbotts Creek. The doctor labeled the condition as "spondylolesthesis." Kate has been departed for decades now, but I cannot help but wonder if she ever had any hint that spondylolesthesis would bring back the memory of a springtime fishing trip that was thwarted by her antics.

Killing Rats

Small animals, especially rodents, provided an unusual challenge to the farm family. A barnyard or hog pens where a surplus of grain existed were perfect sanctuaries for the very large rats. We found that rats thrive unimaginably under such conditions and become pests of the highest order. Not only do they eat grain wherever they discover it, but they can carry diseases transmittable to other animals and perhaps humans. The smart thing is to get rid of them. Several methods have been used to destroy their colonies, such as setting rat traps or placing rat poison strategically. When these fail more drastic measures need to be taken.

One of my early memories is of a skill required to eradicate these pests when normal methods did not work. Rat killing became a kind of sport, especially in the hog lots where the pest would burrow tunnels and trenches around the hog houses. Having a successful rat killing required several very agile people who were good at using long poles or sticks as weapons of rat destruction.

A water hose opened wide would be placed in the entrance to a rat tunnel, and the pole or stick carriers would be ready to deal killing blows when the rat(s) fled their flooded homes. Some rat burrows were very deep and voluminous, requiring gallons of water before the killing would begin, but this technique proved to be effective in most situations. A bystander not knowing exactly what was happening might wonder about the sanity of the group.

One year, our flooding technique failed us, but thank goodness the country mind, so full of common sense, seems to find solutions. A neighbor of ours had heard of a man in the northern part of the county who owned several ferrets. The owner was making the claim that his ferrets would enter the rat tunnels and kill them like aggressive cats. Dad put the ferret owner to the test by inviting him to come to our farm.

He arrived talking about the value of ferrets like a sideshow barker, making statements about how the English Royalty used ferrets to rid the castles of rats, and how many farmers in his area had not seen a rat in years. We could not wait to see his ferrets do their thing, but he did not seem to be in a hurry. Finally, as our patience wore thin, he showed one albino ferret the entrance to a tunnel. In he went, but no rats emerged, and neither did the ferret at least for a half hour. The owner picked him up and offered some explanation for the failure which none of us quite understood.

He left the farm with his cage of ferrets, the rats stayed, and we never sought another ferret demonstration. What Dad did was to increase the size of his cat population, and the rats one by one disappeared. Obviously there is more than one way to "feed" a cat.

Cutting Logs and Sawmilling

Cutting logs with a crosscut saw and sawmilling tested the strength and endurance of any man, and practically every country male gained experience at doing both. Nothing more aptly described hard manual labor than cutting logs and working at a sawmill, especially before the advent of powered chain saws and fully mechanized mills. The entire process of getting sawed lumber from a standing tree was a continuous hand labor challenge. Nevertheless, sawmilling provided income for many families with names such as Parks, Greer, Lohr, Beck, Swing, Rhodes, Miller, Kepley, Smith and Hedrick to name a few. In fact, anyone who owned timberland cut trees from time to time and sold the sawed lumber or used it for constructing homes, farm buildings, fences or in making needed repairs.

The first step in sawmilling involved the use of an axe and a two-man crosscut saw. Using an axe, a man would notch a tree in order to fell it in a desired direction, and with a partner, would cut horizontally through the tree trunk with a saw starting on the opposite side of the tree from the notch. Most crosscut saws were some six to eight feet in length with a handle at each end. Two sawyers positioned themselves on their knees on opposite sides of the tree from the notch and pulled the saw back and forth in a smooth rhythm as sharp teeth ate their way through the tree. The two workers had to synchronize their strokes to make the pulling as easy as possible. The energy required cutting through a tree two to three feet or more in diameter could exhaust both workers temporarily.

Once the tree had been felled, it was cut into logs of various lengths and dragged or hauled to a sawmill location to be sawed into lumber. Most sawmills in our area were portable and could be moved from site to site for better access to wooded areas, and mills had to be securely anchored in place on the ground to work safely and properly. Mules or horses "snaked" or dragged logs to the mill using a log chain and grab hooks. When the distance made snaking impractical, a log cart pulled by a team of animals became a better mode for moving the logs.

When the logs arrived at the mill, a worker using a can hook rolled them one at a time onto a carriage and secured each log into position with a dog clamp. The carriage mounted on a track, pushed the log into a large circular saw powered by a tractor pulley—in the earlier days a steam engine—cutting it into rough boards of various widths and thicknesses. One or two men, "off bearers," stacked the outsides or slabs of the logs and freshly cut boards nearby or placed them on a truck or wagon for a pre-determined destination. By the end of the day, most of the workers had reached the point of exhaustion, and a saying in lower central Davidson County held true, "A sawmill worker has little trouble falling asleep at night."

Drivers of the trucks hauling the sawed boards to a lumber mill for further processing did not have a much easier life, although driving a truck was considered by many to be less work and perhaps enjoyable. A friend of mine who was 16 years old at the time hauled lumber with his father's truck. At the end of his first week on the job, his father paid him five dollars which my friend thought to be not enough. He complained to his father who replied, "Well, you got to drive the truck, didn't you?"

Usually when trees were felled in a farmer's woods, treetops had to be removed. Axes and crosscut saws cut the larger limbs into eight- to ten-foot lengths later to be cut into firewood with a powered wood saw. Limbs that were too small to save were cleared from the forest floor and heaped into large brush piles for burning or rotting. Piling brush had no art to it and was looked upon as an unpleasant exercise. An uncle of mine had patience for piling brush, and when we took a break to eat or rest, he would get on his knees and work.

An all-day stay in the woods could not be accomplished without carrying food for the noon meal. Mom would rise early to pack a box for us, and when the noon break arrived, we were ready to eat heartily. Into the box we went with both hands, uncovering large biscuit sandwiches filled with hard scrambled eggs and fried country ham which had been covered by enough pieces of cloth to hold some warmth. She had also included cooked green beans, baked sweet potatoes, fried potatoes and a fried apple jack. A hungry boy sitting down in the woods at noon for dinner remained grateful to the cook forever for packing such a feast.

Going to Town on Saturday Night

Farming and sawmilling were six-days-a-week occupations, and workers longed for a break from the drudgery, which came on Saturday afternoon, usually early if we had worked diligently during the week. As soon as we stabled the mules or horses, milked the cows, fed the hogs, or handled the last piece of lumber at the mill, our thoughts turned to Saturday night and going to town. We never grew tired of "Going to town on Saturday night" which brought relief, a welcome catharsis for aching muscles and exhausted bodies after working all week from sunup to sundown.

Before being able to drive a car to town, we begged for rides from anyone willing to give us one. We skipped supper at home on Saturdays if we had a few pieces of change to put in our pockets. With luck, the accommodating driver would drop us off near a barbecue place. We went in and grabbed a stool at the serving counter. For 25 cents, a supper could be had, comprised of a tray of barbecue and slaw plus two hamburger rolls. The server would also place a six-ounce Coca-Cola before us as well at no extra charge.

This may not sound like much of a supper to most folks, but to us farm boys, it was about as good as it got. To eat barbecue correctly and enjoy it, we did not rush into it like a starved dog. We took our time and savored every bite. It has been more than 50 years since I left Davidson County, and I have yet to find any dish to match the taste of the local barbecue.

A Saturday night excursion did not end with eating barbecue. On Main Street, the next destination, we mingled with town boys and girls and others who had come from different parts of the county. The corner drugstore did not close until 10 o'clock which gave us enough time for ice cream, provided the funds were sufficient for making a purchase and going to a movie. Funny how we country boys seemed to stand out in such situations, and we did the best we could with what we had to blend into the crowd. Our dress and hairstyles parted in the middle and held in place by an excessive amount of Rose Oil or Brilliantine could not be disguised. For a boy from the country to catch the eye of a pretty town girl as she sipped a soda was as awesome as David slaying Goliath.

"Saturday night" in town culminated with a late movie or late show, a special which had never been shown in a local theater. Admission to the movie cost 25 cents if you were over 12 years old, but cheaper tickets probably could be obtained from one of the ushers, who always seemed to have an endless supply in his pocket. The movie let out at midnight, and we searched for a friend

with a car to take us home. Luckily, my older brother, Homer, was dating Ellen
Kepley, who lived on the way home. With no other option for a ride, I could
always find Homer's 1936 Ford parked in front of her house, climb in the back
seat, and wait until he decided to go home.

Staying Home on Saturday Night

Staying home on Saturday night was not all bad. In fact, it could be very entertaining to play regular or Chinese checkers or permissible card games such
as Old Maids, Setback, or Pedro. Another pastime was to listen to the Grand
Ole Opry from Nashville, Tennessee. We knew the names of all the Opry stars
and many of their songs by heart. Such performers as Minnie Pearl, Uncle
Dave Macon, Eddie Arnold, Bill Monroe, Roy Acuff, and many others became
household fixtures, and even if we could not purchase and play records of their
works, we would get songbooks containing the words and music.

For me, going to Uncle El's store on Saturday night had advantages. Many
local folks also came, and it was fun to sit around and listen to adults tell stories
on just about every subject even if the truth was butchered a bit. Uncle El's
store had a pool table; a rack of pool balls cost five cents. My playing pool bordered on being slightly sinful, or so thought my folks. If I had a loose nickel in
my pocket, chances were it went for a game of pool.

One Saturday night while playing a game, Mom and Dad entered the store
unexpectedly, and the pool stick in my hands dropped to the floor as if it were a
hot poker. It was too late. I was caught red handed at "sinning" and sheepishly
followed Mom and Dad to the car and helped load the groceries they had purchased. Mom's vocabulary in such situations could be amazingly effusive and
effective. "Were you trying to embarrass the family with that pool stick?" she
asked. There were no retorts on my part. After watching the single tail light
on the car fade into the darkness as they drove toward home, I retrieved my
bicycle and followed.

Uncle El's store was scarcely more than one mile from home, and I always
rode the bicycle to get to and from it. About two-thirds of the distance home,
a shortcut could be made by going through the graveyard at Beck's Lutheran
Church and following a narrow road through heavy woods to our barn and
on to the house. My plan was to do the same that night. The path through
the cemetery had been mapped out many times having learned the silhou-
ettes of most of the tombstones. Finding the entrance presented no problem.
Never had I gone this way without thinking of some of the ghost stories heard
around the stove at Uncle El's store, which always gave me pause about taking
the shortcut. The thought of peddling the bicycle an additional half mile that
night ended the mental debate. I would take the shortcut one more time. Upon
reaching the middle of the graveyard, the loudest MOOOOOO ever heard

came suddenly from behind a large tombstone. Most people think jet propulsion was not known in the United States until near the end of World War II, but it arrived that night as my feet "moooved" the bicycle to unimaginable speeds. Later, I figured that one of our dairy cows had broken through the pasture fence and found the cemetery grass to her liking.

Front Porches and Rocking Chairs

For a farmer, the front porch represented a place to seek rest after a hard day's work and a good supper on a warm summer day. Nothing beat the cool breeze of eventide to fan our reflections of the day or what we'd face the next. Front porches were places to greet visitors and to salute passersby on the road or highway. Drop-in casual visitors always felt welcome on the front porch. Sunday afternoon visitors never rejected an offer to sit for a spell.

Front porches did much for us, and whatever the benefit, the most compatible companion a front porch ever had was a rocking chair. Our front porch had four or five of them. Their comfort was great, and more that that, the chairs spoke volumes about the kind of folks my mom and dad were because they had the look of having been sat in for many years. Rocking chairs made our front porch the ideal gathering place. As a youngster, I would sit quietly in a rocking chair for hours listening to the conversations between my parents and visiting uncles, aunts and neighbors.

From this vantage point, military convoys of World War II could be seen passing between army bases in the South. We wondered about the soldiers' destinations and what they would be doing months later. Somehow the wave of a hand back and forth to the men riding in the Jeeps and trucks made me think it was a small contribution to the war effort. When radio broadcasters spoke of war casualties and the names of missing or killed in action appeared on the front pages, I could not help wondering if any of them had seen my greeting from the porch.

If I were to write my philosophy on life, what was learned on the front porch sitting in a rocking chair would be central to its message.

The County Fair

As an outing for farm families, going to the fair ranked high on the list for excitement, entertainment and education. In addition, it was a day to suspend all other activities such as working on the farm for the adults and going to school for the children. Anticipation heightened when we approached the entrance gate. We could scarcely wait to leave our parents' side and rush to explore what the fair had to offer.

"The Davidson County Fair" was located for years on grounds near the Smith Lumber Company on West Center Street in Lexington. It usually ran for a week in the fall of the year, but not on Sundays. School children could come through the gate free of charge on educational day. Most of the schools in the county would close early on that day, encouraging families to take their children. A great emphasis was placed on the agriculture of the county with exhibits of every crop grown, all kinds of livestock and poultry, foods canned and clothes sewn by the women—every element of farming. Blue, red, and yellow ribbons were awarded to the first-, second-, and third-place winners of exhibits and animal shows. Boys and girls in the 4-H clubs participated regularly in the competitions as did the boys in the Future Farmers of America.

Great attractions for young and old alike could be found on the midway at the Davidson County Fair. Amusement rides of many types always included a Ferris wheel, a merry-go-round, swings, bumper cars, and small airplanes suspended on cables or chains. Some years the show included such rides as the octopus, caterpillar, a small roller coaster and loopier plane.

Tents along the midway provided freak shows for those daring enough to view them, juggling acts, dart throwing at inflated balloons, baseball pitching at stacks of milk bottles, penny pitching at kitchenware plates, guessing weight, and testing strength at a booth where participants wielded a sledge hammer. Lucky pitchers and throwers would be awarded prizes of little value if balloons were popped and stacked bottles knocked down, and strong men making a bell ring did not go home empty handed.

The sideshow barkers tried to lure us into the various tent shows which usually housed phony displays; a child spending a hard-earned nickel or dime to enter came away sorely disappointed. Entrance into one tent could only be gained by males 18 years and older. Younger boys developed a great curiosity about this tent, especially hearing the enticer say over the loudspeaker, "She walks, she talks, and she crawls on her belly like a reptile." Adults would never explain what was viewed inside only to say, "You don't want to waste your 50 cents in there." Years later, the curiosity of younger boys grown older verified the statement.

Vendors sold popcorn, hotdogs, and cotton candy at stands throughout the fair grounds. A real treat was a candy-covered apple. Not every child had enough money to enjoy everything. Luckily, some of the entertainment cost nothing. A fireworks display occurred after dark, and there was a high-diving exhibition from a platform 100 feet in the air. A diver, man or woman, would dive from this perch head-first into a large barrel of water no more than 10 feet deep. Such a performance occurred twice a day, and the barker gave a prolonged and scary description of what was to occur before each dive. First, he pretended to have to coerce a reluctant diver to climb the ladder to the 100-foot platform. Eventually, the climbing began, and the barker ranted and raved about the diver's bravery as he or she negotiated each rung in the ladder. About halfway up, the diver would balk, pretending to be frightened by the height. The barker would crack a whip or feign firing a pistol, causing the diver to scamper, squirrel-like, the rest of the way. Reaching the diver's platform, the diver would wave to the crowd as the barker enticed him or her to make the dive. This verbal challenge lasted at least five or ten minutes, and when least expected, the diver came down, looking like a beautiful swan with arms outstretched. He or she landed head first into the water, which splashed at least ten feet in every direction. I remember well one year the barker saying, "Oops, I believe she 'busted' her dictionary," as a lady diver climbed out of the water asking for a towel. To this day, I never figured out exactly what the comment meant.

The end of the fireworks show completed the trip to the fair. We left to go home wide-eyed but tired beyond description. Shame, we thought, that the fair only came once a year. Small carnivals did set up a few thrill rides in the middle of town at least twice a year near Beck's Barbecue stand and the Snack Shoppe. This small imitation of a fair did help hold us over until the big fair appeared again.

(*Left*) Farm teenage boys had a tanned, healthy look from working long hours in fields often with their fathers. (Library of Congress, FSA-OWI photo collection, LC-USW361-946)

(*Below*) Farm children enjoyed the puppies and kittens that seem to be born in abundance. (Family collection)

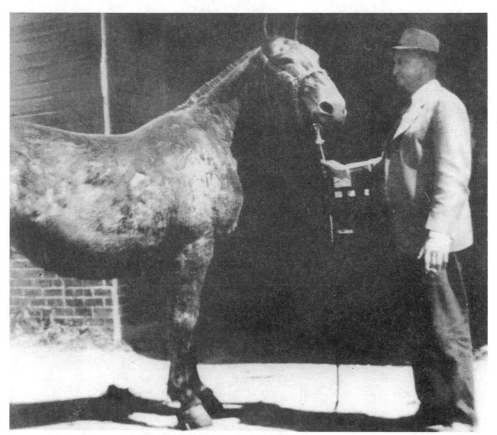

Charlie Misenheimer shows one of his mules at a sale in Richfield, N.C. (E. B. Pickler)

One person and a team of mules can break one acre or slightly more in a day. (Ellen Day)

Many farm boys experienced their first challenge of working a mule with a cultivator in a field of corn. (Terry Scoggin, Madison, Georgia)

Little by little the work mule was replaced by the tractor. (Library of Congress, FSA-OWI photo collection, LC-USW3-034361)

Milking a large herd of milk cows by hand can be one of the most tedious chores on the farm. (Library of Congress, FSA-OWI photo collection, LC-USF34-031572)

Coble Dairy in Lexington gave a great impetus to the dairy industry in Davidson County. (Davidson County Historical Museum)

Raw milk left too long in the can without refrigeration will sour, and cows grazing on onions and a few other plants can give the milk an undesirable odor. (Library of Congress, FSA-OWI photo collection, LC-USF34-039719)

Children visiting a hog farm derive considerable enjoyment from watching the hogs eat shelled corn from the cob. (Family collection)

One of the most relaxing family gatherings on the farm is to cut a cool, ripe watermelon at the end of the day. (Family collection)

Young girls and boy picking cotton in the '20s. (Davidson County Historical Museum)

Cutting ripened wheat with a horse or mule-drawn reaper set into motion one of the great times on the farm. (Howell Living History Farm)

This threshing machine is being pulled by a steam engine, an early source of power. Later to be replaced by tractors that ran on gasoline or kerosene. (Kay McCulloch Kepley)

Farm workers placing individual bundles of wheat on a platform of threshing machine. (Library of Congress, FSA-OWI photo collection, LC-USF34-025654)

Straw and chaff are blown into a pile at the rear of the threshing machine while clean grain is augured into a bucket which is emptied into sacks. (Library of Congress, FSA-OWI photo collection, LC-USF34-025645)

In the middle 1940s, the work of the reaper and threshing machine was done by a single machine, a tractor-powered combine. (Library of Congress, FSA-OWI photo collection, LC-USF34-044634)

Making hay after the threshing season ended provided the feed for the farmer's livestock during winter months. (Library of Congress, FSA-OWI photo collection, LC-USF34-055836)

Farmers with limited hay loft space in barns put hay into tightly-packed stacks. (Photo by author)

Experienced corn shuckers used a long wooded peg strapped around the hand, shucking peg, as an aid to removing the shucks. (Library of Congress, FSA-OWI photo collection, LC-USF33-030717)

Corn shuckers have finished their job and resting before a scrumptious supper. (Library of Congress, FSA-OWI photo collection, LC-USF34-056216)

A job well done; shuckers sit around a table in the farmer's home enjoying a meal prepared by the farmer's wife and women she has engaged to assist her. (Library of Congress, FSA-OWI photo collection, LC-USF34-052663)

After the leaves are stripped from the stalks of cane sorghum, they are taken to a mill for grinding and the cooking of the juice into syrup. (Photo by author)

Tobacco is harvested from the bottom of the plant to the top as the leaves ripen. (Davidson County Historical Museum)

Large families required quantities of fruit to meet their needs, and a peach-apple peeler was an important gadget. (Family collection)

Hog-killing time occurred around Thanksgiving. (Library of Congress, FSA-OWI photo collection, LC-USF34-052999)

Farm girls and horses develop a special relationship. Martha holds the rein of Nell. (Family collection)

Of Kate and me. (Family collection)

After trees are felled and cut into log lengths, they are often dragged or snaked to the sawmill.
(Library of Congress, FSA-OWI photo collection, LC-USF34-043995)

The man with the lever in his hand slowly moves a log into a circular saw cutting it into lumber.
(Library of Congress, FSA-OWI photo collection, LC-USF33-002083)

Furniture factories employed hundreds of workers. (Davidson County Historical Museum)

Many women worked in cut and sew factories. (Davidson County Historical Museum)

Barbecue stands have been a restaurant fixture in Lexington for years. (Davidson County Historical Museum)

Uncle Dave Macon, an accomplished banjo player, was one of the early performers in the Grand Ole Opry. (Wikipedia Foundation)

Meeting in town on a Saturday afternoon. (Library of Congress, FSA-OWI photo collection, LC-USF33-020890)

Merry-go-rounds and Ferris wheels, great attractions at county fairs. (Library of Congress, FSA-OWI photo collection,LU-USF34-046188)

Rural boys and girls joined 4-H clubs. The young lady is giving a cooking demonstration. (Library of Congress, FSA photo collection, LC-USF34-039196)

Boys had a deep interest in developing projects on animal care. A group of boys preparing to show cattle at the fair. (Library of Congress, FSA-OWI photo collection, LC-USF34-045535)

A feature at the Davidson County fair was women and men divers who would dive from a platform 100 feet above the water, a daring deed, into a relatively small pool. (Davidson County Historical Museum)

NINE
LIFE AS CHILDREN
AND TEENAGERS

Small public grammar schools and private academies dotted the countryside of Davidson County in the decade of the 1920s. The Rev. Jacob Leonard in his 1927 history of Davidson County lists 93 schools for the year ending in 1926. The year 1921–1922 marked the greatest progress in rural schools in the history of the county. The public grammar schools offered programs through the seventh grade. Students who continued their education attended one of the few high schools or private academies. During the same decade, the county began extensive consolidation of the one-, two- and three-room schools. Pilot High School became the first consolidated school in the county opening in 1923 with grades one through eleven. Welcome, Arcadia, and Reeds opened in 1925. Southmont led the way for rural schools in making high school education available in 1914–1915. The small town of Denton also opened its high school about the same time. Linwood School opened it doors for students in grades one through eleven in 1930.

With the completion of Davis-Townsend School on September 15, 1930, and the opening of Silver Valley School, the consolidation of all of rural Davidson County was complete. A superintendent of schools directed the programs for all rural schools in the county, which assured uniform curricula and standards.

With the total enrollment in the county schools numbering in excess of 9,000 in 1930, transporting children became a gigantic effort, and a fleet of buses large enough to transport the students was purchased by the county government. Paul Miller of the Beck's Reformed Church congregation was in the second grade when Linwood School opened in 1930, and he describes the bus he rode as an old T-Model Ford with an engine that lacked enough power to climb Miller Hill. When the bus stalled, all the students debarked. The larger boys pushed the bus as the other students watched, walking up the hill following the bus. Most roads were unpaved in those days, which added to the stalling problem when the tires became stuck in the mud.

Getting Our Education

No experience in early decades of life had a greater impact on me than the 12 years spent at Davis-Townsend High School. What we learned opened the world to us and gave us tools to function effectively in society. Similar stories could be told for Linwood, Southmont, Silver Valley, Denton and possibly any other school in the county.

My school education began in the first grade in the fall of 1936 at the Davis-Townsend School. I and all my classmates had to be at least six years of age by the end of September of that calendar year and had to have had a vaccination for the dreaded disease, smallpox. None of us had ever attended a kindergarten.

Our teachers taught primarily for the love of teaching; their salaries were unenviable. Teachers that still resonate for us included the names Helms, Foster, Tippett, Rivers, Click, Harvey, Shirley, Chadwick, Clodfelter, Smith, Ward, Curry, Miller, Dabbs, Lopp, Honeycutt, Michael, Cieszko, Marsh, Sink, Kearney, McCrary, Gathings, and Bunn. Not all were equal as teachers, but they were great human beings who took awkward and naive children from some of the most rural homes in Davidson County, molded them into responsible citizens with self-confidence, and sent them out into the world.

Memory is a wonderful thing. It gives us roses in winter and snow in summer, and memory allows us to replay life's significant experiences. Memories of school days take those of us born in 1930 into another time when the world was simpler. Our most powerful memories of school do not focus totally on the teachers we had and not even the subjects we studied, both immensely important. Instead, most memories are of other students and the relationships we had with them.

When calling up my bank of school memories, I liken them to a shelf full of books between two large bookends representing the first and last grades, the two most vividly remembered. Between the bookends resides the story of what happened during the intervening years. Strange how those 10 years seem to run together while the first and last years retain clarity.

My three older brothers helped condition me for entering the first grade. I was lucky. The school bus driven by a male high school student stopped in front of our home. By the time the bus reached our stop, many boys and girls had already boarded and taken most of the seats. My older brothers knew the system and boarded ahead of me. By the time I reached the top step of the bus, they were seated comfortably, with the oldest brother in a place on the big seat and the other two on the little seat. I was left to find my seat by myself, which caused temporary panic. Much to my relief, one of the older Smith girls motioned to a place on the little seat and suggested I take it. I sat down, looked around, and concluded that practically everyone else was bigger than I, a frightening revelation.

The driver closed the door, let out the clutch, and headed toward school, turning right on the County Home Road. A few more stops were made along the way. A girl smaller than I boarded the bus. I was beginning to feel more confident about going to school. For a couple more miles, the bus moved along the bumpy dirt road. We arrived at the school, the door of the bus swung open, and the driver said, "This is it."

Experienced students hurried off as I looked for help from an older brother. One of them nudged me toward the door, and we left the bus. My brother said as he hurried off, "Look for bus number 38 when it is time to go home."

Since it was the first day of school, a high school student standing in the doorway helped me find the first-grade room. I entered carrying my lunch for the day in a small brown paper bag. The teacher greeted me and suggested I sit at one of the desks until others arrived. Like all of the other boys, I was wearing bib overalls (or overhalls as we wrongly called them), and the girls wore dresses. My memory is fuzzy on this point, but I believe several of the boys were barefooted.

A bell rang signaling the start of the school day, and you soon learned to recognize the ring of the school bell, which always meant something important. The teacher had put each one of us at a desk admonishing us to sit quietly. How much was accomplished that first day is beyond me. I do remember some of the kids crying a bit and others, including myself, not knowing too much about how to use the equipment in the bathroom. The teacher might have handed out a large pencil to each of us, an eraser, a few sheets of paper, and a first-grade reader. She gave us a list of things we needed to take home to our parents. The bell rang a few times during the day to signal two short recesses, lunch, and the end of the school day.

Somehow I found a line of students waiting to board bus number 38, boarded the bus with them, and sat down on the little seat at about the same spot I had riding to school that morning. Nobody had to tell me, but that spot became my personal seat for the remainder of the year. When the bus stopped in front of our house, we debarked, and I scurried up the driveway and went inside the house eager to tell my mom about my first day at school. No day would match it for the rest of my school days.

As the year progressed, Miss Cress, the first grade teacher, taught us how to read from a book about Dick and Jane, and we used the large pencils to print on paper crossed by special lines. Each of us had a box containing at least eight Crayola crayons purchased by our parents if they could afford them. Some parents did not have enough money for the purchase, and the school provided a few used crayons. We learned about colors, and how mixing yellow and blue would turn green as if by magic.

Each day, the teacher led us in singing, and from time to time another teacher came to the room and taught us special things about music. In a few weeks, by playing together on the playground and hearing the teacher call the roll each morning, we began to learn everybody's names. Still, a few students remained unhappy, and the teacher asked some parents to come after school for a conference. One day, a boy wet his pants, and a few students laughed at him, which angered the teacher. The next time this happened, those who laughed had to help clean the floor.

Attending school was fun, and learning new things made us want to come each day. All of the students in the first three grades would assemble in the big auditorium every couple of weeks for what was called chapel. The principal of the school talked to us one day about how glad he was that we were in his school. Most chapels began by saying the Pledge of Allegiance to the flag. We put our hands over our hearts, faced a flag of the United States and said words that were initially difficult to say and then remember. The teacher told us how much the Pledge of Allegiance meant, and we practiced it in our room to get to know it better. As the days passed by, we became better at reading and printing. When the printing or art work with crayons looked good, the teacher would let us take our papers home to show our parents. Miss Cress was a good teacher.

Near the end of the first half of the year, our teacher told us that the principal wanted us to give a play on the big stage of the auditorium, and she began assigning parts to some members of the class. Delores would be the Interlocutor, I was to be Mr. Stone, and someone else was to be Mr. Wood. She said everybody would get to stand on the stage, some with Mr. Stone and some with Mr. Wood. The class would go to the auditorium when no one else was there, and Miss Cress lined us up on the stage as if we were already giving the play. We spent a lot of time getting ready, which she said was important to give a good performance, and we memorized what we were going to say.

The day for the next chapel arrived, and Miss Cress said we were ready to perform. She had made a dress out of red crepe paper for Delores to wear, a brown hat for me and a gray hat for Mr. Wood. We lined up on stage with a large red velvet curtain drawn so the audience could not see us. The principal told the students from the other classes that Miss Cress's first grade would be giving an operetta that day.

Everybody became very quiet while Miss Cress pulled on some ropes until the big red curtain opened completely. None of us had ever been on a stage before an audience. She motioned to Delores to begin as she had done during practice, and Delores looked at me and asked, "Mr. Stone, how are you and all of your little pebbles?" I responded, too nervous to remember what I said, and Delores looked at Mr. Wood and asked, "Mr. Wood, how are you and all of your little splinters?" Being the Interlocutor, Delores asked some more questions, after which Miss Cress pulled on the same ropes to close the curtain. The students in the audience clapped, and we all felt good. When we got back to our room, Miss Cress told us how proud she was of us, and we felt good for a second time.

The year continued learning songs about Thanksgiving and Christmas. One of the big boys in high school helped Miss Cress put up a few decorations, and before we took the Christmas break, she gave each one of us a small rubber car. As she called our names she attempted to roll the car in each of our directions. School dismissed, and she told us she would see us in two weeks and wished us a Merry Christmas.

We took school one year at a time progressing and progressing. The subjects we studied challenged us year after year, most bearing the same title. For example, arithmetic came in each grade in grammar school, as did English, reading, and writing. The name remained the same, but the subject increased in difficulty each year. In the second and third grades, we learned multiplication tables up to the number 10, and by the sixth grade, the top number went all the way to 25. Funny how these numbers have stayed with me, and I notice that many teenagers today cannot multiply 7 x 9 not to mention 25 x 25.

Our first history course came about the fourth grade. We learned about the origin of our ancestors. We read about Sir Walter Raleigh and his deed of putting his coat in a wet spot so the Queen of England would not get her shoes muddy. I never thought of it being a big deal, but someone must have seen value in the act because our state capital was named in his honor. The girls in the class saw something romantic about it, and we boys wondered, what the heck is romance?

The subject was called North Carolina History, and the following year we studied United States History which introduced us to Christopher Columbus. I must admit, Columbus exhibited much courage sailing into unknown waters and wondering all the while if his three ships might fall off the edge of the world. At that time, I could not understand why such a smart man thought he had gone all the way to India. The class probably developed its real love for the United States in the history course. I know I did learning how we fought against England for freedom and won it.

For some reason, I had a special affinity for geography. We began studying the subject in the fourth grade first learning about North America. Each year after that, we would study another part of the world—Europe, Africa, Asia. I really liked studying the different parts of the world, and it was fun looking for them on the big globe located in most classrooms. Two countries became favorites, Argentina and the Congo, although I do not remember why I liked them more than others. Perhaps it was because of the pictures in the geography books. Argentina had large wheat fields, plenty of cattle, and cowboys dressed differently than those seen at the Granada Theater on Saturdays. A picture of a cowboy in Argentina had the word "gaucho" printed under it. I wondered why a cowboy was not a cowboy in every country.

We learned about the Congo when we studied Africa, and I was amused by the Congo because the book said the people lived in the jungle. "Where was

Tarzan of the Apes?" as described by Edgar Rice Burroughs in the Sunday comics, I asked myself. A picture in the book of people living in the Congo has become a permanent fixture in my mind. Two men with no more than a wash rag around their waists had large tin can lids for lips. You could see how they had cut their lips to make the lids fit. I puzzled for years how the two fellows could possibly eat food or drink water. They were members of the Ubangi tribe, the name of a smaller river that ran into the Congo River.

Learning the basic elements of writing correct English gave all of us problems. What were nouns, pronouns, adjectives, verbs, adverbs, prepositions, and conjunctions? How did they come up with the subject and predicate of a sentence? In due time, we knew some of the answers. If we did not develop a good understanding of the English language in a particular grade, we received further instruction the next year. In fact, we studied English every year until we graduated. I was beginning to think learning English was a life-long process.

Beginning with the third grade and for the next three years at least, the "Weekly Reader" newspaper came by mail for each of us at a cost of no more than one penny per week. Even at this low price, some students could not afford to pay for it, and we were encouraged to share it with others. In addition to the Reader bringing the events of the week to our fingertips, we learned to appreciate the misfortune of others and the good feelings that sharing brings.

By the fourth or fifth grade, the school opened a cafeteria, which meant eliminating the need for lunch in paper bags. The teachers said carrying our lunch in a bag did not make sense with hot food available. Parents liked the idea of a cafeteria except for those not able to afford the per-day cost of five cents, but the state or county provided financial assistance for the needy. The first lunch menu I remember consisted of a bowl of tomato soup, crackers, one half pint of pasteurized milk and an apple. Most of us had never tasted soup, and frankly we experienced difficulty adjusting to the new way of getting our lunch. Hot tomato soup smelled strange, pasteurized milk tasted awful, but the apple saved the day. We overheard the teachers praise the soup which puzzled most of us, who also felt the process of pasteurization killed the taste of fresh farm milk. We adapted to cafeteria food, and found that lining up to go to the cafeteria could be fun as we pushed and shoved to get into the line. We also jostled each other during recess, a twice–daily, beloved feature of school.

School without recess periods would be like a baseball without a bat. A typical school day had two recesses, one in the morning and one in the afternoon. In the first two or three years, playing on seesaws or swings were favorite activities as were rope jumping and the game of tag. In the middle school years, group participation frequently occurred in such games as dodge ball, outdoor basketball, red rover, kick ball and softball. Kids also brought marble sacks, smoothed out places on bare ground, and drew a ring in which to play the game.

In high school, the girls often used time at recess to talk about boys, going on dates, or making plans for a social at one of their homes. Boys talked about girls, but also engaged in physical games such as basketball and tag football, which sometimes became rough and resulted in skinned arms and knees and even broken bones. No students could leave the school ground during recess without the permission of the principal, but students of daring sneaked their way to a nearby store to make a purchase. Some of the boys had already developed a smoking habit, and they would play a game of cat and mouse with the principal by lighting up a cigarette in the boys' rest room. Nothing stirred the ire of Principal Gathings more than smoking.

Discipline was strict both in and out of the classroom. Two things absolutely forbidden were cheating on tests and abusive talking in class. Violations of either led to stern punishment usually in the form of a trip to the principal's office, the most dreaded event in a student's life at school. The principal served as the judge and jury in determining the extent of the punishment, which usually came in the form of a paddling or whipping by the principal or the teacher. The principal kept a paddle just for this purpose, and he knew how to use it. Boys received more whippings than girls, probably, which is not to say that boys misbehaved more than girls, but the principal handled punishment for girls in a more delicate manner. But never was any student excused from appropriate punishment.

Occasionally, when cheating on a test occurred, it usually involved a boy copying an answer from a girl's paper. We would hear an ill-prepared boy sitting behind a girl pleading in a whisper to her to lean to the side so he would have a better view of what she had written. Getting caught doing this resulted in an "F" or a zero for the boy and no opportunity to advance his case or mount a defense.

A story made the rounds among students about a boy who got his answer from a girl's paper where she had written, "I do not know the answer to this question." The boy wrote on his paper, "I don't know the answer either."

Classroom teachers used the technique of requiring students to write sentences on the blackboard as punishment. For example if caught talking, chewing gum, or throwing paper, a student might have to write at least one hundred times, a sentence saying, "I must not talk in class," or "I must not do so and so." Often the teacher would require the student to write the sentences on a sheet of paper as homework, writing exactly what he or she prescribed. You cannot imagine how writing sentences at home became double jeopardy, alerting parents about misconduct at school. Usually, when the principal meted out a paddling, our parents gave us another at home. Misbehaving in school had no redeeming features.

The lawn in front of our school had a fence around it measuring no more than 18 inches high. It was strictly forbidden for any student to place his or her foot on the grass on the other side of the fence. For some strange reason the principal never missed seeing this violation, and the person, boy or girl, stepping on the grass received at least one lick with the paddle on the spot. It was as if the principal were more than one person or had eyes in the back of his head. Not only did the lick with the paddle hurt, you were embarrassed in front of the other students. Whatever the type of punishment a student received, a lesson was learned. He or she had to pay the consequences for breaking rules.

Rules for playground and recess behavior seemed to have been written after committing a misdeed. When I was in the fourth grade, I made a great error in judgment by entering into a tussle with a student two years my senior even though he was in my class. He had failed two grades his first six years. The scuffle started in the gymnasium while waiting for the school bus to take us home. Just who landed the first blow, I do not remember, but we went at it for about 10 minutes which seemed much longer since my opponent got the best of me. The principal caught us in the act when he entered the gym to tell us our bus was ready.

Did we escape his paddle? Not in the least, because he had a policy of allowing students to go home in such situations and report to his office the next morning to discuss the ordeal. One of my brothers charged ahead of me when we stepped off the bus at home telling Mom of the fight in an exaggerated fashion. She promptly laid a switch across my behind which already hurt from the tussle, not waiting for my explanation. Having received orders from the principal to come to his office the first thing the next day made the night extra long, but I went to school and received my paddling as expected. Never again did I commit such an egregious error. The lessons learned were many, but one error not made again was to pick on someone older and larger than I was.

By the fourth or fifth grades, boys, for some reason they did not quite understand, began to pay more attention to the teacher, especially if she was attractive and nice. Anything she would ask of the boys was done gladly and immediately. A Miss Tippett had beautiful red hair and a graceful walk. A classmate named James who had failed a grade or two earlier seemed to have a better understanding than I did about the sudden attraction for Miss Tippett. Whenever she smiled she received complete attention, and whatever she said, we boys believed. James remarked one day about how nice she smelled. We did not know it at the time, but growing up had its benefits.

The word debate was introduced into our vocabulary in the sixth or seventh grade. In studying U.S. history, the word was used to describe an argument about slavery between President Lincoln and a senator named Douglas from Illinois. Our teacher wanted us to understand how arguments could be settled without getting into a fight.

To further illustrate the meaning of "debate," the teacher asked two students to debate the question: Resolved, the mule is more valuable than the bicycle. A boy named Horace was asked to take the affirmative (another new word) side and Paul was asked to take the negative side. They were to prepare for the debate as homework, and the rest of us were told to look forward to the next day to hear what Paul and Horace would say. When the history period arrived, the teacher asked Horace to stand before the class and repeat the debate question. He gave his reasons to be in favor of the question.

Too many years have passed to remember much of what he said, but I do remember him saying the mule is more valuable because you do not have to buy tars (tires), a mule never needed painting, and a mule could pull a plow. Horace completed his argument, and Paul stood before the class and said that a bicycle never needed oats, corn, or hay, and the owner did not have to clean out a stable. He ended by saying you do not have to buy harness for a bicycle. The teacher asked us to vote for the boy who gave the better reasons, and we learned two boys can discuss a topic without it ending in a fight.

In addition to our studies, we would assist the teachers with classroom chores such as erasing the blackboard and dusting the erasers. The other students envied the person asked to do the latter because this called for a trip outside the building to stand at the top of the fire escape. For some reason, carrying several felt erasers in your hands made a person feel like King Kong, especially as he or she beat the erasers on the rail of the fire escape until the air cleared of chalk dust.

Report cards came out every six weeks showing grades for each subject, and if the teacher had additional comments about a student's progress, it would be noted on the back side of the card. We took them home for parental review and a signature from at least one parent.

A life-changing comment was written in ink by the teacher on the reverse side of my card after the first six-week period in the sixth grade. It simply said, "Eugene can do much better if he would." This was not so bad, so I thought, but Mom thought differently. As far as I can remember this was the final time she used a dogwood switch on me with authority. She did sign the card, and the next day it was returned to the teacher, who asked if my mother read her comment. Sheepishly, I replied with a yes.

What a wake-up call to action. Reveille sounded with a blast, knocking me for a loop. For the remainder of my school days, the report card was filled with "A's." Miss Click's message was never forgotten. and afterwards studying became fun and all subjects interesting. Getting an education began in earnest on that day, and I suppose it is correct to say Miss Click made a serious scholar out of me. Studying became fun and all subjects interesting. I owe her, my sixth-grade teacher, a tremendous debt of gratitude and realize that "eight little words" can make all the difference in a person's life, especially when re-enforced with a dogwood switch. Next year, having a report card void of the message was a welcome relief.

Beyond the seventh grade, activities inside and outside the classroom multiplied ad infinitum. We students began to appreciate each other, and a few couples paired and experienced puppy-love relationships often felt by adolescents. As if by magic, we moved into the pre-adult stages of life. We were acting clumsy on our feet and in conversation but getting more excited about the future. Annual class picnics became more than just skipping stones on the creek's surface. They had many elements of an adult social.

We loved walking the two-mile hike to an isolated picnic site near a railroad trestle on the bank of Abbotts Creek engaged in grown-up dialogue all the way there and back. Funny stories were told, and dreams and hopes for the future surfaced. A few of us wanted to go to college, others to work in town or stay on the farm while others imagined a marriage and rearing a family.

Our time had come to participate in the varsity sports of basketball and baseball and experience the ecstasy of winning and the agony of defeat. Those lacking athletic skills sat in the stands and cheered for the athletes. Organized football did not come until years later with further school consolidations. Another performance opportunity was the school plays, which challenged us to be good thespians. Play practice after school could be as much fun as it gets. If the play called for a person of color, one of us wore black-face makeup and attempted to alter speech to fit the role.

On the night of the production, members of families filled every seat in the auditorium as we said our lines. Occasionally one or two actors or actresses would forget their lines, and the faculty director prompted and encouraged them through the stage drapes. I can still remember the play parts of Booger-face Boggs and Whaley McWhorter. Those were the days.

A more serious role played by residents, young and old, was a wartime one. During World War II, we were told by the nation's president we should be prepared if the enemy attacked us with an air raid, and we practiced "blackouts" by making sure every light bulb in the county was turned off. Practice began when factory whistles signaled us when to make our homes dark, and ended with a second whistle. Schools also conducted air raid responses. Teachers instructed us to get under our desks as if we would have been saved from bodily injury by the small wooden desk. Fortunately, enemy bombs did not reach the shores of the United States.

By the tenth grade, Mr. Gathings, our principal, asked a student to be responsible for collecting and counting the lunch money from each classroom teacher early Monday morning. My turn to collect for one-half of a school year was a lesson in trust and responsibility.

Our teachers did their level best to help us reach our potential as we studied algebra, geometry, physics, English, history, social studies, sociology, biology, chemistry, science, French, dramatics, and vocational agriculture. All boys, most of whom feared French, took vocational agriculture, pretending their future rested with farming. The class taught leadership skills and the courage to speak before a group. It was not a choice that boys made; girls were not allowed to take agriculture, so they studied French instead.

Our entire class by the senior year numbered only 20 students, all of whom had started together in a class of 40 in two rooms in the eighth grade. The sole exception was a student who had returned from the military service to complete high school. A dropout rate of 50 percent between the eighth and twelfth grades was common in the 1940s for rural high schools, because many students stayed home to work on the farm and others married at an early age. Truancy laws required all students to remain in school until reaching the age of sixteen.

Each classmate had his or her favorite teacher, but we all agreed on Mr. Gathings, the principal we had from the first grade through the eleventh, when he decided to retire. The day was sad when we went home for summer vacation and returned to a total stranger our final year. The high quality of instruction at Davis-Townsend High School prepared us well for the future. Three of us went on to college attending classes with students graduating from some of the largest and best high schools in the state and nation. We held our own, and even excelled in many subjects. Our high school chemistry teacher armed us with a background in the subject vastly superior to what most other students brought with them, and the same thing could be said for U.S. history. Perhaps, the most important ingredients instilled in us in high school were manifested in the form of good common sense and the ability to get along with others.

Of course, some of our teachers possessed their own idiosyncrasies which were fodder for chatter at recess or social functions. One male teacher was a bundle of nerves, and several of the boys decided to jack up his automobile and put it on blocks at a night basketball game. Mission accomplished, the boys hid among the school shrubbery to see how the teacher would handle his dilemma. He got in his car, cranked it, put it in reverse, but the vehicle remained stationary. No rain had fallen for days; yet the teacher started yelling for help, asking for a shovel to extract his car from the mud, which prompted a huge laugh from the observers. The next day in class, the teacher gave the perpetrators a skillfully delivered lecture that shamed all of them while gaining genuine sympathy from the remainder of the class.

The lesson had an impact, driving home an important lesson: For every action, there is an equal reaction. Similarly, we discovered that using vulgarity and profanity had no place at school, either in the classrooms or on the playground.

Our principal taught us about individual freedom and responsibility. Extra-curricula activities seemed to come in droves in the form of public speaking, serving on staffs of the school newspaper and yearbook, playing basketball and baseball, canvassing businesses in Lexington and locally for support for sanctioned activities, taking the senior trip, and so forth. Engaging in any of these was no excuse to shirk classroom responsibilities. School bus drivers had the greatest responsibility of all students, the safety and care of their passengers. Bus drivers were captains of their vehicles at all times, and when they left the school ground, all riders knew who was in charge.

Our teachers knew instinctively that our knowledge of different kinds of music had its limitations largely because of a lack of exposure. We knew church hymns, country and western tunes, and big band music heard in movies and on the radio. Attempts were made by a few teachers to introduce us to classical music by playing recordings in class, and much to our surprise, she played something more than vaguely familiar, the "William Tell Overture." When the phonograph needle touched the record, our first reaction was that the Lone Ranger and Tonto were about to come charging through the classroom on their horses. The "William Tell Overture" was the theme song for the Lone Ranger radio program. The teacher had made her point that we and classical music were not strangers at all. Prior to the classroom demonstration, no one suspected it was a piece of great classical music. The teacher stressed that the world around us is filled with many pleasant surprises, and the challenge is to recognize and appreciate them.

Graduation from school came after 12 long years of doing what was at our fingertips, but in retrospect the time seems as a fleeting moment. We gathered in the school auditorium for the graduation ceremony in May 1948, the last official occasion for all 20 of us assembled as one body. We listened to several speeches and received diplomas from the principal. Our final act was to sing "Farewell to Thee," a tear jerker and a tradition of graduating classes for years. The meaning of feeling "agony and ecstasy" simultaneously found its target as we struggled to say our goodbyes, to receive congratulations, and to promise each other that we would stay in touch.

Of all of the experiences that life affords, those accumulated during the process of getting an education remain unmatched. For some, the time in school did not go well, as disappointments piled up year after year. For others, images of school days rekindle the best of times, friendships, laughter, successes, the building of dreams and the challenge of studying and academic achievements. Good or bad, school experiences helped shape how we emerged as adults. Those students who found school to be some of the best times of their lives began to have reunions soon after graduation.

They kept in touch as vowed on graduation day and found reunions a time to reflect and remember.

Celebrating Special Days

Our lives as children and teens were shaped outside school, as well. Our family homes and our communities were fertile grounds for learning many lessons and forming values that would last a lifetime. Holidays provided peak experiences to be nostalgically recreated. Of all the holidays of the year, Christmas was the best loved, most anticipated, in the South for at least two reasons. First, our ancestors passed the Christian faith to us. We practiced it, and we were committed to celebrating the birthday of Christ. Second, the excitement of the Christmas season was a special time of gift-giving and receiving, and visits with relatives and neighbors. The trimming of a tree, the sumptuous meals prepared when food was available, and the many other festivities conducted around Christmas made it a joyous occasion. During the Great Depression of the 1930s, incomes remained pitifully low for most working families and those living on farms. Very little money was available for purchasing tangible items such as gifts, special foodstuffs for the main meal on Christmas Day, fresh fruit and nuts for unusual treats at Christmastime, or gasoline by those who had automobiles to drive to visit relatives. Yet, those Christmases of scarcity were some of our happiest times, and we remembered them most and still cherish them today. What we had for Christmas in the 1930s and the years of World War II did not come without sacrifice and hard work, and we were especially thankful for what little we had. To make it from year to year required each member of the family to contribute his or her energies and know-how in planting and harvesting crops, tending to the livestock, looking after the sick, doing the washing and ironing, keeping the house clean, doing the cooking and sewing, and taking responsibility for other tasks. Through love and respect for each other, we worked together as a family unit as if it were a small factory producing the bare essentials for survival. In tough times, the toughness in each of us got going, and when Christmas Day arrived near the end of each year, we prided ourselves for having done our best.

Stockings were hung on the mantel by the chimney—"chimley"—with care or a shoe box was placed on the hearth as receptacles for whatever gift "Sandy Claus" might bring. Some families could not afford stockings for both wearing and hanging on the mantel. Having a fire in the fireplace on Christmas Eve caused us to worry for fear Santa would burn himself in the hot coals when he descended the chimney. No one ever explained the connection, if there was one, between Santa Claus and Christmas. We believed the fairy tale about him until an older sibling or playmate destroyed our innocence by revealing the true Santa Claus story. The truth about Santa Claus seemed to make itself known around the age of six, but we really did not mind our parents playing the role as long as he showed up. We knew not to expect much and rejoiced over any surprise. The toe of the stocking or the bottom of the shoe box might have contained a small rubber ball, a few dried raisins with seeds, an orange, and a few pieces of candy. Sometimes Santa would bring a single item such as a writing pad or a small atlas essential for school work. In better years, gifts included several pieces of fruit, a small sack of chocolate drops, sticks of peppermint and horehound candy, or a box of crayons. I can remember one boy getting a used bicycle, and he was the envy of every kid in the neighborhood. Being used made no difference. The kid had a bicycle. One girl was thrilled to receive a scooter from Santa Claus, a gift she would never forget. Whatever we received made us grateful because we knew the parents of some boys and girls could afford nothing at all, and we arose with unparalleled excitement early on Christmas morning to see what was in our stockings and boxes. We knew our parents had done the very best they could.

Finding a red cedar tree on the farm suitable for decorating as a Christmas tree always brought excitement because this signaled Christmas would soon be upon us. Our dad or older brothers would cut and haul the tree from the forest or field to the house, where it would be mounted on a board and placed upright in the best furnished room, the front room, in the house. The decorations were meager at best and homemade except for a box of silver tinsel purchased at the five and ten store in town. Strips were cut from brightly colored sheets of paper and made into circles or large rings looped to form chains and wrapped around the tree. Any tinsel available found its way on the end of the branches giving the appearance of icicles. A few thin-walled silver, red, or gold balls might be added to give the tree a special look, and strings of electric lights became commonplace in early nineteen forties after houses became wired for electricity. Gifts for the adult members of the family were wrapped in special paper and placed under the tree for opening on Christmas Day.

The custom of gift giving started several hundred years before Christ was born which distances the practice as a Christian religious custom. In the United States, gift giving around Christmastime began in the 1820s, though the promotion of the concept started years earlier. By the 1840s, exchanging gifts became mainstream in American society and increased tremendously in the 1930s when Coca-Cola incorporated Santa Claus into its marketing campaigns.

When my generation was coming of age, shooting fireworks on Christmas Day was as traditional in the South as gift giving or going to church on Christmas Eve. Although we didn't wonder about the origin of pyrotechnics, historical evidence shows that lighting fireworks and shooting firearms were practiced for years in the U.S. to noisily celebrate. Early settlers communicated Christmas greetings to their neighbors in this way. It was thought to also frighten off evil spirits. Nevertheless, one of the most eagerly awaited Christmas traditions was shooting fireworks on Christmas Eve and Christmas Day. Approximately two or three weeks before Christmas, we searched through the yearly mail-order catalogs to make an affordable list of the various types of fireworks, because our limited resources kept orders to a minimum. Scarcely anyone had more than a dollar to spend for fireworks, and most of us could not scrape up as much as fifty cents. Fortunately, fifty cents would purchase an incredibly large selection, especially if we excluded the more costly boomers.

Firecrackers called Zebras made a loud noise for their price, and a ten-cent pack contained as many as 100 or more pieces. If you could be content with a much softer explosion, you could get 100 of the so-called penny firecrackers for one cent. With pooled resources among us brothers, we would order a sky-rocket or two, several packages of Zebras, a few Roman candles, fire bombs having enough explosive power to rip an empty tin can to pieces, chasers that would swirl rapidly and give off a loud shrill before exploding, and a few boxes of sparklers for the younger children. In families with only one son, pooling resources was not an option. One such boy in our neighborhood approached us after our order had arrived one year asking to purchase four cents worth of Zebras. His request amused my brothers and me, and from that day forward, he carried the moniker, Zebra. Lighting firecrackers with a match or smol-dering coals was a very dangerous sport, and we took more than our share of risks. Once the fuse of a firecracker was lit, you had only a few seconds to throw it safely away from everyone. In fact, the practice was so dangerous in the hands of novices that the federal government issued a law banning the mail ordering of fireworks products in the 1960s.

While the teenagers and younger boys shot their fireworks, the older men in some communities found their own way to celebrate noisily. They took their guns off the racks and went rabbit hunting with a pack of dogs. Through-out the afternoon on Christmas Day, the barking of dogs trailing the scents of rabbits was accompanied by the sound of exploding shotgun shells echoing across the hills and hollows.

One of the great memories of Christmas was sitting down with all or most of the family at our mom's dinner table covered with a spread of food unequaled at any other meal during the year. Even in the Depression years, we had plenty of food at our fingertips at Christmas because of a good supply of canned vegetables and fruits in the pantry and cured or fresh pork from an early winter slaughter. Fried chicken and baked hen fresh from the barnyard or the chicken house made the top of the menu. Potatoes, both white and sweet, came out of storage to increase the choices. Wheat grain from storage bins had been milled into flour for baking biscuits, pies, and cakes. The Christmas Day dinner is remembered as a highlight of the total celebration.

The last Thursday in November was set aside as a national holiday to be called "Thanksgiving Day" by a proclamation issued by President Abraham

Lincoln. We learned in school about the first Thanksgiving celebration held in Massachusetts by the pilgrims and the Indians sharing an autumn harvest feast. What has evolved over the years still centers around counting our blessings and a meal consumed with the same spirit of celebration and overindulgence.

How we celebrated Thanksgiving Day during the time of our youth is not remembered so much for the food on the table but rather the feelings of gratitude shown by members of the family. We had produced and gathered another crop in preparation for the winter, and when we sat down for the dinner, it was a time to reflect on the past few months and have a thankful heart for the things we had and shared. During the depression, we understood our most precious possessions to be our families and friends, not the materialistic items we touched and felt. During World War II, our thoughts focused on the war itself, and how we wished for a victory soon so the men and women away from our communities could return. Not as much chatter and banter went around the table because of the uncertainty of the future. We feared the worst and hoped for the best. Above all, we were thankful the war was being fought in distant lands and not at home. Even though we often sang the old song, "Count Your Many Blessings, Name Them One by One," during church services, we were not the type of people who verbalized extensively about our blessings. We knew them one by one intuitively and took none for granted.

Together, we feasted on a sumptuous dinner prepared by the grandmothers, mothers, and daughters. By that time of the year, a hog or two had been butchered, so fresh pork, especially fried tenderloin and sausage, filled a large platter bolstered by dishes of vegetables, potatoes, canned sauerkraut, fresh cabbage, relishes, and plenty of homemade biscuits. Many families also added a baked hen and dressing to the menu, and the pies and cakes never disappointed us.

In the afternoon, we sat around a cleaned dining table and shared thoughts and stories about major concerns of the times while the food settled in our stomachs. Later in the day, the men and older boys might have headed for the fields and woods for a rabbit hunt. The women and girls continued the conversation, but the focus moved away from manly concerns to children and grandchildren and activities in the community. Whatever we did, it was a time for being together being thankful for our families.

"Easter Sunday" or "Resurrection Sunday" was the day we celebrated the resurrection of Jesus from the dead. Curiously enough, many people considered it to be the most holy of religious holidays, being the only time they attended church services. Of course, Christmas ran a close second, but it only occurred on a Sunday every few years; Easter was always on Sunday. Christmas had its Santa Claus, and Easter had its Easter rabbit, and if the animal had any meaningful tie to Easter, we never knew about it. Rather than bringing gifts, as we credited a white bearded fellow, the Easter rabbit brought us eggs leaving them in a moss nest in the backyard or in a basket strategically placed in the house. During the depression, most of the eggs were hard-boiled, colored hen eggs, but later when affordable, candy eggs replaced them. Why eggs? All of us had seen rabbits, and none carried eggs. Nevertheless, this mythical creature, the Easter rabbit, made getting up on Sunday morning an exciting adventure. An old sage in the community told a group of my friends and me that the Easter rabbit was born in Germany, and our ancestors brought the idea here. He also said that in ancient times, there was a custom among people in Egypt and Italy of giving eggs. None of us had any idea about Egypt or Italy, but it did not matter as long as the Easter bunny brought us eggs.

Church service on Easter Sunday stuck closely to the resurrection story, and we always sang hymns about the cross and Jesus rising from the dead. Seldom did we miss singing "Onward Christian Soldiers" and "Up from the Grave He Arose." The preacher made the congregation get extra quiet as he told us that one day the people buried in the cemetery a few hundred feet away also would rise up from the dead. The small kids would move closer to their mothers and fathers when the preacher spoke of this promise, and the adults seemed to be comforted by the thought.

Easter Sunday was a time when we would wear our finest clothes, especially the women and girls of all ages. Every woman wore her newest and most colorful spring hat, and the little girls donned either hats or bonnets. Most of the dresses were new, and purses and shoes matched; a pair of white gloves provided accent. Church service was literally an Easter parade, and we loved it. After church, no young lady came to the dinner table without changing clothes first for fear she would soil them.

Four other holidays had special meaning: New Year's Day, the Fourth of July, Labor Day, and Armistice Day, but none received as much attention as Christmas or Easter. We did look forward to a new year each January first. Black-eyed peas were cooked in some homes and served on New Year's Day supposedly to bring good luck during the coming twelve months. We were also told that we should go to the barn on New Year's Eve and observe cows getting down on their knees to pray at midnight, but I never saw one in a prayerful position.

The Fourth of July, the anniversary of our forefathers signing of the Declaration of Independence, usually passed without much fanfare unless we emerged from the fields early enough for a picnic or a watermelon cutting. Labor Day meant absolutely nothing to people living on farms, but people who worked in the factories in Lexington or Thomasville appreciated their day of rest. Armistice Day commemorated the ending of World War I, and occasionally, we would go to town to enjoy a parade of bands and veterans in military uniform. Birthdays of President Washington and Lincoln were honored largely through school activities.

Halloween, the evening of October 31 and eve of all Saints Day, took on special significance even though it was not an official holiday. It originated in Europe, and our ancestors brought it with them in the early 19th century when waves of immigration were heavy. Various countries in Europe had individual ways of celebrating, so what we had was probably a combination redesigned to fit our own desires. Halloween has always had a strong connection with ghosts and the dead, and even the occult sphere. It was understandable why black cats, skeletons, witches, and gravestones symbolized Halloween for us. Pumpkins came into the picture to illustrate the story of a man named Jack who was banned from heaven and hell, and he wandered the world carrying a lantern to brighten it up. This tale was the origin of hollowing out a pumpkin, carving a face on it, and putting a candle inside, hence the name jack-o'-lantern. On Halloween evening, pumpkin faces of every description glowed all through the villages and the countryside.

Halloween for us as children and teenagers presented an opportunity to play tricks on others and to do things to scare them as well. The schools held Halloween Carnivals earlier in the week in darkened gymnasiums decorated with drawings and cutouts of pictures of witches, pumpkins, tombstones, black cats, and skeletons. Booths sponsoring games of chance offered challenges to the attendees. Students in costumes demonstrated witchcraft and supernatural acts. Efforts at deception were commonplace such as representing peeled grapes as eyeballs to blindfolded children. The presence of a large tub filled with water and floating apples tested bobbing skills—the ability to bite and lift the wet fruit in one attempt.

On Halloween eve we dressed up with masks or painted our faces, and made our way throughout the community armed with arsenals of scary tricks, but never collecting treats. It was not the custom. Ringing of doorbells was not an option either, because very few homes had them. Filling paper bags with water and tossing them on front porches ranked high on our lists, and moving furniture from porches into the front yard was another irritant. Some of the bravest and most mischievous boys would toss small pebbles at passing cars.

The adults would tell us stories about how they turned over outhouses on Halloween night when they were young although the evidence of such misdeeds was never presented. Jokes were suggested about turning over an outhouse with grandpa in it. Several of the older teenagers on one occasion made a straw man which they called their dummy. They placed it along the roadside at strategic locations compelling passing motorists to think they had spotted an injured or dead pedestrian, bringing their car to a screeching halt. How the teenagers kept from being arrested could never be explained. One community leader who spied the dummy along the road became so nervous he called an ambulance. Soon it arrived, sounding its siren and pulling to a stop. The crew loaded the dummy on a stretcher and the ambulance left with lights flashing.

The pranksters never saw the dummy again, and out of fear of being caught, they never broadcast their misdeeds in the community.

Mischievous kids made great use of a long piece of kite string and an empty pocketbook, essentials needed to fool someone into thinking they had found money, a common Halloween hoax. Pranksters usually quite young would tie the string to the pocketbook, carefully place it along a path or road where it could be easily spotted, and lie in wait behind a bush or tree. Sooner or later an unsuspecting person would spy the pocketbook and bend down to retrieve it. At that very moment, the kids would gently and slowly tug at the string causing the pocketbook to disappear. Everyone involved had a good laugh at the expense of the passerby.

So it was with Halloween; an evening and night of witchcraft activities, glowing jack-o'-lanterns on front porches and youngsters dressed as ghosts and goblins having fun.

Throughout the ages, Valentine's Day offered the best opportunity to send a message to an existing or potential sweetheart even as far back as the days of the Roman Empire. St. Valentine was a romantic figure, and when imprisoned in Rome was reputed to have written a letter to a young lady with whom he had fallen in love and signed it, "From your Valentine." This simple but meaningful phrase has decorated many notes exchanged between the sexes of all ages. For a young boy or girl whose heart throbbed for someone's attention, this line could conveniently convey heart-felt feelings toward the intended on Valentine's Day. Eager school boys and girls would watch intently across the room to see how the recipients reacted when the valentines were read. We called such admiration in the grammar school "puppy love." Valentine messages could be sent from boy to girl or vice versa. Sometimes messages such as "be my valentine" would be intercepted by a classmate and read aloud, disclosing secret admirers and usually embarrassing both the sender and the intended. We always looked forward to Valentine's Day.

Nicknames

Some of us bore names that would not soon be forgotten, and sometimes served as permanent monikers. Descriptive names added to or replacing the name our parents gave us created distinctive nicknames. In our community, having a nickname became the rule rather than the exception. In some families with as many as 10 children, all of them might have had nicknames. It was not that given names were rejected; rather, circumstances or events often led to a new designation, deemed appropriate and assigned to someone for a lifetime, especially among family members and close friends. My parents gave me the name, Eugene or Gene, but when I was about four years old, the nickname, "Guinea," emerged. As quick as lightning, my uncles, aunts, and cousins made the transition to calling me Guinea. According to my mom, my older brother had difficulty pronouncing Gene, saying Guinea. Charmed, the others adopted the "new name" and it became a permanent tag. Seventy-five years later and after living away from the community for more than 50 years, I am referred to by my cousins as Guinea when I return home. In my case, one nickname was not enough. I was the youngest child in the family for six and one-half years which led to a second nickname, "Babe." My siblings still call me Babe.

Following are nicknames that were common in the area, along with the given names and, if known, an explanation of their origin, included:

Shorty (Bruce): The school principal asked Bruce to press the button on the classroom wall to make the school bell ring saying, "Would you ring the bell, Shorty if you can reach the button?"

Hicks (Wayne): Wayne was driving a team of mules pulling a wagon at wheat threshing, and riding on the wagon was a colored man named Hicks. Wayne in negotiating a sharp curve went too fast and Hicks fell off. Wayne's buddies teased him about his driving ability and called him Hicks ever after.

Moze (Raymond): He moved like Old Man Moze, a character in the comics.

Flukie (Clarence): Clarence placed an automobile generator with a propeller on it on top of a tall pole, and on windy days, he expected it to generate electricity for the home. The *Amos and Andy* show had a character named Flookie who played the role of an inventor, hence the name was transferred to Clarence.

Lefty (Homer): Homer pitched baseball left handed.

Tib (Bryce): His mother gave him his nickname for an unknown reason.

Cooder (Lohr): Someone said he looked like a "Cooder." No such word exists in the English language; however, a German word spelled Koeder and pronounced Cooder means to entice or bait.

Freck (Laura Frances): As a child, she developed a beautiful pattern of freckles.

Mil (Mildred): Mil is a short for Mildred.

Bubber (Lloyd): Bubber is a name for brother.

Shoe Peg, Rooster (Peggy Ruth): The style of her hair formed the shape of a rooster's tail.

Sandy (Lloyd): His hair was sandy in color.

Glad (Gladys): Glad is short for Gladys.

Robbie (Robert): The nickname is obvious.

Teenie (Ernestine): Teenie is short for Ernestine.

Dorsie (Delores): Dorsie is derived from Delores.

Old Woman (Ruth): When she was a young girl, she came into the room wearing a long night gown, and her brother said, "You look like an old woman."

Shady (Bill): Probably because he sat in the shade much of the time fishing.

Red or *Skin* (Dolan): Dolan had bright red hair when he was young.

Gert (Gertrude): Gert is a diminutive of Gertrude.

Tiddlywinks (Leon): Named after a game called Tiddlywinks for some reason.

Buttermilk (Charlie): Charlie was a man of some girth thought to be caused from drinking huge quantities of buttermilk.

No explanation could be found for the assignment of some nicknames. These follow in alphabetical order with the nickname in italic type.

Big Ha (James O.), *Bird Dog* (Tommy), *Boots* (Edgar), *Bud* (Hoyle), *Catfish* (Elmo), *Creasy* (Lindsay), *Dee Bud* (H. R.), *Dink* (Marie), *Doc* (Lloyd), *Doslitchet* (David Doobill), *Ebbin Annie* (Evelyn), *Eck* (Paul), *Fuzzy* (Robert Bruce), *Hobby Pottsy* (Harvey), *Hook* (Bill), *Hunk* (Franklin), *Hurley Miller* (Early), *Jesse* (John), *Machine* (Maxine), *Maggie* (Theda), *Moe* (Carl), *Neats* (Juanita), *Pee Wee* (James), *Poochie* (Loretta), *Roy* (Betty Jean), *Shank* (Joel), *Shorty* (Clois), *Sis* (Martha, Anna Lynn, Helen), *Sooner* (Wade), *Speedy* (Paul), *Squeaky* (Van Hoy), *Tee* (Elmo), *Toby* (Willis), *Tootie* (Mabel), *Whistle* (Ralph), and *Windy* (Dolan).

Being Afraid of Lightning

In addition to having more than one name, most of us shared a common fear when hearing the word "storm" in the summertime. Rain storms filled with lightning and thunder occurred with regularity, which caused concern especially among young folks. Many were literally scared beyond words. We were constantly reminded never to stand under a tree in a thunderstorm or out in open fields, which created a dilemma. If standing under a tree is dangerous and being in an open field is the same, where should we go? No one needed to tell us. We made a beeline to the house if possible. Most of our homes had lightning rods on the roofs which supposedly provided protection. Whether the rods ever did could not be proven, but we dared not be without lightning rods if money were available for their installation.

Being in the house did not calm fears totally, however. Many children crawled under the beds, especially at night. Flashes of lightning lit the sky signaling an approaching storm, and our heads would go under the bed covers if we did not scoot under the bed. We slept with windows wide open and shades up providing a clear view of nature at work.

Lightning strikes happened from time to time, which added to our concerns. A major tragedy occurred when a young woman in her prime of life, Margie Fritts, was killed by a bolt of lightning as she stood outside her house. Walt Younts' barn burned to the ground in the summer of 1942 when lightning struck it. These two incidents made lasting impressions in the minds of all people in the area. The passing of a thunderstorm brought welcomed relief.

To this day, those of us who were living at the time have never forgotten them, and we often think about them when we hear thunder.

Afraid of an Elevator

A trip more than 10 miles away from home was a rarity indeed. My first trip outside the county occurred when Aunt Lucille took me with my grandmother to Charlotte to get Grandma some new reading glasses. Lexington lacked a store that provided such service, which made the trip to Charlotte, some 60 miles away, necessary. I was probably five years old at the time remembering Aunt Lucille had just bought a new 1936 Ford. We arrived in Charlotte around noon "dinner" time, and ate some food from a box that Grandma had prepared for the trip. Aunt Lucille found the place where the glasses were made and we entered the building, then walked into its elevator. A man greeted us and asked, "What floor?" My aunt answered, "Five." Suddenly the floor began to rise, and my aunt took hold of my shaky hand. The man turned a crank and the floor stopped rising. He opened the door, and we got out and went to a room nearby. Grandma coaxed me to look out the window, and all I could see were the tops of buildings and a street way below. Everything looked strange, and I was glad Aunt Lucille asked me to make the trip with her and Grandma. I had fun that evening after we got home telling Mom all about the trip.

The Clock Waited for No One

Another modern marvel enabled us to travel to distant places and provided considerable pleasure. I have enjoyed listening to the radio as long as I can remember, even before starting school. One program heard on WPTF in Raleigh, when I was about five years old, was broadcast from noon to 12:15. It featured the Tobacco Tags, a string instrument group that I seldom missed hearing. One day I let time slip by, not watching the clock, and did not turn on the radio until after 12:15, missing the Tobacco Tags. I pleaded with Mom to turn the clock back so I could hear them, which I believe flabbergasted her. She patiently explained the dilemma, and I learned that time waits for no one. The clock shows the time, but you have to read it.

Not Everything We Were Told Was Necessarily the Truth

We did not believe everything heard on the radio, and we were often fooled by others. Youngsters would marvel at the ability of a snake to crawl fast without any sign of legs. One black snake, called a black racer, has the speed of a scalded rat or faster. How did the snake move so fast, we innocently asked older siblings. In their smarter-than-you style, after consulting with each other, the response came forth gilded with the authority of an accomplished scientist. "Well, a snake has legs, but you cannot see them because the legs are inside his body." They went on to say, "If you throw the snake into an open fire, his legs will pop out," a doubtful but passable answer for a five-year-old boy. For years, every time I passed a burning fire in an open fireplace, my thoughts returned to the absurd explanation of my brothers.

After making a rather loud sneeze, an older brother remarked there is no way to stop a sneeze completely. In fact he said, "If you put tape over your mouth during a sneeze, it will blow a hole in your throat." My gullible self swallowed the explanation as gospel truth. How long this belief remained a part of my being, is a lost memory. I never attempted to hold my mouth completely shut while sneezing.

Games We Played and How We Amused Ourselves

Our creative nature extended beyond tall tales, transforming mundane objects into tools of enjoyment. Imagine a time when the most advanced forms of technology around home were a four-vacuum tube radio and a hand-crank eggbeater. Objects used for play never moved under their own power, and most things having recreational potential had little utility without individual resourcefulness. An old automobile tire, a discarded horseshoe, a garden tomato stake, a ball of cotton string, a small rubber ball or an empty spool once filled with thread held the possibility for unbridled pleasure when placed in the hands of the ingenious.

We created entertainment from materials at our fingertips to escape idleness and boredom. We enjoyed each other although testy conflicts arose frequently on the playground. Somehow, we knew how to get along in our different worlds where opportunities were limited, but the freedoms of choice were unlimited. Dividends of friendship and caring trumped materialism every time. How did we amuse ourselves in a world of scarcity? What games did we play when together? What were the options when alone? Life did exist before television.

Very few things we made could move under their own power, but a toy made from a large empty wooden spool could show you crawling action. In order to make it work as a tractor, it was essential to obtain a sucker or lollipop stick, a piece of naked Crayola crayon, and a narrow strip of an inner tube.

Ridges on both ends of the spool were first notched with a pocket knife until the spool was completely circled. Both ends of the rubber strip were tacked to one end of the spool and the remainder fed completely through the center hole in the spool. The piece of crayon was slid into the loop of rubber exiting the other end, and the sucker stick was placed on the top of the crayon. By turning the stick in windup fashion, the rubber strip became wound and twisted. Placing the spool carefully on a flat or slightly inclined surface, amazingly, the spool would rotate slowly but surely moving the spool in imitation of a caterpillar tractor.

Ground corn or small grain would be placed in large wooden barrels in the feed barn where the feed would be easily accessible to give to the livestock. "Strong bands of steel or hoops" circled the barrels holding the staves in place, and for some reason or another, a barrel would lose a hoop sporadically. Here was another item on the farm offering recreational opportunities. Using a short stick or limb, the hoop could be encouraged to roll, or if the diameter of the hoop had the right dimensions, it could be mounted at an appropriate height on the side of the barn and used as a basketball goal.

Perhaps, the homemade toy that provided the most enjoyment was the four-wheel, wooden go-cart. Building such a contraption required a mental design concept never having seen a model drawn on paper and better-than-average wood-working skill. In all probability, the design changed a number of times as the construction proceeded.

The entire cart was made of pieces of strong wood. Hickory or oak two-by-fours were used for the front and back axle boards, and axles about one inch in diameter and four inches long were carved on the ends of the axle boards. Four wheels of desired thickness were sawed off the end of a sourwood or black gum log some eight to ten inches in diameter and finished by boring a one-inch hole in the center of each. The wheels were held in place on the axles by large cotter pins or wooden pegs. Strips of an old tire circled each wheel, and were held in place by tacking to prevent the wheels from splitting apart. One-inch-thick boards served as the cart's bed. After attaching the piece of steering rope to both ends of the front axle just inside the wheels, the go-cart was tested for downhill travel. Except for a few nails, four strips of an old tire used as tread for the wheels, a bolt to allow the front axle to pivot, and a piece of rope to steer the front, the entire cart came from hand-sawed and hand-constructed lumber.

If a boy made repairs as demanded, his wooden go-cart remained functional for long periods of time. Who knows the number of arms and legs skinned or broken in downhill crashes? Some of the more sophisticated designs had a braking mechanism, but most were allowed to roll freely. Stopping, if possible, might have been accomplished by foot dragging. Somehow we and our group of dare-devil comrades survived even before the protection helmet had been invented.

Many of the games we played required several participants if the contest was to be worthwhile. Equipment necessary for each game was minimal. The main ingredients consisted of participants excited enough to agree on rules often concocted on the spot. The game outcomes produced winners and losers who accepted their fates with the understanding that a chance at redemption would come tomorrow. Participants never relished conceding victory to the opposing team. Without the intervention of darkness, games might never have come to a close.

One of the most competitive and fun games of the '20s, '30s and '40s was known as "town ball," which originated in England before baseball was invented in the United States. In fact, many people refer to town ball as the "father" of American baseball. Only two items are needed to play town ball: a small ball made of either hollow rubber or tightly wound yarn covered with leather or friction tape and a bat shaped like a large paddle. The bases, called corners, are four in number, like baseball: first, second, third, and home.

The giver (pitcher) occupies a position on the field similar to that in baseball. The batter stands in front of home base, holds the bat above the shoulder and swings from that position. The giver throws overhand and "gives" the ball to the catcher over the right shoulder of the batter. All other players on the defensive team, known as fielders, are stationed at strategic positions to catch the hit balls.

If a batter hits a ball, he runs to first corner. Any fielder can get him out by throwing the ball and hitting him before he reaches his destination. Each side can have any number of players which made the game popular for large gatherings. Also, girls participated in the game as regularly as boys. Backyards in our farming community became transformed into town-ball fields if they had enough space. Without much imagination, the images of teenage boys and girls can be recalled slapping a ball with a paddle and racing from home plate to first corner, probably a shade tree.

"Rolly Ball" or "Roller Bat" required a bat of any accepted size or shape and a ball made either of rubber or string. The rules were very simple. A pitcher throws the ball to a batter, crouching as in baseball, and the batter attempts to hit it. Anyone catching a struck ball on the fly comes to home plate and takes the batter's place. If the ball is not caught on the fly, the batter lays down his bat lengthwise at home base, and the person fielding the ball attempts to roll the ball across the bat. If successful, the person rolling the ball assumes the batter's position. Such a pattern of batting, catching and ball rolling continues as long as the participants are willing to play.

Other group games included: red rover, hide and seek, rabbits and dogs, this little finger did it, cow pasture baseball, outdoor basketball, touch football, "ain't no booger bears out tonight" and others—games in which there were winners and losers. It was a matter of winning and losing, but more important, we learned how to play the games and to respect others, lessons that were to carry us through life. Winning simply meant you had bragging rights until being dislodged from a lofty perch. Losing meant you would live another day to get another chance.

Pitching horseshoes gained popularity because people of all ages could participate. Also, the game could be played by one individual for practice or by two or four for sport. Yard space relatively level, free of trees and tall grass was

needed to locate two iron stakes or stobs some 40 to 50 feet apart. The basic ingredients to get the game underway were four discarded horse or mule shoes.
We knew nothing of the existence of today's regulation horseshoes manufactured to certain specifications and uniformity. All we had were worn-out iron
shoes salvaged when the feet of draft animals were re-shod. This meant an
assortment of sizes, shapes and weights, but we played the game with passion
using some type of contest of chance to determine who would get the better
shoes, the larger ones worn by horses. Usually, the winner or winners had first
choice at shoe selection, and no changes of shoes were made until a new winner emerged. The object was to get the shoes close to the stob, around it—a
ringer—or leaning against it, known as a leaner. Ringers counted five points,
leaners three points and the closest shoe earned one point. The first team or
individual accumulating a total of 11 points was declared the winner. Boys and
girls, men and women all pitched horseshoes, and those who had great difficulty in finding the stob or stake received unmerciful teasing. A comment such
as, "You must have left that shoe on the horse," accompanied a toss that sent a
shoe rolling some distance from the stob.

Shooting marbles ranked very high on children's popularity chart and was
especially popular during the '30s and early '40s. To shoot marbles required
little investment, perhaps even less for the skilled players who won a large collection of marbles when playing the game of "keeps." Practically every boy carried a marble sack. Small sacks used to hold roll-your-own cigarette tobacco
were prized by marble players because they came with yellow, ready-made
draw strings, a kind of status symbol. To play the game, marbles would be
placed in the middle of a circle drawn in the dirt, and the object was to use
a shooter or taw (we said "toy") and propel it with the thumb at the group of
marbles. Any marbles driven out of the circle without having the taw roll out
were won by the shooter. The shooter who knocked out the most marbles was
declared the winner.

Having possession of a discarded automobile or truck tire presented at least
two fantastic opportunities for fun and excitement. First, just rolling the tire
by hand could amuse a young person for hours and hours. Second, suspending
the tire with a rope from a sturdy tree limb created a swing for all ages, but the
swing caught more action from younger folks. Back and forth the swing went,
and with some assistance from a playmate, the swinging tire could reach unusual heights. Another thrill developed by twisting the rope and tire until tight
and letting them loose. The thrill came with the unwinding action. Young girls
seemed to be able to amuse themselves with a tire swing for much of a day.

Swinging on muscadine grape vines found in tall trees over gullies and
streams made a backyard rope swing seem like infant's play. As we traversed
the forests hunting for possums and squirrels, muscadine grape vines would

be spotted and mentally rated as prospects for a Tarzan-like swing. At some future date, we would return to the vines and examine them more critically. If they met our criteria, the vine would be cut with a hatchet near the ground and tested. At first, one of us would hold the vine and swing in the direction of a downhill slope. Our weight would carry away from the tree rapidly out over a ravine, returning us to the launch site. After a couple of swings, we knew the vine would support us. Time after time, we returned to the tree, making the vine swing and enhancing our jungle pleasure by making Tarzan-like yells. Some of the vines would last for two or more years before rotting and weakening, rendering them unsafe.

One treasured vine swing was attached to the limb of a tall beech tree on the bank of Abbotts Creek. Swings could be taken over the middle of the creek. To add to the thrill of the trip, the more bold swimmers would let go of the vine at the right moment and plunge into the middle of the creek. We also climbed on the limbs of the birch tree and dived into the creek. Both acts were considerably dangerous, and our parents warned us to stay away from the place. A cousin cut the vine away from the tree, which ended its utility as a launch into the creek. Later in life, the cousin admitted this was probably the meanest thing he ever did.

The same cousin was swimming with another named Sandy in a creek where cows were grazing on the other side of a barbed wire fence. The two of them, wanting to get closer to the cows, made a beeline for the cows in their birthday suits but needed to negotiate the fence to get to them. Sandy made it through safely, but the other cousin snagged his butt on the fence leaving a permanent scar. During World War II, he listed the scar as an identifiable mark in case he was killed overseas.

"June bugs or June beetles" provided an unusual excitement during the hot lazy days of mid-summer. About the time that small grain is ripening or corn nears knee-high, large brownish-green beetles make the farm scene. You recognize them by their loud buzzing noise, large size and by flight patterns of moving in a slow zigzag path about shoulder height or less above the ground. At first you think they might be bumble bees, but after the initial shock, your heart beat calms, and you decide they are June bugs.

With caution and daring, you catch one in your hand and soon become accustomed to the vigorous movement of its legs and feet which can cause discomfort and anxiety for children. You have observed an older sibling or friend make a unique use of the June bug. With patience and dumb luck, the older person attached a sewing thread to one of the bug's back legs. Holding the other end of the thread, the bug resumed his flight being restrained by a taut thread quickly becoming an imaginary "country airplane" flying at full throttle. We always looked forward to the warm days of June and the June bugs.

None of us went to war as youngsters, but we did "pick fights with wasp nests" covered with swarms of adult wasps. Blackberry bushes were natural habitats for red and black wasps. On a normal day, the last thing you wanted to disturb would be a wasps' nest because they angered easily, and their stings made painful and lasting impressions.

On Sunday afternoons when about all types of creative entertainment had been exhausted, someone would suggest we look for wasp nests among the blackberry plants along ditch banks. At first, the idea was rejected, but the longer we thought about it, the more acceptable it became. Soon the most daring fellow of the group started marching toward a ditch in the meadow, and the remainder of us, one by one, marched behind him, probably far behind him.

We had engaged in such devilishness before and understood the likelihood of encountering peril. As we drew closer to the ditch bank and the blackberry briars, we started looking for rocks and dirt clods for weapons. We tried to steady our nerve. This was not going to be a normal playground battle. We could lose it and return home pained and swollen by uninvited stings.

Catfish was the first to sight the wasp nest, and it looked larger than the bottom of a number two wash tub. Catfish possessed a kind of kamikaze mentality, and he tossed the first stone landing a direct hit on the nest. We let all our weapons fly, and soon the air looked like a cloud of red wasps, ones that get angry and vicious. It was time to make tracks, and the eight of us sounded like a herd of stampeded buffaloes as we crossed the meadow to the other side of the road. We stopped and took stock of the Sunday afternoon warriors and discovered to our pleasant surprise that no one was injured.

Cheers went up applauding victory, and we knew we would live to fight a wasp nest another day. Occasionally, a wasp or two could claim victory as they left stingers in someone's flesh. The victim twisted in agony crying for relief. If an adult chewing tobacco happened to be nearby, he would put some of his tobacco juice on the swelling offering some relief. A loser in a fight always pays some price, a lesson well learned.

In late spring, "fireflies or lightning bugs" could be spotted about dusk flying and flashing their abdomens into a bright yellow light which came on and off as if hooked to a programmed switch. Lightning bugs neither bit nor scratched, and the rhythmic pattern of yellow light to darkness fascinated young children and held adults in awe because no one understood how the bugs were able to do it.

Soon barefoot kids with empty jars would start chasing the lightning bugs. With skill and luck, they caught enough of them with their bare hands to light up the jar. It would have a constant yellow glow, and we all continued to wonder about the bugs' secret. Someone said, "That's for the bugs to know and us to find out."

Before the advent of air rifles, a young boy's favorite hunting weapon had to be a "homemade slingshot." Basic items for a slingshot included a forked limb, usually green dogwood, one-half-inch-wide strips of flexible rubber cut from an old automobile inner tube, a tongue from a leather shoe and strong string for tying the rubber strips to the dogwood forks and the shoe tongue.

After locating a forked limb of desired size and shape in a dogwood tree, it was cut from the tree about six inches below the fork, and the two smaller limbs forming the fork were cut of equal length. Bark was removed by scraping with a knife while the wood was still green, and later placed in the oven of the kitchen stove for drying but not scorching or burning. After removing from the oven and allowed to cool, the handle and forks were carefully cut to desired length. Small notches were made near the ends of the two forks, and a strip of rubber tied to each fork. A pad to hold small pieces of gravel or stone was fashioned from the shoe tongue, and the strips of rubber fixed to the tongue through holes cut on each end.

An anxious young boy could not wait to try it out. After placing a small rock in the pad, holding the loaded pad in one hand and the handle of the slingshot in the other, stretching the rubber strips and releasing the pad gave the small rock a propelled ride.

Using a slingshot demanded great care due to its potential to cause harm to other persons or damage to property. The most use we had for a slingshot was to hunt birds, the small sparrows, for example, that nest in trees. Fence posts made good practice targets. Older folks admonished the slingshot carrying boys to be careful, but for some reason chickens seemed to be fair game.

We never went out of the house without being reminded about the chickens. On one occasion a brother went toward the chicken yard with his slingshot only to return shortly to the house dragging a dead chicken. When asked if he had shot the chicken deliberately, he responded by saying, "I did not aim the rock at the chicken. Rather I shot it in the air and it came down and hit the chicken on the head." The story did not pass muster as he was quickly jerked up, reminded of the gravity of the deed, but it was so clever Mom left the due punishment undone.

Before the advent of clothes dryers, the washing was hung outdoors on a "wire clothesline" and left to dry in the wind and sun. Also, the bed clothes would be placed on a line from time to time for airing and sunning to refresh them. Sheets and bedspreads draped over a clothesline offered the chance for a child to part the two sides of the draped cloth and pretend to be walking in a special tunnel. The direct sunshine made the cloth tunnel warm and cozy, and there always seemed to be a unique smell inside. As a curious boy, I experienced exotic peacefulness many times walking through sheet and quilt tunnels. The memory of the smell and warmth remains as if it happened yesterday.

A clothesline filled with clothespins and no clothes presented another temptation. You examined the situation and wondered if you could possibly push all of the pins to one end of the line. Curiosity killed the cat, and sooner or later you had to try it. Grabbing the first pin in your hand, you would walk fast to accomplish the feat. As luck would have it, about half way toward the other end of the line, the clothespins now bunched, would suddenly stop sliding, and your momentum almost tore your arm from its socket.

Learning to Drive a Car

If you lived in the country, learning to drive a car seemed to be no big achievement. By the time you had reached the age to get a drivers license during World War II, you knew instinctively all of the finer points of handling a car, or so I thought. Most likely an older brother or cousin had slid out from under the steering wheel and let you assume his place a year or two early. On the farm many opportunities just happened that put you in a position to learn some of the rudimentary requirements for handling an automobile. Most roads were unpaved and lightly traveled reducing the chances of hitting another car to almost zero, but carelessness at the steering wheel might still put you and the car in the ditch.

Dad's car was a 1938 Chevrolet, and my brother, four years my elder, conceded to let me drive one afternoon on a dirt road about a half mile from home. He shut the engine off before I climbed under the steering wheel. The first task was to get it started by hitting the starter on the floorboard. I cut on the ignition switch, pressed the starter and the car lurched forward but the engine stopped. The clutch, the all important pedal that disengages the gears, had been neglected. The next command was to go easier on the accelerator and put the car in gear, which I attempted by grabbing the gear shift and pulling it toward the lower left corner. You have never heard such loud grinding and scraping of metal. My brother, becoming impatient, reminded me that the car had a clutch. My trembling left foot pressed it to the floorboard and with my right hand, a second try moved the gearshift to the correct position. Slowly, I thought, I let out the clutch as the car jumped and jerked like a crippled kangaroo for at least a hundred or two hundred yards. Finally, the clutch was free of my foot and the car moved along at a snail's pace. Glancing quickly at my brother, he suggested the car would move faster if it were put in second gear. For the life of me, I could not remember the location of second gear. Shifting the gears had been practiced countless times when Hoyle Parks and I skipped the main service at church and played in the car. Where was Hoyle when I needed him? Brother instructed me to press the clutch to the floorboard once more, and he did the shifting to second gear.

The trees along the road were sailing by us now when the order to get the car in high gear was given. Nerves had steadied enough to do the shifting myself this time, giving me a feeling of relief. The dirt road had ruts left by cars traveling over it when muddy a few days earlier. When the tires of the old Chevrolet fell into the ruts, the steering wheel became difficult to hold, and we went from one side of the road to the other several times.

I do not know how my brother knew when I had had enough driving for one day, but he did. He suggested we stop, a maneuver offering a different challenge, which was not negotiated until the second attempt. He took the driver's seat behind the wheel, and we returned home.

What a great older brother. He never told anyone about my initial experience at driving the car which bordered on being dismal. My guess was his older brother or our dad had done a similar favor for him.

Community Baseball

"Community baseball" created home-grown excitement not to be duplicated by any other sport. Several teams were probably formed throughout the area. One formed in Sandy Grove and played its home games in a field next to Elwood Younts' barn. A team was created also in the Linwood/Southmont community which played many of its games in a field next to Sam Tussey's house, and other teams were made up in Holly Grove, Denton, East Lexington, etc. The community around the Junior Orphanage Home had at least part of a team, and from time to time, games were played in Sheet's bottoms along Abbotts Creek when the level of High Rock Lake receded leaving the land dry.

Baseball enjoyed enormous popularity, and folks bragged on the quality of play. We had to scrounge scarce resources to get enough equipment. The cost of a catcher's mitt or a fielder's glove equaled a day or two's wages and more. Many of the bats were made in woodworking shops from willow wood, but gloves, mitts, chest protectors and balls were purchased usually at the Western Auto Store in Lexington. The normal lineup for the Sandy Grove team looked something like this: Hollis Burkhart, catcher; Gladfred Burkhart, pitcher; El Younts, 2nd base; Coy Weaver, 1st base initially but Wayne Younts later played the position; Dallas Swing, right field; Lindsay Younts, left field; Bryce Younts, center field; Bruce Younts, shortstop; and one of the Burkhart boys at 3rd base. Many other boys and younger men played from time to time. Persons that come to mind were: Wade Younts, Homer Younts, Pee Wee Allred, Van Hoy Hines, Bruce Greer, and several of the Burkhart boys. When another pitcher was needed, the team would call on Gurney Burkhart or Walt Watkins. Don Fritts played also as did several of the Greers. Lee Beck appeared one Sunday afternoon in a baseball uniform his mother had sewn, but I do not remember if and where he played. The boys never stopped picking on Lee, and he seemed to relish it.

A few interesting things need telling about playing baseball on the field next to Elwood Younts' barn. The field was anything but level, with the highest point being home plate. A ridge of high ground ran from home plate toward center field sloping the entire distance. An apple tree stood just beyond second base, and downhill slopes toward third and first bases and right and left fields were obvious. If a batter hit a long ball toward right field, it usually fell into a rough terrain, swampy wet and full of bullrushes.

Both Dallas Swing and Coy Weaver were strong as bulls and hit left handed. Their long fly balls oftentimes buried in the wet muck in right field never to be found again. Losing a baseball bordered on tragedy because the team had no budget. A baseball would not be discarded. When its cover became worn thin or stitches broken, we repaired it. If the ball cover could no longer be repaired, the naked ball would be wrapped in black friction tape and used in practice.

All games were played on Sunday afternoons which was pause for concern, because the Sabbath was looked upon as a day of rest. We heard that from the pulpits. You could not go fishing on Sunday either. Was playing baseball considered rest, and was it a sin to play on Sunday? The issue was presented to the minister for his opinion who said he saw nothing wrong with playing on Sunday as long as we did not become too noisy. Elwood Younts kept his store closed on Sundays for a long time, respecting the Sabbath, but at the urging of the players wanting a Coca-Cola or a Pepsi-Cola to drink, he finally opened it. This soon became an every Sunday tradition.

Gladfred Burkhart or "Thucks" as we called him, pitched most of the games, and he and some of the other pitchers had the ability to make the ball curve as it neared home plate. Some people doubted if anyone could make a round object like a baseball curve. They declared such impossible. Isaiah Beck, the community sage, never believed it either even after observing Thucks throw his best stuff. Once some country folks made up their minds on a subject, neither Heaven nor Hell could change them.

Sandy Grove's biggest rival was the Linwood/Southmont or Tussey team that played at Sam Tussey's field. A few players on both teams competed or had competed in basketball in high school, and many of them attended the same churches. They knew each other very well. Players for the Sam Tussey team included Odell Harvey, Bill and Bryan Swing, Dermont Rhodes, Alec Trexler, the Miller brothers, the Parks boys, Tysingers, Briggs and Zeno Greer and others whose names have long since been forgotten. Competition was defined as friendly, and the teams rotated the playing location to take away home field advantages. Records of the wins and losses were never kept officially as far as I know, but the games did become spirited when plays were close or home runs were hit. Luckily, the minister did not show up for the games. He would have probably ruled we were getting close to disturbing the Sabbath with the loud cheering and a few flaring tempers.

World War II continued to escalate in Europe and the Pacific with no reports of it ending any time soon. The young men running the base paths for both teams had already registered for the draft and were prime candidates for military service. Uncle Sam's armed forces needed them, and one by one the teams lost most of their members. Those of us staying on the home front attempted to keep the baseball teams going, but the challenge was too much. Assisting in the war effort overshadowed everything else, and every facet of our lives took on a different meaning.

Professional Baseball in Town

"Professional baseball" was played in Lexington and Thomasville in a big way even though the league was at the Class D level. The Lexington team was associated with the Cleveland Indians organization for many years and later with the Philadelphia Athletics. Both the Lexington and the Thomasville teams were members of the North State League which made for great intra-county rivalry. Young boys followed professional baseball at all levels of play, and each boy had his favorite team.

For some reason, which no one ever knew or explained to me, my brothers and I pulled for the Detroit Tigers in the major leagues. Boys in other sections of our area had their own favorite teams. We read the sports column in the *Greensboro Daily News*, which carried the box scores every day, and knew all the members of our favorite team by name and position. The only glimpse we ever had of a Detroit Tiger player was when his picture was printed in the newspaper, a rare occurrence. Our fascination with the Detroit Tigers may have been spawned by a visit that Ty Cobb of the Tigers made to Lexington five years before my birth. Such events made lasting impressions on a community.

But the real professional team in our hearts was the Lexington Indians. The class of play made no difference whatsoever. The team played their home games at Holt-Moffitt Field located on South Main Street in Lexington.

During a single season, we would go to several games. Just how we got to the games, I cannot remember. Our dad went on rare occasions. Some of my cousins old enough to drive a car also attended games and neighbors would ask me to ride with them. Admission to the games amounted to 25 cents for adults and 10 cents for me, and even this price often presented a problem. Extra change came hard during the late '30s and the '40s, but the Lexington Rotary Club sensing the problem for most children helped form a Knot Hole Gang section in the right field bleachers where children under 12 years of age would be admitted for five cents. After a few innings had been played, admission was free. We loved baseball with passion, and a home run hit over the fence in our Class D park provided just as much a thrill as if it were hit out of that stadium up in New York City. Small-town America found its entertainment in its own way during the Depression and World War II, and the Class D baseball league was much of it. "Take Me Out to the Ballgame" always resonated well.

Before the days of racial integration, the Lexington Indians and Athletics played only white players, but the colored people also had a professional team known as the Lexington Pirates. The colored had a league of their own, and the Pirates' biggest rival was the Winston-Salem Camels.

The supply of practically all consumer goods went from plenty to scarce, and we learned how to live with less or without. Most of the people were able to buy a rationed amount of gasoline for essential travel but none for pleasure driving. Dallas Swing devised a clever activity that would show our support of the troops, conserve gasoline, and provide enjoyment at the same time. He suggested those of us with bicycles assemble at Elwood Younts' store each Sunday afternoon for rides of several miles, and soon the number of regular riders grew to as many as 40 or 50 in number.

The group would depart from the store around 2:00 p.m. and return by 5:00 p.m. traveling a route that passed by Beck's Evangelical and Reformed Church, continued crossing the Abbotts Creek bridge at Sheet's bottom to the Junior Orphanage on Highway 8, to Lexington where a stop would be made for refreshments, after which we would return to Elwood's store exhausted and go our own way.

Some of the riders shared ownership in a bicycle which usually meant riding on alternate Sundays. Sometimes this arrangement, even though it made sense, led to serious difficulties. Two brothers had invested in the same bicycle, one having purchased it and riding it until he wore out the tires after which he put it aside. The other brother rescued it and put it into a very good condition; he joined the Sunday riding group on a regular basis. One Sunday, he failed to meet the gathering, and the other riders waited for a few minutes. When he did not show, an older member of the group went to see if a problem existed. Much to his surprise he found the two brothers fighting furiously behind their house over who was to ride the bicycle that day. It was no small spat. They had literally dismantled the bicycle piece by piece, hit each other with the parts, and put them into two piles according to ownership. It was not a good day for either brother to ride.

Going Swimming

The city of Lexington built a "public swimming pool," which took many of us away from the creeks for our Sunday swims even though pool water had a disagreeable chlorine smell. Chlorine was placed there to guard against diseases and infections that were easily spread in the water.

We rode bicycles as far as six to eight miles getting to and from the pool. The ride and the swim worked up big appetites. Herbert Lohr ran the Southern Lunch restaurant near the Depot. He made hamburgers fried to perfection especially when topped off with mustard, ketchup and slaw and placed on a steamed bun. A crucial portion of the swimming routine on Sunday afternoon was eating a Herbert Lohr hamburger on the way home. They sold for five cents each, and if our pockets contained the right change, we would afford two some Sundays.

Herbert would proudly boast to other customers how we boys loved his hamburgers. On one occasion, an elderly gentleman disputed Herbert's claim telling us he would pay for all we could eat. Well, the gates of Heaven just opened, and a cousin and I devoured two or three and slowly ate at least four more. Herbert's claim was substantiated, but our bicycle ride home went in starts and stops as we sought gastric relief.

Stealing Watermelons

Despite working almost from sunup to sundown, rural boys did have some free time on their hands. The saying, "an idle mind is the devil's workshop," must have been coined to describe a group of hungry teenage boys on the loose. In the absence of organized play, one in the group would always float an idea for consideration. If it was in the late summer, the motion to visit a local watermelon patch always received a second and passed unanimously.

Teenagers knew the location of the watermelon patches in the community because the growing melons had been eagerly watched all summer. Ripe watermelons attracted teenage boys like rotten peaches attracted flies, and under the right circumstances, the boys were known to steal a few. Any patch became fair game, and the boys respected the patches, only taking as many watermelons as they could consume on the spot. The boys assumed they took watermelons without the knowledge of the farmer, but nothing could have been farther from the truth. He knew some were stolen, and he usually knew who had done it. Such type of thievery went uncontested as long as it was not destructive.

A most bizarre thing happened during a watermelon "stealing" when some of us boys on a possum hunt visited a patch on Early Smith's farm in his bottom land along Pounders Fork. We had been on the unsuccessful hunt for a couple of hours when we came upon Early's watermelons. With lighted lanterns and flashlights, we entered the patch which had become smothered by a late burst of tall crabgrass. After stomping down some of the grass and shining the flashlights, two or three good watermelons were found and extracted from the patch. We went to a large poplar tree nearby and used a hunting knife to cut the melons.

Suddenly, Gene Smith yelled in horror as if he had been bitten by a rattlesnake, "I lost my class ring in the watermelon patch," and made a few comments about what his parents might do to him. We dropped our slices of watermelon and returned to the patch as fast as our legs and feet would carry us. If the crabgrass did not look like a jungle the first time we entered the patch, it did the second time. In pitch dark, we wandered around like the blind leading the blind in grass almost up to our waists for at least 15 minutes. With a profound expression of relief, Gene exclaimed, "Here it is!" picked up his ring and calmly walked back to the poplar.

As far as I know this story in no way reached his home and parents, and he never misplaced his class ring again. Months later, Gene was heard saying, "I know what looking for a needle in a haystack means."

Some Words Were Never Spoken

If our spoken vocabulary became laced with certain words or phrases either at school or at home, quick and often painful punishment ensued. Never, yes not ever, would a teacher or parent excuse a youngster calling someone an idiot, liar or fool or referring to a person as being stupid, dumb or crazy. To tell someone to shut up would bring the wrath of the intended. This could very well have been what provoked the fight I had with a larger classmate in the gymnasium when in the fourth grade.

Parental discipline was usually in the form of a swift slap to the face or even requiring the guilty one to wash out his or her mouth with soapy water. Teachers had several options, a trip the principal's office for a paddling or requiring the student to write at least one hundred times, "I will not say (idiot, liar, etc.) again." If the forbidden word was uttered in close proximity of the teacher, a stinging slap might be quickly administered.

Call the Sheriff If Everything Else Fails

Herding a bunch of roughneck boys could cause a mother more frustration than a woman had whose husband had not kissed her in 10 years but shot the man who did. The mother's initial reaction was to grab a razor-sharp dogwood switch from top of the kitchen stove and wave it in the air as if it were a knight's saber. She tried other tricks but to no avail such as, "Wait until Dad gets here, and he will make it rough on you," "If you do not stop fighting, you will wish you had," and "You boys ought to be ashamed of yourselves." No stone was left unturned as the mother searched for the solution to gaining control, and she often used every ace in the hole when in dire straits. Quoting her, "If you boys don't calm down, I'm going to call Sheriff Bowers, and he will get you."

"You boys have no shame." The boys wanted to believe that the lawman was their friend as they had been taught. They admired his technique of gun toting, and he was the nearest thing to a western cowboy in the county. Certainly, the boys did not wish to disappoint the sheriff, and for many years none of them could ever be sure that Sheriff Bowers was not somewhere on the premises.

The Birds and the Bees

Boys and girls alike were curious and unsure about how animals, including people, reproduced themselves. Children and adolescents of the '20s, '30s, and '40s sometimes broached the subject to a few parents who did not want to discuss the topic and ignored most questions or swept them under the rug. By closing the conversation, they may have sent nonverbal messages that discouraged us from ever posing additional questions. For the most part, we were on our own, and we usually looked to peers or older brothers and sisters for answers.

The situation differs today. In the early part of the 21st century, a father thinking the time has arrived for him to discuss the birds and bees with his son might say: "Son, we need to talk about the bird and the bees." The response from the son might very well be: "Sure Dad, what do you want to know?"

Nothing would have been farther from the truth before and during World War II. Our parents, like their parents before them wanted us to know, but usually became emotionally charged and emotionally challenged when dealing with sexuality. They weaseled out assuming "he" or "she" would learn about "it" from somebody else. When an adolescent raised a question about the birds and bees among older peers, the boy or girl was told to shut up and sometimes ridiculed for not knowing all there was to know in the first place. Mothers were likely to communicate in some way with daughters about the biology of their bodies, but sons were left to their own devices. Fathers just never talked.

Our parents would brush questions aside by saying a baby brother or sister was delivered by "the stork," and newborn pigs and calves were found in a hollow stump, along the creek, or around the bottom of a wildflower that looked like philodendron. Parents used the word "found" to avoid telling the real story. My dad would come in the house saying another cow had found a calf, never saying simply she had a calf.

After hearing such non-scientific answers, young boys and girls would look for storks in the sky or when walking in the woods for baby animals in hollow stumps, along creeks, and around the base of the wildflower mentioned earlier. Actually, the plant had enlarged growths near its base, and we imagined they might become little pigs. Any belief possessed about this tale became totally obliterated in a college botany class some years later. The professor teaching the class just happened to hold up a picture of the plant which excited me to no end. After class ended, I stop by the professor to display some down-home knowledge, and said jokingly, "This plant grows in the woods on my dad's farm, and our sows find their little pigs at its base." Not only did the comment uncover ignorance for which I was criticized, but the professor looked at me with dismay and pity. Why I passed the course I will never know, but I did learn the scientific name of the plant, *Hexastylis arifolia*.

If a woman was a bit overweight from being pregnant, the whisper among adolescents might have been that she swallowed a pumpkin or watermelon seed. On the farm, we witnessed animals mating and young ones being born, and after a while we put one and one together to develop some understanding about the origin of babies. However, my first experience at seeing a calf born left me in shock for a month.

Dad owned a bull, one of the few in the community, and many people would bring their milk cows to our farm for breeding purposes. If my Dad or an older brother was not at home at the time, it became my responsibility to introduce the bull and the cow. Country boys and girls often helped city boys and girls overcome their deficiencies on the subject, which might not have been the best way for the city-born to learn the mysteries of reproduction either.

Boys wanted to know about the anatomy of girls and girls about boys. Our age was a time before the existence of magazines that displayed the two sexes more explicitly, and I am uncertain what our reaction would have been to a publication like *Playboy* or *Playgirl Magazine*. The nearest publications to *Playboy* were the catalogs of Sear-Roebuck and Montgomery Ward. Years later during a discussion about "girlie" magazines with a man from a region outside the South, he remarked, "Well, you had the Sears-Roebuck catalog with its lingerie section, didn't you?"

Somehow we made it into adulthood with most of us experiencing a few bumps along the way. Whoever wrote the song, "Let me tell you about the birds and the bees and the flowers and the trees and the moon up above, that's the power of love," would have been welcomed into our lives. We did the best we could with the knowledge we had.

Party Activities for Teenagers

Teenage boys and girls gathered frequently at one of their homes for parties on Friday or Saturday night. We would be served Cokes and cookies and sometimes small sandwiches by the host and play parlor games, which afforded much interaction among the boys and girls. A favorite game called "the five-minute date" was a part of every party, and we usually waited until the host's parents had gone to bed or to the back room before starting the playing. The host would call the name of a boy and girl from a previously prepared list, and the pair would take a five-minute walk down the road or go sit in an automobile or a porch swing. Upon returning to the front door of the house, if the boy got lucky, he could sneak a kiss.

Another popular game, "Spin the Bottle," may have resulted in a boy or girl's first kiss ever. Teenagers would sit in a circle around the room, and a boy or girl would kneel in the middle of the circle and spin an empty Coca-Cola bottle. When it pointed to a person of the opposite sex, he or she was obligated to kiss the person. I can remember very well an evening party that was held at Bill and Bryan Swing's home on the Shamwell Highway. We played Spin the

Bottle in the front yard. How it was possible to spin the bottle in the grass, I never knew, but that was beside the point. I was one of the younger boys attending, and an older girl spun the bottle, stopping in my direction. Having no choice but to step forward with the screaming encouragement of the entire crowd, the older girl named Pauline put her arms around me and planted a kiss on the lips. Later in life I replayed that occasion in my mind, always with pleasant thoughts. The adage of "younger boys liking experienced women" became clearly understandable.

Laura Frances, Betty Jean, and Peggy Ruth

Every community had its lively blend of boys and girls who interacted almost daily whether in school, at church, working in the fields, going to the movies, playing games, gathering at the country stores, riding bicycles or in cars, double dating, sitting around parlors and on porches on a Sunday afternoon, taking picnics, or just plain telling stories and laughing together.

We teased each other about sweethearts, the way we wore our hair, our choice of clothes, how we walked and talked, and any combination of habits that gave each of us our own personalities. Through thick and thin, friendships ran deep and true, and if one of us got into trouble, we came to that person's aid or defense. If an outsider dared make an unwanted intrusion, he or she was sent packing.

Being of the male gender and reared in a family of mostly boys naturally put me in a macho world most of the time. Yet, with more than 30 girl first cousins and a younger sister, my upbringing could not escape the female influence. Three girl cousins living within a mile of my home, ones with which I perhaps interacted most frequently, were Laura Frances, Betty Jean, and Peggy Ruth. This lovely trio fit the mold of being good old country girls, with the highest of compliments.

Girls born on a farm or in the country were sturdy and developed personal responsibilities and work habits that contributed to the well-being of the family and the community. They had a heavy dose of common sense. Good fortune shined on me for having such great relatives, and they became some of my closest friends. We went to church together, played together, worked together, sang songs together and even experienced a bit of mischief together. You could say with assurance we were sandbox buddies.

Many rural youngsters had double names, and these girls were no exceptions carrying double names all their lives. For some reasons, my parents gave their sons only one name, but my mom pondered a double name for me. Expecting me as her fourth child, the odds of her having a girl should have been increased. She even went as far as selecting a girl's name, but Dr. Smith denied her by delivering a boy.

Several months later, Dr. Hunt delivered a baby girl to my aunt, and without laboring over what to call her, my aunt took the name my Mom had reserved for me calling my new-born cousin, Laura Frances. For more than seven decades, I have never let her forget how lucky she has been to have such an elegant name. The right to tease is not forfeited as one grows older.

We might as well have called the girl cousins the Three Musketeers. In looks, they differed, but they stuck together like glue in most things, especially in school and fun activities. Their earliest memories began with the first day in school and when a younger sibling was delivered at home. All shared Grandma Younts in common, and her home seemed to serve as a Sunday gathering place. Here they played and laughed together, at least once a bit roughly when Laura Frances tripped over a string in Grandma's yard and broke her arm. Their parents showed no hesitation in meting out discipline when needed in the form of spankings, maybe an occasional slap, or a switching. As girls often did, they tried to lay blame for some of their misdeeds on a brother. All three were born in the same year in the middle of the Depression in unpainted homes without electricity. Windows had no screens, and during the summer months, families left them open for the fresh air. They remember very well washing clothes on a washboard before the advent of wringer washing machines and hanging clothes on a clothesline to dry.

Oil lamps provided light for school and home studies, and none of their homes had a telephone for several years. When one did come, it was fastened to the wall, and dialing an operator to reach a party was done by a crank. Peggy Ruth remembers when they got their phone and the number: three long rings. All rural telephones were on a party line of up to a dozen subscribers, and you would hear the rings for all of them. Many people on the party line had the habit of listening to all calls, and no one seemed to mind it. Telephone privacy was hardly known under such a system; it could be achieved simply by asking members on the party line to hang up.

Laura Frances and Betty Jean lived on farms where their fathers worked all their lives. Peggy Ruth, who lived on a small farm, had a father who was a mechanic. She did go to the fields to help neighbors at corn harvest time, earning the first money she ever had. Farm girls seldom escaped the drudgery of working the fields, hoeing corn, gathering corn, potatoes, vegetables, and helping in any way they could. If the rest of the family stayed in the field all day, the girls did the same. All took something to eat for dinner which often consisted of baked sweet potatoes, cooked Irish potatoes, pieces of salt cured ham if available, biscuits, and a stone jug filled with fresh well water. The jug would be wrapped in an old ragged heavy coat to help keep it cool, and everybody drank out of the same cup.

Laura Frances and Betty Jean remember that when thunderstorms would come up while they were still in the fields, they hoped against hope their daddies would look at the approaching heavy black clouds, sense the oncoming rain as a certainty, and go home. But daddies on farms typically would stay in the field until everyone became soaked, including the horses or mules. On the way home, the horses or mules would slip and slide on the muddy roads. Despite being wet to the skin, the girls rejoiced at getting out of the field.

Farm girls did not go to the fields every day. They spent a lot of time with their mothers in the home learning how to wash, cook, sew, can food, and clean house. During wheat threshing and corn shucking times, the girls worked alongside the older women in preparing and serving food for the crews of men. All three treasured the great times they had at these gatherings.

Every home in the country had a garden large enough to provide vegetables for the entire family, and the girls played a huge role in hoeing the gardens, harvesting the vegetables, cooking them, and canning them so the family would have vegetables year 'round. Many girls milked the family cow, cooled the milk at the spring, and churned some of the milk into butter. Eventually, iceboxes placed in kitchens or on back porches provided an improved method for cooling milk and other food items. The ice was delivered by trucks from the Lexington Ice and Coal Company, and came in a large block that cost a nickel. As it melted inside the icebox, pans were set beneath the drain to catch the water.

Laura Frances, Betty Jean, and Peggy Ruth played many of the games that boys played, taking great delight in beating them at their own contests. They loved pitching horseshoes on Sunday afternoon using available horse and mule shoes. The three of them would also play cards, mumbly (mumble) peg. They also rolled hoops or nailed them on the side of the barn to create basketball goals. Their dads or older brothers made "Tommy Walkers" or stilts out of 2 x 4s, and the girls excelled in walking on them. Sometimes they would hunt rabbits with the family, especially on Thanksgiving Day. Their houses were set on stone pillars, and the space underneath the house made a great spot for children to play. When work days were over in the field, the girls would fuss with the boys to see who would get to ride the horses and mules home. If a dog or cat died, they arranged a mock funeral, and for a cat once killed by an errant piece of lumber, an epitaph written for the funeral read, "Here lies the body of our dear cat done to death by a slat."

Going to the movies rated high on the entertainment list, and their first movies seen played at the Granada Theater. A ticket cost nine cents on Saturday mornings; most movies had a western theme. As they grew older, the late shows on Saturday night at the Carolina Theater became extremely important. Most of the people attending the late showing were boys and girls of their age. Getting to and from town presented a challenge. The girls then in their late teens, would go to Uncle El's store early on Saturday evening, learn of someone going to town, and hide in the back seat of their car to get there. After the movie was over, they looked over the crowd seeking a ride home. If unsuccessful, they would catch a cab, ride to where the Beck's Church Road intersects U.S. 64, and walk the rest of the way home to save money.

Shuford Swing from the Holly Grove community had a movie projector, and he went from country store to country store showing old films on large cloth screens. He did this all over the southern part of the county, charging five cents per person. Halfway through the movie, he had to change film reels, which meant time for a break to go inside the store to purchase candy, crackers, and soft drinks. Both Shuford and the store owner made money with this arrangement, and it gave country folks a convenient opportunity to view a movie. Teenage boys and girls liked the outdoor movies because they also offered a wonderful chance for close socializing, and often my cousins could be found among the crowd.

Each community had its own Laura Franceses, Betty Jeans, and Peggy Ruths who enriched the lives of everyone. Many of the girls married local boys, but as was often the case, dating someone from another part of the county, the next county, or from another state seemed special. A new face and personality could be mysterious and very attractive, and marriages often occurred between boys and girls of varying backgrounds. It was then that they would "set up house" bringing to their new union the wisdom of their two families and an unshakeable belief that their union would withstand the test of time.

The first graduating class from Dunbar High School in Lexington. (Davidson County Historical Museum)

School bus heading to school down a rural dirt road. (Library of Congress, FSA-OWI photo collection, US-USF34-044064)

The first grade class at Silver Valley Grammar School in 1936.(Peggy Hedrick Wilson)

Students studying a unit about Holland. (Davidson County Historical Museum)

The county's bookmobile visited schools all over the county giving additional reading opportunities to children. (Davidson County Historical Museum)

Southmont had a consolidated high school much earlier than many sections of the county. (Ruth Parks)

Many county schools opened lunchrooms in the late thirties or early forties. Here we see the Southmont students getting a hot meal. (Ruth Parks)

Linwood High School opened in the late twenties. (Ruth Parks)

Friends at Linwood School. (Davidson County Historical Museum)

A special treat for graduating seniors was the "senior trip." These seniors are enjoying a spot near Chimney Rock, N.C. (Photo by author)

Learning about the birds and the bees seemed a difficult challenge for rural boys and girls. A wild plant, *Hexastylis*, found in the woods had small jug-like enlargements near the base of the stem. Older children would tell the younger naive ones that the enlargements would become little pigs; a very incomplete lesson. (Daniel Reed)

Girls basketball team at Davis-Townsend High School. (Kay McCulloch Kepley)

Boys fishing with cane pole, line and hook in a creek. (Library of Congress, FSA-OWI photo collection—LC-USF351-112)

At the end of the day, students lined up to board their respective buses for the trip home. (1947 Yearbook *Daviston*)

TEN

OUR ENDURANCE, RESILIENCY
AND INGENUITY

Our parents and other adults taught us how to be adults through example. Most of them showed how to make the best of any situation and held strong beliefs that difficulties strengthened each of us. Whatever the task, we knew to give it our best. We faced adversity by seeking solutions to problems and inevitably were rewarded by a feeling of accomplishment when successful. Challenges were many and luxuries few, but materialistic things were not all that important. Our most precious possessions were our family and a caring community.

Indoor plumbing did not come to many rural homes in the county until the decade of the '40s. The chamber pot, "thunder mug," or slop jar served as the vessel where most of us did our business when we had to go after dark. Our family pot was kept in a closet beside the fireplace, and we boys showed no mercy on the fellow using it last. He would show wisdom by never entering the closet barefoot. The homes with girls made sure that they and their mother had a chamber pot of their own to share.

During the daytime, the outhouse came into play, although it was used by the more courageous souls at night. The little house was situated over a pit behind the big house. Most outhouses had a wooden seat with at least three holes cut in it, the "three holer"—a small hole for the kids, a medium hole for teenagers and grownups of narrow width and the largest hole for the bigger folks. Each hole was covered by a lid that could be slid to the side when in use.

Of course, no written rules appeared on the wall dictating the hole a user must select. Once inside, you were on your own. Dumping a cup of lime down the hole from time to time kept disagreeable odors at bay. For families with several children, no one was really timid about sharing the outhouse with another person. In large families, children often got on the same schedule. Sears Roebuck and Montgomery Ward catalogs found their way to the outhouse along with discarded newspapers to be used for an obvious reason. Corn cobs served the same purpose, although the young folks often complained about being roughed up. Most corn cobs were used by the daddies and grandpas.

Indoor plumbing came to town homes before it made it to the country. When city cousins visited country cousins, the question sooner or later had to be asked, "Where is your bathroom?" Puzzled looks ran across faces of the town folks when told it was 200 or 300 feet down a path. Most country folks liked the old outhouses, but, one by one, they replaced them with indoor plumbing when able to afford it.

The Saturday Night Bath

A body bath more than once a week would have been an unthinkable luxury for many rural families of the era. One of the great rituals practiced in the country was the Saturday night bath. We took it whether we needed it or not in a galvanized tin washtub, a no. 2, which held up to 15 gallons of water. Young kids and some smaller older folks could fit into it sitting down. In the wintertime, parents would put the tub by the kitchen stove so the bath would be cozy and warm, especially for the children. Hot water from containers on top of the stove or the built-in side boiler would be poured into the tub. By using a soapy wet rag you could scrub all over. A short supply of hot water called for two or more persons to bathe in the same water before it would be dashed over the railing on the back porch. The grown-ups found bathing to be more convenient by standing and taking the wet soapy rag from the tub and drizzling water over the body. Partial bathing did occur during the week, limited primarily to scrubbing the feet in a washbasin before retiring for the night. Bathing the entire body only happened on Saturday.

I cannot remember the first time I ever saw deodorant or heard of its use. As far as I know, not many people used deodorants. Given that we worked hard on the farm and took a bath only on Saturday night, we must have needed them desperately during the week. I would have to speculate that we teenagers began to worry about how we smelled once dating began.

A story made the rounds about an old dirty fellow from the country standing in line to purchase a theater ticket with his body odor overwhelming the crowd. A wise city fellow finally yelled, "Someone's deodorant is not working." The old dirty fellow said, "It's not mine because I don't wear the stuff."

Battling Hot Sticky Nights

Before the days of window fans and air conditioning, the "hot sticky nights" of late July and the month of August could be brutal. We referred to that time of the season as "dog days." John Eller had told someone a few years earlier that the "dog star" rose and set with the sun for about a month and a half from the middle of July to the end of summer.

To say those hot sultry nights showed us no mercy was putting it mildly, and getting a good night's sleep after a long day of drudgery in the fields and the milk barn bordered on the impossible. We would give our hands, arms, and faces a cool washing in the wash pan and go to the dinner table where we consumed a reasonable quantity of late summer vegetables and corn bread washed down with a cool glass of milk. Following supper, after a glance at the local newspaper headlines and listening to the evening newscast on the Philco radio, the greatest challenge of the day became getting enough restful sleep to be able to go at it again the next day. Mornings were cool and tolerable until near noontime, but after dinner, it was a tough stretch all over again.

During the daytime, homes and everything in them accumulated heat —not just the air, but the furniture and every object became overheated. Mattresses and sheets felt as if they had just been removed from a modern day dryer. The combination of such warmth with sticky, sweaty skin left you tossing and tumbling, begging for a breeze of any magnitude to come through the room. We four older boys slept upstairs in a large room without divisions which did allow cross breezes from time to time. Mom believed the sleeping area would be cooler if it were totally closed during the daylight hours and opened just before we hit the hay. Fortunately, pajamas were taboo. We slept in our summer underwear or nothing at all.

Cold Winter Nights

The sleeping experience during the "depths of winter" took just as much courage or even more guts than during the hot summer. Wood was the only source of fuel and was burned in fireplaces and the kitchen stove. We ate supper in the kitchen and gathered around a fireplace in the living room where it was warm and cozy before going to bed.

The thoughts of leaving a heated room, scurrying up the stairs into the bitter cold of a large dormitory-like room and slipping your body between ice-cold bed covers put us in a reluctant mood. There was no good moment to make a run for it. You used every stalling trick imaginable. I would often feign the need to do more homework which might or might not delay the parental order to head for bed.

In the winter, we slept in our long underwear or "long handles," as many called them. Thank goodness for the person who invented them; they were warm and fit tightly against the skin. My big hurdle each night was to get to the top of the stairs and into bed without getting cold. Long handles had a long slit or a trap door in the rear for obvious reasons. Maybe if I could get extra warm air inside the underwear by putting my backside toward the heat of the fireplace and opening the slit, the agony of a rapid run into the jaws of an ice-cold room and bed just might be reduced. Night after night, my hypothesis would be tested. I never detected any benefits from the rear end exposure, however.

The room was as cold as the temperature outside the house, and nothing is as uninviting as a bed above the artic circle. To keep from freezing to death, the corner of the bed covers would be lifted, and in I would go, assuming the smallest fetal position possible and allowing the warmth of my body to begin to make the mattress and covers tolerable. How long I remained in this position, I never estimated, but it seemed forever. Slowly but slowly, the legs and feet would be extended a fraction of an inch at a time warming the rest of the mattress and covers as feet and legs made the journey.

At last, I had a comfortable area the exact size of my body, a place where I stayed for the remainder of the night. Any move to the left or right put me into frigid territory. Covers were drawn completely over my head; a hole at the edge of the covers was just large enough to keep me from smothering.

Going to bed in the cold has its difficulties, but rising from a warm cocoon in below-freezing temperature made the evening antics seem like child's play. During the night, all sources of heat in the house shut down totally, with the possible exception of a few hot coals in the fireplace heaped into a pile by your mother or father before she or he retired for the evening. Once up in the morning, everything I touched was like icicles—the floor, my clothes, the socks, shirt, shoes, overalls, cap,—everything. Thank goodness, we knew nothing of pajamas, because wearing our long underwear to bed was probably the only thing that saved us. Polar bears have their white fur, and we had our white long handles. To this day, I cannot recall when the word pajamas became a part of our vocabulary, if it ever did.

Once out of bed, relief could be found in the kitchen. Mom was an early riser, and starting a fire in the kitchen stove was her first morning deed, an angelic act. People have always wondered when visiting in the country why we gathered in the kitchen. Now you know. The warmth from a wood kitchen stove beats any type of heat I have ever known. Once housewives switched to electric ranges, kitchens lost much of their charm especially during the deep of winter.

Keeping Shoes on Our Feet

Providing shoes for every member of the family became a challenge during the Depression when resources for buying shoes were limited and in World War II when shoes were rationed. In families with large numbers of children, a big thank-you went up during summertime because the children went barefooted. About the only time youngsters put on shoes in the summer was to go to church, and not everyone wore them to worship services. Stretching budgets and leather put a heavy burden on parents to keep feet warm in cold weather. In fact, it became largely a family project. The mother shopped for what few shoes the family could afford and the father kept worn shoes repaired using self-taught skills. Getting one pair of new shoes per year could be cause for celebration during the '30s and early '40s. The owner kept them as long as possible, which meant replacing worn-out portions such as heels, soles, and laces from time to time. Fathers and many older brothers could perform these tasks, but if leather stitching needed to be done, the shoes might have to be taken to a shoe shop in town.

Almost all farm homes kept a shoe-repair box usually on a shelf on the back porch, or at least that is where Dad placed his. The contents of the box consisted of a metal cobbler's foot or shoe "lash," shoe tacks, a tack hammer, an assortment of replaceable heels (both men's and women's), leather for making soles, a trimming knife, a few stick-on rubber soles, and glue. A cobbler's foot was formed with cast iron and had three short legs joined at right angles. Two of the legs bore iron feet, sized to fit inside both large and small shoes. The third leg lay flat on the floor for support as tacks were being driven into shoes. The role of the cobbler's foot, in addition to supporting the shoe being repaired, was to clinch the sharp ends of the tacks as they protruded into the inside of the shoe.

Carefully, Dad would cut a piece of leather the shape of the sole of the shoe needing repair, fit the shoe over the cobbler's foot, lay the piece of cut leather in place, and tack it firmly onto the shoe. Next, he would feel inside the shoe to be sure the cobbler's foot had clinched all of the tack points. Dad's shoe repair never matched the work of a professional, but he kept shoes on our feet.

Stick-on soles had their greatest utility for women's and young children's shoes. They were made of rubber and came in pairs that cost less than 50 cents. The repairman would peel off a thin covering on one side of the sole, add glue to the same side, stick it on the sole of the shoe, and place it aside to dry. In later years when trying to convince people we had meager belongings on the farm, the reference to having to use stick-on soles sometimes would make them believers.

Feed and Flour Sack Clothes

The first feed and flour sacks that bore words and pictures in color began to appear in the '20s, and they found a use for making dresses, aprons, shirts, quilts, and children's clothing. Contrary to what most of us remember, using printed sacks as sewing cloth was not a product of the Depression and World War II. These two events, out of necessity, spurred the practice. Any way you look at it, this had to be one of the most practical innovations for the farm scene during good and hard economic times.

Davidson County had a number of dairy farmers. Feed manufacturers put dairy feed in sacks made of cotton imprinted in bright colors and designs of every flower imaginable which was a two-for-one bargain for farm families. My memory fails me as to whether the price of the 100 pounds of feed increased when put in a colorful sack, but if it did, the increase was small—no more than a nickel.

The Farmer's Exchange in Lexington supplied feed and flour for many farmers, as did the local roller mills. A visit to either took on extra meaning when a new shipment of sacked feed and flour arrived. Selecting the sacks was a family project, and housewives would climb up front in the truck and ride with the farmer to assure that sacks with the most attractive designs were chosen. The wife of one dairy farmer near Linwood was said to have come with her husband to the Farmer's Exchange to find a sack to match one purchased earlier. Much to her disappointment, the sack sought could not be readily found. She demanded her husband move at least 25 sacks or more to find the matching fabric. I can remember going with Dad to the Exchange and observing an increased number of girls in many of the trucks, another good reason for riding with Dad.

Feed stores and flour mills took on an entirely new atmosphere. Housewives would scout among the stacks of feed sacks until a suitable pattern or color was spotted. Into the truck bed the sacks went, and the husband and wife came home with feed for the cattle and cotton cloth for the sewing machine. As far as I know, this was one of the few times the feed store clientele resembled that of a department store. The man handling the bags had to adapt to a new culture. Research shows it took two feed sacks to make a dress and four to make a sheet, and one sack might make an average-size shirt or blouse.

Clothes sewn from feed sacks made their way onto every school bus and into the classrooms. Drab one-color shirts and dresses gave way to red, blue, yellow and green flowers along with squares, rectangles, stripes, birds and boats. Mom made all of her children clothes from feed sack material.

Wearing feed sack clothes caused no stigma whatsoever; yet, neither did they set a trend in fashion. A benefit seldom mentioned was the use made of the string obtained when the band stitching that formed the sack was removed. By tying the ends of strings unraveled from several sacks, you had enough length to fly a kite.

A dairy farmer at Denton claimed in all seriousness that wearing feed sack clothes helped develop a more trusting relationship with his cattle. For example, if he wore underwear made from feed sacks and unbuttoned the sides of his overalls to expose his briefs, his cows would follow him to the milk barn every time.

Hand-Me-Down Clothes

Farm families had large numbers of children, sometimes more than 10, to help with the farm and house work. Clothing and feeding them tested the parents' resourcefulness unimaginably. A common and often necessary practice, hand-me-down clothes, allowed overalls, shirts, blouses, coats, shoes and underwear to be passed down from child to child, which worked very well if sexes and sizes matched.

Having three older brothers made me a natural candidate for hand-me-downs. It is difficult to envision how the practice enhanced the size and condition of my wardrobe. Many items did not fit at all, but Mom, with her ingenuity at using a sewing machine, made necessary adjustments. Most of the overalls had been worn by all three brothers before they reached me. By that time, patches covered the seats, and the legs of most pairs had been cut off above the knees. They had been laundered and hung out to dry in the sun so many times that the original blue color was nowhere to be seen. In fact, my clothes had changed so much in the hand-me-down process that I was setting a whole new trend in fashion and did not know it.

In all fairness to my parents, they made every effort to see that my school clothes were neat. I did not mind wearing my older brothers' clothes, which in many ways was a comforting and secure feeling as long as they were not corduroy knickers. The person who designed and made corduroy cloth, the type available in the Depression, should have been tarred, feathered, and ridden out of town. My three-time-cycled corduroys had completely lost the elastic supports in both legs and would stand up in the corner by themselves when taken off for bed. I can still visualize the difficulty of running the bases during school recess wearing knickers with no leg elastic and feeling like a circus clown.

We Had a Love for Automobiles

Our fascination with automobiles came early in life. None of us had the means to purchase our own, although our fathers and/or older siblings loaned their cars to us on rare occasions, once our driving skills had been demonstrated. The two most popular automobile makes were Fords and Chevrolets. Seldom did a family mix the two, but our family was an exception. My dad was a Chevrolet owner and two of my brothers had Fords. Once a Ford or Chevrolet aficionado, an owner usually purchased the same make the next time around.

The younger drivers and often the older ones, too, would defend the worth of a Ford or Chevrolet, and opinions rarely if ever changed. They would say, "I have a Ford that will do this," or "I have a Chevrolet that can do that." Acceleration capability seemed to be the most worthy virtue a car could have. Fords with their V-8 engines developed in 1932 had an indisputable claim until the Rocket 88 Oldsmobile, which had speed to burn hit the market in the late '40s. One of the boys in the community in Briggs Town drove a Rocket 88 Oldsmobile with a loud exhaust. You could hear him approaching a mile or two away, and no one would challenge him to best his top speed.

Robbie Swing, born in 1916, one of the oldest residents in the area when this book was written, purchased a used Chevrolet as his first car. He described it as a Chevy 4-90; 4 days of running and 90 days of repairing. When the Chevy went its way as worn-out cars did, Robbie purchased a 1934 Plymouth from

Pete Fritts for $300. Robbie had a job at the Lexington Chair Factory. At the salary he made in 1934, he had to work 150 days to earn the $300. In 2006, a worker could earn that much money in about one day and a half; the price of a new car has increased 100 times in terms of dollars.

Automobile factories stopped all domestic production in 1942 and converted to producing vehicles for the war. It was not until 1946 that passenger car production resumed, and the 1946s showed little variation from the 1942s. Bona fide change-over models appeared in 1947. The only cars available for sale from 1942 to 1946 were used, and many changed hands, especially those owned by servicemen going overseas. My brother, Homer, purchased a 1936 Ford from one of Reamer Regan's sons when the son went in service.

We took what was available or we did without. People owned car models never considered in peacetime. One fellow in our area purchased a used Lincoln Zephyr which had 12 cylinders, famous for being a gas hog, getting somewhere around eight miles per gallon of gasoline. Previous owners had apparently driven it to the extreme; it reportedly blew up on a long trip. The challenge to keep the wartime cars running never ended. One week, new cylinder rings might have been needed to reduce exhaust smoke, and the next week, it could have been the brake linings had worn thin or the carburetor was causing the motor to spit and sputter.

The automobile owned when the war started is the one driven for the war's duration, and most of the models had been manufactured in the mid to late 1930s. Our car was a 1938 Chevrolet which had withstood the abuse inflicted by four young boys learning to drive. Once licenses were obtained, the car had little rest until gasoline rationing curtailed driving significantly. Rubber shortages prevented worn tires from being replaced, which called for ingenuity when they went flat or blew out totally. For safety's sake, imposing a speed limit of 35 miles per hour during the war prevented accidents and saved lives.

Getting a flat tire on trips occurred regularly and called for patching the inner tube on the spot because many cars had no spare tire. You jacked up the car, removed the wheel with a lug wrench, pried the tire from the rim and took out the inner tube to locate the puncture. Most cars carried a supply of patching rubber and a tire pump, and ours was no exception.

I can remember while on a date one hot Sunday afternoon in 1946 getting two flat tires on the old Chevy within an hour, which tested my sanity and abilities at the same time. One of the flats was a blowout, and fortunately the car had a couple of blowout shoes in the trunk. I can still see the young lady who was my date using her handkerchief to wipe perspiration from her brow as I changed the tires. It was an exercise of male chivalry at its best.

We learned to do much of the engine and body repairs ourselves. When we couldn't, we took the vehicle to a nearby garage or to a shade tree mechanic. Pete Fritts had excellent mechanic skills, although his customers often complained of him getting the interior of their cars "soiley" from brushing his dirty coveralls against the cars' upholstery.

Jess Kepley made his living by repairing cars under a shade tree in the yard behind his house, hence the term "shade tree mechanic." Practically every community had one shade tree mechanic. Jess lived in Sandy Grove. He built a make-do shed in which to do the repairs, and he shoveled a pit in the middle of the shed, allowing him to slide under the cars. A large oak tree with a sturdy limb stood near the shed. Jess hung a block and tackle from the limb and used it from time to time to lift the front end of cars for ease of accessibility to the engine and front end. Mechanics often drove cars in good running condition to impress their customers. Jess owned a 4-door Buick manufactured in the late 1930s which was his pride and joy. It ran like a well-oiled sewing machine, and on one occasion he went to the Smoky Mountains and returned in a single day, quite a feat in the late forties. The fact it made the trip in one day was a testimonial to his mechanical skills.

During the war, most of the cars found on the highways were manufactured between 1920 and 1942. You would see T-model Fords, A-model Fords, B-model Fords, V-8 Fords, Chevrolets, Dodges, and similar models of Plymouths, Buicks, Packards, Studebakers, Oldsmobiles, Chryslers, DeSotos, and Lincolns, which were fewer in number. Most of the trucks were Fords, Chevrolets, GMCs, or Dodges. New trucks could be purchased during the war if they were to be used to support the war effort, especially in producing and transporting farm products or lumber.

I bought my first car in 1951, but was able to drive some fine automobiles in earlier years. My oldest brother purchased a 1950 new yellow Chevrolet convertible that he let me borrow on occasion. Driving his convertible placed me for one evening, at least, in a most elite class. Thank goodness no accident ever occurred while the car was in my hands, because the excitement of driving such a machine soared to unbelievable heights. Cousin Bill Smith and I conducted some of our social activities together, and he had use of a convertible as well, an A-Model Ford with a rumble seat owned by his brother-in-law. Country courting had added pleasure in that automobile with the top laid back on a warm summer evening and one couple in the rumble seat. It would not run at breakneck speed, but dependability made up for it.

Fathers as Barbers

Another way families "made do" was to develop an at-home competency in a variety of professions. Fathers usually cut their small sons' hair, and mothers did the same for their daughters. Hair clippers, scissors, and a neck cloth were kept in a box in a designated place and taken down at hair-cutting time, which occurred on Saturday afternoons. The fathers had never been schooled in the art of barbering which really was unimportant. One by one his sons would assume a seat in a chair or on a stool with the neck cloth in place to prevent cut hair from sticking to their bodies. The goal was to cut off the long hair with the scissors and go up the neck and sides of the head with the clippers. Most boys did not find hair cuts by their fathers to be pleasant experiences. The scissors lacked sharpness, and the clippers were most likely dull and ice cold. Dull clippers pulled at the hair rather than cutting it, and cold clippers never felt good against the neck and sides of the head.

The sons would squirm, and the father would sternly admonish them to sit still while clipping away. I can still feel the firm pressure of Dad's hand on my head while pieces of cut and clipped hair fell to the floor or lodged on the neck cloth. You learned after a couple of haircut sessions to avoid scratching your nose during the process unless you wanted a mouthful of loose hair. The quality of the haircuts never deserved a blue ribbon, but they made us presentable for church and school, especially after an application of rose oil to hold the hair in place.

A Town Haircut

As boys grew older, around the age of thirteen or fourteen, they would make their first trip to the "barber shop in town," another rite of passage to adulthood. Many of us went to a shop on the main square in Lexington operated by the Corn family, and we sat in a real barber chair with a padded seat, cushioned arms, and a foot rest. The first time we entered the shop, the sight of four barbers cutting hair in unison surrounded by a canyon of gigantic mirrors took us into another world. A radio played quietly to soothe the customers which surpassed in quality the stern admonitions to sit still handed down by a father.

The barber used a handle to raise and lower the chair to get his customers' heads to eye level for ease of cutting—just like I had seen in the movies. Clippers were powered by electricity rather than by hand as Dad's were, and the barber's clippers were sharp, cutting the hair instead of seemingly pulling it out by the roots. Haircuts cost 25 cents each, and Mr. Alec Corn or one of his sons, Skinny, normally cut my hair.

All in all, the experience was pleasant, and there was an added feature beyond what we received from Dad. Once the cutting and clipping were finished, the barber would use a straight razor to shave the neck. I marveled at the way he could sharpen the razor by sliding the blade up and down over a long piece of leather.

Each barber in the shop proudly displayed his diploma from a barber school in a frame on the wall behind him to bolster the confidence of his customer, I supposed. A saying made its way among barber shops, "Shave and a haircut— two bits." Two bits meant 25 cents.

Some great conversations, many of which were educational, were held between the barber and his customers usually in hushed tones inaudible even a few feet way. As the barber made his cuts, he and the customer shared in an engaging conversation, the content of which remained where spoken. What was said in the chair stayed in the chair, a code of conduct which bonded the barber and the customer. He would often ask his customers about their personal interests and their families. I often wondered if learning to conduct a conversation was a unit taught in barber school.

The barber excelled as an expert in practically every human endeavor but especially in current events. Sports usually got top billing as he talked about the college football teams and outstanding players in the country, displaying an excellent memory. Strange, but I can remember very distinctly a statement he made about a great running back attending the U.S. Military Academy at West Point, Glenn Davis, who was dating Elizabeth Taylor at the time. Hollywood and sports always seemed to have a magnetic attraction for each other.

There were other barber shops in Lexington. One shop had a lady barber who cut men's hair. The term, women's liberation, had yet to be invented, but she liberated a barber shop in town and also gave good haircuts.

A story about a one-arm customer going to the barber shop to get a shave and a haircut made the rounds. The customer sat down in the barber's chair, and the barber leaned him back and started to shave his face. Soon, the barber nicked the face with the razor and offered an apology to the customer. Two or three more nicks were inflicted followed by apologies. Thinking he needed to divert the customer's thoughts, the barber asked, "Is this your first time in the shop?" "Yes," replied the customer. "My arm was cut off in a sawmill accident."

Local Barber Shop

Immediately after the war, when Cousin Bruce, or Shorty as most folks called him, was discharged from the Navy, he decided to make a career of being a barber. He attended a barber school in Winston-Salem located on Trade Street. After graduation, he set up shop in Sandy Grove near Uncle El's store, bringing hair cutting and a local industry practically to our doorsteps. Besides, a barber shop added prestige to the community.

We rejoiced at knowing we could get a haircut locally and by a relative, too. Barber shops in rural areas seemed to attract customers in bunches which added a social benefit to getting a haircut. As you waited your turn in the chair, which might be an hour or two on a rainy day, enlightening discussions could erupt among the customers at any minute. If you listened you might learn much about the community, its citizens, and even the facts of life (advanced versions also).

Topics ranged from "how is your momma and them" to the general status of community events and activities. We would learn who were getting married, who should get married and who were not, how much hogs were bringing at the market, when would farmer Smith's cow freshen, how soon the first frost might occur, who has been catching fish from the creek, who has been telling the biggest whopper about fishing exploits, and who has been hunting lately and for what. Nothing matched the barber shop as a source of information, especially with such amazing detail and accuracy. It had all of the trappings of being a "man thing."

Shorty had a policy that benefited bridegrooms-to-be. He would give each a free haircut so they would look extra special on their wedding day, and when they stepped out of the chair, he would comment, "This one's on me, but don't come in here expecting another one."

Women could cross the threshold of the door to the shop which happened on the rarest of occasions. When it occurred, male talk dropped to a whisper immediately. Suddenly, many customers remembered a chore left undone at home as they grabbed coats and scurried out the door. Barbers did not give perms in those days, and a woman was not seeking one either. She merely liked the man's cheaper rate.

Our world lacked most of the modern conveniences of the twenty-first century, but our world had a sense of community where everyone knew everybody and cared for each other deeply. If one person was in trouble, the entire community was in trouble. If one family was hungry, the entire community was hungry. Not having a bath tub, an automobile, or knowing about electricity made no one a lesser person. Character was judged by what people did and said, not by what they owned. We struggled at times to get from one week to the next, but at the end of the day, we honored honesty and truth.

1930s vintage automobiles along Main Street. (Library of Congress, FSA-OWI photo collection, LC-USF34-056217)

Friends and Peggy sitting on her 1938 Oldsmobile. (Family collection)

Sue and Raymond standing beside a 1941 Ford.
(Peggy Hedrick Wilson)

Fancier automobiles came on the scene after World War II. Two blondes and a redhead in an early 1950s convertible. (Family collection)

Hopalong Cassidy and his horse, Topper, in a parade down Main Street in Lexington. (Davidson County Historical Museum)

Band playing in parade down Main Street in Lexington. (Davidson County Historical Museum)

Children never missed an opportunity to tell Santa Claus what they wanted for Christmas.
(Davidson County Historical Museum)

ELEVEN
COUNTRY STORES, COMMUNITY FOLKS
AND DOCTORS

Entrepreneurs built "country stores" scattered throughout the area, locating the stores at busy intersections and crossroads, and in the heart of small communities. One characteristic was common to most of them: they were one-person owned and/or operated. Country stores operated for years included: the Dale Tysinger Store, located at the corner of Beck's Church Road and Shamwell Highway; Elwood Younts Store in the middle of Sandy Grove; "Sleepy John" Hedrick Store, located near Hedrick's Grove Church; McCulloch Store, beside the Davis-Townsend High School in Holly Grove; Otis Younts Store, across from the same school; Hepler's Store on N.C. Highway 109 between Silver Valley and Thomasville; the Charles Lohr Store on Highway U.S. 64; and the Ivey Briggs Store and Garage on U.S. 64 nearer Lexington.

Coppleys' Store was located in the Linwood community, and stores existed in Southmont, Denton and Cotton Grove communities. A poor memory prevents the recollection of who operated them although I do remember Handy's Store just outside Denton. A very strong wind blew it off its foundation when I was very young.

A variety of items for sale could be found on the shelves of the country stores depending on the size of the store and number of persons frequenting it. All of them sold gasoline and oil purchased by customers who would stop on their way to and from work. While there, they would go inside for a few personal items or something needed at home, especially if they were headed that way. Most store owners accepted credit, and they often provided items without charge for worthy causes.

Country store owners possessed a genuine interest in the people of the community. Paul Miller verified this claim in a story he told about an experience of his senior class at Linwood High School. The University of North Carolina invited his entire senior class to come to Chapel Hill to attend a football game that the university would be playing against the Citadel. Five cars existed at the school, but nobody had enough money to pay for the gasoline to make the trip. Mr. Coppley understood the problem, and he filled up the tank of every car without charge enabling the students to make the trip. Not a single student in the class had ever been out of the county before going to Chapel Hill. In addition to the education gained from the experience itself, a great lesson in generosity and caring was learned by the students and followed them the rest of their lives.

Ivy Briggs' Garage served a useful purpose, being the only attempt at providing full-blown garage service for miles around it. Pete Fritts handled most of the mechanic work, and Ivy's son, Arlan, assisted him mostly in doing body repair work.

Charles Lohr was my grandfather, and it is difficult to remember everything he carried, but among the items on his shelves were loaf bread, crackers, baking powder and soda, a few canned goods, potted meat, Vienna sausage, peanut butter, cigarettes, cigars, snuff, pipe tobacco, chewing tobacco, a variety of candies, chewing gum, aspirin, soap and washing powder, and a few toiletries. On racks standing near the counter would be small bags of salted peanuts, oatmeal cookies, Moon Pies, peanut butter nabs and BC and Stanback headache powders. Soft drinks such as Coca-Cola, Pepsi-Cola, Dr. Pepper, Seven Up, RCs, Nehi orange and grape, ginger ale and Cheerwine were standard items. Grandpa's store was minimal in size which limited the scope of his inventory, but some of the larger stores carried a broader selection of items. Customers could get the soft drinks either warm from a crate or cold from a drink box filled with ice water some five to six inches deep. In the very early days, a chunk of ice from the iceman kept the water cold, but in due time, the water was cooled with electric refrigeration. All soft drinks sold for five cents a bottle, most of which held six ounces except for bottles of Pepsi-Cola and RC which held 12 ounces.

Jargon used in making soft drink purchases had a local flavor. For example, a thirsty worker entering the store might ask for a bottle of dope or by the brand name. Many people called the colas "dope" since they were thought to have some medicinal benefits. The word dope meant something entirely different from its meaning today. Sometimes a dose of BC powder, an analgesic, might be poured in an opened bottle of drink, a convenient method used to wash down the powder and mask its bitter taste. Many men often poured a small package of salted peanuts into the bottle before drinking the contents. The term "belly washer" for obvious reasons was often used when asking for one of the 12-ounce drinks, and younger children usually preferred the larger bottles—more bang for the nickel. If they were consumed on the spot, the empty bottles went into a crate specifically made to hold them. If they were carried home, the buyer paid a one or two-cent deposit which was refunded once the bottle was returned to the store owner.

Country stores served as a gathering place for loafers, many of whom might hang around the store for hours, even days, at a time. Except for buying a soft drink and a few other items, the store operator would just as soon they leave. During the cold winter days, loafers would sit around a pot-bellied stove conversing from time to time, but more often than not they napped to while the time away. When more than one loafer showed up for an afternoon or the day, they would become involved in games of checkers or even card games such as setback or Pedro. Each country store had a checkerboard, and some of the loafers were admired for their skill at the game. Lee was not necessarily a loafer, but he was without doubt the community checker champion around Sandy Grove. He could not be beaten unless the opponent used some kind of trickery when Lee lost eye contact with the board. Each checkerboard had its own personality having been crafted from a piece of plywood or heavy cardboard, and caps from soft drink bottles were used for the checkers. Opponents would sit there literally hour after hour challenging each other, and at the end of the day, one player would declare himself champion. If Lee had notched a walking cane for each time he won, it would have appeared as if a beaver had chewed it up.

Loafers, though out of work, showed ingenuity at creating games of chance.

For example, the bottom of a glass Coca-Cola bottle contained the names of the city and state where it was first filled by a bottling company. Since empty bottles were rarely discarded, over time, a bottle might be transported to locations very distant from its origin. Two or more loafers would make a game out of seeing who could lift an empty bottle from the crate with the most distant name on the bottom. Monetary stakes might have been placed on the game if the store owner permitted such. Often the payoff would be a nickel or a full bottle of the drink.

One hot summer day a traveling salesman from near Statesville, North Carolina, explained a game played near his home called "fly." Players would each place a penny or a nickel on the closed end of a nail keg and stand by quietly waiting for a fly to land on one of the coins. The owner of the coin first chosen by a fly would scoop up all the rest for himself. I saw "fly" played but a few times since it had all of the trappings of gambling. My grandfather for one did not allow gambling of any sort in his store. Grandpa himself played solitaire when business was slow, and Cousin Bruce would ask him if he had won. He would say, "Yep" and Bruce would ask, "Did you cheat?" and he would say, "Didn't have to...much."

If you were looking for persons with a great sense of humor, country store patrons seldom took life too seriously, particularly the loafers. They never overlooked an opportunity to mete out surprises on each other. Sitting around a warm pot-bellied stove on a cold winter day induced restful afternoon naps, and a loafer who managed to stay awake under such circumstances found clever ways to disturb his sleeping buddies. The perpetrator would take an ice-cold Coca-Cola or Pepsi-Cola from the drink box, open it, and empty the contents into a "sleeping beauty's" shoes, soaking his socks. Sleeping with cold feet had its difficulties especially if they were soaking wet. The victim would rise in surprised horror looking for the perpetrator who had feigned a deep sleep. Another trick was to gently rub a chicken feather on the upper lip of a sleeper after having applied a few dashes of red pepper on his fingers. Tying the laces of two shoes together while a person slept and yelling for him to come outside created considerable consternation as the sleeper attempted a quick move when he awoke.

Each store sold only one brand of gasoline and oil, probably Esso, Texaco, Gulf, Sinclair, or Pure Oil. Pumps used in the '20s and '30s and early '40s to dispense the gasoline into the tanks of cars operated by gravity flow. A tall glass tank of some 10 to 15 gallons capacity sat on top of the pump which was filled by back and forth action of an attached handle. It was impossible to overfill the glass tank because any overflow would go back into the underground storage tank setting the reading of the gasoline gauge at zero gallons. In dispensing the fuel into a vehicle, the store operator would watch the markings on a stick inside the glass to determine the volume dispensed. Eventually the old gravity flow pumps were replaced by some powered by an electric motor.

Elwood Younts built the first phase of his Sandy Grove store in 1939 with the dimensions of 12 by 16 feet plus overhang in the front where the gasoline pumps were located. Elwood's store developed a large customer base quickly, and he expanded the size of the structure at least five times or more over a period of a few decades. Folks referred to the store as the "Jot 'Em Down Store," the name of a store in the Lum and Abner radio show. Elwood showed successful entrepreneurship which became legendary.

A very unusual store in the shape of an airplane was located west of Lexington. We loved passing by the store if for nothing else than to see its construction and to imagine what it would look like soaring into the sky.

A store operated by Ralph Garner on Highway U.S. 64 just below Odell Fouts' home distinguished itself by selling beer for many years until a change in the law closed it down. Selling beer in a community of church-goers during the early '40s reeked with deliberate boldness. Eventually, the good guys won out, but the establishment made its mark while it lasted.

I cannot remember how I came to go there one Saturday night, but it happened. A few couples were dancing in a large room in the back dance hall, I presume swaying and even staggering at times to music from a jukebox. The visit did not last long but long enough to make me bugged-eyed and allowing me to recognize the couples. Of all the things I did as a teenager, this came as close to sinning as anything. Going to beer hall and observing dancing had to be a bit much.

Arriving home I reported the night's activities to Mom who quizzed me as if she were the head of a tribunal. I was too frightened not to tell it all; she took exceptional interest, especially in the names of the dancers. Actually, she showed some delight in hearing my story I thought, and related it to some of our neighbors. No punishment came from the experience, and a few weeks later I took advantage of an offer to go to the dance hall a second time, a decision I would live to regret. When I got home that night and excitedly began reporting to her, she explained in no uncertain terms my life would be over if I went there again, which I never did. Just when the store closed is a lost memory, but never did I pass by the place without thinking that the devil himself must have lived there.

Lexington's most famous café could have easily been the "Red Pig" located on North Main Street. It sold beer and became the place for drunks to frequent. To hear our parents describe the place, Satan himself must have lived in the back. In no uncertain terms were we to even walk by the place.

Listing Taxes

One of the great sayings in our community was, "Nothing is more certain than death and taxes." Taxes were one of the few things the government required people to pay, but the citizens understood their taxes paid for government services such as schools and roads even though griping about paying taxes seemed an eternal exercise.

My mother listed taxes for property owners in Conrad Hill Township during the 1940s and perhaps some in the '30s as well. Each year every property owner would have to appear before her to verify real estate he or she owned and give a listing of all personal property including automobiles, household contents, jewelry, livestock, grain in storage, dogs, and valuable clothes such as furs. All males of voting age, 21, were required to list their poll. Mom went to specific locations around the township carrying enormous size books that contained a page for each property owner. If she was at Hepler's Store, local citizens would meet her there; she moved about until the entire township was covered. Severe penalties came to those owners failing to list their properties. She would ask about everything and answers usually were given freely except when the question concerned dogs.

The tax for male dogs was $1.00 per year and $2.00 for females unless spayed; then the tax was the same as for males. I traveled with Mom from time to time and found the answers to the question about dogs to be amusing because people hated to pay tax for having a dog. Mom would ask, "Do you have any dogs?" and after a stumbling pause, the responder would say, "Well, there are one or two that hang around my yard, but I do not know who exactly owns them," often suggesting an owner's name. If they said they owned dogs, Mom would ask how many females they had, which also caused some pause before answering. On one occasion, the person listing his property said he did not have any dogs, and his young son who was with him spoke up saying, "You forgot about old Red, Daddy."

Sometimes Mom would say she was not feeling well that day and asked if I could do the listing for her. Naturally, I went to the location for the day and took down the information filed. Much to my amazement, I learned that many of the property owners could not sign their names, and when I signed it for them, they touched the eraser of the pencil exhibiting tremendous trust. The only thing that many others could write would be their name, and in signing their page in the book, great care was taken to get it done properly. Such personal pride I have yet to witness in anyone else.

Persons with Special Personalities

Every region or community had persons who possessed unusual traits or characteristics that made then stand out from the rest. We thought of them as "special people" for any number of reasons. People were not homogeneous; we were different physically, psychologically, and temperamentally. Recognizing such differences in a loving and caring way added to the integrity and enrichment of the way we interacted. We accepted people for what they were and who they were. We worked with each other, played with each other, and joked with and about each other. At the end of the day, we distinguished funny and amused from being hurtful and kept respect for everybody no matter how different they might have been. A great uncle once said folks in our section got some of their sense of humor from their heritage. He had always heard that Germans could find humor in the unique habits of others. Perhaps, our ancestors handed down a tinge of the trait from generation to generation.

Old man John lived near old Highway 90 in the vicinity of Hedrick's Grove. He was known as a sage and a weather prophet and would spend much time in my Grandpa's store. John's physical trademark was a very long thick white beard, the kind you imagined on Santa Claus. He is but a faint glimmer in my memory because he passed away before I became seven years old, but the vision of his beard has stuck with me. People living in the community talked about him long after his death. In one of his colorful moments, he boldly predicted it would snow the next day. Folks in earshot of the prediction waited for the results. Well, no snow fell, and when his reputation as a weather prophet came under question, he laughed and said, "Didn't you read the paper? It snowed in Chicago."

He said if it thunders in the wintertime, it will snow in three days. A practice of his was to plow land when snow was on the ground claiming this would put nitrogen in the soil. Grandpa's barn had a small swamp behind it, and John claimed he witnessed a man, his team, and a load of coal sink out of sight in the swamp. Recounting another sighting, he would open his eyes wide telling about the big fish—five feet long—he had seen in Pounders Fork Creek.

An interesting fellow named Wiley lived in the Holly Grove community. Wiley liked his booze and was arrested for loitering under the influence. The judge sentenced him by telling him to get out of town, but in two weeks, he was seen roaming around Holly Grove again. Someone asked him, "Didn't the judge tell you to get out of town?" He replied, "Yep, but he did not tell me for how long, so I came back." Wiley would show up at high school functions, and you could hear his cackle-like laugh all over the auditorium.

For the sake of the story, we'll refer to another distinctive persona as Roscoe. He lived in a house off the Beck's Church Road, and if there were a village drunk contest, Roscoe would have vied for the title. Of course, anyone who drank any type of alcoholic beverage in those days was referred to as a drunk. Well, Roscoe was known to have a beer or two on occasion, and when in this condition he had a propensity to get in fights and curse a bit. This may not sound too extreme, but Roscoe did provide entertainment for many of us teenage boys. He used to walk on a path through the woods behind my dad's barn to get to Grandpa's store. One day, while three of us were playing near the path, Roscoe came walking past us, staggering slightly and mumbling under his breath. We asked Roscoe what was the matter. He said he had paused in the woods to relieve himself and the zipper of his pants caught some skin.

Before Roscoe married, he showed up drunk at my Grandpa Younts' house in Sandy Grove and started a fight in the yard with two or three other guys. A fellow named Jake entered into the brawl and brought an innocent bystander into the fight.

Roscoe and his wife owned hound dogs known for killing chickens. The dogs attacked my uncle's chickens three or four times. The uncle asked one of his sons to see if he had seen the dogs get the chickens. His son went out of the house in the rain with a shotgun in hand and heard a chicken squawking. Looking up, he saw Roscoe's dog coming out of a ditch and through the creek with a chicken in his mouth. He killed them both. No one took kindly to dogs that killed chickens or sucked eggs.

Lee was the community checker champion. Lee was also an inventor of sorts, and he slaved over making a foolproof rat trap about which he boasted unashamedly. The night came for him to put his trap to the test. He carefully baited the trap with cheese, expecting to find several rats struggling for breath the next morning. The sun came up, and when he checked the trap, the cheese had been eaten. Except for a few rat droppings, all evidence of rats would have been destroyed. Back to the drawing board seemed to be the next logical step.

Lee found many uses for possum grease, or so he claimed. Applied properly, it would ease aching joints, cure eczema, and remove warts. He worried about President Franklin Roosevelt being crippled by polio and wanted to help the man. Once during a visit to a local store, he told the manager that he believed he could cure the president if he could talk with him. The manager said, "Well, there is a phone on the wall; let's call him." He cautioned Lee that the president would listen to him, but due to security reasons, the president would not answer him. Lee admonished the store operator to make a call to the White House which the operator pretended to do. He handed the phone to Lee who talked at least 20 minutes explaining the virtues of his possum grease ointment.

Shorty never forgot the time Lee came into his barber shop, and Elmer rose from his chair to shake Lee's hand and said, "I'm Elmer. I'm glad to meet you Mr. Possum Grease."

Lee had a horse named Charlie that he claimed could talk. He'd ask the horse if he wanted corn, and the horse would paw his foot.

Lee's mother would take him fishing getting as close to the creek as her car would go, and Lee would get out. You had difficulty seeing Lee under all of the junk he had—an old steam cage, fishing poles, and a lasso to mention a few items. He would not tell the crowd in the barbershop the purpose of the lasso. Instead he whispered in Shorty's ear that he tied one end of the lasso around his waist and the other end around a tree on the creek bank to keep him from slipping in the water.

Once in a while a city boy would come to live with an uncle or grandparent, and the country boys would watch for the city fellow's first goof-up. A boy from out of state up North came to live with one of the Everhart families near the County Home. He had never lived on a farm before and knew nothing about the care and feeding of animals. One morning a member of his host family encouraged him to give a cow in the stable a bucket of water to drink. She watched carefully as the water was carried to the cow only to see the city boy return to the house almost immediately. She went to the barn and saw he had poured the water in the feed trough. Her only comment was, "Why didn't you just pour the water in the hay rack?"

Willie was a man who could have been anybody's uncle, and he was indeed an uncle to over 40 nephews and nieces, never short on intelligence and conversation but long on procrastination. The story of his life—particularly his livelihood—should have been made into a movie because of so many experiences he had in making a living. Nothing seemed to worry him, and if he had no more than a nickel in his pockets, you would think he was a Texas millionaire. He seemed to rehearse life each day, and he played the parts to the fullest. He spent much of his early working life as a "peddler," traveling over the back roads of much of Piedmont North Carolina. Nephews would travel with him from time to time because they enjoyed his humor and listening to his sales pitches before the store owners. The Uwharrie River, or "Underwear River" as he would call it, had to be forded at a crossing in Randolph County due to the absence of a bridge. Carefully he would guide his old 1935 Chevrolet through the stream, the water-covered exhaust pipe making the sounds of a gurgling whale causing him to laugh heartily as the car emerged from the other side. The companies he represented changed as often as sheets in a first-class hotel, but you had to give him credit for keeping his ears and eyes opened for opportunities.

At the beginning of World War II, the Department of Defense advertised for carpenters to come to Fort Bragg to help build barracks for army trainees. The pay would be 90 cents per hour, a tidy sum in 1942. Willie had never heard of such good wages, and he proceeded to round up carpenters' tools from his father's decaying tool shed and drove to Fort Bragg. His brothers-in-law remarked that he would be back soon, because he didn't know a thing about carpentering no matter what his tools look like.

A foreman assigned him to a crew, and it started building a few barracks. Within two weeks, the foreman recognized Willie had a fear of heights if ascending above two feet off the ground and sent him home. When he got home, he told tales of fellow carpenters knowing little to nothing about handling a hammer as if he were a pro. Willie noticed one man throwing practically every other nail away. When questioned about what he was doing, the man said, "Many of these nails have heads on the wrong end, so I am getting rid of them." Willie said, "Save them. They are for the other side of the building." We loved that man, and after he moved up North for an extended career, many of us made our first trip of any distance to pay him and his family a visit. Usually, we took in at least a couple of major league baseball games. In his latter years, the South called him home to Davidson County where he and his wife spent the remainder of their lives in a new home about two miles from his birthplace.

Jack worked mostly at sawmills when he worked at all. One of my cousins worked with him, and Jack was the boss. His basic weakness just happened to be whiskey which affected his thinking. One day he announced repeatedly that he wished to hang himself. The owner of the sawmill grew tired of him mouthing about it and put a rope in a tree saying he would drape it around his neck. All he would have to do is jump from the back of a truck. Jack declined to take advantage of the offer. The owner went to get him for work one morning, and his wife said. "Why he's drunk, and he can't go to work." She pointed to a pear tree beside the house where Jack had hung a rope on a limb to hang himself. The sawmill owner replied, "You had better get a bigger rope because the one he selected won't do the job on someone as cussed as he is."

Jack and his drinking buddies were constantly getting into trouble driving their old automobile from one side of the road to the other and steering it through front yards and side ditches. Pedestrians seeing them coming would climb road banks to get out of the way and shake fists as they passed by. When he didn't show up for work, a trip to the jail house would often find him behind bars. When he sobered up, you never saw a man who wanted work more than Jack; this fervent search was a common trait of habitual drunks needing money to purchase a pint or two.

Some respected professionals showed considerable versatility in their work. Preacher could lay a good sermon on the line which he did Sunday after Sunday. Beyond preaching, he also knew about all there was to know about raising chickens, and he volunteered to teach a poultry short course at Grandpa's store. Notice of a short course was posted in the store windows for the customers to read. Prior to the night of the course, preacher asked one of the boys in the community to bring a crate of chickens from his farm to serve as teaching props.

The evening for the course arrived, and attendees found two crates of chickens, one brought by the preacher and the other by the boy. Preacher began by describing the appearance of sound, healthy chickens, taking one from his crate to make his points. He then turned to the other crate and lifted out another showing surprise at the sorry appearance of the boy's chicken. Preacher asked the boy about his chickens to which he replied, "Well, most of 'em in the coup looked a bit puny." Without saying a word, preacher slid his crate of chickens about ten feet from the boy's crate. In a few minutes he left the store, saying something about not wanting his chickens to meet up with anything inferior.

Jess, the shade tree mechanic was fearful of the unknown—particularly things "that go bump in the night." His buddies also played numerous tricks on him, and he had musical talent, playing at various events.

While working on an automobile late one evening, the wind came up and blew limbs across his workplace causing a noise that disturbed Jess. Without investigating the source of the noise, he threw down his light cord and left the door wide open. The next day, he was in a state of denial about it all. Older teenagers stole his "taters" from under his house and made a trail out of them to the barn like the Little Riding Hood story. The same boys would slip into this henhouse and make strange noises. Afraid to come out of his house, he would ask his wife, "Did you hear that?"

Roby Smith came to see Jess and asked what was wrong with his car. Jess said, "You go ahead and drive it, and when it stops running, bring it back and I will tell you." He and a cousin named Steve played musical instruments, and they would be asked to play at corn shuckings. Jess related the following story at Shorty's barber shop:

We had an engagement to play for a corn shucking, and went to a bootlegger's house for some moonshine to fortify ourselves before the performance. He did not have moonshine and sold us a half gallon of blackberry wine. Both of us took a long drink, and the old man said, "Boys, you had better go kindly easy for it's got a pretty good hammer to it." As we were driving along the Baptist church cemetery, one of us said to the other, "You feel anything?" The other said "Nope" as the other said "I don't either." We pulled up at the bridge and took another drink and had a long laugh. Much later, they found me at the foot of an old maple tree and Steve at the edge of the road. The feller having the corn shucking had to go into town to get some other musicians so they could have the dance.

Nobody in lower Davidson County had a memory like John especially with dates. John, a mill worker was known for his nearly flawless recollections. If he ever heard when you were born, the date was saved in his memory bank as if it were a high-powered computer. Ask him about birthdays, not only of people but cattle and horses as well, he could reel them off with alacrity. A serious argument broke out between two Bobs at El Younts' store one Saturday evening over the date of a certain event. Back and forth they went, Bob one claiming one date and Bob two another. Just before fisticuffs might have been tried as a solution, John overheard the squabble stepped in and said, "I know when it was. It happened two weeks after Curt Lohr's cow had her second calf." John had spoken, and nothing more needed to be said.

John also had considerable physical stamina. He worked the second shift at Erlanger Mills, and he would often walk the distance of some 8–10 miles from his home in Briggs Town to Erlanger. If no ride was available after finishing his shift after midnight, he would walk back to Briggs Town. John was known by everyone for miles around.

One of the most interesting characters ever to grace Davidson County was the Goat Man who came from out of state. He owned a small wagon and moved it from place to place using a team of goats. In addition, 10 to 15 goats trailed along behind the wagon. The wagon, its contents, and the goats comprised all of his worldly possessions. Stories about the Goat Man substantiate his claim of traveling to every state in the continental United States. On one of his trips through North Carolina, he passed along the highway in front of Grandpa's store stopping for a few hours before moving on to some undetermined destination. His appearance and life style were suitable for folklore at its best. We often wondered about his origin and purpose in life. Based on the description given by Grandpa, I learned the meaning of the word "vagrant" and determined his was not the life for me.

Peddlers

Peddlers of home products made their rounds from home to home throughout the country. One who developed notoriety sold an ointment named Rawleigh's, and to us farm folks, he was simply known as the "Rawleigh Man." Other peddlers roamed the countryside selling anything from lightning rods to Rosebud salve to hair products. Encyclopedia and Bible salesmen, usually college students working their way though college, came around during the summer, and they received a better reception than others because they were viewed as trying to improve themselves.

An uncle really liked a story about a vacuum cleaner salesman who stopped by a farm house to make a sale. Before knocking on the house, he went by the barn and gathered a bucket of horse droppings. When he got into the house, he went to the living room, and without saying a word, he scattered horse droppings over the woman's best carpet. Next he proclaimed to the housewife. "If my vacuum cleaner doesn't take up every particle of these horse droppings, I will eat every bit of it myself." The housewife said, "Well, you had better start eating, because we do not have electricity."

Countryside Signs

As automobiles became more comfortable and the roads were improved, folks would take longer trips. Advertising agencies soon learned product messages could be relayed to travelers effectively by posting signs along the highways. The Burma Shave Company caught the idea early, and over the countryside, in farmers' fields, red signs with white lettering placed about 100 feet apart told us about the product. Each sign contained one line, with the fifth always advertising Burma Shave. Here are some of the actual signs:

DON'T LOSE YOUR HEAD
TO GAIN A MINUTE
YOU NEED YOUR HEAD
YOUR BRAINS ARE IN IT
BURMA SHAVE.

TRAINS DIDN'T WANDER
ALL OVER THE MAP
'CAUSE NOBODY SITS
IN THE ENGINEER'S LAP
BURMA SHAVE.

SHE KISSED THE HAIRBRUSH
BY MISTAKE

SHE THOUGHT IT WAS
HER HUSBAND JAKE
BURMA SHAVE.

CAUTIOUS RIDER
TO HER RECKLESS DEAR
LET'S HAVE LESS BULL
AND MORE STEER
BURMA SHAVE.

CAR IN DITCH
DRIVER IN TREE
THE MOON WAS FULL
AND SO WAS HE
BURMA SHAVE.

Large and sometimes grotesque advertising signs mounted on poles or pillars along the highways never distracted us because they were not yet invented. On the other hand, farmers often rented space on the sides of their barns to companies who painted signs advertising their products. Cigarettes, chewing tobacco, and snuff appeared in very large illustrations in colors that matched their packages on the store shelves. Camel, Lucky Strike, and Phillip Morris cigarettes led the parade of barn advertisements. Mail Pouch Tobacco and Prince Albert for roll-your-own cigarettes and pipes had their share of barn sides as did Brown Williams Chewing Tobacco and Tube Rose Snuff. The advertisement slogan, "See Beautiful ROCK CITY—ATOP LOOKOUT MOUNTAIN" greeted travelers on the sides and roofs of barns all over the South.

Going to the Doctor

Road and barn signs entertained and distracted us as we traveled to the offices of our doctors and dentists. Our family doctors for the most part lived in either Lexington or Thomasville, and if someone needed a specialist, Charlotte or Winston-Salem became the destination. Since there were so many in my family, there were probably more trips to see the doctor than I can recall, but we only went when absolutely necessary. Health insurance had yet to be invented for country folks, and thank goodness, the cost of an office visit was seldom more than five dollars, still a tidy sum for a person earning a couple of dollars a day.

When I was about eight years old, a large boil appeared on my rear that refused to open using normal home procedures. Finally, Dad put me in the car one day to go see Dr. J. A. Smith, our family physician, in Lexington. He carefully examined the boil and with a calm voice said it had to be lanced. At that moment if I could have escaped from his office, I would have, but Dad was sitting between me and the door. Dr. Smith came at me with a syringe needle the length of a ruler and gently plunged it into the boil as Dad held me still. After a bucket of tears, the pain subsided from whatever anesthetic was in the syringe; next he took a blade some two or three inches in length and lanced the boil. The boil released its poison, and relief came quickly.

Further encounters with the doctor, Dr. Smith again, included a stay in the hospital as a ninth grader to have my appendix removed, requiring a recovery of nearly ten days before I could go home. A brother was bitten by a black widow spider while playing in corn shucks and was rushed to the hospital for treatment; otherwise, death would probably have been certain. Another brother suffered a serious wound in his thigh when horned by the bull in the stable one morning. He, too, required the care of a doctor. The aforementioned incidents were not unique to my family but serve as illustrations of the kinds of medical needs requiring a doctor's attention in rural areas. Doctors made house calls at that time, especially to deliver babies and to tend to people with bed-ridden infirmities. Again, the charge for doing this was minimal compared to today's fees.

The Tooth Puller and the Dentist

Trips to the dentist in the 1920s, '30s and '40s rarely occurred except when a toothache became unbearable. If the person with the ache could afford it, he or she sought relief from a dentist. Otherwise, the tooth met its demise by assistance from a "community tooth puller" or total decay.

A story in the community about an old man having an unbearable toothache and his family calling for the community puller lends some credence to the rarity of dentist visits. For the sake of retelling the story, the name of the man was Claude. The tooth puller arrived with his handmade tooth pliers, a mark of his trade, and little else. Claude needed relief from the pain and opened his mouth, pointing to the aching tooth. Quick as a duck jumping on a June bug, the puller fastened his pliers on Claude's tooth and gave a man-sized yank, only to have the pliers slip from the tooth. Chaos ensued. Claude jumped from the bench where he was sitting and circled the room for what seemed like several minutes, yelling at the top of his voice and begging for help in any form. His wife remembered a jar of moonshine whiskey Claude kept in the pantry, and she made a beeline for it. In desperation, Claude took a long snort, as it was called then, and finally calmed down.

Returning to the bench, Claude placed the jar of moonshine nearby just in case. Reluctantly, he opened his mouth again, and the tooth puller approached him cautiously fitting the pliers around the tooth as best he could. Claude grimaced, anticipating another yank on the tooth, which came like lightning. Yet, success was not yet to be had. The pliers slipped a second time, and Claude reached for the moonshine, having another drink. The process repeated itself several times: yanking on the tooth, slip of the pliers, swallow of moonshine. Claude got to the point where he couldn't care less, and when in a limp condition, the tooth fell out hitting the floor. The tooth puller reeking in sweat, Claude drunk as a sailor, and his wife saying halleluiah made for a fitting conclusion.

Baby teeth of children, as they became loose, were pulled by parents or an older sibling, often by tying a string around each tooth and tugging or using pliers. A local blacksmith pulled a lot of baby teeth using a special pair of pullers he made in his blacksmith shop.

I was 15 years old when I made my first visit to the dentist to get a six-year molar extracted that was too decayed to save. Dr. Sowers, the family dentist, put an injection of Novocain along the gum line near the base of the tooth to deaden it and used carefully designed pliers to make the extraction.

If teeth were brushed at home, it was done with soda using a crude brush often made from a sourwood twig, but some of us did have the manufactured brushes. We were afraid to have our teeth cleaned by a dentist because we believed it would wear the teeth down. Our school had educational programs on proper dental care conducted with puppet shows coming from the state health department in Raleigh. The puppets had the names of Jack and Judy. Little by little we learned how important it was to save our teeth, but many people by the time they were 25 or 30 years old had to have most of their teeth extracted and replaced with a set of false ones.

Dr. Sowers filled a few cavities for me after my sixteenth birthday. He pumped a foot treadle that turned the bit very slowly causing pain slightly less than excruciating. He reserved his pain killer for tooth extractions, but with determination and patience, he would remove the decay and place a filling in the drilled hole. Dentists and pain seemed to fit naturally in the same sentence, and visits to see them commonly incited fear and trembling.

Dr. Sowers practiced his trade for years, and just before retirement, a woman patient of some age needed stitches put in her gum, but the good doctor could not see to thread the needle. The woman informed Dr. Sowers she could thread the needle if she had her eye glasses. Looking through her purse, she remembered she had left them in the car parked along the street. The crisis needed solving. The woman carefully disconnected herself from the dental chair, walked down two flights of stairs to her car, returned, and threaded the needle. Her gum received the needed stitches.

The people of lower central Davidson County, North Carolina—from farmer to sawmill worker, carpenter to brick mason, shade-tree mechanic to checker champion, loafer to drunk, preacher to peddler, barber to tooth puller, housewife to school teacher, doctor to dentist, furniture maker to textile weaver, from leader to follower, and many more—were the heart of life as we knew it in the '20s, '30s, and '40s. Their heritage is our heritage and their stories are our stories, combining to create memories of human frailties and strengths. All of us have our own memories tucked away in the recesses of our minds that can be replayed at will on a quiet summer afternoon or a rainy winter day. We exist in each other's memories of lives filled with success, failure, humor, tolerance, hard work, joyful play, and the spirit of community.

Abraham Lincoln said, "Die when I may but let it be said of me by those who know me best that I planted a rose where a rose would grow." This has been the calling of the generations in south Davidson County.

Larry Johnson, a local Davidson County artist, painted Ivy Briggs' Service Station on Old Highway 64. (Family collection)

Old country store and gasoline station at Jackson Hill, Davidson County. (Davidson County Historical Museum)

C. T. Taylor's service station in Lexington. (Davidson County Historical Museum)

Service station shaped like an airplane. (Davidson County Historical Museum)

The window of a small town grocery store. (Library of Congress, FSA-OWI photo collection, LC-USF351-268)

A spacious barn roof served as an excellent site for outdoor signs. "See Beautiful Rock City" was one of the better known advertisements. (Photo by author)

Signs we read as the automobile sped along the highway. (John Colclough)

TWELVE
IN THEIR OWN WORDS

Several people in the lower Davidson County region who lived during the 1920–50 period were interviewed to gain additional perspectives about conditions of the times as they experienced them. Excerpts taken from the interviews serve as authentic testimonials presented in their own words without comment.

PAUL MILLER

Paul Miller has lived his entire life in the community below Beck's Reformed Church. Larry Younts interviewed him on October 15, 2004.

INT: When were you born, and what are some of the earliest things you remember?

PM: I was born in 1923. I remember well before I went to school that the two oldest boys were going to school.

My daddy liked to take me with him. He had a 1920 T-model Ford and that thing didn't have a cab on it, or doors, nothing but a windshield. He'd haul lumber down around the Denton area. My grandpa and my daddy were timber brokers. They never had a sawmill, but Grandpa being a store man had made a little money over the years and so people would come to him to sell timber. People would have it sawed and have it stacked. Nobody hauled green lumber. Everybody didn't know where the market was and didn't have any way to haul it except wagons, so the first ones that had trucks could get in the business pretty good. Uncle Allison Miller was considered one of the wealthiest men of his time in the sawmill business. He had two sawmills and two steam engines. Clyde and Early and his boys kept them both trucks and at one time, so my daddy said, he had 12 head of horses and mules. Clyde and Early had the best trucks. They had the old model Dodges. Now, I don't know how old they were but they were better than the T-models. They actually had a transmission in them, and they would pull. You could put on a pretty good load but you couldn't make no speed on the road because they had solid tires. If you had any speed you couldn't stay in the trucks with old solid tires.

My daddy would bundle me up, I can still remember that, with old coats and everything in the world and take me with him to Denton to get a load of lumber. A lot of times they'd haul the lumber to this plant over here what they call Walls Town. It burned down. I remember well when it burned down. That was some trip on an old open air truck. He'd take a mule's hitching rein to kind of tie me in because he knew if I got warm and went to sleep I'd fall out.

At one time, he had the big business with Morris Cabinet Company in High Point. Well, High Point was a long drive from Thomasville and they would haul out lumber. That old T-model wouldn't pull but about 1,000 board feet because it didn't have the pulling power. They would haul out from the people they bought the timber from to Thomasville, stack it there in the rail yard so the box car could get to it. As well as I remember, box cars then would haul about 30,000 board feet of rough lumber. He would do that during week days and on Saturday he would take Arnold, Harold, Odell Harvey and J. L. They were big enough to work. They would hand load that stack of lumber on the yard onto the box car and ship it to High Point.

I never will forget in this box car they would get ready to load in there was a pile of something in the corner of it, looked kind of like cow manure. So my daddy said you boys find some broken timber around here and scrape that mess out. We ain't going to throw no lumber in on that. My brother tasted it. Just happened to put his finger in it, and it happened to be molasses. You know they used to haul a lot of Cuban molasses and Arnold and Odell were kind of devilish. They got the idea they were going to have some fun. My daddy let them do it. They took that molasses and smeared it all over the railroad tracks, and they knew about what time the local would come there. That old engine hit that molasses it went chug chug chug chug chug, and it didn't go nowhere. The engineer looked outside, shook his head, because he figured somebody had done that, and he had to make several tries before he could get traction through it.

As far as teaching us to work, he put us to work when we were big enough to do anything, chores or helping. If it wasn't to do the job, it was helping. Helping mama hunt the eggs, feed the pigs. We always kept several cows. We learned to milk cows real early.

INT: You were born in 1923. Did you have a doctor come out to the home?

PM: Yep, old Dr. Terry. I was born at home, and I lived there until I got married.

INT: Did your daddy farm, too?

PM: Yeah, he farmed and he cut logs a lot of times and cut cord wood. There was always a big sale for cord wood in Lexington. They used to haul it to town in wagons. Take all day. Load up a cord of wood in the morning, go to town and I think they sold it to a furniture plant on Highway 8 right about where that concrete plant is. There used to be a big factory there. I think it burned down. Then trucks and things started coming in.

INT: You had plenty of food, plenty of clothes? Do you ever remember being without anything?

PM: No. Now, money was not plentiful, but when I got big enough to go to the field—with my mama, she liked the outdoors—they had me an old wore out hoe and a broom handle in it and they knew I wasn't going to do a professional job at it, but I went along digging some grass, teaching us how to work. We raised everything that we ate. We had fattening hogs, cows, and that's where I learned most of how to do things. I learned from my parents. They knew when to start turning the crops. People depended on the garden because you didn't go to town to buy canned goods. We were continuously planting crops all summer long. Potatoes, popcorn, peanuts, and molasses cane. Your grandmother made molasses if I'm not mistaken because I think we went up there and bought some.

INT: How many acres did your daddy own?

PM: 160 acres. 100 acres up here and 60 acres down.....most all of it was from the old first ancestors of George Miller. He was buried down there at the old place. I don't know exactly, but he was in the Revolutionary War. He and Peter Hedrick came over about the same time. They came from Germany, and they had military training from way back there. The Continental Congress didn't have no money, and they immediately put these people that had a little military training at the rank of Captain - the names of Captain Peter Hedrick and Captain George Miller. After it was over with, the only thing they got out of it was a huge tract of land. Peter Hedrick got 4 miles up and down the branch. George Miller got no telling how much down on the farm that we farmed. Hundreds and hundreds of acres and my daddy inherited most of that. Uncle Allison and my daddy just kept breaking it down through the years, and Sandy Miller got the old original part of it. That was Harold's daughter.

INT: When you were growing up did you have corn shuckings and wheat threshings?

PM: Now that was fun. Everybody had a big corn pile, and they would ask their neighbors...you know communities worked together. Everybody was in the same boat. They were farm people. Nobody was rich. They dug their living out of the ground. We went as far as Matt Tysinger's and Edward Rhodes' all back up and down the line here and sometimes they'd be big piles of corn and shucking was usually done in cold weather too. It was fun. The men would kind of get on one end and the women on the other end. That was gossip time. They could talk and do like they wanted to.

INT: When you were little, what did you do for fun?

PM: We made our own fun. We played in the big woods out behind the house and we'd play cowboys with old wooden pistols and go hide. There was a gang of boys—me, Reid Harvey (we were about the same age), Reid had a little brother that was retarded (Hill Harvey), Gene Miller and Harvey Parks. We were together all the time shucking corn, wheat threshing. Noland, he was the youngest boy. James Oswald Lloyd was the oldest one. He was older than my brother Arnold and Odell Harvey. They'd all grown up and their way of amusement was different from us children. We'd have a time on Sunday. As we got bigger we got up to Pounders Fork and some of the boys found a hole that was deep enough to go swimming. Traffic wasn't too heavy. There were some old vines and we'd swing across that thing and think we were Tarzan. We'd have the biggest fun over nothing. The next year we went up there and the first one got 'holt of the swing to swing across the thing had rotted and they fell in. Last year's vine would fall every time.

INT: Seems like in those days everybody had a nickname. Did you have a nickname?

PM: My brothers called me Pike. Some called me Peter Paul. In fact, Robin and her friends still call me Peter Paul. It's the funniest thing. Hill Harvey was a year younger than I was, but he was always in the crowd with us playing. He didn't get to go to school, his mentality wasn't good enough to go—fairly good brain and an incredible memory. I tell you these names he came up with. He could say Paul, he couldn't say Reid—he'd say Weed and Wobin. Rodney Miller knows about this, and me and Reid Harvey and Dolan Parks and I don't know of anybody else that would really remember that but Hill had names that are not in any history books, and I wouldn't know how to spell them but I still remember what he called them. I'll start with Will Greer and his wife. Will Greer's name was Chukakootie, his daddy was Papa Tom, mama was Mamma Lilly, my daddy was "Big Lee's Wife."

INT: When you were growing up, do you remember any of the old people speaking in German?

PM: No, I think most of them knew English.

INT: Daddy and others say they can remember Grandmother Younts speaking a little and Joe Ben and Minnie Swing at church speaking German to each other.

PM: Joe Ben and Minnie, I thought when I was growing up their names were Joe Ben and Minnie Ben. They were brother and sister, the last ones that drove a horse and buggy to church. He'd hitch them up there above where the old hut used to be. They said he had a car one time but he was such a reckless driver and the law took it away from him.

INT: You mentioned earlier going to Fairview School. Do you remember any of the teachers that you had?

PM: Yeah. My first grade teacher was out at the rest home with Mama. It was Sally Miller's sister, her name was Ginny Morris. She married Carly Davis. She drove a T-model coupe all the way from Denton. She taught three grades. Old Fairview School had three rooms and seven grades. Then another teacher had the fourth and fifth and the other teacher had sixth and seventh. Lloyd Beck taught the last year out there. Clifford Greer taught school out there. Will Greer took him, when he was Deputy Sheriff, carried him to Lexington High School for four years. He carried him and Raymond Harvey both. Raymond Harvey said Will gave him a whipping one time and he still remembered it. Did you know Edward Rhodes taught school there one time? He taught my daddy. The county picked up anybody with a little education that would do it. My mama said she remembered carrying third grade books. That was as far as she got but she could read and write, she could do arithmetic—simple mathematics. She educated herself just like Abraham Lincoln.

INT: Who was the principal of that school?

PM: I'm not sure. But, I remember in the first grade, and it had benches where three sat at one desk. And the rest of us scattered about. It was heated with an old wood stove. The worst punishment you could get was the teacher put you between two girls.

INT: Did you ever get punished like that?

PM: Yeah. I remember that.

INT: What was Christmas like for ya'll during the Depression?

PM: Well, it wasn't too plentiful but we thought it was real good back then. Everybody got a stocking and it usually had an apple, orange and tangerine and a few Brazil nuts and they always bought Red Bird stick candy. And maybe something like a pair of socks or something like that. It was a little Christmas but what our parents could afford.

INT: Did you have a Christmas tree?

PM: Always had a Christmas tree. Mom usually didn't have anything like tinsel…strings of icicle looking stuff….and she'd string popcorn and put on it. Maybe a few little glass balls.

INT: Do you remember the Christmas plays you had at church?

PM: I was always in them because mama told me I had to. I enjoyed doing it, just little old things down at the old church. They'd take down that old ragged curtain. The old church is where Reverend Hiatt married me and Marie and that's where we went to church for years. That's where John and Maxine met each other and got married. That was a long time ago, of course we were married 61 ½ years. Upstairs they had an old wire and a green curtain, and they'd take that thing down and some way or another fix it on the pulpit and it would open up and they would change scenes. There was a little class that would come out and say their speeches….then maybe have Christmas cut-outs from pretty colored paper…we'd stand up there "C" for Christmas…It was simple but it was a lot of fun.

INT: Do you remember what kind of choir did you have?

PM: Well, they had a choir. I remember when they played the old organ. Jesse Staley was the one I remember first played the organ. She knew music. My mama always said "you couldn't stall her on nothing"—she could play anything. Then later they got the piano and Treva Greer played the piano. Mabel Harvey and the choir was up on a couple of steps higher and they put a pipe around it and a curtain so it wouldn't show themselves. Had old homemade benches made out of the forest pine I guess off the place. A lot of people paid a lot for them old benches.

INT: Do you remember when you had your first date? How old you were?

PM: I tell you what. I didn't become 16 until my senior year and of course you always claim a sweetheart in your high school days but that didn't amount to nothing. I guess maybe the first date was my senior year banquet. My junior year I wasn't old enough to drive. We had a banquet up here at the old hut. Katherine, the teacher and my mama helped and Minnie Briggs, and I forgot who all prepared the food. Senior year we had it in our new gym, and I was old enough to drive then. I went around and picked up several people who didn't have a way, but everybody back then, by golly, didn't have a car. That was 1940, we were coming out of the Depression. People raised their kids back then.

I guess I was in high school when the county let schools have 4–6 weeks in the fall of the year of one-half-day school because the parents couldn't make a living if they didn't have some help. Everybody had cotton picking time, dug sweet potatoes, corn pulling time, and all such as that. Cotton was the money because people didn't raise tobacco around here. I think my daddy and Jim did until the Depression come along, but that was the thing. Everybody had big old patches of peas because they had to prepare themselves for winter, so to speak, butter beans, pinto beans, popcorn, peanuts, everything had to be hand picked. They gave 4–6 weeks of one-half-days. I think we got out at 1:00. Mama always had a big pan of baked sweet potatoes or, old people dried a lot of apples and made what we called flap-jack pies. Man alive! You'd be hungry and you'd eat your way through them. I thought sweet potatoes were the best tasting thing, and she kept them warm for us too. Then we'd light out to the cotton patch or to the corn field or potato field. Life was hard but it was still good.

INT: How did World War II affect you?

PM: When I was 17 years old I didn't have money to go to school. The government offered training at Lexington High School at night of sheet metal work because they knew they were going to have to have airplanes. You could go, and they had teachers there to kind of teach you how to cut metal with right and left hand tin snips. I didn't know they had a right and left of anything —how to cut and shape metals and rivet and all that stuff. Whenever we got done, they helped us fill out applications. The closest air factory then was Martin Aircraft in Baltimore, Maryland. Even my brother, Arnold, went up there. The wages were better than they were here but living expenses was high too.... Then the war really hit on December 7th in 1941, and they were wanting to get those planes out. I worked up there......me and Marie got married....That was my real first date. I started going with her, I had broke off with a girl (or she broke off with me) because I think somebody had a prettier car. Then I met Marie and I suppose that was the best deal I ever got in my life. Never dated anybody else. I got a furlough, 3 days off, to get married. One day to come home, a day to get married, and day to come back and all on an old steam train. That was the first train I was ever on. Nasty thing took all day. Then I worked up there, in fact, we never did know....they wouldn't tell us, but they had security.....let me tell you. You go in there carrying a lunch bag you better open that thing up. Now, we ate in the cafeteria. We had 30 minutes to eat and honest to God, we walked from here to Dolan Swing's shed over there and in a crowd and sat down and gobbled down your food and be back on the job in 30 minutes. The plane they made was the B-26. It was a medium bomber, but it was the biggest thing that I ever saw. It was called a Marauder Bomber. It had two motors and was a big son-of-a-gun. Do you remember Marie Swing's husband....Dolan Swing's sister's husband?

I'm not sure how long I worked up there. My daddy had a stroke and heart attack, and it was less than a year, I reckon. They wanted me to come home. I talked with them up there at the aircraft factory. He had his land broke to put in crops. Leon was young then, and Harold was already in the Army. They drafted him and Arnold. I think George Coble got him to stay; he was a good mechanic, so he had him stay to keep the trucks rolling, and we came home and at that time, I got a deferment from the aircraft factory to go home. Then I just kept working on the farm because at the time of the Battle of Bulge everybody about my age that hadn't been called—Joe Beck, me—they were pulling everybody. We all passed and the Battle of the Bulge smoothed out and they sent me a card and said we're not going to draft you. I was ready to go. Joe Beck went and, of course, he got hit with shrapnel in his foot, and Bill Rhodes I think he got scarred over there too. A lot of families—Lindsay, Willie—they took just about everybody. I didn't balk on it because when they called, I went, and then they sent me—after that—looked like it wouldn't be necessary to give me another deferment.

INT: What one or two people had the greatest influence on your life?

PM: My parents. They taught me everything I ever knew. My daddy, everybody always give him praise for being honest and hard working. They believed in everything that was right. That gives you great influence.

INT: Do you see any similarities between when you were little and the way life is now?

PM: Oh my yes; you know, I have given any number of talks down at the school. They wanted me to talk about how life was when I grew up. You see, kids now don't know anything at all what I was talking about, but they were real interested. A lot of those kids don't know where eggs come from—they say the grocery store. I always enjoyed that. I had the best listeners you ever had. I'd start off about my early days with riding on a truck and crossing a foot log at school and pushing the school bus up the hill, and it was a good life but it was a hard life. There was so much difference, some of the teachers were young girls....I'd tell them about butchering in the fall of the year and how we'd butcher hogs and nobody heard tell of that. We couldn't wait until my daddy then dressed the hogs, and I would hunt the huge bladder and wait for them to cut that out for me and get some kind of reed or something and blow that thing up like a football and tie a string around it and that's the way we played kickball because we didn't have a ball. Then it dried out and looked kind of like a piece of leather. We made our own pleasures. Some of the older boys would come in and bust the thing.

I believe in a way that neighbors loved each other more so than they do now. I think money and modern times have divided a lot of people. People don't visit anymore because TV has got most people at home looking at programs. I remember when Sunday afternoon was the day to go visiting. Of course, we'd go with our parents to see relatives.

I remember the first car my daddy ever had an old T-model Ford and then later he had a 1927. I wasn't too old then. My mama remembered the first automobile she ever saw as a young girl; old man Lee Parks and John Hedrick had an old thing with buggy wheels on it and a little motor sitting on it just popped and cracked and had a steering wheel that was like a lever.

ROBBIE SWING

Robbie Swing was born in 1916 and has lived most of his life in the Sandy Grove community. The author held a session with Robbie in October 2003 and remains grateful to him for his candor in responding to the questions asked.

INT: What year were you born; who delivered you?

RS: I was born in 1916, and a mid-wife delivered me by the name of Nevie Beck.

INT: What is the earliest memory you have?

RS: When my younger sister was born. I was four years old at the time.

INT: Young children have fears. What frightened you most as a child?

RS: A steam engine. The thing made a terrible racket coming down the road, and if it blew its whistle, I could not get in the house fast enough.

INT: Wheat threshings?

RS: Well, all I know about wheat thrashing was to help haul the wheat, pick up the bundles. I never did work around the thrashing machine, but Dallas Swing and Howard and Erman now they'd cut bands....

INT: Emmit Swing did most of the threshing in this community. How did Emmit get into the wheat threshing business?

RS: He worked for Isaiah Beck who had a thrashing machine and a sawmill too.

INT: Tell me about Isaiah Beck.

RS: We called him Izer, but his name was Isaiah. Yeah, well, he was a little old fellow and if you worked for him, he'd always give him more and paid him more than he asked. He had a blacksmith shop and he had a clover huller. A thrashing machine and a clover huller are two different machines. The thrashing machine had spikes on it.....and he took them all out and there must have been probably a hundred or more. And he'd take them out and take them to Sam, the welder, and have them sharpened at the blacksmith shop. So I was with him, and we went to pick them up, and Isaiah said "how much do I owe you?" and Sam stuttered around a little bit and said "fifty-cents". Isaiah had a habit to go "humph" before he spoke and said "Humph, no wonder you ain't got nothing, you don't charge what you're worth."

INT: How often did you go to town when you were little?

RS: Oh, we went to town often....went with my daddy because he'd carry a load of wood in town about every Saturday.

INT: What'd he pay you?

RS: We delivered a lot to a blind man up there on toad hill. The old man was living on welfare and he was 2/3 blind and he paid my daddy. My daddy would charge him $1.50 a load for wood, pine posts. A lot of times he didn't have the money, and he'd pay my daddy fifty cents a week.

INT: What was the first crisis in your life? You said the steam engine is what drove you crazy. That was a crisis every time it came down the road I guess.

RS: Yeah, it scared me. The next thing that scared me was the old T-model. There was one day, it had to be a Saturday, settin' under the old oak tree up here at Uncle Andrew's, and we was the first one that got a T-model and I was alone with my daddy, and I think we'd been to the mill. And as we come back by Pearce, or whoever was driving wanted to stay there and I was about 12 or 14 years and said "Robbie you can drive it home." And I said oh yeah; you know, I thought I could drive it. So, I got in that old T-model and come back and down to the house and out in the barn yard I made a circle, and I stopped. I had done just fine. And my daddy said come on up here a little bit closer and I put it in gear—and if you pushed it in too far you pushed it in low gear—he said pull up a little further and when I throwed it in gear or whatever I done, I don't know what I did, but I couldn't get it stopped I reckon. I thought I was going back up the road, and my daddy said "HEY, can't you stop it? Can't you stop it?" He just reached over and got the steering wheel and cut it up through the garden, and we ended up in the garden about middle ways.

INT: Do you remember the first car in the county or anything like that?

RS: No, but I remember some of the ones that did have a car. Now, you take Jake Burkhart had a Dodge. Emmit had that old big Buick, what model would that have been? In the '20s I suppose.

INT: Did you grow any cotton around here?

RS: Yeah, my daddy used to grow an acre or two.

INT: Did you pick cotton? What do you remember about picking cotton?

RS: It was a back-breaking thing. I didn't like to pick cotton. And I'll tell you, you know whose planter we used to plant it with? We borrowed Charles Lohr's. He had a cotton planter. We took the picked cotton over towards Southmont to get it ginned.

INT: Did you grow any tobacco?

RS: Roy Burkhart and my daddy built a tobacco barn right down here on my daddy's land, and they tried to raise some tobacco three or four years but they never did make any money out of it.

INT: Did you milk cows?

RS: Yeah, we always had two or three milk cows. My daddy sold milk to Dave Burkhart. You know, Dave ran the dairy up here. And my daddy sold milk to Dave.

INT: Running a dairy; what did he do with the milk? Bottle it?

RS: Back during the Depression, my daddy would load me up with molasses and roasting ears and stuff like that—anything that we had that we didn't need, and I'd get an old Hoover cart and hitch a pony up to that cart, and I'd go up through "colored town" and sell that stuff. On a good Saturday morning sometimes I'd make $4 or $5.

INT: Hoover cart? Named after President Hoover.

RS: Yeah, made out of the front end of a T-model; the wheels came off of a T-model.

A lot of people had them up and down the road here. I wasn't the only one who didn't have a car. I couldn't afford gas.

INT: The church. You started going there when you were just a little tyke.

RS: Always been going.

INT: How important was your church in this community?

RS: Very important. I have gone to church in a two-horse wagon. We would have the Big Meetin'—you didn't call it revival. Rev. Sammy Peeler was our preacher and before him his brother, J. C., was the preacher. Everybody went in buggies. Those who came from the south side of the church sat on that side, and we sat on the north side because we come from the north side.

INT: Did you tie the horses up?

RS: Yeah, they'd have hitching places kind of like you have parking places now.

INT: You either had buggies or wagons.

RS: You had a lot of people walk, too. Leonard's, they lived over behind the church over there. They'd pass through the woods, and it was a couple of miles.

INT: What about the big oak tree cross the ditch and up back of the hill from the church spring?

RS: I think about it about every time I go to church and go by that hill. That was a tremendous tree, and it had a lot of memories.

INT: Did we kill it?

RS: I think we probably did.

INT: We talked about the Lutherans and the Reformeds and how they grew up in a close relationship.

RS: I don't remember when they were gathered together in the same church. You see they used to meet in the same building, but not at the same time. When the Lutherans moved out, they lost the right to the property.

INT: Let's talk about World War II.

RS: I was drafted. I was 25.

INT: Did you go to Italy?

RS: Went to France, and then after we won that we went over to the Philippines. Dolan Swing and I stayed together all the time.

INT: Were you in the infantry?

RS: No. Engineers.

INT: How many of those people in that engineering company you reckon are still around? Did you ever have a reunion?

RS: Not many of them. Yeah, we had a reunion. We have a little reunion of the local, the ones that left a couple of months ago and there were four of us showed up. Supposed to be five of us living.

INT: How far did your daddy go in school?

RS: My daddy could read and he could figure a little but he was limited.

INT: Did your mother have more schooling than he did?

RS: Somewhere along the line she picked it up. I remember her teaching us.

INT: What did she read to you?

RS: All our little first books, and I remember, she would read the Bible a lot.

INT: Did she read the Bible to you? Did she teach you how to pray?

RS: I've heard her pray more than one time.

INT: What did you do the first day you got out of the Army?

RS: Bob, my son, was born while I was in the Army. He was 14 months old before I ever saw him. I probably played with him the next day. I know when I got in they cracked the door and he was standing there, and he started crying.

INT: Lets talk a little bit about Bible School in the summertime. Where did you learn to swim? Or did you?

RS: Yeah, I learned to swim and I've got to tell you this....right after they backed up High Rock Lake. Do you remember right next to the creek, that low land they backed it up and made a swimming hole out there. Dolan and I and Carly Beck and Howard and Erman was in the swimming hole and me and Dolan....Howard and Erman and Dallas were further away from us and saw an old log laying up next to the bank. We started to cross over and get that old log, and Dolan was in front of me and there was a ditch going down through there. Dolan slipped off in that ditch, and it was over his head, and that red hair floating up and down and he managed to hit the bottom and bounce up, and if it wasn't for me, he'd of drowned. I slid off into it, but somehow I got back up on the bank and called Dal. If he hadn't been as big a man he is, long legged, we couldn't have done it. I saved his life, I'm sure I did.

INT: Did you have a community loafer? People who didn't work? Who was the community character?

RS: I don't know, about everybody around here had a regular job they were doing. We had one fellow that, and he was a farmer, he walked around. Daddy and I would be plowing, and he'd come down and say "Well, its just a little dry or I'd be plowing or it's a little too wet, and I'm not going to do it..." and this and that. We'd come to the conclusion, and figured out, that old man when he planted a crop he planted it right, and to my knowledge he was the best two-horse farmer up and down the road.

INT: Did John Eller have any family?

RS: Yeah, he had...... didn't Charles Smith marry one of his daughters?

INT: What did you do on Saturday nights when you were growing up?

RS: Nothing much, just the usual. Tom Swing and I ran around together a lot. He bought a Chevrolet. He carried me around a lot in that car, or I'd have to have walked. He was 6 months younger than me.

INT: Remember Beck's BBQ? What about the county fair?

RS: Yeah. I worked at the county fair. Setting up the big tents, hitched up the elephants to pull the tents up, and they'd give us a free pass. But brother when I tell you about those elephants, I stayed away from them.

INT: Parades?

RS: Always had a parade. Coming down Main Street. To start with, you know when they brought the animals in, they had to bring it all in by train. They unloaded everything down near the Southern Lunch. That's where the depot was. A lot of people would go to town and stand along the street to watch them parade up to the fair grounds. And that was the prettiest music, that pipe organ—steam organ.

INT: Where are the fairgrounds? Were they out West Center Street?

RS: They had one there but it was several different places. The first fairground was up there where Craver's antique furniture was on the right—in fact, I think part of the old exhibit building is still standing there. There is where the first fairground that I ever remember and then it got smaller or something and it was different places. Do you remember when the horse would dive off a platform into a tank of water?...well, do you know who built that thing? Jake, Roy Burkhart and maybe Sam, they helped build the platform that the horse ran up.

INT: Let me ask you about diseases during childhood. What do you remember?

RS: Well, I tell you, the thing I remember most about diseases was pneumonia, whooping cough and flu.

INT: Did they have diphtheria?

RS: I don't remember them calling it diphtheria, but they had some kind of name but I don't remember.

INT: You remember when they first vaccinated for smallpox. Did you ever see anybody that had smallpox?

RS: I don't remember.

INT: I remember diphtheria, whooping cough. When you had whooping cough you only had once. Measles you only had once - chicken pox, all of that.

Once you caught it, you never got it again.

INT: Who cut your hair?

RS: Jess Kepley cut my hair more than anybody else when I was growing up. He didn't cut it, he pulled it out.

INT: Did he cut the hair in the community or just because he liked to do it?

RS: He cut several heads.

INT: Did you pay him anything? Or did he just like to cut hair?

RS: I don't know if he liked it or not but he about had to.

INT: Do you see any similarity in life today and what it was like back when you were growing up?

RS: A whole lot of difference existed. I asked my daddy one time, me and my brother Red did, for a few cents. Cheek Miller who lived up there in the old Finch house had made a little money, and Cheek said he wanted to have a cook-out and we said we'll chip in a little bit and after they added it up mine and Red's come to 20 cents. And we asked daddy for 20 cents, and he said "Boys, what do you think I'm made out of? Money?"

INT: When did your daddy's house get painted for the first time?

RS: That had to be probably....I can remember when they painted the inside. They painted the inside before they painted the outside. It had to be at least 80 years ago.

INT: They didn't paint because they didn't have money or that paint was unavailable?

RS: Well, they didn't think it was worth it. The roof was out of old split shingles, and then he had a tin roof put on it.

INT: Did any houses burn down in this community when you were growing up?

RS: Lightning struck our old house one time and set it on fire. They put it out and we repaired it. Old Jake Burkhart burned his down one time. His pipes froze up and he took a blow torch to it setting the house on fire..

INT: What was the convenience that you thought was the best thing ever invented?

RS: I believe running water, because I despised to draw water for cows.

INT: How did you get to work?

RS: I rode with Charlie Morgan; he lived over here in Eb Young's old house.

INT: What was gas per gallon?

RS: I believe it was 16 cents, one grade.

INT: What did the tank look like?

RS: It had a glass thing, and then you pumped it up. It had marks showing one, two, three, etc. gallons.

INT: Did anybody every fuss that you hadn't quite put enough in?

RS: Sure did.

INT: What did you like the best in school other than recess?

RS: Spelling was my poorest subject. I still can't spell. We'd have spelling matches and I spelled like it sounded. I taught myself. I learned to figure because I had to in the building business.

INT: Did you like English?

RS: Yes, I went to school about 6 years and never missed a day.

INT: Did you read and write?

RS: Yes.

INT: What did you read when you were a child?

RS: I liked to read these wild western stories. Zane Grey.

INT: Do you remember your first washing machine? Did it have a wringer on it?

RS: The first washing machine we had, it wasn't a machine, it was run by hand. Fifty gallon barrel cut off and put a dasher on it and turn it by hand.

INT: Did you make it?

RS: No. Jack Tysinger, Sylvanius, made them. He made the first one, and it had a handle on it.

INT: Did you ever wash clothes on a washboard?

RS: My mother did.

INT: Did you ever make soap?

RS: No, but my mother did.

INT: Do you remember Lee Beck and his checker playing?.

RS: You know what his nickname was? Nozzle.

INT: You brought the pool table into Grandpa's store didn't you? You brought "sin" right into the community. What about Television?

RS: Dolan Swing had the first television that I ever remember seeing. He worked in the furniture store for Thurman Briggs, and he got hold of a little television, must have been a 6-inch screen.

INT: I see you like to play practical jokes on folks. Do you remember any others?

RS: I like to scared Helen Fritts down here to death one time. You know there used to be a path from Dave Burkhart's all the way through here over to Crawford Swing's. Anyhow, she was over at the house late one evening, and I got a little sheet and went there and laid down beside the path, and when she come by I jumped up and like to have scared that girl to death! She never forgot it because every time we'd see each other we'd talk about it.

INT: When did you smoke your first cigar?

RS: I don't know, but I have smoked them—smoked as a boy. I used to smoke rabbit tobacco. First cigar, I was probably 16 or 18 years old.

INT: Why did you quit cigarettes?

RS: Too tight to buy them.

INT: Why were you so tight?

RS: I like having money.

INT: I remember wheat thrashing and one year we'd start down at the Curt Lohr farm, and come up this way, and the other year we'd start up here and go down that way. Do you remember that?

RS: Charlie Fritts was the first one that had to have his wheat thrashed first? You'd have to thrash his first or he'd get mad at you.

INT: The Vo-Ag teacher taught how to grow chickens, and he used to come out in the community. Charlie Fritts was at one of the meetings. Lohr Younts saw him and told folks there was a man so dried up that looked as old as the hills.

RS: Ruby Briggs, Ivey Briggs' daughter, I thought she was right pretty. Her daddy was a big hunter, and he and a bunch of them went down east, and they killed an old bear. Ivy had the hide tanned and the head mounted and made a rug out of it. I told Beulah the other night, we were talking about it. I had a date with Ruby once, and I was asked what we did. I said, "We didn't do much; we just sat there on the sofa and looked at that old bear."

VIRGINIA LOPP WHITE

Virginia Lopp White was born on June 12, 1926, in the Holly Grove Community. Larry Younts interviewed her on October 31, 2004.

INT: Where and when were you born?

VW: I was born June 12, 1926. At that time all babies were born in the home, most of them anyway. Dr. J. A. Smith was the attending physician. He even named me. My mother was 30, and my daddy was 40 when they got married, and you would think they would know how to name a child but they couldn't think of a name. So he named me Virginia Duette. Some of Dr. Smith's family also had that name.

INT: What was your earliest memory of childhood?

VW: I don't remember anything that stands out so much. I guess probably going to church. We always went to church. What was so special about this memory was, of course, there were always Sunday school parties. I don't remember much about the preacher. The first preacher I remember was Dr. Andrews and his little car. He would get in that car and gun the motor. He'd have that thing cranking up something fierce. I grew up in Mt. Tabor. In those days the Sunday school teachers would give the girls little dishes or bowls or bottles or vases.

INT: Do you remember the first crisis in your life?

VW: The first I remember was my baby sister who is eight years younger than me had pneumonia. We were so scared. It was snowing and raining and, of course, in those days the doctor had to come out to the home. We did not have a telephone. My daddy rode out to Mrs. Frank Younts' house, the house right next to the school, and they had a phone and called Dr. Smith. As well as I remember he came out, but I know my grandmother and Mrs. Younts came and spent the rest of the night. I just remember that if something happens to her the world just may as well stop. I was like her second mother. That is the most traumatic thing I think I recall. She made it.

INT: What were the first memories of your parents?

VW: I guess, I remember that we always had a big open fireplace in our family room/sitting room, and Daddy would always take our shoes and line them up where the soles would be against the fire so that the soles of our shoes could be warm when we got up.

INT: How did your father and mother earn their living?

VW: They never did public work. Before Dad was married, he worked in Indiana on the building of railroad tracks. My mother never worked, she was always home. They always had gardens. Dad actually dealt more in timber and truck farming. He went to Lexington to sell timber. Each year when they would have wheat threshing, Mr. Carl Smith had the threshing machine and he would bring it down and all the neighbors would get together and help each other. He'd bring the machine and they'd go from farm to farm threshing the grain. I remember that Dad would always let us bring a water bucket and a dipper, and I'm assuming everyone drank from the same dipper. He would always say don't get too close to the horses. And there was always a lot of food, and the women would get together and do a lot of cooking big meals. Wheat threshings were big things then.

INT: You describe the way you lived, you had plenty of food and plenty of clothes?

VW: I never remember not having as much food or clothes as we needed. My dad had had the house built when they got married so I never lived in another house until I started to Ashmore. I lived in the city, and I thought I had really come up in the world. We would walk up town and go to the movies and sometimes we would see the same movie if it played 3 or 4 nights we'd see it 3 or 4 nights. It was a social gathering.

INT: Did you have anything that frightened you when you were young?

VW: We think of tornadoes and storms here as being so bad, but I can remember one time—and I don't remember how old I was, probably 6 or 8—Dad had what we called the tool shed and it had the big "A" roof but it didn't have a door to it. It had sides. He'd keep the wagon and rakes and farm equipment in there. All of a sudden the storm came up and it just lifted that roof as if a huge hand took it up and lifted it all the way up across the road into a field. That just like to have scared us to death.

INT: Were there other things you were afraid of? Ghosts? The dark?

VW: No. When it would thunder and lightning my mother would make us be quiet. She never let us make noise and so we'd go to sleep. Now, she may have been afraid, but she never let us know it. I followed the same pattern with my boys, I never let them see that I was afraid of thunder and lightning, but I'd make them be quiet. Now don't ask me why, but I'd make them be quiet.

INT: Did you have to help out on the farm?

VW: Oh yes, I learned to milk a cow, water the chickens and get up the eggs and feed the chickens and carry in a load of stove wood every day; and carry a bucket of water from the well to a big tank that was on the stove in the kitchen so we would have warm water. I was probably 6 years old. My mother would get the meal pretty much ready before we'd go to the field and most of the time we'd take a cow which we hated to do that. They'd have those big metal chains and we'd take a cow and hitch it out where there was good grass while we were working in the fields. We didn't farm on a big scale but it was mostly corn. They called it truck farming, I believe - lots of vegetables.

INT: You mentioned wheat threshings, did you have those or corn shuckings as social events?

VW: No, we never had corn shuckings. I witnessed corn shuckings that other people had, but wheat threshings was all we had.

INT: What things did you do for fun when you had time?

VW: We loved to go to the library. We'd go get library books and when we'd bring them home if we were supposed to go hoeing in the garden we'd look up and see one little fluffy cloud and hope it would rain so bad so we could go inside and read our books. We had a wooded area that joined our house that we could make play houses. We'd have extra bricks, and we'd outline the rooms.

INT: You said you went to corn shuckings and wheat threshings at other places. What were they like? Were they fun? Did you look forward to them?

VW: I sort of looked forward to them. I remember going to my aunts (Grady Lopp), and if you were old enough to have guys there that you were interested in. There was always good food and lots of it. Never music at the ones I went to but I understand there were some, and the young folks would dance.

I never went possum hunting. I never did much fishing. One time Dad said while he was plowing he would let us fish and it was like a bank here and then it dropped off and there was another bank. Well, my sister fell. I thought she had drowned. I kept saying "come back here, hold my hand...." And finally I did get her back up. Then there was a swinging foot log, and this was planks on wires and then there was one wire stretched that you held to and it went across Hamby's Creek. Well, Dorothy and I were sitting up there on that foot log. Dorothy fell off down in the water. I didn't look to see whether she floated on down the creek or not, I just got off that log and run screaming to daddy "Dorothy's drowned. Dorothy's drowned." Well, he looked at me and just kept right on going. I thought what in the world is wrong with that man? Well, I didn't see that she'd scrambled out and was following me like a drowned rat. It was probably 10 feet from the bridge to the water, and, of course, the post or whatever held it there collected trash or whatever and there were little fish around there.

INT: Tell me about when you first went to school.

VW: My first school was Davis-Townsend, and in the beginning, they didn't have indoor bathrooms. I was so scared to go to the outside johns. I was scared to death to have to go way out there. I think I went about a whole year before they had the inside bathrooms. I remember just being among people because at that time there weren't any houses around our house very much. You didn't have a next door neighbor. So, this was a big gathering of 24 children or so every day. Miss Helms was my first grade teacher. I was always one of the bigger, taller girls, so anytime we had a school play I always got to play the mama or the grandma which I didn't like very much.

I remember we had what we called operetta and I remember that brings back a memory. Evidently I had a cold or something and the teacher wanted us to just wear white socks and not shoes. My daddy said no, you are sick and that will make your cold that much worse. The teacher told me if I had white shoes I could wear a pair of white shoes and not go in my stocking feet. Why this was such a big deal I don't know, but that was the first pair of white shoes I ever had. Daddy went out and bought—he did it, not my mother—he went out and bought me a pair of white shoes. They looked like boys shoes as I think about it now.

I always liked school. Miss Brady was my third grade teacher. I had scarlet fever when I was in that grade, and it was like having the plague. I remember they kept me in one bedroom, and there was a window that looked out on the back porch. Miss Brady brought out a fruit basket, and she came around on that porch and looked in at me through that window, but she would not come in to where I was. My mother would put on sort of a uniform to tend me, and then she'd take it off before she did anything with anyone else.

Fourth grade was my toughest year that I had. Miss Ward, I always thought she smelled so good. She always used cologne or whatever. I graduated in 1943. I went only 11 years.

INT: During the Depression, what do you remember about celebrating Christmas?

VW: I don't remember it being any different because we always got dolls. We always got tea sets. Every year and sometimes we got clothing but mostly we got toys. Sometimes whatever the fad was, of course nuts, fruits and candy we always had those things but we probably got more than a lot of people because my daddy was 40 when he got married and I guess he had accumulated a little more. I don't remember anything different. The only thing I remember about the Depression was this older man that lived down the road. He would come, and I don't know if she gave him the basket or whether he brought the basket, but she would cook food and give him a basket full of food. That was in the 30's. As far as us, we had as much as we did any other time.

We always had a Christmas tree. Never put it up until Christmas Eve. We always had a cedar tree. Dad had a staple in the ceiling and he'd put a string at the very top of the tree and hook it to that staple so the tree did not fall over. All of our gifts were tacked on the tree, even our dolls. Mrs. Santa Claus always put a thread on the package and tied it on the tree.

Decorations were paper bells. Now you see them at brides' parties, little white bells. We always put one of those to every window shade at every window. Always had a big bell in the center of the sitting room, Never put that tree up earlier because it was such an inconvenience and we always had one that went from the floor to the ceiling and never put it up until Christmas Eve. This was a special time for sure.

INT: Do you remember when you went to Bible school? What were your favorite hymns?

VW: "Trust and Obey" and "Work for the Night Is Coming." Those are the two I remember and of course, "Jesus Loves Me."

INT: Tell me about your first date.

VW: Back in WWII. Five couples in our class married each other. I was seeing Johnny Hedrick, and then Johnny went into service. I continued to write to him. My daddy's theory was—I was 16 when I graduated high school—boys and books don't mix. I'm sending you to school to get an education so I did not date until after I was 16. I didn't go to college. If he had encouraged me, I think I would have gone, but back in those days everybody went to business school just about. Cost would have been a factor I guess. In those days if you got a high school education that was a big check mark. That was almost an equivalent a college education today.

INT: Did you always have a car?

VW: We always had a car. We had a T-model I can just barely remember. The T model that had curtains. In the wintertime you snapped curtains on the sides. Then we thought we really came up in the world when we got an A-model. We were embarrassed to death for him to pick us up at school in that T-model but when he got the A-model we thought we were really climbing up in society. Then, of course, we got a Ford.

INT: How old were you when you owned your first car?

VW: I never had a car. In fact, a car was never put in my name until I was in my 20s.

INT: You graduated from high school during WWII, how were you affected by WWII?

VW: I didn't have any brothers, but I had several fellows that I corresponded with and that kind of thing. No one close to me lost their life, but I can remember the maneuvers and they would come through here. The trains would bring the guys home through here, and I think they would spend the night.

INT: Tell me about television.

VW: We moved here in 1951, and we got one of the first televisions around. Shuford Swing had the television shop where David Smith now has his electrical engineering shop.

INT: Do you remember the first program you saw on television?

VW: I don't remember the first, but I remember the Dinah Shore Show, Chevrolet sponsored that, a musical—Gunsmoke, Have Gun Will Travel, and lots of westerns. No soap operas.

INT: What one person or two had the greatest influence on your life?

VW: I would probably say my parents and then the cousin that was the school teacher, and I went with her when I went to Ashmore. She took in the cousins. Two cousins went to stay with another cousin there. She introduced us to a whole new world by living in the city. We could walk up town to the 5 and 10 store and that kind of thing was a whole new world. This was 1944, and I got a job and continued to stay with her until 1946 when I got married.

INT: Before you moved there and were still living at home. What did you do on Saturday nights?

VW: Studied our Sunday school lesson. Washed the lampshades, the lamps that were sitting on the dining room table, and we always had at least two sitting there because that's where we studied. We had to make sure they were washed and dried with newspaper. Usually my mother would make a cake and she started cooking a lot of her Sunday noon meal on Saturday.

INT: What about Sunday afternoons?

VW: Sunday afternoons we would like to go visit aunts and uncles. We loved to go to Aunt Libby's which was down in the Silver Hill section and my Uncle John because they all had children that were my age or a little older. Talking about our first cars, I remember when we went to Aunt Libby's that her son and his friends had cars.

INT: What part of your early life do you remember most vividly?

VW: School and the activities. I thoroughly enjoyed when we had the junior/senior banquet which had to be in late 1939 or early 1940 I guess. At that time, we would have them in the gymnasium at the school, and they would allow the juniors to do the decorating. I recall one year it was supposed to be the wishing well. Anyway, we had a makeshift well, and we had made paper flowers that we strung all over that was absolutely beautiful.

INT: You told me you had scarlet fever and your sister had pneumonia. Were those the most dreaded diseases when you were small?

VW: Probably. I remember we had measles but that was just expected that you had measles and whooping cough. Mumps, we did not get mumps. My boys gave me mumps when I was working, we were living here. My poor mother didn't get mumps until she was well into her 60s because my younger sister, Betty, got them at school and brought them home.

INT: What similarities do you see growing up early 1920s 1930s and life now?

VW: I remember when this road was not paved, and if it rained, school buses lots of times wouldn't go on some of these secondary roads. I remember one time it had rained so, I guess dad must have brought us to school. It was Valentine's day. Mr. Gathings had a car that had a rumble seat where you could open up the back. Anyway, he had a couple of boys to get there so that when we got stuck those boys would get out and push.

INT: He was well liked, wasn't he?

VW: He was different. And you might find him on a ladder looking through the transom to see that everything was going okay in the room. He'd do crazy things like that. I never will forget one time someone asked the question in class "can I go do so and so" and he said "I don't have the foggiest idea whether you can or not, you might try". He was talking about the grammar you know.

INT: People I have talked with see very few similarities in growing up then and growing up now. Which style of life would you prefer to live?

VW: Today, of course, because of the conveniences. I remember we used to in the summertime when it was hot, we would put our pillows down at the foot of the bed because that was closer to the window and cooler. As far as the morals of the people though, now I would go back to those days. But as far as conveniences and so on, I would pick today of course

DERMONT AND GLADYS BECK

Dermont and Gladys Beck, husband and wife, were interviewed by Larry Younts on October 23, 2004. Dermont was born in 1918 and Gladys in 1915.

Dermot–D

Gladys–G

INT: Tell me when you were born and who delivered you? Did you have a doctor come out?

D: Dr. Alex Smith. They named me after him.

INT: I think that was common back then that they would name them after doctors and politicians because they were famous. That has changed today.

G: You don't want to name them after politicians today.

INT: Where was your home place?

D: On old 75.

INT: How much did the doctor charge back then, do you remember?

D: Yes.

G: I don't know but I do know it wasn't much. If we did not have money, Doctors took chickens or whatever, maybe a ham for trade.

INT: How many were in your family?

G: Seven children. Mama's first baby died at birth, and there were eight including that infant.

INT: Dermot, I have a rough idea how many were in your family.

D: 14 children

INT: What did your parents do to make a living?

D: Farming. My daddy later was a deputy sheriff and served about 15 years. He had a sawmill and cut logs with a cross-cut saw.

INT: While he was being a deputy sheriff, ya'll had to do the work, didn't you? Just about everybody out this way did some sawmill work. Gladys, did your family do sawmill work?

G: Not particularly. His dad did, and Clyde and them sawed some for him. Also, when he built the house that is presently up there, and he had lumber sawed to build it off the farm.

INT: Do you remember life being hard?

D: Yes. It was during the Depression—Hoover days.

INT: So in your mind you knew it was a Depression. You knew things weren't like they should be.

D: No money. My mother peddled every Saturday. She'd take cakes, eggs and milk to the black section in Lexington.

G: I think a lot of the wives of the farmers did back then....I know my mother did that too, but we didn't sell in the black section: we sold in the Na-komas Mill area.

INT: You don't ever remember being hungry? What did you eat?

D: Vegetables in summer and hogs in the winter; also chickens.

INT: Did you butcher cows too?

G: No, back then we didn't have refrigeration and most times back then the meat was canned to preserve it.

D: We had a cow for milk.

INT: So even back then, to make money or to trade was always centered around Lexington? Never Thomasville?

G: Yes. We sold lumber in Denton and some to the Thomasville Chair Company.

INT: Back then, did you make most of your money off lumber or farming?

D: Didn't make much money, but farming was what we lived off of. Then we took lumber to make a little money. We sold some wheat but saved 100 bushels to carry us through the winter until next harvest.

INT: Years ago they had a separate kitchen. Do you know why they did that?

D: Smell of something cooking.

G: I have no idea why but I thought maybe back then some people had servants, and maybe the servants didn't want to live in the main house. I don't know.

INT: I always heard there was a fire going and maybe it wasn't safe to have it where you were sleeping. When you were growing up, do you remember ever being afraid of anything?

D: Yeah. Mad dogs.

INT: Was that a common thing?

D: Yeah.

INT: You had a lot of wild dogs?

D: Yes. We would see them and holler, mad dog, mad dog!!!

INT: I remember daddy saying they scared him with a story about a headless dog. Down in front of Edgar Morris' and the Lutheran Church on Beck's Church Road. I think every generation has something like that they make up to scare the little ones with.

G: I was scared when I was little to hear hoot owls on the hill.

D: I never went to town on Halloween. Trick or treating didn't exist back then.

INT: Hoyle told me that he went to town a lot. His daddy worked in town, and he was a car salesman which was unusual. You didn't go to town often? Do you remember going to see movies at the theaters?

G: No. I drove a wagon to town selling wood and saw the theater but didn't go in; had no money.

D: I saw my first movie in the service during WWII in Germany. Just the troops could go in. Not the German citizens that were there.

INT: Where were you trained?

G: Fort Leavenwood in Missouri and Fort Bragg

INT: Before we talk about the war, what do you remember first when you worked in the fields about plowing?

D: Plowing corn when I was young.

INT: Did your family farm mostly, Gladys?

G: Yes. We farmed. Terry farmed for a long time. Up there by Abbott's Creek down there where you can see it from I-85, the fields back in there. He grew corn down there and we'd go chop Rankin's grass, and the next time we'd go back to the field, the grass had come right back. He leased that land from the Finch's I guess.

INT: There was a reed patch over there years ago, and we'd go cut cane poles at the corner there somewhere.

G: Cane poles, like fishing poles? My dad owned some land on Abbott's Creek on up toward new I-85, and we'd go up there and cut cane poles for fishing.

We used to go down to Abbott's Creek on his land and fish a lot. On Ascension Day we'd always take a lunch and go fishing. Ascension Day is in the Spring. We'd go sometimes to Pounders Fork down there where it enters Abbott's Creek.

INT: What kind of fish did you catch?

G: I don't remember, but we ate them...those keepable.

INT: From four-mile branch you could catch eatable fish? What kind were they?

D: Catfish, carp, bass, suckers.

INT: In four-mile branch? They had more water in it then, didn't they?

D: Yes. We'd catch eels also. We would seine the creek over a long distance.

INT: Why do you think four-mile branch had so much more water back then than it does now?

G: More rain.

INT: What was your favorite time of the year growing up?

D: Springtime.

G: I like the springtime, too, because then we could all pull our shoes off and go barefooted.

INT: What about harvest time?

G: We always had a cotton patch. That was our money for our winter shoes and things like that. We had to pick the cotton. I didn't enjoy it much back then, but I think I would now.

INT: Most people in this area had nicknames. Do you remember nicknames? Did you have a nickname?

D: Yeah. Mutt.

INT: Hoyle told me today that his nickname today was Spiegel because he always was wanting to look at the Spiegel catalog. Do you remember his nickname being Spiegel?

D: Treva's was Cheese. She liked a lot of cheese. Dolan was Dough. All of us had a nickname. We needed 14 nicknames for 14 children. Hoy's was Skeeter. Darwin's was Date.

INT: What is the first thing you remember about going to school? Where did you first go to school?

D: Hedrick's Grove. They took an old church building to make it into a school. I also went to a school on Deaton Young Road.

INT: Do you remember what year you went to Davis-Townsend? It was built about 1929 or 1930. Did you finish at Davis-Townsend?

D: Yeah.

INT: Hoyle told me he remembered going the first year because they had finished the road, they had a new school and they had new school buses, and that was pretty exciting.

G: I started school in Burkhart School. The old school, I know I went with Edmund to school one day. That was before I was old enough to go to school. They'd always take me to school when they could take their little brothers or sisters to school. It was a one-room schoolhouse and as I remember, this man—a Surratt I think—he wasn't fit to be a school teacher. He'd get out there in his old car and the big boys would run around in the school yard with the other kids out there playing and they'd run to the schoolhouse. Mr. Carl Smith's chickens would lay eggs under the schoolhouse, and they'd run and get the eggs and eat them—raw.

INT: Did you go there in the 1st grade?

G: Not in that old school. The teacher got so homesick. My brother researched, and said one evening she came back to the schoolhouse and set it on fire. So they built a new school below where this was, back of where Mt. Tabor church is now.

INT: Why was it called Burkhart's?

D: Some of the Burkharts helped build the school.

G: My dad, Mr. Lee Crotts, Carl Smith and others did some carpentry at the school. Dad built our house. I wasn't six years old yet when we moved out of the old house where my Grandma Fritts was raised.

INT: What do you remember about church back then?

G: When we were going down to Jerusalem United Church of Christ we had one Sunday a Lutheran preacher and the next Sunday Church of Christ preacher. It was in the 50s.

INT: Did you enjoy going to church twice in one day?

D: No. Parents made us.

INT: How did a family of 14 get to church? Some were grown when the others were born but you still had a big crowd.

G: When we were small we didn't have a way to go to church. We would walk to Mount Tabor like we were going to school. After we got a car, we went to Holly Grove because we were Lutherans. We walked to Bible school at Holly Grove from our house on the road which was several miles.

INT: So, it made no difference if you went to a Lutheran church or….were the services much different?

G: I enjoyed going to the United Church of Christ at Mt. Tabor. The Smiths up there were such good singers, and the pastors would always have the children up front to have a children's sermon.

INT: Who were the good singers at Mount Tabor?

G: Carl Smith, all the Smith boys. George, Paul….and the songs were easier then.

INT: Do you remember the revivals? Revivals were in the summertime, right?

D: We had them at Jerusalem.

G: I don't remember revivals at Holly Grove. I do remember up at Mount Tabor. Seems like they were in the Fall of the year after the sun went down at night. I remember getting in the buggies and going to Pilgrim Church of Christ. Grandpa and Aunt Hester would get in one buggy, and Edna and me and Aunt Lillie and Uncle Ray would get in the other buggy and go through the woods to the church at night.

INT: Do you remember how old you were when you had your first date?

D: Fifteen years and she was 13.

INT: When did the two of you have your first date? How did you meet?

G: Woodrow, his first cousin, brought him up here. Woodrow was dating my youngest sister and he brought him up to meet me. I don't remember when. I was 27 and he was 30 when we got married.

D: I was in service for 3 years and that delayed us getting married. I didn't want to stay longer than 3 years—one-and-a-half years in Germany and one-and a half years in the U.S.

INT: Do you remember the first time you drove a car? What kind of car?

G: I was 18 or so.

INT: Was there a law back then requiring a license?

G: You had to get a permit, but I didn't have to take a test.

INT: Did you drive to town the first time you drove?

D: Left from here and drove to Lexington.

INT: How many cars do you think you would pass between here and Lexington?

D: Four or five.

INT: Do you remember how fast you drove that old T-model?

D: No speedometer, 20 or 25 mph. Roads were bumpy.

INT: How were you affected by WWII other than being in the service?

G: Rationing. Everything was rationed. Couldn't get gas which we didn't need much because my three brothers were down at Wilmington at the shipyards, working down there. They never were called. Money was short. I was working. I had a bicycle and my dad would ride that to town.

INT: Do you remember your first television?

G: We had one when we were married. I think we've got the first one we got when we got married and it was working. It's still upstairs.

INT: Was there any one thing that happened in your youth that stands out that you remember that had a big influence on your life; perhaps one particular man or woman?

D: John Younts, I always admired him. Good neighbor, helpful man, Christian.

INT: Were Saturday nights special?

G: Saturday night baths! And get ready for Church. Roll our hair.

INT: What did you do on Sunday afternoons after church?

D: Played baseball and went walking in the woods.

INT: Do you remember diseases when you were young that you dreaded or were most afraid of?

D: Scarlet fever caused me to fail two grades and the flu. In 1918 so many people died from the flu or pneumonia.

INT: When it was hair cutting time, who was in charge?

D: My dad cut it at first, and we didn't like it so we started cutting each others.

G: Dermot cut hair when he was in service and before and also since for the younger boys and any of the neighbors.

D: I signed up for barber school but I had to wait a year. I had to work, and I went to Cobles.

INT: Coble Dairy had a big impact in this area. How many people do you think worked there?

G: Dermont was in the refrigeration department. He would go out and service coolers and ice cream boxes.

INT: I know a lot has changed since 1918, but do you see any similarities? How is life the same?

D: Trying to hold onto some of the old ways; still driving a 1988 car with less than 50,000 miles.

INT: Do you see people being a lot different today?

G: Moving too fast.

EDMUND SMITH

Edmund Smith was born on March 30, 1926, in the Mount Tabor Community and has lived there all his life except for a stint in the United States Army in World War

II. Larry Younts conducted this interview on October 10, 2004, with the assistance of Edmund's wife, Mary.

INT: Edmund, tell me where you were born, and what year you were born.

ES: I was born March 30, 1926, in the first house west of Mt. Tabor Church. No attending physician. There was a Burkhart woman down there that did that, a midwife. She delivered me

INT: What is your earliest memory?

ES: The first thing I really remember….it was snowing. In March, 1930, there was snow 'that' high and Papa had to leave the house and go through the feed places where we keep the hoops and stuff, his car shed, smokehouse and where we had our wood. Mama had on the side of it a place where she could put her wash tub and get out of the cold. She had a big cast iron pot and used a scrubbing board and went from there to the barn and from there to the chicken house.

INT: So how big do you think that snow was? That was 1930.

ES: Well, I couldn't see out of it. I was four years old.

INT: Was that the biggest snow you remember?

ES: No, they had one bigger than that, earlier than that. I was that little and I wanted to go with him…Mama would say "you'll freeze to death out there." I couldn't see out. I only made it to the wood shed. I went back to the house where it was warm. I can still remember that, after I wanted to go so bad to get out in the snow.

INT: Dermont and his wife were telling me about a big snow and somebody came over to the house and wrapped burlap sacks all the way up to his waist around both legs.

ES: Burlap and used reaper string and fix it up to here, and you could keep your head and legs warm with that.

INT: What were your most pleasant memories of your childhood? What do you remember the fondest?

ES: Hunting with my daddy. When I wasn't big enough…..rabbit and squirrel. You could go over the Byerly bridge up above where Bob Fritz lived. Papa would get me up if I wanted to go, and we'd have fried eggs, and we always had meat because we had our own hogs. We'd get over there at the Byerly bridge and it would still be dark and we'd wait and those squirrels would start at daylight and they come out and he was knockin' them off. I don't know how many we'd have but I was carrying the bag. We'd come down behind Walt Clotfelter.

He was down there fussing at his daughter about corn or something and Papa and me creeped around back and when we got down there he was still hollerin' up there at the house. He had a hog in a wire thing....and Papa said "You get in there," (there were some squirrels in a tree or something), and Papa would see one, and POW one would come in there and they were still fussin'. They didn't even hear....and when he shot a fourth one, it hit an old tin on the shed, and they stopped and listened, and we got down on the ground....so I crawled in that pen and got that one and Papa said that's enough. I crawled in the hog pen to retrieve them.

INT: When you were young, I know out there where you lived there were a lot of ghost stories about Abbotts creek. Was there any specific thing that you were frightened of?

ES: Nothing but the doctor. That's the truth. When I got over yonder, I was 18 years old and fighting the Germans. I could get up and move around, and I loved the dark because they couldn't see me. I was afraid of it when I was young, but I got over that when I went to the war.

INT: What were the things that made you the most happy?

ES: When we got everything done and we went down to Jim Crotts'. Colan and Bruce were the same and me and Hoss. You know where they live? Mama would say, "You gonna have to get back to do chores." We didn't have watches. She would call us and holler for us, and we would holler back. Then we would come home. Can you believe that?

INT: Do you remember how old you were when you started helping with farm work?

ES: Hoeing and stuff, I would say eight and nine...but I can tell you when I got 13 years old I cut bands on the thrashing machine, enough for 1,300 bushels of grain on one day. Out in that sun and heat. It took a long day. It liked to have killed me.

INT: When harvest time came did ya'll have wheat threshings and corn shuckings?

ES: Yeah, Grandpa and Bob.....lord have mercy.....people would come from all around there. You don't ever get that much done in one night. It was a social. We had music. David Leonard and all his boys could play. Fred Smith he played the violin. There was some dancing. I carried a red ear of corn with me. You know what that meant, don't ya?

INT: What other things did you do for fun?

ES: We had too much work. They turned us loose on Sunday after church. We didn't have a car we just walked across by David Leonard's and hunt muscadines. On Sunday afternoon we'd get home from church we'd go through the woods and shake 'em and come home with a whole bunch in a sack. Later on there was a tree back of Papa's barn, and we would pick up hickory nuts and store them.

INT: Tell me about your school. Did you go to Burkhart School?

ES: No. Colan would have went. Lindsay would come over there with the dogs, and we'd go possum hunting. And if the dogs was running and stuff, we'd sit down and talk. We'd go all the way down to Bob's and Abbotts Creek, and that was a real treat to get away.

INT: Did you ever cut logs? Make your toys? Cutting logs.

ES: Yes. All of our cutting was with a cross-cut saw. Playing checkers in the house. We didn't have a radio. Baseball games—we used to make our baseballs. We'd wind up kite string tight. We didn't have nothing that was bought.

County fair. I never will forget when me and Hollis Crotts jumped across the fence and a fellow with a ball bat come after us. He said you get out the way you come in. We did.

INT: Do you remember who your first-grade teacher was?

ES: I can tell you who she was. It was Ward Everhart's sister; called her Miss Everhart. She wasn't married. I liked school, but I know some that didn't.
I tell you, Charles Black, he had this pea marble shooter. The school bus would go way out yonder toward Thomasville and come back. It was a lot of time, and we'd shoot them marbles. He thought he could beat me, but I knocked his all out of the ring, and I had my two pockets plumb full of marbles. He really cried. He was a bully, but his brother, Harry, was a bigger bully than he was.

INT: Do you remember the first Christmas present you ever got?

ES: Yes sir! A cap pistol, made out of silver, and you'd run the little caps on a thing. It was a bought one. We had a Christmas tree. I believed in Santa Claus until I was six or seven, and then those big bullies with big mouths told me.

INT: In the church, did you have Christmas plays?

ES: Yeah. I could sing. I was in a couple of operettas. Miss Shore went around and asked me to sing at each one, and like a fool I would sing at the church and I got caught in there. I was the Lord Mayor. They made me a skirt out of crepe paper. You did not talk. You sung to the girls and everything.

INT: Did your friends or your brothers make fun of you?

ES: Yeah, but I didn't care. I enjoyed it at that age. I was in fourth or fifth grade. In fact, there was a fellow who lived down yonder, and he was one of them that sung. I can't remember his name.

INT: You went to church every Sunday, and you went to Bible School.

ES: Every Sunday. Pastor Andrews was our preacher. He'd come up there and bring all of his spoons, and he'd pick off peaches, and when he'd holler GO, you'd take a spoon and peach and run, and if it dropped out, you'd have to back up and start over. He sat down there, and enjoyed seeing who could run it down there.

INT: Do you remember the first time you drove a car?

ES: I was 10 or 11. We were out at George's, and Baxter had an old 1945 green Ford. He said "You want to drive that home?" and I said "Sure." I got in there, and back then you had to put the clutch in. When we got down there and cranked it up, but I was looking at my feet and run off in the culvert.

INT: How old were you when you got your first car?

ES: I went to work in the summer at the Dixie. I was 17 when we graduated—we just had 11 grades—and I bought a '36 Plymouth mohair—four door for $225, and it had a brand new set of tires on it.

INT: You were born in 1926, so you were only about 15 when WW II started. You graduated in '43. Did you go right into service then?

ES: Not exactly. When I was 18, March 30th I went up there, and the next month I went down to Camp Croft and went in the infantry. I was in training 15 weeks. They needed infantry bad so we didn't get all of our training. We went on the Queen Mary. There were 14,000 soldiers on that one ship. We were the last ones to get on there. They waited until dark. We got there in four days and nights. The rolling of the ship made me sick. I had never been on the ocean before. We'd zig and zag.....They took us to England. When we landed we got on an LST and went to France. Four days after we got to France I was in a foxhole trying to kill them Germans. They were beating the tar out of us.

INT: When you got discharged, what did you do the first day?

ES: I can't remember. I came home from Texas, and James Black found it out someway, and when I come out of a building, he was sitting out there propped against his car. He'd come to get me. When I come home Mary was down there at Mama and Daddy's, and it was early in the morning. We were already married.

INT: How would you describe the community where you were born and raised?

ES: We didn't have no stealing. It was a world away from what it is now. Everybody was poor; everybody knew everybody, one big family.

INT: What one person or two had the most influence on your life?

ES: No one person—Grandpa and Grandma Smith. We would go down there and he was old. There was a maple tree out in the front yard. We'd go down there early, get the horses out—they plowed corn. Grandma stayed in the house...she had two pie safes...made you cakes and pies. We'd come in at dinner and eat and go out there in the front yard and lay down under that maple tree. Now that was the stuff. About 2:30, Grandpa'd say, "Time to go back." That followed me all along. When I turned 16, down at Dixie they were needing people to work, and when I'd get done eating dinner some of them would be playing cards and stuff, but I'd lay down like we did with Grandpa. When that horn would blow, I'd get up and go back to work. That followed me all my life.

INT: I asked you earlier what you were afraid of. Do you remember the diseases?

ES: Oh, lord, yeah. I had everything but whooping cough. Bob come out and said to not come up here because they had it. We stayed outside. To this day I haven't had whooping cough. I had the mumps. Colon and Baxter didn't. Colon and Baxter got 'em when they were in Okinawa at the same time.

INT: When you were little, who cut your hair?

ES: Mama. Jim would cut Papa's and Papa would cut Jim's with one of those things that pulls more hair out than it does cut off.

INT: Do you see similarities between life now and when you were growing up? How is life the same today for your grandkids as it was when you grew up?

ES: We do more for them than they did for us because they needed us to help work. I'm glad I went through what I went through. Somehow because from here on out, I just do not believe it could get worse than what it was in the Depression.

INT: You aren't confident about the future?

ES: Not right now, I ain't. I'll let you know after November.

INT: Did your parents peddle? Did they take produce or cut wood? Sawmill?

ES: Papa had a sawmill; ran the belt off the tractor to run the saw. If somebody wanted a car shed or a corn crib, they called, and I'd have to go down there and tail that dad-gum thing. I didn't weigh over 100 lbs., but we had to work. It didn't hurt us.

INT: On Sunday, did you go visiting much other than just in your neighborhood?

ES: We didn't go far. We would go into the woods and stuff and go down to Grandma's. Johnny Hedrick would come down...all of us got together and we'd come down to our house, we'd go down to Mary Jane's one Sunday and June and Charlie's one Sunday. Sunday afternoon was good.

INT: What is the longest trip you remember taking when you were young?

ES: One time we went to Virginia to an apple orchard. That was the only time I had ever been out of the state of North Carolina before I went in the army.

LAWRENCE BECK

Lawrence Beck was born on January 15, 1918, and was reared by his grandfather in the Holly Grove community. Larry Younts conducted this interview on October 1, 2004.

INT: I'm going to ask you when and where you were born.

LB: I was born January 15, 1918, down at the old homeplace. J. A. Smith was the doctor.

INT: By the old home place. Where do you mean?

LB: Next house down.

INT: At John's house, your dad's house? Did Dr. J. A. Smith deliver all of ya'll?

LB: He did me.

INT: Do you remember what he charged back then to come out?

LB: $25.

INT: What's the first thing you remember about childhood?

LB: I started staying with Granpa when I was small and went to the Holly Grove School. During the summer I'd stay up there. I went to school down here for a time before going out to Grandpa's full time. I started at Davis-Townsend in the sixth grade.

INT: Your grandpa you are talking about John Lee Lohr on Holly Grove Road?

LB: I'd hitch up a horse and a plow at 12 years old. Had some pretty land back there, and plowed with two horses. If it wasn't too hot, you could plow about an acre a day. Back then you had corn and wheat. You'd clear off rows four feet apart; ain't like it is now. I used a four-shank cultivator to plow corn. Today you put your corn about 18 inches apart Then you'd gather your corn and you'd have to pull two rows on each side of your pile come through there with a wagon and put it on a wagon and then he'd take it to the barn and push it off the back of the wagon. Next, you'd have corn shuckings.

INT: How did tobacco do out in that area?

LB: Not good. They had sandy land and it wasn't too rich a land. And when you thrash wheat you'd go help your neighbors, and they'd come help you haul wheat in. No charging, just neighbors helping neighbors.

INT: What are some of the most pleasant things you remember about growing up out there?

LB: I guess that I met my wife probably.

INT: Do you remember where you met her?

LB: Yeah, we were about 15 years old. We went to Holly Grove Church, but at a meeting on Sunday night down at Mount Tabor, I met her there and that started that off.

INT: You were about 11 or 12 when the Depression started. Do you remember the Depression changing the way you live in any way?

LB: Yeah, you'd see hobos walk through and catch these freight trains and go from place to place. Some of them came along the Holly Grove Road. They'd stop and ask for things. Now if they wanted a meal, they'd chop wood for you or something. These people were good. There wasn't no meanness going on.

INT: I've seen the house where you were living in at that time, tell me a little bit about it.

LB: We had a log house, two stories and it had winding stairs. If you had hired help to get the crops in or cut wood, they'd sleep upstairs. I had my own room at the end of it built on to it and then a kitchen and dining room was to the left of it. They slept on this floor, and I slept right up here in my own room.

INT: You were small out there, do you remember anything that frightened you? Like the dark, or ghost stories that were told that you remember?

LB: No, wasn't nothing to harm you. I used to walk the roads and you'd never meet a car. Nobody out there to bother you; maybe a dog or something. I tell you, Efird Conrad loved to take me possum hunting. On Sunday us boys would just walk around, sometimes we'd go to the river or the lake.

INT: You said you started plowing when you were 12 years old. Tell me about the start of a day on the farm.

LB: I'd milk a cow before breakfast. Feed the hogs before I went to school. When I came home from school we'd put wood on the porch, milk the cows, feed the hogs and do all the chores outside before dark. The barn was about 300–400 foot from the house. We had chickens up there. A hen would make her nest and lay about a dozen eggs, set on them until they hatched giving her a bunch of biddies.

INT: Did you play baseball?

LB: No.

INT: Did the Conrad boys play baseball much?

LB: Yeah, they played baseball but mostly basketball. We rode the bus. Only hard surface road that was here was old 29 that goes by Pilot school now and Holly Grove Road went down by the church and go toward Asheboro. Holly Grove road was not paved.

INT: Did you go to the mill?

LB: Now, I'd go to Holly Grove mill and hitch the smallest horse to a buggy and take two bushels of wheat and get our own flour. Grant Everhart ran the mill and then Jim Whitlock.

INT: Did you do much hunting growing up?

LB: Yeah, there were a lot of birds at that time, quail. They'd come from High Point and lease the land out here, and Charlie Everhart kept the bird dogs.

INT: Did you do much fishing?

LB: Yeah. There was an old mill pond. We'd catch little mixed fish. Abbotts creek had some good size suckers. We had some clean streams then and could lay down and drink the water if it ran through sand first. We had a swimming hole down there close to where the viaduct is now—on Avery Lopp's land— Efird's boys and I, we'd go down there and skinny dip.

We didn't have running water at the house; we'd have to heat water to take a bath. We had a lot of snow. Sometimes you'd go to bed and wake up the next morning, and there'd be ice in the kitchen where the water froze.

INT: You were talking about going to school earlier, you said you went to Hedrick's Grove through the 5th grade. What can you tell me about that? Do you remember who your first-grade teacher was?

LB: I remember a couple of teachers I had. I had Thelma Anderson and Leila Hedrick and Robert Beck was principal up there. We went to school for 6 months. It started about October and ended about May. We went for 11 years total. I graduated from Davis-Townsend in 1936.

INT: Describe Principal Bivens.

LB: He was a little short fellow, moving around all the time. He was principal of the school and also English teacher. He didn't have an assistant. There were 14 in my graduating class—11 boys and 3 girls.

INT: Do you remember what Mr. Bivens did when he wanted to punish somebody? I've heard a story about that.

LB: I used to be a witness sometimes. He'd spank them and then pull down their britches and see the damage, and then he'd give them a dose of salts before they'd leave there. He stayed there until Mr. Gathings took over. Bivens was a likeable old fellow from Monroe.

INT: Who was the first woman you ever dated? You said you met your wife when you were 15 years old.

LB: That's the only one I ever dated.

INT: How old were ya'll when you got married?

LB: Both 18.

INT: When WWII came along, how did that affect you?

LB: I went to Ft. Bragg in April, 1945, and I drove down there in one of these trucks like they haul furniture in now. I was 26 years old, had three children, and I got a deferment for six weeks and during that time the war ended and I didn't go.

INT: When did you start sawmilling? Who did you work with?

LB: Daddy always bought timber. When I was married I was hauling logs out here. Clyde Beck and Thurmond were sawing up there then. I saw Clyde before he died, and he said you were the little kid I picked up one morning to haul logs for us. When we got married, we had lumber cut for this house down at Denton. We moved in here in 1937. We didn't have a well dug. James Hedrick helped build the house. I mixed up the mud. Back then you didn't have mortar mix, you had to mix lime and cement sand.

INT: So you got the first bricks from Cunningham. How long did it take them to build it?

LB: About a month probably. I was one of the first to build a house. Picked the spot out of a cow pasture.

INT: Was there one single event that happened in your younger years that stands out above everything else?

LB: Met my wife. I knew her 70 years. We were married 67 years. Back then everybody grew a big garden and all kinds of vegetables. You didn't have bugs eating up your stuff. People didn't have fescue back then either; all they had was crabgrass and meadow hay. Do you know what meadow hay is? A lot of times we'd cut tops off the corn down to the ear and have that for the cows to eat.

INT: When you were young, did you ever get a major illness or disease? Do you remember being afraid of an illness?

LB: No. Just mumps and measles. I had chicken pox one time real bad.

INT: How is life today the same or different from when you grew up?

LB: When I grew up, neighbors helped neighbors. Now you're in awful shape if you depend on neighbors. That is the main thing I see. If somebody was sick somebody would come in and gather your crops for you. If your barn burned down they'd help you build your barn. Now everybody has got more selfish.

INT: What was the best about growing up back then?

LB: People back then didn't have so many bills to pay. They didn't have a water bill or light bill no telephone bill.

INT: I've always heard people say that in those years you had a lot of time but not much money. Today, people have more money but no time.

LB: And they've still got 24 hours in a day.

INT: Time hasn't changed. I believe I would prefer the other way.

LB: You know people used to come down and didn't think nothing about staying a half a day and talk, just didn't worry about it. You can't do that now because everybody's got somewhere to go.

INT: When you were growing up, no woman worked in a job?

LB: No. WWII brought that up.

INT: During the Depression when you had a farm, what happened to it during the Depression?

LB: I helped them clear a lot of land. When this house was built there weren't no bulldozers, no cement blocks. You had to dig your hole, dynamite the rock, build a form away from the wall about 4–6" and throw flint rock in among that and pour concrete in it and mix it up and pour it in there. Never had a crack in the wall.

INT: And Isaiah Beck did all of the planing for the people in this area?

LB: Yes. He did every door frame and every window frame. I never had to replace a thing. He cut every one by hand. Then chainsaws came out long about WWII and cut all trees. I borrowed $600 and bought this house. That's the biggest debt I've ever had. It was an awful debt trying to raise a family, too.

ELIZABETH BYERLY TAYLOR

Elizabeth is a member of the class of 1948 at Davis-Townsend High School. Some of her thoughts given here were in response to a written questionnaire from the writer.

INT: When were you born? Attending physician?

EBT: I was born at the home of my parents on November 20, 1928. Dr. Sowers was the doctor. Practically all children were born at home then.

INT: Memory of first crisis in your life?

EBT: The death of my mother in 1939. It was hard to understand why she had to die.

INT: How did your parents earn a living?

EBT: My father worked at Carolina Panel Company and farmed on the side. Like practically all mothers in the rural areas did then, mine did not work. She stayed home.

INT: How did you live? Did you have plenty of food? Clothes, etc?

EBT: We owned our home and had plenty of food such as it was, mostly grown on the farm and such. We had work clothes, school clothes, Sunday clothes and two or three pairs of shoes—nothing like children have today. Everyone knew times were tough in the 30s and 40s. Most people understood where they stood, just making ends meet.

INT: Describe the house where you lived.

EBT: Our house had five rooms (a path out back), a fireplace in a large room called a living room. A wood cooking stove in the kitchen, wooden tables and chairs for eating. No electric lights until I was 13 years old. The roof on the house was tin, and the side boarding was not painted until sometime after the mid-forties. The house sat on pillars without a foundation.

INT: What frightened you as a child?

EBT: I was afraid of snakes, lizards and airplanes flying overhead.

INT: What made you happy?

EBT: Playing with other children, going to Bible school in the summer, getting candy and ice cream—vanilla—made me happy.

INT: Your memory of the farm activities? Of country living?

EBT: When you think of hunting, fishing, horse shoe playing, watermelon patches, swimming in the creek and hog killings, you are thinking of country living in the 30s and 40s. I loved them. They were the good old times if you didn't have a reason to know better.

INT: Do you remember your first-grade teacher? Did you like school?

EBT: My first-grade teacher was Miss Helms, and I really liked school. Miss Chadwick which I had years later in the eighth grade was my favorite teacher, and I liked the principal, Mr. Gathings.

INT: What about going to church and revivals?

EBT: Before my mother died, we attended revivals at Beck's Evangelical and Reformed Church, my mother's church. After she died, we went to Mt. Tabor Church, my father's church.

INT: When did you see a television program for the first time? What was it? Your first car?

EBT: I saw my first television show after I was 20 years old. I do not remember the program. I got my first car in the 1960s when I was working.

INT: What did you do on Sunday afternoons?

EBT: Sundays were for church going and resting from the drudgery of work. On Sunday afternoons while growing up, a group of us neighborhood kids would get together and walk to see other people. We had no cars, neither the boys nor the girls. Everywhere we went we walked.

INT: Did you go to outdoor movies?

EBT: Shuford Swing showed movies at the store beside the school house. I really enjoyed seeing them mainly because all my friends would be there.

INT: Did you ever pick blackberries?

EBT: I picked blackberries and dewberries for Grandma who canned them or made pies.

INT: Do you remember the Rawleigh man?

EBT: The Rawleigh man was remembered by everybody. He sold Rawleigh's salve which was good for colds and most things. It was a standby medicine for cuts and bruises. Grandma also made a lot of medicines to treat us. My most horrible experience from taking medicine was when Dad held me between his legs and poured three spoons of 666 down my throat.

INT: Do you remember rationing in World War II?

EBT: Yes. We had ration coupons for many things—gasoline, sugar and shoes, for example. I lost the shoe ration book one Saturday going to work with my dad. I was going to get a pair of shoes when he got off work for dinner. Someone found it, thank God, or my hide would have been at stake.

INT: When people died, do you remember the all-night wakes and the burials?

EBT: I do remember the wakes and stayed up all night at some of them; the funeral services when the whole congregation in the church would get up and walk past the open casket to view the body; sitting by the graveside while the dirt was thrown over the casket; no vaults, just a casket. This was not a pretty sight for children especially when a parent has died.

INT: Your best friend in school?

EBT: My best friend in school and ever since has been Betty Ann Crotts

(Lambeth now) who lives a few miles from me. We still see each other often and go shopping together. My relationship with Betty Ann started in the primary school which proves friends made in school become friends for life.

INT: What about childhood diseases?

EBT: We all had diseases as children. In my second grade, I got diphtheria and almost died; missed so much school I had to repeat the grade. My brother and I had scarlet fever while our mother was sick before she died. You were quarantined for all the contagious diseases even though you might have been living a mile from anyone else.

THE GOOD OLD DAYS ???

Remembered and written in 1986 by Delores Beck Rose for her children. Delores gave permission to use her story as another person's view of life during the Depression and World War II.

The house where I was born in 1930 still stands. It is almost hidden from view among the trees at the end of a long driveway. There is a rolling ridge behind the house called "Three Hat Mountain." To get to our house, we had to cross a small creek that ran across our driveway. There was not a bridge, which meant we had to drive through the water. In dry weather this was no problem, but when we had heavy rains, the water would run down off the mountain and turn our quiet stream into a much deeper, rushing body of water. I remember several times, coming home from school, Mother would meet my sister and me at the creek and we would walk through the water up to our waists, holding hands to keep from being pulled down. Soaking wet, we would run to the house and strip off our clothes in the kitchen by the wood stove. After scrubbing dry and getting into dry clothes, we were treated to a nice hot bowl of vegetable soup. There was always a big pot simmering on the stove when the weather was cold and rainy.

Although I was born in the old house, my memories of living there don't really start until I was twelve years old. The house belonged to my mother's parents. When my parents were first married, they continued to live there for several years. I must have been about two or three years old when we moved away. We lived in several places from this time until I was about twelve. I remember well where we were living when my sister was born. I was six years old and the day I started school was the day she was born. I was not the least bit impressed with that tiny, red-faced person who had come to live with us.

She cried often and loud, and I resented sharing my parents with her. Thankfully, that has long since changed, she is my best friend now.

The other house I remember was where we were living when we found that we were going to have to move back to the "Old Place." We were living next door to a family with two boys about my age and a girl who was close in age to my sister. This family had a pony and a barn and several other old buildings, which were perfect for playing. We had so much fun riding in the pony cart and making playhouses and living in our own "pretend world." We marked off the rooms in our playhouses with white flint rocks and used beautiful green moss from the woods for carpet. People lived so closely. Now, not many children have the woods and fields for a playground. I think it is sad that so many of today's children don't know how to invent their own fun and games.

Sometimes we did get into dangerous situations. We had a deep well between our two houses that both families used. We had no electricity or indoor plumbing at that time. One day my sister, who was about five at the time, got curious about the well. We found her sitting on top of it with the lid open, looking down to see where the water came from. Scared us all to death! There was another incident involving her and an old mother hen. That very protective mama hen jumped on my sister and scratched and pecked her while she was screaming her head off. After she was rescued from the clutches of the hen, my sister stayed away from the chickens!

About this time our lives were about to be changed. Mother's stepfather had developed a health problem and my grandparents needed us to move back to the "Old Place." Mother, being the only child, we had no choice. I was not happy at the thought of moving from this place with friends next door. Grandpa's house was rather isolated, not another house in sight or children nearby. My sister and I would have to walk about a quarter of a mile to catch the school bus. Thinking of rain and snow, this didn't sound too great. In spite of all the negative reasons I could think of, we moved. Looking back, I'm so glad we did. I couldn't know at that young age how much that move would enrich my life and how much I would learn from my grandparents and living on this farm.

The old house as I remember it, when we moved in was weather-beaten, unpainted wooden boards with a front porch and a wooden swing suspended by chains. In the back there was a large screened porch with two doors going outside. The main part of the house was over one hundred years old at that time. Rooms had been added through the years. On the front were a parlor or "front room" as it was known then and also a bedroom where my grandparents slept. There was a door leading from their bedroom into their sitting room. Both the parlor and their sitting room had fireplaces, which was the only source of heat except for the kitchen stove. A door opened from their sitting room into a large dining room where there was yet another fireplace. There was a small kitchen that you entered from the dining room and a door out of the dining room onto the back porch. On the second floor there were two bedrooms, the stairs went up from the sitting room.

Since there was no electricity in the area at that time, we used kerosene lamps and the fireplaces and kitchen stove for heat. Behind the house down a hill and across a pasture was the spring where we got our water. We carried water to the house in two buckets, and due to the distance, you didn't go with only one. There was a shelf on the back porch where the water buckets sat and a sink with a drain was beside the shelf. The spring was a beautiful place, and I wish I could describe it well enough for you to really see it in your mind. This spring met a need other than water; it gave us a form of refrigeration. There was a building over the spring and a cold stream of running water came from the spring and went through the springhouse. In there, Grandma kept the milk, cream and butter in pottery crocks, setting them right down in the water and it kept all of it cold and fresh. Hanging beside the spring was a long-handled gourd that we used to dip out a drink of water. The spring was lined with rocks and the water was always ice cold and clear, the best water I've ever tasted! Everything was done the old-fashioned way.

The laundry was done at the spring. A fire under the big black iron pot heated the water and there were tubs on a bench to wash and rinse the clothes. A washboard was used to scrub the clothes clean, and of course every piece had to be wrung out by hand. I wonder how many people under the age of thirty even know what a washboard is today? We've come a long way, baby!

Grandpa had four horses, three cows and pigs (I don't know how many). My grandmother had chickens, which provided eggs and fried chicken for Sunday lunch. From the hogs we had cured ham, sausage, bacon and liver pudding. Breakfast on the farm was usually ham or sausage and eggs, homemade biscuits, jelly, preserves and butter. We had milk straight from the cow, no pasteurized or homogenized process on the farm. All of our vegetables were grown in the garden. We grew fields of wheat and corn to feed the animals, and we even had a strawberry patch. That heavenly taste of fresh strawberries with thick sweet cream over them, I'll never forge it! My Dad worked in a furniture manufacturing plant in a nearby town and helped with the farm work in the evenings and on Saturdays. Grandpa wasn't able to do very much by this time, but he worked as long as he could.

When the grain was ready for harvest, one man with a threshing machine and a crew of men went from farm to farm cutting the grain. When they came to our place, we naturally had to feed them lunch. Such a meal, you can't imagine. We had fried chicken, biscuits, chicken and dumplings, corn-on-the-cob, green beans, beets, cucumbers sliced in vinegar, potatoes (sweet and white) and all kinds of cakes and pies. Those men could really put away the food. We had a building called a wheat house, and in it were two sections to store the grain when it was harvested. This new grain had to be stirred every day to keep heat from building up in it. This was a job that my sister and I couldn't wait to get into.

We would jump in the bins and have a ball, walking through the grain, digging our arms down to the very bottom and up again. We pretended we were swimming, and neither of us had ever been swimming or even know how. This is a good example of making your own fun on a farm. There was one job that I just hated, and that was thinning corn, chopping out extra plants so it wouldn't be too thick. People don't even do that anymore. Mother, Grandma and my sister and I would go to the cornfield early in the morning, taking our hoe and a jug of water. My sister wasn't big enough to do this so she played in the shade while we worked. Those corn rows were the longest I've ever seen and I despised every minute of it...

Soon after we moved back to the farm, Daddy bought a wooden ice box. This wonderful contraption had a handle on top to open the part where the ice was kept. On the front was a door which opened to the inside where the shelves were. We now kept our butter and milk and cream in this instead of in the springhouse. Under the icebox was a drip pan to catch the water as the ice melted. The icebox was kept on the back porch and many times I forgot to empty the pan and water would run across the porch floor. If we wanted iced tea, we used an ice pick to chip off enough ice to fill our glasses. Believe me, that was a treat! Looking back on those years, we sometimes call them "the Good Old Days."

Well, much of life was very good, but there were times that were downright miserable. One good example was having to go to the old outhouse on cold, rainy or snowy days and nights. Another part of those "Good Old" that wasn't so good was trying to keep warm by a fireplace when the temperature was below freezing and the wind was howling around the old house. I remember how I dreaded going upstairs where we slept. There was no heat up there and we would jump into bed and rarely move once we got the bed warm. My sister and I slept together under at least three quilts in really cold weather. Eventually, Daddy closed some of the fireplaces and put in wood heaters. When summer came, it was so hot upstairs, we were miserable with the heat. My dad's father, Grandpa Beck, came and helped him put in some more windows, which gave us some relief. About that time we had the outside of the house painted, I was so proud to have a house that was painted like my friends at school had. The Rural Electrical Association was coming through the area and we had the opportunity to get the house wired for electricity. At first, all we had were lights, just bare bulbs in the ceiling and a pull chain for on and off. One good thing brought on more, now we could get a pump and have running water in the sink on the back porch. The best thing of all was that beautiful white electric refrigerator that my dad bought from the Western Auto Store. We were all so proud! I felt like we were rich! It was wonderful, now we could have ice any time, cold cokes, and even have ice cream any time.

We still didn't have a sink in the kitchen. That came years later when the little kitchen was converted to a bedroom and the dining room became the kitchen. With electricity came a more convenient way to do the laundry. This was a round tub washer with an automatic wringer. It was on the back porch along with two large tubs for rinsing. This was not an automatic washer, they hadn't been invented at this time or if they had, we hadn't heard of them. Our washer had an agitator that swished the clothes back and forth until they were clean. There was a lever on the washer to stop the agitator, and each piece of laundry was put through the wringer that was attached to the washer. As each piece of laundry came through the wringer we rinsed them in one tub and ran them through the wringer again and back into the second tub of rinse water and again through the wringer and out to the line to dry. We had to heat water on the stove to put in the washer, but there was a pump and drain pipe that emptied into a bucket, which we poured out through the sink drain on the porch. Not many people do their wash this way any more. But it sure beat doing it at the spring and using that washboard. Before we had an electric iron, we used the old flat irons that were heated on the kitchen stove. It used a thick pad of cloth around the handle, iron until it cooled off, then set it back on the stove and got a hot one while the other one heated again.

By now a few years had passed and I was beginning to think about having a boy friend. I wanted to fix up the "front room" so I would have a place to entertain company. I nagged my parents until they bought some living room furniture. We got a couch and two chairs. They were upholstered in a burgundy colored mohair fabric, which was the popular thing back then. I thought we were really coming up in the world! There was one particular young man that I really liked. He lived a couple of miles up the road from us. He wasn't old enough to drive a car yet, so he would ride his bike to see me on Sunday afternoons. I remember those first dates well. Sitting on that scratchy mohair couch, we were rather shy, but we did have a good time. Before dark he would get on his bike and pedal on home. He lived on a farm and had chores to do.

Because we were so isolated, I spent a lot of time alone. I did a lot of reading in my free time and I loved to walk out in the woods. I used to walk up the mountain behind the barn on across the pasture to the creek and sit by the water, dreaming of what I would do when I grew up. There was no danger back then for a young girl to walk through the woods or down a country road. We never locked our doors. In fact, we had no locks except for hooks on the screen doors. This is one of the things in the "Good Old Days" that was truly good. I wish we could trust everyone enough to live that free from fear today. My favorite season of the year was autumn because it was so beautiful around the "Old Place." The trees turned such brilliant colors and the temperatures were pleasant for sleeping upstairs. Walking in the woods was such fun when the leaves were falling.

My next favorite season was winter. My sister and I would play in the snow until we got really cold and wet, then Mother would call us into the house. She always made snow cream and that was a special treat. Mother's snow cream tasted delicious; sometimes she made vanilla, sometimes chocolate or banana. We weren't afraid to eat the snow back then. There was no pollution in the air to make the snow dangerous to our health; another point for the "Good Old Days."

When I was fifteen years old and my sister was nine, a big surprise happened! Mother told us that she was going to have a baby. We were shocked to say the least, but then happiness and great anticipation set in. This was going to change our lives considerably. Daddy built a small living room onto the front of the old house. This gave Mother and Daddy the old front room for a bedroom. Mother was not able to continue going up the steep stairs to the bedrooms upstairs. We used their new bedroom downstairs as a sitting room or den, giving our grandparents and us more privacy. My brother was born on February 7, 1946, and we were all so very happy, especially my dad. I'm sure he wanted a son, already having two daughters. The baby was born three or four weeks early, very tiny but he made it. We all spoiled him. There were so many of us to help in spoiling him, but also we all helped take care of him. Being fifteen, I was able to help Mother a lot with the baby. Sometimes when I think of him, he almost seems like my child. As I remember the old home place, I can see the house with a big maple tree out front. Then there was a smokehouse with a grapevine growing on the side next to the house. On the other side of the smokehouse, sat the garage, where my Grandpa's old "T" model Ford was kept. He used to drive it to town on Saturday, taking milk and cream and vegetables to sell to the city folks. He loved that old car and drove it as long as he was able. Around on the other side of the house, you walked through a gate into the barnyard.

There was a wood shed and a big chopping block in front of it. The chopping block was where Dad split fire wood and also where many fryer chickens lost their heads on the way to becoming our Sunday lunch. Walking past the wood shed, there was a chicken lot, then the wheat house and the outhouse. Just past them was another building called the buggy shed, where an old buggy rested, having seen its best days. This building was always a fascination to me. Besides the buggy, there were old farm tools, old bottles, a wagon and a plow or two. Then there was a barn. I can still remember the smell of hay and horses and cows. There's a special aroma about an old barn, and I don't mean unpleasant. In fact, it is really rather pleasant. In the barn was an old corn sheller that removed the kernels from the cobs of corn. I haven't seen one of those since the "Good Ole Days." We had a building called a corn crib; this was made especially for storing the feed corn. It was made of narrow strips of wood with open spaces between the strips.

There is a special place in my memories for my grandmother's flower garden. This was her pride and joy. She spent many happy hours out among her beautiful flowers, chopping away the weeds, pinching off dried blossoms, and planting new flowers. When anyone came visiting, Grandma always took them on a tour of her garden. If anything was blooming, the visitor usually left with a bouquet or maybe some bulbs or plants for their own garden. I can see her so clearly, with her wide-brimmed straw hat covering her snow-white hair. With her hoe in hand, she was doing what she loved so much, working with her flowers.

Grandpa passed away the year before I got married, in November, 1951. As was the custom at that time, his body was brought home and the open casket was placed in the living room. Relatives, friends and neighbors came, brought food and helped with the chores. Several people would always stay all night. This custom called "sitting up with the dead," has been discarded and is rarely done anymore. After the funeral, the next day, we came home from the church, and we all felt that empty feeling in the old house. I remember it was the same when Grandpa died about five or six years later.

In March of 1952 I got married and moved away from "The Old Place." My husband went into the army in November of that same year and I came back home to live for two years while he was away. At this time the little kitchen was converted into a bedroom for me. The dining room became the kitchen and dining area. Daddy built cabinets and put in a sink and a water heater. These additions were a great improvement to the old house. While my husband was in the army, my sister got married. There was a period of time after he came home that we all lived with Mother and Daddy, along with Grandma and my brother. That's really an extended family under one roof!

When my husband came home, we began construction on our house. We moved in March of 1956. Our daughter was born in March of 1957. When she was almost two years old, Grandmother passed away. After she was gone, Mother was not happy living in the old house. My sister and I were both living away and Daddy was away at work all day and my brother was in school all day. So the old place was sold and my parents built a new house near me. Since that time, I haven't been able to "go home again." But the memories of growing up in the country are always with me. I'll never forget those days down in the country at "The Old Place." When my daughter was five, we had a son born in December, 1961. I often think of how I was raised, how different the lifestyles are today, and that is my reason for writing this account of my growing-up years. I want my children to know what life was like when Mom was a kid.

EPILOGUE

In *A Tale of Two Cities*, Charles Dickens, referencing the French Revolution, wrote, "It was the best of times, it was the worst of times, it was the age of wisdom, it was the age of foolishness, it was the epoch of belief, it was the epoch of incredulity...it was the spring of hope, it was the winter of despair...."(1) Someone could have penned similar words in 1950 for Davidson County having just passed through a roller-coaster ride of 30 years. The decade of the twenties began on a high note filling the people with confident enthusiasm only to be followed by a sagging economy. At decade's end, as the country songwriter wrote, "Wall Street fell but we were too poor to tell."

The thirties ushered in a worldwide depression unlike any ever experienced, and low incomes in the United States put millions in poverty, but the people in lower middle Davidson County seemed to survive better than those in most parts of the country. Our people were self-reliant, producing from the land much of what they consumed and possessing a character of hope at a time when despair might have been the easier choice. All the while, the Nazis in Germany and the Japanese in East Asia were building machines of war and training millions of men in an effort to expand their reaches.

The inevitable, war in Europe, came on like gang busters at the close of the thirties and expanded rapidly in the forties to include the Pacific region. On the home front and in the armed forces, the people of lower Davidson County rushed to do their part to bring the enemies to their knees. Peace came again, and the Depression had run its course. The health of the economy grew almost daily.

As we moved beyond the 1950s, the roller-coaster years drifted behind us, and we went full speed ahead into the future honestly thinking the world had really been made safe for democracy. Scarcely had our lives been placed in order when the Korean War broke out; never mind the armed might we had demonstrated the previous 10 years. Our fighting forces went to Korea helping to preserve a divided nation as our leaders continued to search for stability. Not again we thought, but as we moved through the decades to the present, a similar pattern of world events kept repeating itself. An arms race took on a torrid pace as friend and foe stockpiled weapons, and enemies unleashed many of them as armies battled up and down the Vietnam peninsula only to witness the forces of the United States come home in defeat. All-out wars were avoided, but skirmishes small and large around the globe kept us on edge.

The modern technology of television brought every home in lower David-son County into the middle of state, national, and world events, and we be-came engulfed with entertainment opportunities. Economies swung back and forth, and on balance, standards of living rose, even if not in equal proportions for all.

The first part of the 21st century arrived appearing vastly different from 1920 to 1950. Every aspect of our lives had changed beyond belief. Things not even imagined in 1920 have become commonplace, and current popula-tion numbers make those of the past seem miniscule. For every person in the United States in 1920, there are now almost three in his or her place, and two-thirds of these are likely to be of a different color, have a different religion or speak a different language.

Demographers predict that by the year 2050, the Caucasian segment of so-ciety will be in the minority. Who would have imagined we would be hear-ing many of the languages of the world being spoken on our streets and in our schools? If the current pace persists, can anyone predict an end in sight? Change remains omnipresent, and the United States is expected to grow by over 40 percent more people over the next 40 years. There are no reasons to expect that growth and changes will be different in Davidson County. What kind of world will the young people face? Where will they live and how will they earn a livelihood? Where will they receive their education? How will they develop reliable and meaningful values?

Those of us born in the '20s, '30s and '40s in lower Davidson County came into a stable and enduring culture and environment, and they served us well. The basic values of our heritage that have remained solid from generation to generation may be hitting a bumpy road. A scientist studying the values that society holds in the 21st century observed that among the recent generations the percentage of persons giving sway to other ideals is increasing. He makes the observation that a youngster today forms much different views of the world when he or she gets a dirt bike or a new car for Christmas as opposed to the rubber ball or a few pieces of fruit that their parents found under the tree. He speaks of the watering down of integrity and the simultaneous increase in greed—more focus on self and not on others. The reduction of tolerance and civility toward each other among families, in communities, and among revered institutions makes us wonder about the future.

Individuals and institutions prospering tomorrow will be those that pos-sess two characteristics: (1) the ability to accept a changing world and (2) genu-ine concern for **all** human beings because we are all brothers and sisters. The future belongs to those who believe in these and subscribe to them.

The values learned in the '20s, '30s, and '40s are endeavors to which people give top priority, and they request institutions and their leaders to hold them in security. Good institutions have to have integrity—be fit for the job—but above all the leaders of our institutions have to be honest. The seven churches, described in the early part of this book and many others could be added to the list, gave so many persons the foundations for living a useful life—useful not only for themselves but to others as well. The challenge to the church in the 21st century is tough—to continue to accept change in a changing environment and to be a change agent for good—to have a deep and abiding concern for all human beings in a society more diverse than any previously known.

Perhaps 50 or 75 years from now someone born in the first part of the 21st century will write a treatise about his or her memories of growing up in North Carolina. They will surely be much different than the ones described in this book, but we have to wonder if the writer will speak of his or her experiences as occurring in the good old days. He or she will worry about present conditions and what is going to become of the younger generation. A wise man once had something to say about this. "The younger generation is going to grow up and start worrying about the next younger generation." Things are not what they used to be, and perhaps they never were.

ENDNOTES

Chapter One

The basis for this chapter came from a visit the author made to his old home place in 2004. He made observations of the grounds and buildings recalling how visible entities impacted him during the 18 years he spent there before leaving for college. Out of this visit came the decision to write this book with the objective of leaving something for the people of his home region so they might have a better appreciation of their heritage.

Chapter Two

1. Sink, M. Jewell and Mary Green Matthews. *Pathfinders Past and Present: A History of Davidson County, North Carolina.* Hall Printing Company. High Point, N.C. 1972.
2. Hammer, Carl, Jr. *Rhinelanders on the Yadkin.* Second Edition. Rowan Printing Company. Salisbury, North Carolina. 1965.
3. Leonard, Jacob Calvin. *Centennial History of Davidson County, North Carolina.* Edwards & Broughton Company. Raleigh. 1927.

Chapter Three

1. Leonard, Jacob Calvin. *Centennial History of Davidson County, North Carolina.* Edwards & Broughton Company. Raleigh. 1927.
2. Sink, M. Jewell and Mary Green Matthews. *Pathfinders Past and Present: A History of Davidson County, North Carolina.* Hall Printing Company. High Point, N.C. 1972.
3. Described in Sink and Matthews from information provided by Dr. John Varner of Lexington, N.C. and Mrs. Bobby Hepler of Thomasville, N.C.
4. Described in Sink and Matthews from information provided by Bryum Tysinger of Silver Hill and Raymond Doby of Alleghany Township.
5. Described in Sink and Matthews from information provided by Bert M. Lanier, Denton, N.C.
6. Described in Sink and Matthews from information provided by Mrs. Helen Surratt Perlman of Southmont and Mrs. Clarence Sink of Cotton Grove.
7. "History of Beck's Lutheran Church." Unpublished information.
8. Younts, Larry. "History of Beck's United Church of Christ." Unpublished information. 2001.
9. "A Journey through Time. Hedrick's Grove United Church of Christ, 1891–1991." Unpublished information.
10. "A Brief History of Mt. Tabor United Church of Christ, 1883–1983." Unpublished information.
11. "Holly Grove Evangelical Lutheran Church, Centennial, 1885–1985." Unpublished information.
12. "History of New Jerusalem United Church of Christ." From *The Dispatch* (1956) and "A Story of the Southern Synod" (1968).
13. Hendricks, Garland A. Saints and Sinners at Jersey Settlement. *The Story of Jersey Baptist Church.* The Delmar Company. Charlotte, N.C. 1988.

14. Hammer, Carl, Jr. *Rhinelanders on the Yadkin*. Second Edition Rowan Printing Company. Salisbury, North Carolina. 1965.

Chapter Four

1. *The Dispatch*. Lexington, N.C. 1882.

2. *20th Century Day by Day*. Dorling Kindersly. London. 2000.

3. Leonard, Jacob Calvin. *Centennial History of Davidson County, North Carolina*. Edwards & Broughton Company. Raleigh, N.C. 1927.

4. McCrae, John. "In Flanders Fields." May 3, 1915.

5. Sink, M. Jewell and Mary Green Matthews. *Pathfinders Past and Present: A History of Davidson County, North Carolina*. Hall Printing Company. High Point, N.C. 1972.

Chapter Five

1. *The Dispatch*. Lexington, N.C. (1882). 1930–1939.

2. *20th Century Day by Day*. Dorling Kindersly, London. 2000. pp. 380–501.

Chapter Six

1. *The Dispatch*. Lexington, N.C. (1882). 1940–1949.

2. *20th Century Day by Day*. Dorling Kindersley, London. 2000. pp. 504–671.

3. Berstein, Mark and Alex Liberlozzi. *World War II on the Air: Edward R. Murrow and the Broadcasts that Riveted the Nation*. Sourcebook, Inc. Naperville, Illinois. 2003.

4. North Carolina State University Library. Special Collections Section. Raleigh, N.C.

5. Brokaw, Tom. *The Greatest Generation*. Random House. New York. 1998.

6. King, John E. "From Falls City, Nebraska to Lexington, N.C. via the European Theater of World War II." Unpublished manuscript. 1994.

7. Smith, John William and Rose Mary Schneider Smith. Personal communication. 2006.

Chapters Seven, Eight, Nine, Ten, and Eleven

Much of the information contained in these chapters resulted from the early-life experiences of the author and information obtained in face-to-face conversations with people living in Davidson County, N.C. in 2005–2006.

Chapter Twelve

Interviews were conducted in 2004–05 with persons living in lower Davidson County. Those selected for interviews were: Paul Miller, Robbie Swing, Virginia Lopp White, Dermont and Gladys Beck, Edmund Smith and Lawrence Beck. Elizabeth Byerly Taylor provided a response to a written questionnaire. "The Good Old Days???" was written in 1986 by Delores Beck Rose for her children. It is her story of her life during the Depression and World War II.

Younts farm, Davidson
County, North Carolina,
early 1940s.